MW01381321

Luyia Nation

ORIGINS, CLANS AND TABOOS

Shadrack Amakoye Bulimo

Order this book online at www.trafford.com
or email orders@trafford.com

Most Trafford titles are also available at major online book retailers.

Cover illustration: Leopard, the Luyia tribal totem and Sasha Atemo Bulimo

Maps: Henry Miheso

Printed in the United States of America.

ISBN: 978-1-4669-7837-9 (sc)
ISBN: 978-1-4669-7836-2 (hc)
ISBN: 978-1-4669-7835-5 (e)

Library of Congress Control Number: 2013903757

Trafford rev. 04/30/2013

 www.trafford.com

North America & international
toll-free: 1 888 232 4444 (USA & Canada)
phone: 250 383 6864 ♦ fax: 812 355 4082

Also by Shadrack A. Bulimo
Luyia of Kenya: A Cultural Profile

Dedication

To Abaluyia who toil in search of meaning and purpose of their lives. To my late parents, Jackson Andebe Bulimo and Dorcas Tabitha Ong'ayo, who inculcated the values of honor, respect, and dignity by which I have lived my life; to my wife Jacqueline Ajando Bulimo (neé Salano) whose companionship, warmth, and encouragement egged me on; to my daughters, Lynda Asiko and Sasha Atemo, whose catalytic questions inspired this book in the first place.

CONTENTS

LIST OF TABLES

LIST OF MAPS

FOREWORD

Juvenal Shiundu

It gives me great pleasure, honor, and privilege to introduce *Luyia Nation,* a book which is the result of many years of research, carried out both in Kenya and abroad by the author, Shadrack Amakoye Bulimo, who is also the editor of Abeingo Community Network portal. The book gives a detailed account of the origins, clans, and migrations of the eighteen subnations of the Luyia people. The period covered includes the arrival of the first Whiteman (missionary and colonizer), introduction of Christianity, education, political administration, and transformation from kingdom to present-day rule.

The book draws inspiration from earlier works of scholars such as Prof. Gideon Were, Dr. John Osogo, and Dr. Gunter Wagner supplemented by interviews and Internet research to offer a comprehensive exposition in a way that no other single book has done before. In addition to the great deal of attention given to the way of life of the Luyia, the author has offered comparative analysis of closely related tribes like Abagusii (Kisii), Baganda, Bagisu, Basoga, Basuba, and the neighboring Luo.

The author records how the Luyia have a deeply rooted cultural heritage which is currently under siege by the praxis of neocolonialism and risks being swept away as a culture of a bygone era. This book seeks to document and preserve the Luyia cultural heritage for the benefit of our children and future generations.

This scholarly yet pleasantly readable book will interest both the general reader as well as the serious student of history and anthropology who wishes to learn and appreciate the importance of preserving cultural resources. For Luyia kinsmen, the book is an adjuvant that should provoke deeper research on precolonial traditional way of life to correct any misrepresentations recorded by alien researchers and scholars. In saying so, I recall that Akinwande Oluwole "Wole" Soyinka, the Nigerian writer, once offered a sagacious advice to historians in a play to welcome his country's independence when one of his characters reiterated the injunction: "Leave the dead some room to dance." Historians of Africa have tended to "bury" the dead as a justification for our cultural idiosyncrasies vis-à-vis the modern world culture. In this book, the author has shown that in the Luyia culture, there has always been "some room for the dead to dance."

This book is invaluable to anthropologists, historians, sociologists, and general readers and will remain so for many years to come.

Juvenal J. M. Shiundu
Founder member and former Chairman of
Abeingo Community Network
London, UK

PREFACE

The Luyia nation is relatively new by historical standards cobbled together as a political necessity a little less than three generations ago. The Luyia nation is still evolving in a slow process that seeks to harmonize the historico-cultural institutions that define the eighteen subnations in Kenya alone. Available historical and anthropological records indicate that geophysical spread of Luyia-speaking people extends beyond the Kenyan frontier into Uganda and Tanzania with some Luyia (Luhya) clans having extant brethren in Rwanda, Congo, Zambia, and Cameroon. Although this book makes reference to the Luyia beyond the Kenyan frontiers, its scope, however, is limited to Kenyan Luyia even though some like the Samia are victims of the idiocy of a colonial system that subdivided one people into two.

On the key question of origin and ancestry, most Luyia point to *Misri* (Egypt) as the land of their primeval ancestors. Postindependence scholars and historians like Prof. Gideon Were expressed scepticism about the Egyptian links instead positing that West and Central Africa were the more likely lands of origin. However, thanks to further anthropological research, I have found compelling evidence that links the Bantu, including those in West Africa to ancient *Misri*.

This suggests that dispersal from Egypt took two different routes—one directly southward along the Nile like the Nilotes (Luo and Kalenjin) and westward through West and Central Africa.

Notwithstanding the theory of *Misri* ancestry, a major historical and cultural change in Buluyia occurred a little more than a century ago. The major force of this seismic shift was of course native contact with the Western world. Although Europeans had had centuries of contact with native Africans through their exploration and slave trade exploits, much of the interior of Africa remained a "dark continent" riddled with bizarre stories of cannibalism and heathenism. Keen to exploit the resources of Africa beyond the coastline, European powers began sending expeditions to hinterland. In the case of Kenya, the first Whiteman to land on Luyia territory was Welshman, Henry Morton Stanley—he of the infamous "dark continent" epithet. He landed at Igoye, Busia County, in 1875 as he voyaged round Lake Victoria (Lolwe) on his way to Uganda in search of Scottish explorer, Dr. David Livingstone. However, it was Joseph Thomson, a Scottish explorer who first traversed through Luyialand on foot in 1883. His meeting with Nabongo Mumia, the king of Wanga, laid the foundation for British colonialism in the whole country. The Wanga kingdom, an extension of the interlacustrine kingdoms of the Great Lakes was the only organized indigenous government in Kenya. The British quickly leveraged tools of imperialism—the church and provincial administration—to bag the prize of Kenya colony in a process that European powers formalized at the Berlin Conference of 1885. The conference split Africa into spheres of European influence that ended the so-called Scramble for Africa.

Before 1895, the affairs of British overseas possessions in East Africa (Kenya and Uganda) were managed by a royal chartered company known as Imperial British East Africa Company (IBEAC). When IBEAC went bankrupt, the British colonial office reorganized these possessions and established direct rule under what it called East African protectorate. Further changes occurred in 1920 when Kenya was excised from Uganda to become Kenya Colony and Protectorate with a governor appointed from London. A two-pronged strategy was used in the colonization and expropriation of resources in East Africa. While colonial administrators parlayed law, order, and taxation, the church went beyond the realm of spiritualism, establishing schools, health centers, and industrial training units. Christianity became a major force of western acculturation through its network of educational, health and vocational training outfits.

Beyond the socioeconomic impact of European imperialism, evolvement of the Luyia nation is underpinned by other factors not least the assimilation of non-Bantu clans from the Luo, Kalenjin and Maasai. Several clans in Kisa, Wanga, Bunyala, Bukusu, Butsotso, Idakho, Isukha, and Marama were originally Luo, Kalenjin, or Maasai. A whole subnation, the Tachoni, was originally highland Nilotes which metamorphosed into Bantu more than four hundred years ago through large-scale intermarriages with Bantu tribes. The fact that these clans were originally Nilotic does not make them less Luyia any more than Luonized Bantu clans like Jousere of Alego are less Luo. Consequently, the Luyia Nation can be seen as a confluence of Bantu and Nilotic septs bound by a common linguistic and cultural orientation whether primeval, adopted, or assimilated. Observance of the principle of seniority, clan taboos, and prohibitions are the hallmarks of clandom among the Luyia.

The 863 Luyia clans (excluding Songa) are amorphous units united only by common cultural and linguistic bonds. The political union between these clans is a nettlesome issue that has eluded the community since formation of the super-ethnic polity more than seventy years ago. Luyia ethnicity did not exist prior to 1943; instead, there lived in close proximity, a phalanx of closely related tribes sharing common linguistic and cultural traits. Most of these groups were exiguous and acephalous; besides Abawanga, they did not have a centralized system of traditional governance. However, around the time of Second World War, most clan heads realized that political parameters had shifted dramatically and only organized societies with a definite ethnic identity could hope to reap political benefits associated with economies of scale.

The seeds that grew into the Luyia nation were inadvertently sown by British politico-ethnographers who called all tribes in western Kenya Wakavirondo, a pejorative terminology resented by the Luyia, Luo, Kalenjin, Kisii, Kuria, and Iteso. The fight to redeem ethnic pride was somewhat achieved when the name *kavirondo* was expunged from official use and replaced by Nyanza. Administratively, what was then North Kavirondo became North Nyanza under which most Luyia tribes belonged. The interwar period witnessed an unprecedented growth in groupings fighting for or asserting their rights. In 1940, Abaluyia Welfare Association was born to, among other things, popularize the name Abaluyia as a first step in creating a super-ethnic identity. Shortly afterward a language committee was formed, and following its recommendations in 1943, the Luyia nation was formally born.

Midwifing the super tribe was the easy bit; nurturing and developing sociocultural institutions to anchor a system of impregnable national ethos has evaded Abaluyia tribesmen for three generations. Over the years, talk of Luyia unity has waxed and waned depending on political temperatures prevailing in a cyclical pattern that continues even today, especially during electioneering. Luyia unity is a favorite subject among politicians whenever elections are looming, but the same leaders are unwilling to jump into one political vehicle to harmonize the region's socioeconomic interests. In this regard, politicians, important opinion leaders in any society, are rather like vultures preying on dead matter and caring less about unity of purpose as a long-term goal that can potentially secure the region's political, social, and economic empowerment.

In 2005, a community organization, Luhya Elders Forum, otherwise known as Luhya Council of Elders, was formed to bind together community leaders from all Luyia subnations as a common front in the fight against HIV/Aids, poverty, and ignorance. The organization's leading lights were Burudi Nabwera (Tachoni) as chairman with Martin Shikuku (Marama) and Ibrahim Ambwere (Maragoli) as founding members. The organization which is part of a wave of ethnic chauvinism across Kenyan tribes has the potential to marshal support of the community and become a vehicle to drive unity and development in Western.

This book is an invaluable compendium to readers in Bantu anthropology, history, and culture. The title draws inspiration from autochthonous authors, principally Prof. Gideon Were and Dr. John Osogo whose historical accounts of Abaluyia in the postindependence era were groundbreaking. Then there is linguist, Dr. Rachel Musimbi Kanyoro (neé Angogo) whose research on Luyia tongues ignited the debate on whether Luyia is indeed a single tribe or a conglomeration of different tribes. Dr. Gunter Wagner's seminal work on Luyia culture in the 1930s is a classic point of reference for which we remain indebted. The postindependence period has also witnessed a few indigenous writers, and scholars publish books on the history and culture of particular subnations—Fred. E. Makila (Bukusu), Namulundah Florence (Bukusu), Joseph Malusu (Isukha), Dr. Daniel Wako (Khayo), Demmahom Olovodes Lihraw (Tachoni), Osaak Olwumwullah (Bunyore), and Simani Sangale (Tiriki). I want to thank paremiographers, Rev. Tim Wambunya and Abraham Mirimo for recording Luyia sayings and proverbs.

Shadrack Amakoye Bulimo
April 2013

ACKNOWLEDGMENT

In researching material for this book, I consulted and sourced information from various authorities, government departments, libraries, and cultural institutions and corresponded with hundreds of people from all Luyia subnations. For reasons of space it is impossible to cite every person who made a contribution to this book but I would particularly like to thank Daniel Manyonge Khakina for carrying out research on the Bukusu and Tachoni; Solomon Barasa Wanyonyi for cross-checking aspects of Bukusu culture, Alan Alwala Efetha for providing botanical translations, and John Alusa Baraza for clarifying information on the Isukha and Idakho. In no particular order, I also wish to acknowledge the contribution of the following people: Prof. Chris Lukorito Wanjala, Solomon Barasa Kukubo, Topi Lyambila, Dr. Mellitus Nyongesa Wanyama, Paul Kakai Chetambe, John Wafula, Dr. Genevieve A. Mwayuuli, Beatrice Khamasi, Hon. Athanas Keya Manyala, Isaac Maringo Shiluli, Solomon Alusa, Gerishom Majanja, Prof Joshua Akong'a, Kwendo Opanga, Dr. Musa Mwendwa Ndengu, the late Jonathan Pritt Musaa, Amanda Anaminyi, Roy Nasibi, Julius Otieno Musandu, Todd Odhuno Were, Saulo Oduor, Gache Bucheko, Benson Buchichi, Bishop Arthur Okwemba, Samuel Ebole, Rev. Tim Wambunya, Shabanji Opukah, Justus Suchi Obadiah, Eric Amulaku, Dr Dick Makanji, John Khakhudu Agunda, Dr Wilberforce Ojiambo Oundo, John Oguttu, Jeff Ogambo Ganiko, Stephen Otoro, Moses Ochunju, Hedrick Ouma Wandera, Gillian Mutere, Juvenal Shiundu, Edmund Kwena, Rev. Martin Olando, Dr. Rachel Musimbi Kanyoro, Neccy Kikaya, Dr. David Kikaya, Livingstone Ominde, Bishop Titus Khamala, Phillis Gruesges, Benson A. Mulemi, Alex Muturi, Alex Machanga, Paul Sifuna Oshule, Kenneth Musaya, Darlington Sakwa, Peter N. Wanyonyi,

Acknowledgment

Geff Yabuna Ngilandala, Andrew Mungoma, Michael Were, Robert Ayieko, Dr. Francis Juma Ogeke, Michael Aderi and Anthea Neves. I am highly indebted to these people for volunteering their time and resources to help me compile this title.

ABBREVIATIONS

AD	Anno Domini (In the year of our Lord Christ)
AICMR	African Institute for Contemporary Mission and Research
Aids	Acquired Immune Deficiency Syndrome
aka	Also known as
BBC	British Broadcasting Corporation
BC	Before Christ
BWA	Buluyia Welfare Association
CDC	Commonwealth Development Corporation
CMS	Church Missionary Society
DC	District Commissioner
DFID	Department for International Development, a UK government agency
DMS	Digital Mapping System
DO	District Officer
EAC	East African Community
EADB	East African Development Bank
EAT	East African Time
FAM	Friends African Mission, the local branch of Quakers
FAO	Food and Agriculture Organization, a United Nations agency
FC	Football Club
FIFA	*Fédération Internationale de Football Association* (French) or International Federation of Association Football (English)
FORD	Forum for the Restoration of Democracy in Kenya
GMT	Greenwich Mean Time
GTI	Government Training Institute
GTZ	German Technical Cooperation

Ha	Hectares
HIV	Human Immuno Deficiency Virus
ICC	International Criminal Court based at The Hague, Netherlands
IDRC	International Development Research Center, a Canadian agency
IFC	International Finance Corporation, part of the Bretton Woods triad incorporating World Bank and the International Monetary Fund (IMF)
IIBRC	Independent Interim Boundaries Review Commission
ILO	International Labor Organization, a United Nations agency
IMO	International Maritime Organization, a United Nations agency
IT	Information Technology
KADDU	Kenya African Democratic Development Union
KADU	Kenya African Democratic Union
KANU	Kenya African National Union
KAR	Kings African Rifles
KASU	Kenya African Study Union
KAU	Kenya African Union
KCA	Kavirondo Central Association
KEFRI	Kenya Forestry Research Institute
Km	Kilometer
KNUT	Kenya National Union of Teachers
Legco	Legislative Council, the precursor to Kenya's House of Representatives
MMUST	Masinde Muliro University of Science and Technology, Kakamega
MP	Member of Parliament
MW	Megawatts

NARC	National Alliance Rainbow Coalition, a Kenyan political party
NCCK	National Council of Churches of Kenya
NCU	Native Catholic Union
NKTWA	North Kavirondo Tax Welfare Association
NSSF	National Social Security Fund
ODM	Orange Democratic Movement
PAG	Pentecostal Assemblies of God
PC	Provincial Commissioner
PS	Permanent Secretary
SACIM	South African Compounds and Interior Mission
SIL	Summer Institute of Linguistics, specializing in worldwide language research
SKTWA	South Kavirondo Tax Welfare Association
Sq	Square
UNESCO	United Nations Educational, Scientific and Cultural Organization
WECO	Western College of Arts and Sciences, the precursor to MMUST
WUCST	Western University College of Science and Technology
YWCA	Young Women's Christian Association

CHAPTER 1

Geography

Background

The Luyia (Luhya) populate western Kenya and parts of Rift Valley, especially the adjoining Trans Nzoia District.[1] According to 2009 National Population Census, the Luyia number 5,338,666 with an estimated one million living outside native territory. They are the second largest tribe in Kenya after the Kikuyu constituting 14 percent of Kenya's total population of 38,610,097. Administratively, Luyia territory is now divided into five counties—Kakamega, Vihiga, Busia, Bungoma, and Trans Nzoia,[2] of which the first three

---

[1.] Although Luyia territory stretches from Busoga in eastern Uganda and covers Kayunga, Bugwere, Samia Bugwe, Mbale and parts of Tororo, the scope of this book is limited to Kenyan Luyia. Except where stated the terms "Luyia territory" and "western" refer primarily to Kenyan Luyia.

[2.] Although Trans Nzoia is of mixed tribal heritage, the majority of residents (up to 70 percent) are of Luyia origin.

were formerly in Western Province and the latter in Rift Valley.[3] Out of the thirty-two districts in Western (including Trans Nzoia), two each are occupied by Nilotic tribes—Iteso (Wamia) and Sabaot (Sebei). In early colonial era, the Luyia and Luo were clustered into one administrative polity known as Kavirondo. In 1920, when Kenya became a British Protectorate and Colony, Kavirondo, until then part of eastern province of Uganda Protectorate was split into North and South Kavirondo. South Kavirondo became Luo territory while North Kavirondo was Luyia reserve and pockets of smaller Nilotic tribes primarily Iteso (Teso), Sabaot, and Terik. In 1948, North Kavirondo was renamed North Nyanza after the word *kavirondo* (see p.120) was deemed pejorative by indigenes. In 1953, Elgon Nyanza was carved out of North Nyanza, and at independence in 1963, North Nyanza African District was renamed Kakamega while Elgon Nyanza was split into Bungoma and Busia to form the three districts of Western Province.

[3.] Counties were established under a new constitution promulgated in August 2010 to replace provinces as the main administrative units. The forty-seven counties nationwide represent the districts existing as of 1992 (cutoff point). The original districts at independence in 1963 were forty-two. District creation was used as a political tool by Kenya's political elite. During Pres. Daniel Toroitich arap Moi's twenty-four-year reign, he created twenty-eight districts while President Emilio Mwai Kibaki went potty, dishing out 195 districts in seven years to bring Kenya's total to 265 by 2010. In August 2009, the high court ruled that all districts created after 1992 were illegal as they contravened the Districts and Provinces Act No 5 of 1992 but that did not stop President Kibaki from creating further districts.

Map 1 shows the territorial homeland of Luyia
tribesmen in Kenya.

(i)   Physiography

Luyia territory borders Ugandan districts of Busia, Tororo, Manafwa, Sironko, and Mbale[4] to the west and northwest. Busia is a typical example of the idiocy of the so-called Scramble for Africa under which European colonial powers sliced the continent into spheres of influence at the Berlin Conference of 1885. The border of Uganda and Kenya demarcates Busia almost into half-splitting families (see p.289) into two different nationalities. The people of Samia Bugwe in Uganda belong to the same ethno-linguistic lineage as the Samia of Kenya while Abanyala have large brethren in Uganda's Kayunga District and Sigulu Island in Lake Victoria. Bunyala district (hived off Busia in 2007) has the largest water mass in Buluyia by virtue of bordering Lake Victoria to the southwest and is also the river mouth of Nzoia in the lowlands of Budalang'i division. The Luyia border Ugandan tribes of Teso (Kenya and Uganda), Bagwere, and Nilotic Padhola while only Mount Elgon (Masaba) separates the brotherhood of Bukusu and Bagisu (collectively known as Bamasaaba). To the north of Trans Nzoia, Luyia border Kalenjin tribes of Pokot and Marakwet and to the east and southeast, Uasin Gishu and Nandi districts, respectively, and Luo of Nyanza to the south and southwest.

The total area of Western is 10,796.3 sq km (4,168.5 sq miles) which includes Trans Nzoia's 2,487 sq km. Together, Luyialand is only 2.2 percent of Kenya's total land mass (582,600 sq km). Out of the total area, 137.2 sq km is water, and 15 percent is occupied by non-Luyia tribes principally Iteso and Sabaot. From the lowlands of Busia (3,984 ft) in the West, the land rises to an altitude of

---

4.   The name Mbale is very common across Luyialand. There is a township called Mbale in Maragoli and Nambale in Bukhayo. There is even a clan known as Abambale in Idakho. Wherever this name appears, it illustrates a connection with Mbale, Uganda.

14,177 ft above sea level at its highest on the peak of Mt. Elgon in the north. The outlying areas on slopes of Mt. Elgon vary between 7,500 ft and 6,000 ft in the hills of Cherengany (Cherengani) and highlands of Trans Nzoia. Mt. Elgon (Masaba)[5] is the most discernible physical feature in Buluyia famous not only for its height and snowcapped peaks but also for numerous caves and holds spiritual value for Bamasaaba people living on both sides of the Kenya-Uganda frontier. In 1960, rock art predating colonial era was discovered in the caves in the first recorded instance of ancient rock art in Kenya (Bulimo 2013: 607). Elgon, like Mt. Longonot[6] near Nakuru, is a dormant volcano lying on the Great Rift Valley fault line. The dominant tree around Mt. Elgon forest is alpine of which *albizia* is the principal species.

The territorial headquarters of Western is Kakamega Town with an elevation of 4,999 ft above sea level and lies between Latitude (DMS) 0° 16' 60 North and Longitude (DMS) 34° 45' 0 East at a time zone of EAT (GMT+2-3). The indigenous name for Kakamega is Eshieywe although the colonialists first called it Fort Maxted. However, the origins of the name Kakamega can be traced to the Nandi who called this area *kikome kaa* (dead homestead), probably because they had abandoned it after Bantu Luyia from Uganda pushed them farther south into the Nandi escarpments and Uasin Gishu plateau. The Nandi, like Luyia, use the spire that protrudes from the roof of a hut to symbolize a homestead with a man. If a

---

[5.] The mountain straddles the border of Kenya and Uganda. People living on either side of the border call the mountain Masaba and themselves Bamasaaba (Bukusu and Gisu). Mubukusu and Mugisu, the eponymous founders of the two tribes, were brothers. Except for certain subtle nuances, Lubukusu and Lugisu languages are similar. In addition to linguistic similarities, the two tribes share common cultural attributes.

[6.] The name is derived from Maasai word *oloonong'ot*, which means "mountain of many ridges" and last erupted in the 1860s. It currently houses Kenya's only Earth Station and besides, the area is gazetted as a national reserve.

homestead does not have this symbol of manhood, the Nandi call it a dead homestead (*kikome kaa*).[7]

Luyialand is a land of astounding physiographical diversity. From high altitudes of Mt. Elgon in the north, a visitor is treated to a plethora of physical vistas ranging from the highlands of Kiminini, Saboti, and Kwanza in Trans Nzoia to windswept savannah grasslands of Bungoma broken only by undulating valleys and hills of Mwalie, Sang'alo, Musikoma, Kabuchai, and Chetambe. A visit to Mwibale Rock (*Mwibale wa Mwanja*) on the border of Bukusu and Bunyala is a must for tourists on a cultural tour or anthropological study. Mwanja, a Mulwonja clansman, was the owner of the land on which the mythical rock stands. The rock is believed to be the site where a Bukusu wrestler defeated a Nilotic wrestling champion, a symbolic psychocultural comeuppance which reestablished Bukusu superiority over Nilotes with whom they waged constant warfare. Not far from here is *Sikele sia Mulya*, a footprint in Sang'alo named after another Mulwonja clansman, Mulya. No one knows whether the footprint is real or mythical or how it got there in the first place, but in a society enveloped in sociocultural idiosyncrasies, *Sikele sia Mulya* continues to be a source of cultural and ritual fascination. Locals, however, believe that when Wele (God) made the stone, Mulya was the first man to walk across it with his wife and cattle, thus creating the "permanent" imprint. On a good day, you can see flashes of Mulya, his pregnant wife, and some cattle, or so it is believed. Similarly, a cave at Mwalie Rock (also known as Mango's cave) near Malakisi

---

7. A popular meaning of Kakamega, often said in jest, relates to an incident in which a Whiteman or a skeletal stranger was given a meal of ugali. Curious villagers peeped through holes in the hut as the stranger ate. Each time he went for a helping, the people said *khakhameka*. The *khakhameka* exploits of the stranger spread far and wide throughout the village becoming a hot subject in local gossip fare. A Whiteman heard people say *khakhameka* all the time and concluded the people of this place must be known as kak-a-mega.

holds cultural significance for Babukusu. It is believed to be here that Mango, credited with introducing circumcision to the subnation, trapped and killed the dreaded *yabebe* serpent that had terrorized the land for a long time, according to Bukusu mythology (Bulimo 2013: 271). Ecotourists, who come to Kakamega Forest, will not be disappointed with a visit to Buteyo Miti Park in Sang'alo, a privately owned arboretum and reputedly one of its kind in Africa.

As you continue travelling south, the rolling savannah landscape of Bungoma is broken by a pristine tropical forest, the second most significant feature in Western physiography after Mt. Elgon. Beginning in Kabras and enveloping Isukha and Tiriki, Kakamega Forest is the easternmost remnant of the Congo-Guinean equatorial rainforest that once stretched from West Africa through Cameroon, Congo, Uganda, and Kenya with an altitude ranging from 4,593.2 ft-5,577.4 ft. Buyangu Hill is the highest point in the forest, and from here, visitors marvel at the panoramic canopy of the tropical dense forest, their peace disrupted only by the chirpings of rare snake-eating birds like the banded snake eagle. The forest is truly primordial with rare species of flora (380) and fauna, some of which are only found in West Africa including the "flying" poisonous snake. With over 350 species of rare birds and four hundred butterfly species recorded, Kakamega Forest is a favorite with ornithologists from all over the world. In addition, the forest is sanctuary to rare primates like the blue monkey, olive baboon, and red-tailed monkey. Although the forest has 125 tree species, croton is dominant comprising between 40 and 50 percent of forest timber.

A major attraction in the western Kenya tourist circuit, Kakamega Forest has had significant patches cleared over the last one thousand years for settlement and farming. When it was gazetted as a national forest in 1933, it consisted of the main block (23,785 ha) and two smaller ones—Kisere (400 ha) and Malava

(780 ha). In 1966, it was gazetted as a national reserve to protect the rare animal and plant species found here. Further fragmentation continued between 1933 and 1985 reducing the main block of forest to fifteen thousand ha by the year 2001. Currently, the forest consists of 8,245 ha (main block) and six outlying fragments ranging in size from 65 ha to 1,370 ha. These include Malava, Kisere, Lugari, Kaimosi, Bunyala, and Maragoli forests. To the west of Kakamega Forest is a long patch of rainforest known as North Nandi Forest and concave-shaped South Nandi Forest to the south. Besides these two, there are also three small patches—Tarosia (north of Nandi North), Kaglerai (north of Nandi South), and Ururu (West of Nandi South). Together, the Nandi forests add a welcome break from the rugged terrain of Uasin Gishu plateau and the cascading heights of neighboring Nandi escarpments. All these vegetative covers are in close proximity to Kakamega forest and were part of the original Congo-Guinean equatorial rainforest alluded to above.

(ii) Geology

The rocky hills of Bunyore and Maragoli in the south provide the visitor with a postcard image of a beautiful landscape that contrasts sharply with the Uasin Gishu plateau. The lava sheets which characterize Uasin Gishu plateau and Nandi escarpments are replaced with porphyritic granites concentrated in the localities of Bunyore, Maragoli, and Tiriki and sparsely strewn across Idakho, Isukha, Marama, and Wanga. Some of the giant boulders in Bunyore and Maragoli are a natural wonder. Blasted from the earth's crust during the tectonic formation of Lake Victoria millions of years ago, the giant boulders balance so precariously they simply take your breath away. If you turn westward and travel through Luanda[8] Township toward Busia, you cannot fail to notice the pyramid-shaped Esibila hills in Bunyore famed for rainmaking rituals by Nganyi rain magicians (Bulimo 2013: 41). The hills are of such ritual significance to Abanyole that they were gazetted for protection by the Ministry of National Heritage. Busia welcomes you with Samia hills, rich in iron ore deposits which made local Samia people the best iron smelters in Buluyia in the pre-European days (see p.286). Besides Samia hills, one also stumbles upon another magical feature, a series of hills and rocky outcroppings collectively known as Teso hills of which the tallest is Cheremuluk Rock, which has a historico-cultural significance for Babukusu. It was at a cave in the rock that circumcision rituals began before the Bukusu were driven out by invading Iteso from Uganda.

Besides tectonic activity, Western landscape is underlain by rocks of the basement and pre-Cambrian systems attributable to volcanic eruption of Mt. Elgon, especially the area between Nandi escarpment and south east of the mountain. The pedological composition of Western reveals three major soil types, according to FAO classification—nitisols (dark red with 30 percent clay), ferrralsols (strongly weathered soils with a chemically poor but physically stable subsoil), and acrisols found around the fringes of Kakamega Forest. The highlands of Trans Nzoia have two distinctive soil subtypes—the alpine meadow and shallow stony soils with touches of alluvium deposited by slow moving water and peaty swamps in the valleys. The most arable soil in the region is the dark red friable clays and sandy clay loams. The southern and eastern parts of Buluyia like Maragoli, Tiriki, and Bunyore consist primarily of granite soils. The rocky terrain of South Maragoli gives way to fertile red soils in North Maragoli suitable for tea

---

[8.] The name Luanda is derived from the word *olwanda* which means rock. It is a very popular name in Luyialand as well as Luoland with many places called Luanda or Mulwanda.

plantations. The topography of upper Nzoia basin is characterized by alluvial soils deposited by slow moving water, but as the river turns south, it moves faster depositing fluvial soils (fluvisols) mainly around Bungoma, Mumias, and upper Busia. Fluvisols have high fertility due to large amounts of humic substances as well as loamy and sandy fractions.

The swampy areas of Busia in the lower Nzoia basin are dominated by wetland soils (gleysols) and organic soils (histosols) which are imperfectly drained. Around riparian ridges of Lake Victoria in Busia, one finds solonchaks (solonetz) which, when dry, cause structural problems due to an imperfect drainage, salinity, and sodicity. Here also one finds what is commonly known as black cotton soils (vertisols) with a high propensity for water retention suitable for cassava and cotton plantation. These soils can carry crops through a long drought but crack badly when dry. Moreover, the swelling nature of vertisols means they are poor candidates for engineering projects such as road building. The dry lands of Busia County are also characterized by sandy soils (arenosol) formed by colluvial substrates deposited from chipped basement rocks. The sugar belt region of Mumias is dominated by loamy soils which support a number of crops besides sugar while neighboring Khwisero has predominantly shallow soils pointing to highly eroded activity and hence poor crop development in the locality. Butere is fertile with a variety of rich soils most of which belong to the well-drained loamy type.

Most of Buluyia is savannah country consisting of rolling pastoral grasslands broken by rocky hills referred to above. The grassland regions of Western are dominated by the star grass, blady grass (*imperata cylindrica*), napier or Uganda grass (*pennisetum purpureum*), and muteete grass (*cymbopogon afronadus*) found in the granite areas of Maragoli and Bunyore.

(iii) Climatology

Western lies just north of the equator and experiences two main seasons. The long rainy season falls between March and June with September to November having short rain spells. Agronomists advise farmers to plant maize, the chief subsistence crop, at the beginning of February in expectation of the rainy season which peaks during April and May and tapers off thereafter. Maize (*amatuma*) is planted twice a year with the second planting season occurring in September and harvesting in January. The dry season is normally around December to February with January experiencing dry easterly winds from Nandi escarpments. The average temperatures are highs of 30^0 C and lows of 18^0 C during dry season and 28^0 C and 16^0 C during the cold season typically July and August with an annual precipitation averaging 1800mm (70.9 inches). Humidity ranges from 75 to 90 percent in most parts of the province with ultraviolet radiation index (UV) averaging zero throughout the year. Proximity to the equator means that night and day have near-equal hours with sunset clocking at 6:40 p.m. and sunrise at 6:45.a.m. The county of Kakamega is mainly hot and wet most of the year thanks, in large measure, to the pristine tropical rainforest while Bungoma and Trans Nzoia, on the foothills of Mt. Elgon are colder but equally wet. Busia County in the lake basin is the hottest and hilly Vihiga the coldest. Due to proximity of Kakamega Forest, the localities of Kabras, Isukha, Navakholo, Idakho, Butsotso, and Tiriki receive plenty of rain, thus retaining lush green outlook throughout the year.

(iv) Hydrology

The average annual rainfall is thirty inches with the highest recorded (seventy-six inches) in the northeastern flanks of Lugari, southeastern Kakamega, and Kaimosi. The highlands of Trans Nzoia on the foothills of Mt. Elgon also receive heavy rainfall. Central areas like Sang'alo and Bukura and western parts of Luyialand, especially Busia, receive less rainfall. Where it rains heavily, it is often accompanied by thunderstorms and occasionally hailstorms and lightning. The heavy rains are drained in all-seasonal rivers principally the Nzoia, Yala (Lukose or Obaro in Bunyala), Jordan, Ezava (Echava), Lusumu (Isiukhu), Lwakhakha, Malakisi, Kamukuywa, Kuywa, and Sio. River Nzoia is the largest in Luyialand and divides the territory into two almost equal halves running in a south westerly direction before draining into Lake Victoria at Port Victoria in Bunyala. Rising from Mt. Elgon, it is the longest (334 km) with several tributaries joining it as it snakes its way toward the Budalang'i basin. It is eighty yards (73.2 m) wide at its mouth and is characterized by rapids, rocks, and falls (Nabuyole falls, formerly Broderick being the main one) which render it unsuitable for navigation.

River Nzoia is the third most important physical feature in Western and an economic lifeline to millions of people in the region. It flows through densely populated areas, its waters irrigating fields throughout the year. But while the river is a blessing, it is equally a curse. The savior turns into a genie when it breaks its banks and bursts through hapless dykes (levees) built in 1977 in Bunyala bringing death and destruction to whole villages. The first incidence of flooding was recorded in 1947, but since then, River Nzoia has released its torrent on Budalang'i with frightening consequences fourteen times as of 2011.[9] In recent years, the tempestuous river has tended to annualize demonic visitation on Banyala tribesmen who view it as a curse. The

---

9. According to records, Budalang'i was hit with fatal flood from River Nzoia in 1947, 1951, 1957, 1958, 1961, 1962, 1963, 1975, 1977, 1978, 2003, 2006, 2007, and 2008.

deposition of alluvium in the floodplains is largely thought to be responsible for clogging the river mouth, thus causing the flooding. Mt. Elgon from where the Nzoia rises is also the source of another major river known as Suam which becomes Turkwell downstream and empties in Lake Turkana (formerly Rudolf). The government of Kenya entered into a partnership with a French company to build a hydroelectric dam along the Turkwell, but the $450m Turkwell Gorge Dam project, completed in 1993 stands as a white elephant, a symbol of grand corruption by the Moi Government. It was meant to generate 160 MW of electricity but at its highest, only managed eighty-five MW, thanks to a seasonal river whose flow had fallen by 13 percent in 2008.

The second largest river is Yala (Lukose or Obaro in Bunyala) which originates from Nandi hills and passes through Idakho and Kisa on its way to Yala Swamp. It is 212 km long with a catchment area of 3,262 sq km across Rift Valley, Western, and Nyanza provinces. River Yala is fed by several streams and brooks of which the main ones are Etsava and Jordan[10] which crisscross Maragoli and Bunyore. It is 30-40 yards (27.4-36.6m) wide at low water, and for the last 17 miles it meanders through the immense Yala Swamp before joining Nzoia delta near the shores of Lake Victoria. About 8 km from the lake, it suddenly turns north and, within a short distance of the Nzoia, forms Lake Gangu (Anyuoka) which is part of small satellite lakes in the region—others being Lake Kanyaboli and Sare in Siaya and Lake Wamoro in Busia. The Yala then flows out of Lake Gangu and joins the swampy delta of the Nzoia. In 2009, the Kenyan government commissioned a feasibility study aimed at building a multipurpose dam on River Yala. Known as Nandi Forest Multipurpose Dam Development Project, the station

---

[10.] River Jordan (Echorotani) holds spiritual value for Bunyore Christians. It is not clear what the original name was, but Church of God missionaries christened it Jordan and used its waters for baptismal rituals—a rite that continues to this day.

is projected to generate 50 MW of electricity with an irrigation scheme covering 17,000 ha of farmland.

Other rivers which trace their source to Mt. Elgon include the Sio and Malakisi. The Malakisi meets Lwakhakha River near Tororo in Uganda to form the Malaba River which subsequently flows westward into Lake Kyoga. The Sio flows through rolling savannah plains of Kenya, and for the last twelve miles of its course, it forms the southwestern frontier with Uganda separated from the Nzoia valley by Samia Hills. It passes through an extensive wetland before emptying into Lake Victoria. Of the remainder, Lusumu which starts off as River Isiukhu in the hills around Kakamega Forest is a major tributary which confluences with the mighty Nzoia about five kilometers from Mumias. Other tributaries include Lairi and Viratsi which forms the border of Mumias and Ugenya at Buholo. Central Bungoma is also drained by Chwele, Khalaba, and Kuywa tributaries of the mighty River Nzoia.

(v) Administrative and political geography

Administratively, Western was originally one of the eight provinces of Kenya. At independence in 1963, the province, then known as North Nyanza, was split into three districts—Kakamega, Bungoma, and Busia. In 1988, Lugari which began as a settlement scheme in 1962 for squatters on former white settler farms was excised off the larger Kakamega. It included the divisions of Matete, Likuyani, and Lumakanda which also serves as the district headquarters. However, in 2009, Matete and Likuyani were hived off to become independent districts. Lugari has one eponymous constituency created in 1987 and falls under Kakamega County.

In 1990, Vihiga District was created from Kakamega to cater for Maragoli, Tiriki, and Bunyore localities by the Moi Administration. But since 2007, under the Kibaki government there was an explosion of administrative subdivisions. In 2007, two farther districts were hived off Vihiga—Hamisi (Tiriki) and Emuhaya (Bunyore) with headquarters at Kima while Vihiga remained largely for the Maragoli. Vihiga with headquarters at Mbale was further subdivided to create Sabatia District, thus restoring the old rivalries of North and South Maragoli chieftaincies and giving Avaloogoli two districts. Vihiga is now a county following promulgation of Kenya's new constitution with four constituencies—Emuhaya in Bunyore, Hamisi in Tiriki, and Vihiga and Sabatia in Maragoli. A fifth constituency (Luanda) was created following adoption of Ligale Report by Kenyan Parliament in June 2011.

As well in 2007, the larger Bungoma was divided into five separate districts—Bungoma North (Kimilili and Tongaren divisions), Bungoma East (Webuye and Ndivisi divisions), Bungoma West (Malakisi and Sirisia divisions), Bungoma Central (Chwele and Nalondo divisions), and lastly Bungoma South district comprising Bumula and Kanduyi divisions. Mukuyuni is the capital of Bungoma North, Webuye (Bungoma East), Sirisia (Bungoma West), Chwele (Bungoma Central) while Bungoma Town—the regional commercial hub—is headquarters to Bungoma South district. Bungoma Town (population 55,867 in 2009) is the largest municipality in the larger Bungoma. Other urbanized areas include Kimilili (population 41,115); Webuye (23,381); Chwele (7,206); Tongaren (2,793), and Malakisi (3,512). The neighboring Trans Nzoia, although officially classified under Rift Valley, nevertheless has majority Bukusu tribesmen with the major towns being Kitale (75,782) and Kiminini (5,523). Further subdivision occurred in 2009 when Bumula was hived off Bungoma South as an independent district while Kimilili was excised from Bungoma North to make the total number of districts in the larger Bungoma area seven. Bungoma County includes Mt. Elgon District and originally had six constituencies—Webuye, Sirisia,

Kimilili, Kanduyi, Bumula, and Mt. Elgon.[11] Before counties were introduced and new districts created, the original Bungoma District had ten administrative divisions comprising forty-four locations and 114 sublocations covering an area of 2,068.5 sq km.

Kakamega was further split in 1998 when Butere/Mumias District was created with its headquarters in Butere to serve the Wanga, Kisa, and Marama. It absorbed the localities of Mumias, Butere, Matungu, and Khwisero. Butere/Mumias was further split in 2007 into Mumias and Butere districts, and in 2009, Khwisero district was cut off Butere to cater specifically for Abashisa (Kisa) while Matungu District was hived off Mumias to give Abawanga two districts. Apart from the Bukusu who have six districts, the Wanga and Maragoli are the only other subnations with more than one district. In 2007, Kakamega was again further subdivided into Kakamega Central District covering the metropolitan Kakamega Town and the divisions of Lurambi (Batsotso) and Navakholo (Abanyala), Kakamega East (Isukha) with headquarters at Shinyalu, Kakamega North covering Malava, and Kivaywa in Kabras and Kakamega South (Idakho) with headquarters at Malinya. In 2009, Navakholo District was hived off Kakamega Central to cater for Abanyala ba Ndombi. Kakamega County now covers twelve districts[12] with nine constituencies—Shinyalu, Ikolomani, Malava, Butere, Lurambi, Mumias, Matungu, Lugari, and Khwisero. Following the adoption of Ligale Report by Kenyan Parliament in June 2011, Kakamega received three new constituencies. In

---

[11]. Mt. Elgon District is populated by non-Luyia tribe known as Sabaot (Sebei). Following adoption of Ligale Report by Kenyan Parliament in June 2011, Bungoma County got an additional three constituencies. In addition to Tongaren and Kabuchai, Webuye constituency was split into Webuye East and Webuye West.

[12]. The districts in Kakamega County are Kakamega South, Kakamega North, Kakamega East, Kakamega Central, Mumias, Matungu, Butere, Khwisero, Lugari, Navakholo, Likuyani, and Matete.

addition to Navakholo and Likuyani, Mumias constituency was split into Mumias West and Mumias East taking to twelve the number of constituencies in the county.

In Busia region, the original administrative polity has also been divided into several districts—Bunyala, Samia, Butula, Nambale, Teso East, and Teso West. Bunyala and Samia districts were created in 2007 as part of the political plenitude dished out by Pres. Mwai Kibaki in the run up to the general elections of December 2007. Bunyala District headquarters are at Budalang'i and include settlements of Sio Port (Bujwang'a) and Port Victoria. The new district covers an area of 185.6 sq km with a population of 66, 568, according to population census of 2009. Abanyala also occupy Sigulu Island and Kayunga District in Uganda. The district has one division, Budalang'i with six administrative locations and seventeen sublocations. Samia district headquarters are at Funyula with Nangina being the other major division. In 2009, Butula (Marachi) and Nambale (Khayo) were also created leaving Busia largely as a metropolitan area consisting largely of Abakhayo and Iteso. Teso District was hived off Busia in 1995 before being further subdivided into Teso South and Teso North districts in 2007. Busia County originally had five constituencies (Funyula, Budalang'i, Butula, Nambale, and Amagoro). However, the geopolitical map of the county changed in 2011 when two more constituencies were added. Amagoro was abolished and in its place created Teso North and Teso South while creation of Matayos means Bakhayo now have two constituencies.

Map 2: LUHYA SUB NATIONS

Map 2 shows the geographical location of Luyia subnations.

(vi) Economy

Western Kenya is dubbed the bread basket of Kenya but is also ironically a basket case as majority of people live below the poverty line characterized by a high dependency index. While the average national poverty index[13] is 53 percent, in Western this rises to as much as 60 percent in some parts of Bungoma. Although significant parts of Bunyore, Maragoli, and Tiriki have one of the highest rural population densities in the world as you move northward into the highlands of Bungoma and Trans Nzoia, the country opens up to smaller spatial distribution. The average population density is 522

---

[13]. Poverty index is given as $17 per month for rural populations and $363 for urban dwellers. This is the money required to sustain the barest minimum livelihood.

people per sq km which you find in parts of Bungoma. However, in Vihiga, this rises to 1,101 and Bunyore 1,067 while the lowest is in Bunyala and Samia at 354 and 353, respectively.

The majority of Luyia are subsistence farmers occupying smallholder acreages averaging two acres in which they grow crops like maize, beans, cassava, millet, sorghum, sweet potatoes, onions, bananas, and vegetables for domestic consumption with any surplus sold at local markets. They also keep one or two cattle in their homesteads for milk and several chickens for their poultry needs as a matter of custom. Some of these markets are weekly while others are twice weekly and, in dense populated areas, daily. Besides agricultural produce, people also trade in livestock (especially cows, goats, sheep, and chickens) and items of craftsmanship like pots, baskets, and iron implements including knives, hoes, and *pangas* (machetes). Some of the biggest markets include Mbale in Maragoli, Lubao in Isukha, Luanda in Bunyore, Mumias, Bungoma, and Busia. Started in 1952, Lubao, on the Kakamega-Webuye road is the only market in Kenya that sells dogs in addition to cattle and general merchandise. It derives its name from several timber (*mbao*) businesses that thrived in the area. Other local businesses include shops, bars, restaurants, kiosks, and related support services like *boda boda* cycle taxis, most of which operate in the informal sector (*Jua Kali*).

The general economic profile of Luyialand obtains in Idakho and Isukha, but as you turn westward into Butsotso and Wanga, the country begins to open up to medium-scale farmlands. This is sugar country powered by Mumias Sugar Company, Kenya's largest cane miller established in 1973 and touted to be a lifeline for an estimated fifty thousand people, especially farmers in the neighborhood and those as far as Siaya and Busia. Sugar is the most important cash crop in the economy of Western. Although Mumias is the flagship of the industry, Western has three other millers notably Nzoia in Bungoma, West Kenya Sugar Factory, and the controversy-ridden Butali—both in Malava, Kakamega North District.

Besides sugar, Western is also home to Pan African Paper Mills (popularly known as Pan Paper), the only pulp paper manufacturing plant in Kenya situated at Webuye, Bungoma East District. Started in 1974, Pan Paper was established as a joint venture between the Kenyan government (34 percent), the International Finance Corporation (IFC), and Orient Paper Mills, part of the Birla Group of India. The factory was declared insolvent in 2008 following massive debts, its huge chimneys billowing smoke of burnt dreams and economic aspirations of the Luyia people. Despite high-profile government promises to revive the plant, including one by Pres. Mwai Kibaki in 2010, the factory remains shut, a hollow symbol of broken promises. The collapse of Pan Paper rekindles memories of another failed attempt at industrialization in Western. Gold mining which started in Kakamega (Idakho, Isukha, and Butsotso) in 1932 lasted only twenty years leaving behind shattered dreams of a people in what academics dubbed "a failed Eldorado" (see p.325).

Beyond the spectacular beauty of the flora and fauna of Kakamega Forest, the facility is an important source of tourist revenue and rainfall that waters the economic terrain of Western. The forest in popular with birdwatchers and ornithologists and is sanctuary to some of Africa's rarest snakes, some of which are only found in West Africa. An agricultural research station is housed on the eastern fringes of the forest and a tourist lodge, Rondo Retreat Hotel, nests inside the forest. Its unique flora and fauna are a source of fascination and scientific research. The so-called African viagra, *omukombera* (*mondia whytei*) is found here. Locals forage into the forest for firewood and medicinal herbs. Previously, they hunted monkeys for bush meat, but this aspect of Luyia culinary culture is outlawed and is no longer practiced. Despite its huge economic value, Kakamega Forest, gazetted as a national reserve in 1966 is threatened with extinction due to land grabbing, illegal lumbering activities, and human encroachment. Historians, researchers, and cultural tourists who wish to learn more about the ancient Wanga Kingdom will find a trip to Nabongo Cultural Center in Matungu, Mumias, extremely rewarding. Besides hosting the burial chambers of Wanga kings, the facility has a library with a collection of rare photos, artifacts, and books.

Bungoma and Trans Nzoia are famously tagged the granary of Kenya. Formerly expropriated as white highlands, here you find large-scale commercial farming principally maize, sunflower, coffee, tobacco, potatoes, beans, and dairy. Besides Nzoia Sugar Company and Pan Paper Mills, Bungoma also has three coffee processing factories at Chwele, Chesikaki, and Namang'ofulo and a Tobacco Leaf Center at Malakisi. There is also a small but growing tourist industry in Bungoma largely associated with the biennial circumcision festivals of the Bukusu and Tachoni. In addition, Bungoma is also home of the late Cardinal Maurice Otunga, Kenya's first cardinal for whom the long process of beatification may yet declare him a saint. As and when he achieves sainthood, his Chebukwa village in Matili will become a revered shrine attracting pilgrims and the Catholic faithful from around the world. The economic benefits of Saint Otunga are not lost to residents of the county. Bungoma Town and Webuye are already major commercial centers in Western lying strategically along Trans Africa Highway toward Uganda. Cultural tourists and anthropologists should also find a visit to Mwibale and Mwalie rocks as well as Lumboka and Chetambe ruins a compelling addition to their itinerary. The former are associated with circumcision and ethnic war mythology while the latter were walled forts (*tsingoba*, Bukusu: *chingoba*) destroyed by British colonialists in 1894 and 1895 respectively as they sought to colonize the belligerent Bukusu.

After coffee was liberalized in 1949 by the colonial government, suitable areas identified around the country included Bungoma. By

1951, Arabica coffee was being planted in Kimilili, the experiment involving 361 households on a small scale. The experiment soon proved so successful that Western's first coffee factory was built at Chwele in 1954 and a second one at Chesikaki, also in Bungoma the following year. Farther afield, coffee was also grown in the Mt. Elgon area around Chepkube with another factory constructed at Emanang' and Namang'ofulo. However, the success of the agrarian revolution in Bungoma could not be replicated in other parts of Western. In Bunyore for example, peasant farmers planted coffee on small acreages encouraged by a coffee processing factory built at Es'saba sublocation. However, the factory closed without processing a single coffee bean in the 1980s.

Kakamega Town today. The colonial administration transferred provincial headquarters of North Kavirondo (later North Nyanza) from Mumias (Elureko) to Kakamega in 1919.

Fishing is a major economic activity in Busia accounting for about 40 percent of the gross economic output of the county mainly from Lake Victoria but increasingly also from fish-farming in commercial ponds. The warm climate of Busia is ideal for cassava plantations which locals grow for subsistence purposes as well as selling extra produce at local markets. Cassava farming may yet be commercialized in an agrarian revolution expected to change lives of an estimated thirty thousand people, thanks to an initiative by two international organizations. Alliance for a Green Revolution in Africa (AGRA) and Farm Concern International (FCI) are pioneering this initiative aimed at improving food security for small-scale farmers. Besides food, agro-processing centers will be set up to process cassava extract for use in the manufacture of animal feed, glue, biofuel, and glucose syrup. Busia residents also grow sugar which they transport to Mumias Sugar Company about 45 km away. A sugar factory conceived about twenty years ago in the county has not materialized; a victim of political gerrymandering. Cotton farming was introduced in Busia around 1908 and peaked in the 1970s but has since faced daunting challenges finally collapsing in independent Kenya when Kisumu Cotton Mills (KICOMI), the only nearby ginnery collapsed in late 1980s. A small ginnery at Luanda near River Sio in Busia started by a colonial industrialist, Mr. Small, could not sustain large-scale cotton farming. Busia is also the cradle of the famous *boda boda* cycle taxis that now dot the entire country. The business started with a small army of cyclists ferrying passengers and goods on no-man's land between the border of Kenya and Uganda in 1970s. Although perennial floods from Nzoia River cause havoc to the local economy, residents of Busia have stayed put confident that they can turn around their economic circumstances given an enabling environment free of political manipulations.

In Vihiga County, reputedly the world's most crowded rural locality, the principal economic activity is petty trading on several market centers littered in the county of which the primary ones are Luanda in Bunyore, Mbale, Chavakali, and Majengo in Maragoli and Shamakhokho in Tiriki. Besides petty trade, there are also smallholder tea plantations, especially in North Maragoli and Hamisi as well as French beans and mushroom farms. Tea produced on these holdings is processed at Mudete Tea Factory in Sabatia, North Maragoli. Quarrying for construction materials has lately become a major preoccupation and a source of employment for the youth. The process is, however, still manual-based, but with appropriate investment in quarrying and stone cutting machinery, this is likely to be an area to watch given the huge availability of granite rocks in the vicinity. Subsistence dairy farming is widely practiced with experiments at cheese-making from goat milk taking place.

Located on Kisumu-Kakamega road, Chavakali is one of the major market centers in Luyialand.

Overall, living standards in Western are generally low with majority of residents having no access to running water (less than 3 percent) and electricity although this is now changing under the rural electrification programme by the Kenya Power and Lighting Company (KPLC). Although the main mode of sanitation is pit latrines, a sizeable number of people still use the bush to relieve themselves (the national average is 20.7 percent of rural Kenyans). Despite relative poverty, the picture changes drastically when it comes to mobile (cell) phone usage. Over the last ten years, mobile telephony has exploded throughout Kenya with 63.2 percent of Kenyans recorded as having a cell phone according to 2009 census. The impact of widespread telecommunications technology is not lost to scholars, pundits, and planners who see the trend as godsend in terms of communicating development issues. In 2008, the Kenyan government identified Internet as an essential adjunct in development communication and through the Kenya ICT Board embarked on creating digital villages in all constituencies. With broadband technology, a reality since 2010 coupled with Microsoft's Swahili software, it is only a matter of time before rural Kenyans get linked to the international information super highway. At the moment, access to a computer and Internet is still a novelty for most rural dwellers with only 3.6 percent of Kenyans having a personal computer in their households (2009 census). Private Internet kiosks meanwhile are filling the gap in information deficit, but costs are far too prohibitive for most folk.

(vii) Education

Western has 2,059 primary schools (including Trans Nzoia's 265). Butere District has the largest number (187) followed by Vihiga (175) and Bungoma South (163). In secondary education, Western has 602 schools (including 79 in Trans Nzoia) with Vihiga leading (51), Mumias in second place (47), and Lugari in third (40), according to records obtained from the Teacher's Service Commission. Mumias has the lowest ratio of primary schools to secondary (1:2) while Butere has the highest (1:6). In addition, there is one national university (Masinde Muliro University of Science and Technology) with campuses at Bukura in Butsotso, Kibabii, and Webuye in Bungoma and Ebunangwe in Bunyore and one private one—Friends University Kaimosi, a Quaker institution. The region has two government teacher training colleges—Eregi and Kaimosi and several private ones. Kibabii Diploma Teacher Training College was elevated to a university status as a constituent campus of MMUST in 2011 and admitted its first batch of university students in 2012. In addition, Western has one polytechnic (Sigalagala) in Shinyalu, one of the oldest technical training institutes in the country elevated to a polytechnic in 2009 and five technical training institutes—Shamberere in Malava, Matili in Kimilili, Bushiangala in Ikolomani, Sang'alo Institute of Science and Technology in Kanduyi, and Kisiwa Institute of Technology in Sirisia. In terms of vocational training, there are three medical training colleges for nurses at Webuye District Hospital, St. Elizabeth Hospital Mukumu, and St. Mary's Hospital Mumias.

Table 1: Schools in Western districts including Trans Nzoia

District	Primary	Secondary
Bunyala	33	7
Bungoma East	89	35
Bungoma North	109	38
Bungoma South	163	33
Bungoma West	125	38
Busia	143	38
Butere	187	31
Emuhaya	90	22
Hamisi	81	26
Kakamega Central	96	35
Kakamega East	51	27
Kakamega North	112	24
Kakamega South	97	20
Kitale Municipality	27	9

Kwanza	89	19
Lugari	107	40
Mumias	74	47
Trans Nzoia East	90	27
Trans Nzoia West	59	33
Samia	62	11
Vihiga	175	51

Source: Teachers Service Commission (2010)

(viii) Health

The main hospital in Western is Kakamega Provincial which began life as Government Native Hospital in 1922, the region's main referral health institution. Besides Kakamega, mission hospitals were also established at Kaimosi in Tiriki, Mukumu in Isukha, Nangina in Samia, Kima in Bunyore, Mwihila in Kisa, Lugulu, and Misikhu in Bungoma. The government, on its part, established district hospitals of which the main ones are Mbale in Vihiga, Busia, Bungoma, Webuye, Butere, and Lugari. The region's only eye hospital is situated at Sabatia, North Maragoli. In Trans Nzoia, the main hospitals are Mt. Elgon and Kitale district hospital. The following is the updated list of all thirty-nine government and private medical institutions in Western.

Table 2: Medical Facilities in Western

Bukaya Medical Center, Imanga
Bungoma Medical Center
Butere District Hospital
Central Maternity & Nursing, Kakamega

Bungoma District Hospital
Busia District Hospital, Busia
Butula Mission Hospital, Busia
Cherangany Nursing Home, Kitale

Elgon View Medical Cottage, Bungoma

Friends Kaimosi Hospital, Tiriki

Friends Lugulu Hospital, Webuye

Holy Family Hospital, Nangina

Kima Mission Hospital, Bunyore

Kimilili District Hospital

Kiminini Cottage Hospital

Kitale District Hospital

Kitale Nursing Home

Lugari District Hospital, Kipkaren

Lumboka Memorial Hospital, Bungoma

Lumino Maternity & Nursing Home, Mumias

Manyala Subdistrict Hospital, Butere

Misikhu Mission Hospital, Webuye

Moi's Bridge Maternity & Nursing Home

Mt. Elgon Hospital, Kitale

Mwihila Mission Hospital, Yala

Nala Maternity & Nursing Home, Kakamega

Namasoli Health Center, Yala

New Busia Maternity & Nursing Home

Port Victoria Subdistrict Hospital

Provincial General Hospital, Kakamega

Sabatia Eye Hospital, Wodanga

Sister Fridas Medical Center, Kitale

St. Damiano Medical Hospital, Bungoma

St Elizabeth Hospital, Mukumu

St. Mary's Hospital, Mumias

Tanaka Nursing Home, Busia

Vihiga District Hospital, Maragoli

Webuye District Hospital

(ix) Role of the Church

The church has played an important role in economic development of western Kenya. Besides spiritual nourishment, the church pioneered educational and health services at the beginning of the twentieth century. Although Catholics were the earliest arrivals, they were soon eclipsed by Quakers who, besides health and education, also introduced vocational training that imparted employable skills to natives, e.g., carpentry, masonry, and machining. The main church denominations include

Quakers, Catholics, Anglicans, and Pentecostals. Salvation Army, Methodists, Seventh Day Adventists, Lutherans, Jehovah Witnesses, etc., were late arrivals. Out of the latecomers only Salvation Army has a sizeable following, especially in Maragoli. In addition to conventional Christian churches, there are also independent faith movements, notably African Roho and Israel Nineveh sects. The most famous of indigenous religions is *Dini ya Musambwa*, started by Elijah Masinde in 1946. The sect was outlawed by the colonial government, and its founder detained at Manyani for opposing colonialism and preaching against established religious order. Although *Dini ya Musambwa* continued to spread beyond its aboriginal roots in Bukusu despite Masinde's incarceration, it faced insurmountable challenges as a proscribed sect even after independence and has since the founder's death in 1987 gone underground.

Like the Scramble for Africa, Western religions carved out spheres of territorial influence among Luyia and neighboring Luo. Under this pact, CMS was assigned to evangelize among the southern Luo and Marama, Church of God Bunyore (later Kisa and Butsotso), Quakers Maragoli, Bukusu, and Tiriki while Catholics were to concentrate on Wanga, Isukha, and Idakho. Church of God East Africa, which started as South African Compounds and Interior Mission (SACIM) but later bought by missionaries from Anderson, Indiana, USA in 1926, is headquartered at Kima in Bunyore and Quakers at Kaimosi in Tiriki. Salvation Army headquarters are at Madzuu in South Maragoli.

(x) Transport

Long before rail and all-weather roads were constructed, there existed an old caravan route that started in Mumias and ran across Kabras across Kipkarren and Sosiani rivers through Nandi escarpments to Lake Baringo. From here, the route turned southeast to Ngong and continued past Mt. Kilimanjaro toward the coast. It was this route that initially opened the interior of Kenya and Uganda to Arab and Swahili traders and eventually to colonial conquest. It was thanks to this old caravan route that the first Whiteman to set foot in Luyialand, Joseph Thomson arrived at the court of Nabongo Mumia in December 1883 from Uasin Gishu. Even men of religion, especially Bishop Hannington graced this route sojourning at Mumias on his way to Uganda where he was murdered. In 1895, Captain B. L. Sclater was assigned to enlarge the road to 12 ft to accommodate the Mombasa Oxcart Service (managed by Smith, Mackenzie, & Co.) to Port Victoria in Bunyala. Captain Sclater was ordered to shorten the route by turning West at Eldama Ravine and cut through Nandi country. Once past Nandi, Captain Sclater built a buying post at a place that later became Kakamega. The widened route reached Mumias toward the end of 1896, and a ferry was installed on River Nzoia. On 31 December 1896, Captain Sclater drove the first cart to Port Victoria, and from now on, this became the regular route to Uganda (Burgman 1979: 3).

The first all-weather road in Luyialand is the Kisumu-Kakamega Road built in 1936, but by 1966, three years after independence, Western Province had only twenty-eight miles of bituminized roads, according to *Hansard*.[14] Since then, road network has expanded significantly linking most parts of Western by tarmac or murram roads although maintenance is far from satisfactory. The major arterial roads include Kisumu-Kakamega-Kitale, Eldoret-Bungoma-Malaba, Kisumu-Yala-Busia, Kakamega-Mumias-Bungoma/Busia, Chavakali-Kaimosi-Kapsabet-Eldoret, and Eldoret-Lugari-Turbo-Bungoma. Some important feeder

---

14. *Kenya Gazette*, House of Representatives, Official Report of the National Assembly, Fourth Session sitting on Thursday, June 9, 1966. The answer was given by then minister for roads and public works, Mr. Dawson Mwanyumba in response to a question from Martin Shikuku, the MP for Butere.

roads include Luanda-Siaya, Luanda-Emusire, Ekero-Ebuyangu, Majengo-Ebusakami, Chavakali-Standi Kisa-Khumusalaba, Sigalagala-Butere-Sidindi, Ejinja-Bumala, Musikoma-Sang'alo-Ingotse, Chwele-Sirisia-Malakisi, Mayanja-Namang'ofulo-Lwakhakha, Ndalu-Kakamwe-Tongaren, Bungoma-Bumula-Kimaeti, Lugulu-Naitiri-Tongareni-Ndalu-Kiminini, Mabanga-Nalondo-Sirisia, Kimaeti-Malakisi-Kolanya-Lwakhakha, and Busia-Bumala-Funyula-Sio Port-Port Victoria.

While most railway line extensions were to the agricultural-rich white highlands, the Kisumu-Butere line completed in 1932 was the only one that served aboriginal reserves in the whole country. It was to be the last railway construction project in Kenya for eighty years (as at the time of this book's publication). The Nakuru-Kampala section of the Uganda Railway reached Kitale in 1926. Western has no airport but is near enough to two international airports—Kisumu (52 km away) and Eldoret (106 km away) from Kakamega town, the provincial headquarters. Port Victoria in Bunyala provides the only avenue for maritime transport linking Luyialand to major port towns along Lake Victoria like Kisumu, Mwanza and Bukoba (Tanzania) and Entebbe, Jinja, and Port Bell near Kampala. However, this aspect of communication is yet to be exploited although changes are expected in a harmonized customs union under the aegis of a resurrected East African Community environment.

CHAPTER 2

Concept of Time

A. Calendar

(i) Seasons

Unlike today, the Luyia of long ago did not have mechanically powered or electronic clocks to tell time. Time and seasons were calculated on the basis of major activities taking place in the community. Because farming was the mainstay of tribal economy, agricultural seasons were predictably the most important periods in the community calendar. There were three main agricultural seasons in a year: *eshimiyu* (dry season, December to February), *irotso* (long rainy season, March to June), *eshirumbi* (short rains, September to November). Crucial agricultural activities included clearing bushes (*liremula*), ploughing (*lilima*), planting (*liraka*), weeding (*eliaka*, variation: *mukhwaka*), eating first fruits (*amacheko*), harvesting (*lichesa*, variation: *likesa*), and annual thanksgiving sacrifices (*emisango*). Although farming was undertaken twice a year, the primary agricultural season was between January and July. January and February represented a period of clearing bushes and ploughing so that at the onset of long rains in March, the fields must have been seeded. April was weeding time, and by July, the crop was ready for harvesting.

August was a very important month in the calendar of the community. Apart from festivals celebrating rich harvests, it was a time for annual sacrifices to thank gods for the bounty as well as undertake customary rites of passage especially circumcision and weddings. August represented a period when people took time off work to rejoice, socialize, and feast. The large amount of grains in most homesteads meant that clansmen had more than enough food so they organized feasts and brewed alcohol for friends, kith, and family. The second season (*eshirumbi*, variation: *esirumbi*) was secondary and started in September to benefit from the short rains of October-November with harvests in December and January. Generally, people observed certain signs in the cosmos to determine seasons such as direction and velocity of wind, prolonged sunny spells, gathering of clouds, shading of leaves, blossoming, and withering of flowers, movement of animals to new grazing fields, etc. Beyond agriculture, time, and seasons were manifested and perceived variously by different vocations. Hence for shepherds, time was measured in terms of new pastures, watering points, and increase in parasites. For hunters, the concept of time was manifested in finding new hunting fields, movement, and availability of prey, preparing trenches and nets, training dogs, and sharpening weapons (Lihraw 2010: 186).

(ii) Clock

Time on an hourly basis was recorded by the sun whose movement influenced daily activities and behavior of animals. The first cockcrow is always at 3:00 a.m. while birds start singing from

5:00 a.m., and by 6:00 a.m., chickens start cackling to indicate they must be let out to go foraging and return at sunset (6:00 p.m.). Meanwhile, wild dogs, foxes, hyenas, and other nocturnal beasts come out from around 9:00 p.m. to forage, scavenge, and hunt. Accordingly, there are nine main divisions in a day (*eshitere*) and night (*ishiro*) as the table below shows.

Table 3: Luyia clock

Name	Time	Activities
Masherebende	3-4:00 a.m.	First cockcrow
Mabwibwi (Mapwepwe, Makuvulivuli)	Sunrise (5-6:00 a.m.)	Birds singing, cockcrow
Muchuli (Itsuli, Echulichuli)	Early morning (6-7:00 a.m.)	Chickens leave pen
Musenya (Mwisamula)	Morning (8-10:00 a.m.)	Milking, cattle leave for pastures
Mushiteere (Mwihangilwa)	Noon (12-1:00 p.m.)	Lunchtime
Musitsyambo	Afternoon, including early evening (2-5:00 p.m.)	Cattle go to drink water and return to kraals
Elabukabuka	Sunset (6-7:00 p.m.)	Chickens return to pens
Ingolobe (Mukolooba)	Evening (7-9:00 p.m.)	Meal time, storytelling
Musilo (Mushiro, Butukhu)	Night time (10-3:00 a.m.)	Sleeping, wild dogs and foxes come out

Among the Tachoni, time was also captured in terms of meals taken (Lihraw 2010:187). If someone said they will come at *sisingosia* or *sisichuli*, it means breakfast, *siemwisamusia* (around 10:00 a.m.), *siemwihangilwa* (lunch), and *siechifusi* (supper).

(iii) Days of the week

All Luyia subnations had names for six days of the week except Abanyala who, additionally, had a name for Sunday. The Luyia name for Sunday nowadays is *Eliokhuulukha* (rest day), a name evidently adapted from Christianity.

Table 4: Days of the week

Day	Luyia Name
Monday	*Elie imberi (Elie Ibarasa)*
Tuesday	*Eliakhabiri*
Wednesday	*Eliakhataru (Eliakhabaka)*
Thursday	*Eliakhane*
Friday	*Eliakharano*
Saturday	*Eliakhasasaba*
Sunday	*Olwomudiira* (Abanyala), *Eliokhuulukh*a

(iv) Months

The Luyia calculated months by observing four quarters of the moon. In fact the word for moon and month in Luyia is the same—*omwesi* (variation: *omweli*). The first quarter represents first week of the month while half moon generally means the month is halfway. Each full cycle makes a calendar month. In postcolonial era, the Luyia adopted the European numbering order. However, in pre-European days, the Luyia had indigenous names of which Abanyala and Samia are best documented (table 5 in brackets, respectively). The rest of the Luyia had numbers only up to six, and ascribed names from seven onward seem to be derived from Kiswahili.

Table 5: Months

Month	Luyia Name
January	*Okwokhuranga (Dulienge, Ndakweyee)*
February	*Okwakhabiri (Wefu, Omunyalasa Ngokho)*
March	*Okwakhataru (Muungu, Khula)*
April	*Okwakhane (Mwerasi, Nagakha)*
May	*Okwakharano (Nangeka, Ofwombole)*
June	*Okwakhasasaba (Musaru, Mubwiru)*
July	*Okwamusafu*
August	*Okwamunane (Fulula, Munaabakesa)*
September	*Okwatisa (Namafumbye, Kwalulukha)*
October	*Okwelikhumi (Ofwombole, Sesera'ano)*
November	*Okwelikhumi na ndala (Mubiru, Wefwekho)*
December	*Okwesikuku (Olusisi, Okwamakuyi)*

(v) Recording time from major events

Although some subnations used customary ritual festivals like circumcisions and annual harvest thanksgiving sacrifices to record time, major catastrophes like famines, wars, epidemics, droughts, and floods left a lasting imprint in the memory of tribesmen. These events then took on a life of their own, and when trying to recall other happenstances or occasions, e.g., birthdays, they would say so and so was born during *khaoya* (rinderpest) epidemic. Besides calamities, other occurrences that left a lasting memory include coming of the Whiteman, arrival of the railway and first car, establishment of formal education, appointment of paid *milango* (headmen), conscription into the two world wars, etc. Some of these major events are captured in the timeline below.

B. Timeline of Major Events

1050: Wanga, the tribal founder of the Wanga subnation dies.

1710: Wanga Kingdom splits into two following a quarrel between Wamukoya and Kweyu over who should inherit *obunabongo* (kingship) from Osundwa.

1750-1770: Various wars in what is now Bunyala (Buongo) between Abakhoone and Abasamia. It was during these wars that a large contingent of Abanyala (Banyala) fled to safety and settlement in Kakamega.

1840:

- Abanyala fight Luo of Alego in the War of Obuyu during which Abanyala occupy Usonga where they still live up to today (Abasonga).

- The great famine of *Lumala* (total destruction) breaks out and lasts ten years leaving untold destruction of human and animal life.

1844: Lumboka fort (*olukoba*) in Bungoma built in honor of a Tachoni army strategist, Lumboka Sibionei. It was to later play a historical role as a symbol of Bukusu resistance to British rule before being overrun by colonial forces in 1894.

1846: Famine of *Khafululu* (wild vegetables) hits the Bukusu during circumcision of the last Kinyikewu age set.

1850:

- Abanyala recall Abakhoone clansmen fearing *Khafululu* famine was a punishment from God for expelling them.

- Arab and Swahili slave traders and ivory hunters make expeditions to Luyialand first during the reign

	of Nabongo Shiundu intensifying when Nabongo Mumia took over.
1862:	Chetambe Fort in Webuye built measuring five kilometers long, 10 meters deep and 100 meters wide. The fort was to later play an historical role as the last bastion of Bukusu resistance to colonial rule finally coming down in 1895's War of Chetambe.
1875:	The first white man in Luyialand, Henry Morton Stanley, lands at Igoye near Port Victoria's Berkeley Bay as he voyages to Uganda in search of Dr. David Livingstone.
1881:	Mumia Makokha Shiundu is crowned *nabongo* (king).
1883:	

- The first white man to pass through Luyialand on foot is Joseph Thomson, a Scottish explorer immortalized by Thomson's gazelle. He holds talks with Nabongo Mumia having journeyed to Luyialand from Uasin Gishu.
- Dr. Carl Peters, heading Germany's Emin Pasha Expedition signs a treaty with Sakwa (Nabongo of Wanga Mukulu) under which Germany was to offer protection to his chieftaincy.

1885:

- Bishop James Hannington meets Nabongo Mumia and seeks help in travelling to Uganda. Months later, he is murdered on orders of Kabaka Mwanga II in Busoga. His remains are removed to Mumias where he is buried.
- Berlin Conference subdivides Africa into European spheres of influence, thus ending the so-called Scramble for Africa. Kenya and Uganda become British protectorates while Tanzania is annexed by

Germany. The Berlin conference renders Carl Peter's treaty with Sakwa of Wanga Mukulu irrelevant.

1890: The famine of *Oswekha* breaks out in Samia.

1894:

- The first administrative station is established at Elureko (Mumias) by Sir Henry Colville, commissioner of the protectorate of Uganda. F. Spire is seconded to the station together with a garrison of fifty Sudanese soldiers. Luyialand then was part of the eastern province of Uganda Protectorate.
- The War of Lumboka in which thirty pro-British Sudanese and Zanjibari soldiers are massacred by Bukusu warriors.
- British government takes over administration of its East African possessions from the bankrupt Imperial British East Africa Company.

1895:

- Charles William Hobley (nicknamed Obilo) takes over from Spire as a subcommissioner for North Kavirondo.[15]
- The War of Chetambe—a defining moment in British colonial history in Luyialand which ended Bukusu resistance to British rule.
- St. Joseph's Mill Hill[16] missionaries (Catholics) under Bishop Hanlon arrive at Shianda, Mumias.

---

15. North Kavirondo is used here loosely. It was not until 1920 that Kavirondo was formally split into North and South to denote Luyia Bantu and Nilotic Luo administrative polities.

16. Mill Hill is a suburb in North London, UK, and it was here in 1869 that Irish Catholics established a theological college which produced missionaries that later constituted the spiritual arm of British imperial conquest around the world.

1896:   Nabongo Mumia sends his army to attack the Kager Luo at Buholo killing several people including the father of Alfayo Odongo Mango, the founder of Roho sect. The Ugenya Luo have never forgotten this battle dubbed Musanda massacre.

1897:

- First national population census reveals that Kenya has 2.5 million people.
- Sudanese soldiers mutiny against the British in Western. Nabongo Mumia quickly assembles one thousand men to replace them thus earning respect from the British.

1899:

- Introduction of hut tax, first levied in kind (timber, goats, hoes, fowls, grains, eggs, etc.) or in the form of labor but later collected in cash when the traditional barter exchange system was replaced by cash. The legal tender at this time was the Indian rupee (three rupees per year).[17]
- The colonial administrator, C. W. Hobley launches massive operation against the Luo of Sakwa, Uyoma and Seme who were hostile to British caravans transiting to Uganda. Hobley's contingent included Ugandan, Wanga, and Maasai troops.

1901:

- Railway line reaches Kisumu (Port Florence) bringing with it Indians who penetrate deeper into rural Buluyia establishing *dukas* (shops).

---

[17]. In Luyia ethnolinguistics, the term *etsilupia* (rupees) is used synonymously with *amapesa* (money) borrowed from Kiswahili word *pesa*. Other words denoting money include *amadongolo* and *amang'ondo*.

1902:

- Administration of Western Kenya (stretching to Naivasha) is excised from Uganda's eastern province and transferred to East Africa Protectorate following reorganization of administrative boundaries by British colonial office and named Lakes Province (later Nyanza). Until now the British Empire in Eastern Africa was ruled from Zanzibar.
- The first Christian mission—Friends Africa Mission—starts at Kaimosi led by Arthur B. Chilson (minister), Edgar T. Hole (architect and businessman), and Willis Ray Hotchkiss (minister and industrialist).

1903:

- Kisumu-Mumias caravan route is constructed.
- The first Indian *duka* (shop) opens at Kakamega.
- Resistance to hut tax in the form of food items so colonialists switch to timber, trees, goats, cows, and even crocodile eggs.
- Quakers start a mission hospital and a primary school at Kaimosi in Tiriki.

1904:

- Robert Wilson of the South African Compounds and Interior Mission (SACIM) arrives on a reconnaissance trip and is welcomed by Friends missionaries at Kaimosi.
- Mill Hill Fathers mission at Shianda, Mumias, is elevated to a full parish.

1905:

- Mr. Robert Wilson of SACIM returns with his family and Otieno Andale, chief of Abamutete offers him 30 acres of land at Kima to establish a mission.
- Missionaries decide competition for native souls is unhealthy and confusing. So they agree to apportion

areas of jurisdiction with CMS (Anglicans) starting a mission at Maseno led by James Jamieson Willis and Hugh Saville to evangelize among the Luo; Catholics among the Wanga, Isukha, and Idakho; SACIM among Abanyole and Quakers in Maragoli and Tiriki.

1906:

- Mill Hill Fathers start a mission at Mukumu in Isukha.
- Babukusu destroy bridges across River Nzoia to stop tax collectors reaching them.
- Maseno Boys High School starts, later to develop into one of the best centers of academic excellence in Kenya.
- The rupee is introduced as a unit of exchange replacing the Indian rupee which had so far been used as currency.

1907:

- Native Courts Ordinance promulgated as a conflict resolution organ with village elders, headmen, and chiefs empowered to settle disputes as they had done in the precolonial period. The ordinance also established tribunals at the divisional and district level. Appeals against their decisions were handled by DOs or DCs.
- Ivory trade banned and a prison opened at Elureko (Mumias).
- Widespread famine (*irotso*) nicknamed *Opande* breaks out.
- FAM starts a mission at Lirhanda, Isukha.

1908:

- Introduction of maize, groundnuts, and cotton.
- More Indian shops opened at Yala, Marama, Malakisi, and Kakamega.

- North Kavirondo divided into subdistricts.
- Famine of *Demesi* in Kakamega and *Achoka* (*Odongo*) in Busia; Achoka, the rain magician was killed for "forsaking" his duty.
- Demarcation of modern Buluyia into eight locations by acting DC, Geoffrey Archer. Included in North Nyanza (Buluyia) were Luo territories of Gem, Alego, and parts of Ugenya.

1909:

- Mumia appointed paramount Chief of Nyanza (ruling over Ugenya / Gem Luo and Luyia).
- Plague (*libumba*) first reported in Maragoli and begins spreading to other parts of Buluyia.
- Witchcraft Ordinance enacted to stamp out the widespread belief in the occult.

1910:

- Combined hut (*obushuru bwe inzu*) and poll tax (*obushuru bwo murwe*) ordinance and fees introduced at markets in Mumias.
- Clashes between Abashisa (Kisa) and Abanyole over land at Munjiti.
- Motorable road connects Kisumu and Kaimosi
- Rinderpest (*khaoya*) epidemic kills 50 percent of livestock within six months. An estimated fifty-five thousand head of cattle die in two years. The epidemic leads to *Khaoya* famine.
- Harassed by tax inspectors, people begin searching for work outside Luyialand.
- Clyde Talivern Miller settles at Nyang'ori (then known as Matriin) as a farmer. He starts a Pentecostal movement but is deported in 1924 back to England after marrying a local black woman following divorce from his wife.

- Nabongo Mumia acquires a bicycle, the first Muluyia to do so.

1912:

- In neighboring Luoland, JoRoho sect is founded by Alfayo Odongo Mango (1884-1934) and his nephew Lawi Obonyo (1911-1934) as a religious revivalism movement to agitate for return of Luo territory annexed by the Wanga.
- Savings bank opened at Kakamega with chiefs and salaried employees becoming pioneer customers.
- St. Joseph's Mill Hill Fathers start mission at Eregi in Idakho.
- FAM starts a mission and hospital at Lugulu, first as a first aid station then upgraded to a dispensary in 1946 and to a health center in 1967 before becoming a fully licensed hospital in 1977.

1913: The appointment of Nabongo Mumia as paramount chief of North Kavirondo District, Nyanza Province in 1909 is regularized in a gazette notice of 1 February 1913 by then acting Governor, L. G. Bowring. The entry was "Official Headman" as the title paramount chief had no constitutional basis.

1914:

- Outbreak of First World War. Strong men recruited to fight or work as porters (Carrier Corps)[18] in the Kings African Rifles (KAR).
- Kakamega School founded but does not admit students until 1933.

---

[18] Carrier Corps was transliterated to Kariokor by Africans and is immortalised by an estate in Nairobi and Dar es Salaam, Tanzania bearing that name.

1915:

- Outbreak of smallpox (*inundu*) in large parts of North Kavirondo.
- First motor car in Buluyia owned by John Ainsworth, the DC.

1916:

- Sewing machines (*echerehani*) are introduced in Buluyia by Singer Company.
- Butere Girls School started by Irish CMS missionary, Ms. Chadwick, devoted to reading, writing, singing, and scripture. In 1931, it becomes a day primary school, and in 1937, the first thirty-six boarders arrive. A secondary school wing is started in 1957.
- Ndombi wa Namasia is appointed chief of Abanyala (Navakholo). The subnation would later be known as Abanyala ba Ndombi in his honor.
- Fr. Peter Nicholas Stam associated with spread of Catholicism in Buluyia is seconded to Mumias from Nyahururu as a locum tenens but stays for twenty-five years as the linchpin of catechumenism.

1917:

- Major famine (*irotso*) known as *keya*[19] breaks out throughout Luyialand. It was otherwise known as *enjala ya motokaa* (famine of the vehicle) in respect of the first vehicle to appear in Western.
- Spanish influenza kills 3,500 people.

1918:

- First World War ends.
- FAM establishes a mission at Malava, Kabras.

[19.] The famine was named *keya* (a transliteration of KAR) because it broke out at a time when most strong men had been recruited to serve in the First World War under the Kings African Rifles (KAR) regiment. Boys born around this time were named Keya.

- Witchcraft Ordinance Act is revised.
- Famine of Ngaira in Kakamega followed the death of a famous rainmaker called Ngaira. In western Buluyia, it was called Famine of Obando (porridge)
- Kabuchai Tax Collection Center built in Bungoma.

1919: Headquarters of North Kavirondo moved from Elureko (renamed Mumias in honor of Nabongo Mumia) to Kakamega.

1920:

- British East Africa Protectorate split into Uganda Protectorate and Kenya Colony and Protectorate.
- Western Kenya (Kavirondo) which was formerly Eastern Province of Uganda reverts to Kenya Colony.
- Kavirondo split between North and South Kavirondo districts.
- Nabongo Mumia acquires a motor car, the first Luyia to do so.
- The rupee is replaced by East African shilling.
- Girls' school started at Kaimosi. It would later evolve into Kaimosi Girls High School in 1960.

1921:

- Campaign against bubonic plague is launched. By 1929, about 9.5 million rats had been killed.
- Boys' school started at Kaimosi. It would late evolve into Kaimosi Boys High School only to be transferred to Bukusu in 1956 and renamed Friends Kamusinga Boys High School.

1922:

- Government Native Hospital commissioned in Kakamega (precursor to Kakamega Provincial General Hospital).
- Famine of rats breaks out when *m.v Malach* ship docks at Sio Port. To contain the spread of plague, the

administration introduces a system where tax is paid in terms of dead rats (thirty rat tails paid poll tax).

1923:

- Young Kavirondo Association formed. Later changes its name to Kavirondo Taxpayers Welfare Association (KTWA).
- Bukura Agricultural Institute is established to offer training and agricultural extension services.
- Busia Market founded.

1924:

- Pentecostal Assemblies of God (PAG) from Canada start work in Nyang'ori by Keller who had defected from Church of God at Kima. He introduces drumming which attracts locals to his church and annoys Quakers.
- First three dispensaries opened in Kakamega.
- Native Catholic Union formed to compete with CMS.
- Veterinary Training School opened at Sang'alo, Bungoma.
- First interracial marriage recorded when Clyde Talivern Miller, the founder of Pentecostal movement at Nyang'ori marries a local black woman after divorcing his wife. The marriage did not last as Mr. Miller was immediately deported to England.

1925:

- Local Native Councils (LNC) established after an amendment in 1924 in the Native Authority Ordinance. By 1938, 22 LNC's had been created to deal with issues like education, health and labor.
- KTWA is split into two—North Kavirondo Taxpayers' Welfare Association to cater for the Luyia and South Kavirondo Taxpayers' Welfare Association for the Luo.

- Church of God starts a parish at Ingotse in Butsotso.
- Female circumcision is outlawed among the Tachoni.

1926:

- Nabongo Mumia is retired from the post of paramount chief and paid headmen (*milango*) introduced.
- Native appeals tribunal is set up at Kakamega.
- Uganda Railway reaches Kitale.
- American missionaries from Anderson, Indiana, take over Kima Church of God in Bunyore from SACIM after the latter runs into financial straitjacket.

1927:

- Maragoli begin to migrate to Migori and Kanyamkago in South Nyanza due to pressure of land.
- Outbreak of *liboyi* and *majengo* famines.
- Pentecostal revivalism and revolt against Quakers in Kaimosi.
- St. Joseph's Mill Hill Catholics start mission at Nangina in Samia.
- Introduction of ox-drawn plough and hand-driven mill (*ereko*) that eventually replaced *oluchina* (grinding stone).

1928: Girl's school founded at Mukumu by the Catholic Order of Ursulines of Bergen, Holland.

1929:

- Introduction of a regular ambulance service in Luyialand.
- African Spiritual Church (*Dini ya Roho*) formed by revivalists expelled by Quakers.

1930:

- Native Appeals Tribunal's Ordinance 1930 reduces the number of elders sitting on a tribunal and makes it mandatory that a literate member records proceedings.

- Permanent agricultural office set up at Kakamega as well as a sanitary inspectorate.
- Teacher training college established at Ikoshe, Mumias, on land "donated" by Bishop Peter Nicholas Stam.

1931:

- Girl's school started at Kima by Mrs. Twyla Ludwig later to develop into Bunyore Girls High School.
- Teacher training college started at Kaimosi. It would later be upgraded to an advanced teacher training college offering P1 certificates in 1960.
- Gold discovered in Kakamega.
- Mill Hill Fathers, a Catholic order, start mission at Kibabii, Bungoma
- Locust invasion destroys crops leading to a major famine dubbed *enjala ye chisike* (famine of locusts).

1932:

- Government African School opens in Kakamega with Harold Arthur Waterloo Chapman as the first headmaster.
- Gold mining begins in Kakamega by Rosterman Gold Mines Ltd.
- Colonial government outlaws use of compulsory labor on public projects.
- Kenya Uganda Railway line extended to Butere terminus.
- Outbreak of *Nyangweso* famine.
- Tobacco farming introduced but is abandoned seven years later in 1939.

1933:

- North Kavirondo Chamber of Commerce founded.
- Kakamega Forest gazetted as a national park.

1934:

- Archdeacon Walter Owen expels JoRoho founder, Alfayo Odongo Mango from the Anglican Church (CMS) and denounces him as a deceiver. Days later, Mango and his nephew, Lawi Obonyo, plus seven of their followers are massacred at Musanda by a Wanga mob.
- A political organization, North Kavirondo Central Association is founded to agitate for indigenous rights.
- Natives allowed on district education boards for the first time.

1935:   Veterinary School set up at Maseno.

1936:

- The first all-weather road in Western, Kisumu-Kakamega, is built.
- Twenty-four native courts are amalgamated into six divisional tribunals.
- *Milango* headmen replaced by *olugongo* headmen later changed to subchiefs.
- Salvation Army starts a mission in Malakisi, Bungoma, before spreading to Maragoli and Tiriki. It is headquartered at Madzuu, South Maragoli.
- Kabuchai Tax Center in Bungoma is converted into an African Native Court. Elijah Masinde employed here as a process server. He would later be tried in the same court when he founded *Dini ya Musambwa* ten years later.

1937:

- First flooding of River Nzoia recorded in Bunyala, Busia. Subsequent flooding incidences recorded in 1947, 1951, 1957, 1958, 1961, 1962, 1963, 1975, 1977, 1978, 2003, 2006, 2007, and 2008.

1938:

- St. Elizabeth Hospital also referred to as Mukumu Mission Hospital founded by a Catholic Order, Ursuline Sisters of Bergen, Holland.
- Church of God starts a parish at Mwihila in Kisa.
- Local Native Council (LNC) changes to African District Council.
- Catholic mission starts at Butula, Marachi by Father Bunck.
- Catholic mission starts at Port Victoria, Bunyala.

1939:

- Second World War starts. Able-bodied Luyia men recruited to serve in Burma (Myanmar), India, Egypt, Sri Lanka (Colombo) Somalia, Ethiopia (Abyssinia), and Madagascar (Malagasy) as pioneer corps (transliterated to *Panyako*).
- Nyang'ori transferred from Central Nyanza to become part of Tiriki Location.

1940:

- Abaluyia Welfare Association is formed, the first serious attempt at Luyia unity.
- Siriba Teachers College established

1942: African Israel Nineveh Church founded by Daudi Zakayo Kivuli (1896-1974). His wife, Rebecca, took over as High Priestess; but when she died in 1983, her grandson, John Mweresa Kivuli II (1960-), took over and is still the current High Priest. Followers are noted for wearing white turbans and behave like ancient Jews.

1943:

- Outbreak of *esikombe* (cup) famine in large parts of Western otherwise known as *enjala ya Panyako* (famine of Pioneer Corps).

- Friends Bible Institute (now Friends Theological College) starts at Lugulu but is transferred to Kaimosi in 1949.
- Goibei Girls School started by Canada's PAG.
- Abaluyia as an ethnic group is born bringing under its umbrella some eighteen closely related subnations.

1945:

- Second World War ends and African men return to start campaign for independence.
- WWW Awori becomes the first known Luyia journalist as editor of *Habari*, an indigenous publication agitating for independence and human rights for Africans.
- The East Africa Yearly Meeting of Friends (Quakers) is created.

1946:

- Kenya African Union (precursor to KANU) is reestablished with James Gichuru as president, Joseph Otiende vice president, and WWW Awori treasurer.
- *Dini ya Musambwa* (Religion of Ancestors) launched by Elijah Masinde as a protest movement against Christian churches which preached against ancestral sacrifices and polygamy.

1948:

- North Kavirondo is renamed North Nyanza after the word Kavirondo is deemed pejorative.
- Second national population census results reveal Kenya has a population of 5.4 million up from 2.5m in 1897. Asian population in Kakamega District is recorded at 604.
- Britain sets up East African High Commission (EAHC), the precursor to East African Community which pools common infrastructural services in Uganda, Kenya, and Tanganyika. These included the

University of East Africa, railways, harbors, airways, postal, customs, and meteorology.

1949:

- Nabongo Mumia dies aged one hundred years and is buried at Itokho in Mumias (then known as Elureko). He is succeeded by his son, Shitawa.
- Colonial government liberalizes coffee growing, allowing indigenes to plant the crop for the first time.

1950:

- African Courts Ordinance abolishes native tribunals and replaces them with African courts. Expatriate judges and magistrates continue to adjudicate on cases involving non-Africans using relevant English and Indian laws.
- Alupe Leprosy Hospital built in Amukura, Busia, to serve East Africa.

1951:

- WWW Awori is appointed to represent North Nyanza in Legislative Council (Legco) becoming one of only four Africans in Legco. The first African, Eliud Mathu, a Kikuyu was appointed in 1944, followed by Walter Odede (Luo) in 1947. Also appointed with Mr. Awori is JS ole Tameno (a Maasai).
- Coffee growing experiments start in Kimilili and Mt. Elgon areas.
- African Sports Stadium built in Kakamega (renamed Bukhungu).

1952:

- Kakamega goldmines are shut when production declines to 13 percent of its peak in 1939.
- Dog market starts at Lubao, Kakamega. It is the only one of its kind in Kenya and largest dog market in East and Central Africa.

- Mau Mau rebellion breaks out against British colonial rule.

1953:

- Outbreak of *Mau Mau* famine. In Bungoma, they called it *enjala ya Kamuria*, named after a popular Indian trader in Kimilili who saved many families.
- Elgon Nyanza (Bungoma) carved out of North Nyanza.

1954:

- Nyang'ori High School started by PAG, initially as a teacher training college.
- First coffee processing factory set up at Chwele, Bungoma. In the same year construction of a second coffee plant at Chesikaki, also in Bungoma commences.
- Famine of sisal (*enjala ya kamakongwe*) breaks out after Bukusu men abandoned food crops having discovered the commercial value of sisal. Many were working in plantations in Taita Taveta.

1956:

- The African Interior Church registered by the Colonial government as a breakaway sect from Church of God.
- Kaimosi Boys High School transferred to Bukusu and renamed Friends School Kamusinga.
- Bungoma granted urban council status and becomes headquarters of Elgon Nyanza District.

1957:

- The first elections for Legco are held with Masinde Muliro beating WWW Awori to represent North Nyanza.
- African Divine Church founded in Boyani, Maragoli, by Saulo Chabuga. By 2008, it had spawned 21,648 churches in Kenya, Uganda, and Tanzania.

1958:

- St. Peter's Mumias Boys High School started—replaces a teachers' training college which is moved to Kibabii, Bungoma.
- Pascal Nabwana becomes the first African to be elected chairman of an African District Council, Elgon Nyanza (later Bungoma District).

1960:

- Kenya African National Union (KANU) is formed with James Gichuru as president, Oginga Odinga as vice president, and Tom Mboya as secretary general.
- Kenya African Democratic Union (KADU) is formed with Ronald Ngala as president, Masinde Muliro vice president, Daniel arap Moi as chairman, and Martin Shikuku national youth coordinator.
- Chavakali Boys Secondary School started as the first day secondary school in rural Kenya.
- Great floods kill several people in Bunyala and Samia.
- Kaimosi Teachers College starts as the first advanced teacher training college in Kenya producing P1 teachers.

1961:

- The first general elections in Kenya are held. KANU wins by nineteen seats against KADU's eleven. When KANU is called upon to form a government, Jaramogi Odinga Oginga refuses to do so first demanding Jomo Kenyatta's release from detention.
- Priscilla Ingasiani Abwao from Maragoli becomes the first Kenyan woman to sit in Legco following her nomination by colonial governor, Sir Patrick Muir Renison. She was also the only woman to attend Lancaster House constitutional talks in London.

- Kaimosi and Mukumu girls' schools are elevated to high school status.

1962:

- Outbreak of *esipindi* famine.
- Third national population census reveals Kenya's population to be 8.6 million up from 5.4m in 1948.
- Lugari Settlement Scheme starts to settle squatters.
- South Nyanza Abaluhya Union changes name to South Nyanza and Kisii District Abaluhya Union (East Africa).
- Abaluhya Peoples Association is deregistered.

1963:

- Fresh elections are held in May 1963, and KANU wins with eighty-three seats against KADU's forty one. On June 1, Kenya becomes independent (*uhuru*). The first Luyia to win in an urban constituency is James Harry Onamu from Tiriki (Nakuru West).
- North Nyanza is renamed Kakamega District while Elgon Nyanza is split into Bungoma and Busia to become the three districts of the newly created Western Province.
- Lugulu Girls High School is established.

1964:

- Lugari Farmers Training Center is started by Quakers in conjunction with National Council of Churches of Kenya (NCCK) and the Ministry of Lands and Settlement.
- Elgon Nyanza African County Council is renamed Bungoma County Council.
- Abaluhya United Football Club, the precursor to AFC Leopards, is born. It was an amalgamation of Marama, Samia United, and Bunyore (Division One clubs) and lower divisions clubs such as Kisa, Tiriki,

Bukusu Brotherhood, Busamia, Lurambi, Butsotso, Bushibungo, and Eshirotsa. Jafred Ambani is widely recognized as spearheading the unity initiative. The first chairman is Edward Kidoyo.

1965:

- Musingu Boys High School founded. The name is derived from a big tree known as *omusingu* found in the neighborhood.
- Kabuchai Native Court in Bungoma moved to Sirisia. The original site is converted into a health center.

1966:

- St. Cecilia Nangina Girls' High School, Funyula, is founded by Catholics but later taken over by the government.
- First Kenyan coins introduced in denominations of 5, 10, 25 and 50 cents, and 1 and 2 shillings. Before that, Kenya used the East African shilling as legal tender.
- Kakamega Forest gazetted as a national reserve.
- African courts abolished and replaced with district courts.

1967: East African Cooperation (EAC), generally known as community, is born taking over nearly the entire range of joint services and institutions belonging to the former East African Common Services Organization (EACSO).

1968:

- County and urban councils started under the auspices of Local Council Commission (LCC).
- West Kenya Agricultural Show starts. It was later renamed Kakamega Agricultural Show and held under the auspices of Agricultural Society of Kenya (established in 1908).

1969:

- General elections for the second Parliament are held. Sixteen Luyia are elected to Parliament, fourteen in Western Province, and two in Rift Valley (Kitale East and Kitale West, renamed Cherengany and Saboti, respectively in 1988).
- Fourth national population census returns a population of 10.9 million up from 8.6 million recorded in 1962.

1970: Namirama Friends Girls Secondary School in Navakholo and Shikoti Girls Secondary School in Butsotso established.

1971:

- Friends College of Research and Technology started in Kaimosi.
- Samitsi Friends Secondary School in Kabras and Sidikho Secondary School in Nambacha, Lurambi, established.
- Maragoli Girls Secondary School established by Mill Hill Catholic missionaries.

1972: Western College of Arts and Sciences (WECO) founded in Kakamega. It became a state university in 2007.

1973:

- Mumias Sugar Company (established in 1971) starts operations with the Kenya Government holding majority shares (71 percent), CDC (17 percent), Kenya Commercial Finance Company (5 percent), Booker McConnell (4 percent), and EADB (3 percent).
- Bungoma becomes a municipality.
- Abaluhya United Football Club changes name to Abaluhya FC

1974:

- General elections for the third Parliament are held. Sixteen Luyia are elected: fourteen in Western, and two in Rift Valley (Kitale East (Cherengany) and Kitale West (Saboti) in Trans Nzoia.
- Pan Paper Mills, Webuye, is established as a joint venture between the Kenya government (34 percent), IFC, and Orient Paper Mills, part of the Birla Group of India.

1977:

- East African Cooperation (community) crumbles following political tension in the region and pursuance of different economic paradigms with Tanzania emphasising *ujamaa* (socialism) while Kenya is decidedly capitalist and Uganda a under Idi Amin's military dictatorship.
- Construction of dykes in Budalang'i to control flooding of River Nzoia.

1978:

- Nzoia Sugar Company starts operations in Bungoma with the third largest capacity after Mumias and Chemilil.
- Catholic Diocese of Kakamega is created under the leadership of Bishop Philip Sulumeti (a Teso) who resigned in 2012.

1979:

- General elections for the Fourth Parliament are held. Seventeen Luyia are elected: fourteen in Western, two in Rift Valley (Kitale East and Kitale West), and one in Nairobi (Bahati).
- The Friends Church in Kenya (FCK), an umbrella organization for all Quakers in the country, is initiated.

- Fifth national population census returns a countrywide population of 15.3 million up from 10.9 million in 1969.

1980: Abaluhya Football Club changes its name to AFC Leopards Sports Club after Moi regime outlaws tribal names.

1981: West Kenya Sugar Company is launched in Kabras with the smallest milling capacity of Kenya's seven sugar firms.

1982: Coup attempt by rebel air force soldiers against the government of Daniel arap Moi is crushed on August 1.

1983:

- General elections for the Fifth Parliament are held. Seventeen Luyia are elected: fourteen in Western, two in Rift Valley (Kitale East and Kitale West), and one in Nairobi (Bahati).

- Outbreak of famine dubbed (*mugorogoro*) after rains fail. The famine was called *mugorogoro* (variation: *ekorokoro*) after the 2 kg tin container in which grain was measured in village markets and shops.

1984: First case of HIV/Aids reported in Kenya four years after the first case in the world emerged.

1985: Major changes in national education system launched; 8-4-4 system replaces 7-4-2-3 inherited from the British colonial government.

1987:

- The Catholic Diocese of Bungoma is carved out of Kakamega.

- Four new constituencies are created (Sabatia, Shinyalu, Malava and Lugari) while four are renamed with Samia becoming Funyula; Busia East, Nambale;

Bungoma East, Kimilili, and Bungoma Central, Sirisia.[20]

1988: Controversial *Mlolongo* (Queuing) General elections for the Sixth Parliament are held. Twenty three Luyia elected: nineteen in Western, three in Rift Valley (Kwanza, Saboti, Cherengany), and one in Nairobi (Bahati).

1989: Sixth national population census reveals Kenya has 21.4 million people up from 15.3 million in 1979. The Luyia overtake Luo to become second largest tribe after the Kikuyu.

1990: Vihiga District (incorporating Bunyore, Maragoli and Tiriki) is carved out of the wider Kakamega District.

1991:

- Maseno University established out of a merger between Siriba Teachers Training College and GTI.
- Bushiangala Technical Training Institute in Ikolomani, Idakho is founded

1992:

- Multiparty elections are held for the first time since independence but a divided opposition loses to incumbent, Daniel arap Moi of KANU. Twenty three Luyia elected; 19 in Western, three in Rift

---

[20.] In Luyia dominated Trans Nzoia County in Rift Valley Province, a new constituency known as Kwanza is created while Kitale West and Kitale East are renamed Saboti and Cherengany respectively. Although Masinde Muliro won in Cherengany in 1988, he lost the seat in an election petition filed by a former headmaster, Kipruto arap Kirwa, a Kalenjin tribesman who won in the subsequent by election in 1990. Kirwa dominated Cherengany politics until 2007 when he was bundled out by Joshua Kutuny, another Kalenjin.

Valley (Saboti, Kwanza and Nakuru West) and one in Nairobi (Bahati).[21]

- Serious tribal clashes between Kabras and Nandi.

1995: Teso District is created from the larger Busia District.

1997:

- Three new constituencies are created (Khwisero, Matungu and Butula) while Bunyala is renamed Budalang'i.
- General elections for the Eighth Parliament are held. Opposition fails to unite again, and Moi wins to serve his last term as president. Twenty-five Luyia elected: twenty-two in Western, two in Rift Valley (Saboti and Kwanza), and one in Nairobi (Westlands).

1998: Lugari District is carved out of the larger Kakamega District.

1999:

- Seventh national population census returns a Kenyan population of 28.7million with Luyia numbering 3.5 million.
- Butere/Mumias District carved out of the larger Kakamega District.

2000: An interdenominational pastoral research institute in East Africa, AICMR is started in Butere.

2001: Negotiations begin to reestablish economic integration in East Africa under the old name of East African Community (EAC).

2002:

- Musalia Mudavadi defects from Rainbow coalition and is appointed vice president becoming the first

---

21. In 1994, Westlands MP, Amin Walji, dies and in the ensuing by-election, Fred Gumo (Omunyala) wins raising the tally of Luyia MPs in Parliament to 24.

Luyia to hold the highest political office (lasted but a whole three months!).

- General elections for the Ninth Parliament are held, and KANU is finally vanquished after forty-two years in power. Twenty-five Luyia are elected as MPs: twenty-two from Western Province, two in Rift Valley (Kwanza and Saboti), and one in Nairobi (Westlands).
- WECO is elevated to a university status as a constituent college of Moi University, Eldoret. It becomes known as Western University College of Science and Technology (WUCST).

2003:

- Kenya's vice president, Michael Wamalwa Kijana, dies in London; Moody Awori from Samia is appointed to replace him.
- Free primary school education launched nationwide.

2005: Constitution referendum on the so-called Wako Draft defeated. President Kibaki sacks entire cabinet for the first time in Kenya's history.

2007:

- General elections for the Tenth Parliament are held. The presidential results are disputed leading to a civil war in which 1,600 people die and 600,000 displaced. Twenty-six Luyia MPs are elected: twenty-two from Western Province constituencies, two in Rift Valley (Kwanza and Saboti), and two in Nairobi (Westlands and Embakasi).[22]

---

[22] Embakasi MP-elect, Mellitus Mugabe Were, was murdered in January 2008 as politically motivated violence erupted following disputed presidential results.

- Masinde Muliro University of Science and Technology (MMUST) established as a full university from the former WUCST.
- New districts created—Bungoma split into five districts: Bungoma North, Bungoma East, Bungoma West, Bungoma Central, and Bungoma South. Emuhaya and Hamisi districts are carved out of Vihiga District. Butere/Mumias District split into Butere and Mumias districts.

2008:

- Former UN secretary general, Kofi Annan, negotiates a truce between Mwai Kibaki and Raila Odinga leading to the establishment of a coalition government.
- Free secondary school education introduced nationwide.

2009:

- Friends University Kaimosi is started by Quakers.
- Eight new districts are created—Sabatia hived from Vihiga, Matungu from Mumias, Khwisero from Butere, Matete and Likuyani from Lugari, Navakholo from Kakamega, Bumula from Bungoma South, and Kimilili from Bungoma North.
- Eighth national population census reveals Kenya has 38.6 million people with Luyia numbering 5.3 million up from 3.5m in 1999.
- Sigalagala Technical Training Institute is upgraded to a full polytechnic status, becoming the first national polytechnic in Western.

2010:

- New constitution promulgated replacing the 1960s' Lancaster House document with far-reaching governance changes including abolition of provinces, creation of forty-seven counties, and a bicameral Parliament.

- Commercial flights (Flight 540) start flying directly to Kakamega from Nairobi.
- *Chang'aa* and *busaa* (traditional gin and beer) are legalized.
- Rebirth of EAC; thirty-three years after it collapsed granting free movement of labor, capital, and goods across Tanzania, Uganda, Kenya, Rwanda, and Burundi.

2011:

- Kakamega Boys, Bunyore Girls, Lugulu Girls, Friends School Kamusinga, and St. Brigid's Girls in Kiminini are elevated from provincial to national school status.
- Kibabii Teachers College is elevated to a constituent college of MMUST.

2012:

- Death of Nabongo Japheth Wambani Rapando of Wanga Mukulu. His fifth-born son, Maurice Rapando, is selected to succeed him.
- Musalia Mudavadi quits ODM to launch presidential bid under a new political vehicle called United Democratic Front of Kenya (UDF).
- Joseph Martin Olukhanya Shikuku, the quintessential Luyia politician dubbed People's Watchman dies aged seventy-nine.

2013:   General elections are held on March 4 under a new constitution to elect a president, senators, MPs and county governors in a reconstituted bicameral legislature and devolved government. Musalia Mudavadi is among the eight presidential candidates. He came a distant third after Uhuru Kenyatta (winner) and Raila Odinga. Thirty five Luyia MPs were elected-thirty in western, four in Rift Valley (Kwanza, Saboti, Kiminini and Endebess) and one in Nairobi (Westlands).

CHAPTER 3

Luyia Origins

A. Meaning of Luyia

(i) Fireplace theory

The word Luyia is derived from *oluyia* (variation: *oluhya*) which in its generic sense means fireplace or hearth, but it has two other meanings which we shall presently consider. Some scholars[23] say the name derives from the verb *okhuyia*,[24] which literally means "to burn" (Osogo 1966: 6). In precolonial Luyialand, members of a family, lineage (*esilibwa*, variations: *inzu, omuliango*), or clan

---

[23]. The leading proponents are Dr. John Osogo, author of *A History of Baluyia*, and Simon Kenyanchui, author of *Makers of Kenyan History: Nabongo Mumia*.

[24]. The word *okhuyia* also has a figurative meaning. When people say *njichanga okhuyia*, they mean, "I am going to get drunk."

congregated around a bonfire in the evening to exchange news, tell stories of warfare, and discuss important clan matters or simply catch up with daily fare of gossip. If a stranger joined them, they would ask, "From which *oluyia* do you belong?" Translated loosely, this means, "From which fireplace do you belong?" In those days it was essential to guard against enemy infiltration and account for everyone as raids from neighboring clans and tribes were common. Although such congregation was largely an adult male affair, boys, especially those who had undergone circumcision as a rite of passage were not only welcome but encouraged to join elders to receive instruction in tribal history, customs, and traditions. It was also their duty to kindle fire (*omulilo*) and keep it burning. Seldom were women welcome—their roles limited to serving food and traditional brew (*amalwa*, Bukusu: *kamalwa*). Besides offering protection from elements, *oluyia* served as an integral cultural vehicle for oral transmission of vital customary values from generation (*olubaka*) to generation. Accordingly, there were two types of fireplaces, which bring us to the second definition of the term *oluyia*.

Each traditional homestead had a fireplace in the yard (*mukichi*, variation: *mulwanyi*). Where a polygamous man had several wives, each had her own hut in the compound forming a semicircular pattern with the fireplace situated in the middle, preferably in front of the hut of an elder wife. This type of fireplace was kindled twice a day—at dawn and dusk, the early session lasting a short time and serving only to warm the owner of the homestead before he sets off for his daily schedules. The fireplace had strict sitting arrangements with the homestead's owner taking a central position facing the gate (*eshilibwa*, variation: *esilibwa, ekilibwa*). His role as the protector of the family informed this arrangement. Sitting in this position enabled him to see who was approaching the yard. In his absence, his elder brother or son occupied the central position.

In addition to family hearths, each clan community or lineage had a village common where a fireplace loomed like a sphinx. The clan fireplace later assumed a meaning and functionality beyond merely a place to kindle fire to warm congregants and eat food, consume alcohol, or gossip. Of course, all these were part of the culture, but when important announcements or decisions about the community were to take place, clansmen received summons to assemble at the village common. In this sense, *oluyia* served as a village court where important matters were discussed, argued, and adjudicated. Such matters included war or peace declarations with neighboring clans or litigation for transgressions and misdemeanors by clan members. If clansmen differed on whatever issue such that they could not agree among themselves, they often sought intervention of clan elders and a neutral place to hold judicial hearing (*omuse*) and summon witnesses was the village common. Although the name *oluyia* implies fire, the village sitting depended on the occasion. In the case of *omuse* (*baraza* in Kiswahili), this would usually be held around late morning when it would be pointless to kindle a fire as it is quite warm at this time of day. Another important feature typical of a Luyia village common is a large tree, which besides providing shelter from the scorching sunrays replaces the bonfire as the focal point of *oluyia* during daytime. In this sense, when people say they are going for a meeting at *oluyia*, they mean the village common rather than the literal fireplace.

The third meaning of *oluyia* is both micro and macro. The people who share a fireplace or a village common, as a lineage or clan, belong to the same *oluyia* (micro meaning). Thus, when a group of clans (*tsimbia*; variation: *tsinono*, *chikholo* in Lubukusu) come together, they form *abo-luyia* (subtribe) or *aba-luyia*, the macro tribe. As we shall see in the next section, the name Abaluyia (Abaluhya) did not come into existence until 1930s. Nowadays, Abaluyia or simply Luyia generally means the people who speak any of the various closely related eighteen dialects. The territorial region is Buluyia, and the language they speak is Oluluyia (Oluluhya).[25]

(ii) Genesis of Luyia as a tribe

It is widely believed that the word Luyia was first suggested by the local African Mutual Assistance Association around 1930 (Encyclopædia Britannica 2009) and adopted by the North Kavirondo Central Association in 1935 (Ogot 1967: 139) although elders from some subnations rejected it. What resistance there was soon waned as the name slowly gained currency, but it was not until 1943 that Luyia was formally adopted to describe a federation of lexically related Bantu subtribes living in Western Kenya as a distinct tribal group. Before that British colonial administration classified the Luyia as Kavirondo alongside Nilotic Luo, Nandi, Teso, Kisii, and Kuria. Later, Kavirondo was modified to separate Bantu Kavirondo from Nilotic Kavirondo, a term both Nilotes and Bantu tribes found deeply offensive as we shall see later on (see p.120).

In 1940, Abaluyia Welfare Association was formed which popularized the name, and shortly afterward a Luyia language committee established to formulate an orthography (Osogo 1966: 8). However, another scholar, John Kesby argues that it is was

---

[25.] Oluluyia is a macrolanguage spoken by a cluster of closely related tribes with each dialect qualified to be called Oluluyia in a *pars pro toto* context. Attempts to have what is often referred to as standard Luyia have often hit a snag because no one dialect is easily understood by all the subnations. Subnations that live in close geographical proximity tend to understand each other more easily creating a pattern which can be subdivided into four cluster areas: Logooli, Nyole, Tiriki as cluster one; Isukha, Idakho, Kisa, Wanga, Butsotso, Marama as cluster two; Bukusu, Tachoni, Kabras, Nyala (Kakamega) as cluster three and Samia, Marachi, Khayo, and Nyala (Busia) as cluster four.

the colonial regime which first came up with the name Abaluyia (Kesby 1977: 90) as far back as 1929 but his supposition seems far off the mark as it has not been corroborated by any other scholar or authority.

Besides the Wanga whose *obunabongo* (kingship) predates the Europeans, beyond clan system, the rest of Luyia subnations were acephalous communities without clear structures of political command. This put them at a disadvantage in emerging political dispensation of the preindependence epoch. Many Luyia men had been recruited in the Kings African Rifles Regiment (KAR) to fight in the Second World War. Fighting alongside British soldiers and recruits from other imperial subjects in places like Burma, they became politically sensitized, having been exposed to the advantages of an organized army.

At the end of Second World War in 1945, the political landscape was changing and clamor for indigenous rights rising. Resistance against hut tax and other oppressive laws had until now been largely pent up. Apart from the Bukusu who had resisted early British colonial rule but were subdued in what came to be known as War of Chetambe in 1895, there was no organized resistance to the British in the wider Buluyia. It was no coincidence there was little resistance when these tribes confederated and assumed a super tribal identity shortly after the end of the Second World War. With that, the ethno genesis of Luyia as a super tribal group in Kenya was complete. It was a name they easily identified with; practically all subnations had the tradition of *oluyia* (hearth) firmly established in their culture. What little resistance there was came from certain sections of Maragoli who whispered that they are not Luyia. However these sentiments were largely uttered in jest as there is no known record of any formal promotion of Maragoli ethnocentrism or any attempt to have Maragoli expunged from the super tribal identity. The name's acceptance across the board is best illustrated by the following quotation: "This entirely accords with the experience of the present writer (Aidan W. Southall) who, arriving to teach at Makerere College in 1945, found that the whole group of Bantu speaking students from North Kavirondo called themselves Abaluyia and were never known as anything else."[26]

There are at least five other tribes with 60-100 percent lexical similarities to Luyia subtribes in Uganda (Gweru, Nyole, Gisu, Samia, Banyala) and Haya in Tanzania. Unlike Kenya, they have no super tribal identity although *Ethnologue's* sixteenth edition has suffixed most of them under Luyia.[27] The Samia and Banyala transverse the colonial frontiers of Uganda and Kenya and although grouped under the Luyia in Kenya, in Uganda they are classified as independent tribes.

B. Who Are the Luyia?

(i) The great scholarly debate

Scholars are divided on whether indeed there is such a tribe as Luyia or even the exact number of Luyia subnations. Dr. Musimbi

---

26. *The Illusion of Tribe* by Aidan W. Southall published in *Perspectives on Africa: A Reader in Culture, History, and Representation* by Grinker R. R., Lubkemann S. C., and Steiner C. B. (Eds), Blackwell Publishing Ltd, Chichester, UK, 2010.

27. The ISO 639-3 standard defines three-letter codes for both individual languages and macro languages. The latter are defined in the standard as "multiple, closely related individual languages that are deemed in some usage contexts to be a single language." Using the three criteria listed above, some varieties may be considered separate languages and identified by distinctive ISO 639-3 codes, but for other purposes those individual languages might be grouped together and spoken of as a single language based on the shared heritage and identity of the speakers or other common features such as a common writing system and literature.

Kanyoro[28] who carried out extensive linguistic research in this area holds the view that the Luyia are neither a single entity nor do they constitute a homogeneous group of people. But because they are Bantu and therefore different from their Nilotic neighbors (Luo, Kalenjin and Teso), the bestowal of a common identity was administratively convenient to colonial authorities. She argues that the term "Luyia" refers to a nonexistent language as not all Luyia people understand each other and certainly from the point of view of literature provision, e.g., the Bible, all the subgroups should be treated differently.

However, a pioneer Luyia paremiographer, Abraham K. L. Mirimo (1998) has stated that although Oluluyia has several dialects, all share a core lexical structure and only minor inflections in suffixation and prefixation divide them. These lexical variations notwithstanding a thorough linguistic analysis reveal that they have a common denominator in their written form with the differences seemingly pronounced only when spoken. Both scholars are right. Yes, there are differences, but these pale so fast in comparison to similarities. As a people, the Luyia are truly a diverse group made up of kindred tongues with customary threads and physical textures woven together into a rich cultural tapestry; forming one people. The Luyia are generally defined as an ethnolinguistic cluster of several closely related Bantu-speaking peoples found primarily in western flanks of Kenya and Rift Valley. These are Bakhayo, Banyala, Banyala ba Ndombi, Banyore, Batsotso, Bukusu, Idakho, Isukha, Kabras, Kisa, Marachi, Maragoli, Marama, Samia, Songa,[29] Tachoni, Tiriki, and Wanga.

[28.] Dr. Musimbi Kanyoro (neé Rachel Angogo) is currently the director of Population Program at the David and Lucile Packard Foundation in Los Altos, California. She previously served as secretary general of the World YWCA besides being a board member of several nongovernmental bodies.

[29.] The Songa are offshoots of Basoga of Uganda. In Buluyia, they are, to all intents and purposes, almost extinct having been assimilated by the populous

If scholars differ on whether Luyia is in fact a tribe, their academic dilemma is compounded by the number of dialects uncomfortable with existing classification. For instance Bakhekhe of Busia considers themselves a separate dialect (olukhekhe) from the Samia and so also are Abaholo in Wanga, Abanyang'ori (Terik) in Maragoli, etc. In Butere, the people are classified as Marama, but in actual fact, Marama refers largely to a cluster of clans generally referred to as Abamukhula (forming roughly 45 percent of the total population). Other clans such as Aberecheya or Abashirotsa find it rebarbative if called Abamarama. Then there are *ex-situ* clans which live across several subtribes such as Abakhoone (found among Babukusu, Bakhayo and Abanyala); Abatura (Wanga, Marama, Isukha, Bukusu, Marachi and Tiriki); and Abang'aale (Bunyore, Samia, Tachoni, Butsotso, Marachi, Bukusu and Kabras).

Because of this confusion, early researchers estimated the number of Luyia subtribes to be anywhere between fifteen and twenty-six (Kanyoro 1983: 4). Dr. Kanyoro identified seventeen subgroups in her linguistic research, but although she told me she knew about Abasonga, she did not have adequate information about them to offer any specificity. Her reluctance to include Abasonga among Luyia subnations is understandable as this group has, to all intents and purposes, been assimilated into Nilotic Luo. Apart from a few old people who still speak Oluluyia, the main body of Abasonga consider themselves as Luo. They live as a colony among majority Nilotes in Central Nyanza at a place called Alego Usonga. Although the Nyala of Busia and Kakamega were initially one people, they have lived apart for so long that they consider themselves separate entities. That puts known Luyia groups in Kenya at between 17 and 18 if you disregard Bakhekhe, Batura,

---

Luo in Alego (hence Alego-Usonga). Remnants are found among Aberecheya clan of Marama.

and Baholo. Some of the Kenyan Luyia, especially the Samia and Nyala, overflow into Uganda, victims of the Berlin Conference of 1885, which created artificial frontiers and spheres of European influence in Africa. Besides these two, there are also Abanyole (Abanyuli), remote kinsmen of Abanyole of Kenya, Abagisu (related to Bukusu), Abagweru and Abasoga who qualify to be grouped under the macro tribe of Abaluyia. In Kenya, one also finds close lexical and cultural similarities between the Luyia, Kisii, Kuria, and Suba while in Tanzania, the Haya, Jite, and Zanaki of Bukoba region easily qualify for a place in the Luyia nationhood.

Luyia, like the Maasai, practiced a policy of assimilation. Between 30-40 percent of Luyia are not originally Bantu but assimilated from Nilotic Luo, Kalenjin, and Maasai. Citing research by Prof. Gideon S. Were on western Kenya, Prof. Bethwell Ogot,[30] the historian, gives examples of Abatachoni, large sections of Babukusu and Abatiriki, as having been of Kalenjin stalk. Several Luyia clans such as the Abashimuli of Idakho, Abamuli (Bunyore, Tiriki, and Bunyala); Abakhobole (Kisa); and Abamani (Kisa and Marama) are of Maasai or Kalenjin origin.

(ii) Characteristics of a Luyia

Luyia men are generally tall, athletic, well proportioned with thick lips, broad noses and black eyes. The body color is obviously black, but one finds Luyia people with various hues mainly chocolate and light skinned. Luyia men have a reputation of being great lovers—a perception that is propagated by women from other Kenyan tribes. Luyia women, on the other hand, are generally physically strong with big buttocks—an outstanding feature of their

---

[30.] Prof. Ogot was giving a keynote address entitled: "Building on the Indigenous in Constitution Making" published in Report of the Constitution of Kenya Review Commission 2003. Prof. Ogot was then the Director, Institute of Research and Postgraduate Studies, Maseno University.

physique. A woman with flat buttocks struggles to get a suitor. Men with beer bellies are associated with wealth (*obuhinda*) while those with a bald head (*esiole*) are perceived of as either clever (*abachesi*) or *abahinda*. Favorite colors of the Luyia are blue and white while red is associated with death or danger. If it is raining and someone is wearing a red garment, they would say of the individual that he is attracting lightning and try to get away from him before disaster strikes. Similarly, they avoid *likulukulu* (turkey) which, when raining, is said to attract lightning because of its red neck.

For leisure the Luyia love dancing, football, bullfighting, and cock fighting (Bulimo 2013: 613 and 615). They love listening to radio, and their favorite program is usually *tuma salaam* (send greetings). They are acclaimed musicians and entertainers with *isikuti* (small drum), *litungu* (seven-string lyre), *eshilili* (one-string lyre), *oluika* (horn), *ebikhuli* (rattles), and *obukhana* (eight-string instrument) forming the repertoire of traditional Luyia music instruments. The Luyia signature tune is *mwana mbeli* (firstborn), a praise song mainly sang in weddings and other festive ceremonies. They love *boda boda* (bicycles) as a mode of transport which they decorate with various colors and fabrics. The favorite dish is *ingokho* (chicken) with *obusuma* (ugali). Some subnations and clans eat foods that others may consider peculiar. Such culinary peculiarities include consumption of white ants (*tsiswa*), grasshoppers (*amatete*), crickets and locusts (*chisiche*, variation: *chisike*), army worms (*tsikhungu*) and caterpillars (*amasaa*), rats (*tsimbeba*), monkeys (*amakhondo*; variation: *amashene*), doves (*amakhuli*), and mongrels (*amasimba*). While entomophagy is deemed a culinary peculiarity by the West, for centuries it has formed part of an essential diet in many parts of Africa, Asia, Australia, Mexico, and South America. The nutritional value of insects is slowly beginning to make inroads into the West where it is a taboo. Influenced partly by migration, intrepid Westerners will try fried crickets found in many Thai restaurants across Europe and North America. But perhaps, the turning point is a major four-year study by Prof. Marcel Dicke, the entomologist who heads the world's first university center focusing on insects as a food source at Wageningen University in Holland. Prof. Dicke wants to persuade Europeans to ditch prejudices about insect consumption especially as traditional foods like meat, fish, and chickens become more scarce, expensive, and environmentally unsustainable. According to UN's Food and Agriculture Organization (FAO), more than a thousand insect species are eaten around the world in 80 percent of mostly tropical countries as a vital source of protein.[31]

The tribal totem of the Luyia is a leopard (*ingwe*, variation: *wangwe*, *ingoi*) which says a lot about their character. Although egalitarian, like a leopard, they are fiercely independent and democratic. The leopard skin is a prized possession in Luyialand as it is a symbol of power—only *nabongo* (king), clan heads (*abaami*), or decorated warriors are allowed to wear it in public, especially during official functions or sacrifices. Many Bantu tribes in Uganda, Congo, Cameroon, Zimbabwe, Zambia, and South Africa also revere leopard as a cultural symbol or totem. Anybody else, including witchdoctors can only wear leopard regalia in the privacy of their homesteads.

Abaluyia are generally perceived to be honest people who never recant their word, agreement or promise, a characteristic spotted by early European explorers who compared them to Waswahili characterized as the "lying, dishonest, jolly, philosophical, useful scoundrels" (Purvis 1900: 3). A Luyia individual will never attack an enemy from behind true to the tribal war cry *omundu khu mundu* (man to man)—a characteristic mark of courage and fearlessness. Besides the war cry, across several subnations, one finds a proud

---

31.   Article published in the *Guardian* of UK on March 31, 2011, entitled *Insects will be important part of UK diet by 2020, says scientist*, written by Rebecca Smithers.

people othering social identity by the catchphrase: *nifwe baliho, nifwe khuliho khandi nifwe balibaho* (we are the ones here today, tomorrow, and forever). Although *ingwe* (leopard)[32] is the tribal totem, the Luyia have not adopted a single flower as a symbol of tribal identity nor do they have a flag or a mace as an emblem of tribal authority. Some subnations and clans have distinctive totems while others may have lost this aspect of their cultural heritage.

Ingwe the leopard is the tribal totem of all Luyia tribesmen.
Picture credit: Jan Erkamp

---

[32] Luyia men call each other *ingwe* (leopard) when appealing to their tribal instincts.

(iii) Importance of chicken in Luyia society

Chicken (*ingokho*) is considered the most important animal in a Luyia homestead. In the olden days, women did not eat chicken or eggs although they reared and cooked the birds for their husbands. They only started eating chicken under influence from missionaries in the early part of twentieth century, but even then, the culinary practice did not become widespread and acceptable until the 1950s. When an important visitor comes to the homestead, a chicken is always slaughtered in his honor. Even though meat from cows, sheep, or goats may also be cooked, it is a rule of custom that distinguished guests are served with chicken as the main entrée. And in very traditionalist Luyia homes, a chicken meal is accompanied not by maize[33] meal but *obusuma* (ugali) made from *amabele* (millet).

The only clan that tabooed eating of chicken is Abakhoone which settled in Bunyala from Bunyoro in Uganda. Abakhoone were a dominant warlike clan which embarked on territorial conquest as soon as they arrived, driving aboriginal clans away to distant lands. Their two-hundred-year reign of terror ended dramatically after being tricked into eating poisoned meat by a platoon of enemy clans. Emaciated and dying, Abakhoone warriors watched helplessly as enemy clans exacted sanguinary revenge. Reading danger, Abakhoone families escaped and hid in bushes but were hunted and killed after cackling of chickens gave away their hiding place. Since then, Abakhoone resolved that they will not eat chickens again (Osogo 1966: 47).

Apart from providing a delicious meal for families and visitors, chickens were also used in sacrificial offerings. Among the

---

[33] Maize, native to South America, was introduced in Kenya by the British in the early twentieth century. Before maize, the traditional grains that formed a staple diet were sorghum (*obule*) or millet (*amabele*).

Tiriki for instance, a cock (*etaywa*) was dedicated to look after a sacrificial shrine (*lusambwa*) which every family head built in his compound. This cock was revered and was never slaughtered either for consumption or as a sacrificial offering. By virtue of staying at *lusambwa*, it was thought to be in constant communion with ancestral spirits (*misambwa*; *kimisambwa* in Lubukusu) and acquired a soul of its own. If it died, another unblemished *etaywa* was carefully selected to perform this role. However, if the owner of *lusambwa* died, the *etaywa* was slaughtered and eaten by the man's close relatives. Most Luyia families used chicken's intestines (*amala*) to foretell what the future portends usually following a succession of mysterious mishaps. The bird selected for the sacrifice must be unblemished and usually either white, black, or brown in color. *Omusalisi* (sacrificial priest) or village elders of high moral rectitude ripped off intestines and carefully observed the shape, coloration and amount of air in the *amala* for telltale signs of future outlook. Besides *amala*, the bird's legs also provided clues as to what the future portended. A dead chicken's legs are supposed to remain prostrate, but if they coil, this is a sign that trouble looms ahead and the family must seek help to forestall mystical attack. A similar objective was achieved by slaughtering a goat, sheep, or cow; but this was for more serious mystical attacks.

Chickens were also used to symbolize peace. If a wife committed a cultural taboo and was driven away from the matrimonial home, elders intervened to reunite the couple. The symbol of this reunion was a cock (*etaywa*) which the wife was given by her father to take to the husband and restore peace in the homestead. When fighting to assert territorial rights, roosters never attack from behind. They face and size each other before sniping in deadly combat. However, sometimes they simultaneously simply drop their necks and walk away in mutual respect. This is rare, and when it happens, it symbolizes a peaceful resolution to whatever problems the clan community or family may be going through at that point in time.

The prized birds in Luyia society. Besides providing a sumptuous meal, chickens play an important role in security, timekeeping, and procreation. Photo by Gotodie

Chickens were crucial in maintaining security in the homestead, especially from wild animals. Through their particular way of cackling, they alerted inhabitants of the presence of unwelcome guests such as predatory snakes, foxes, hyenas, and leopards. But by far, the most important role chickens played was that of timekeeping. Chickens always left huts at six in the morning just when wild birds started singing and returned at sunset. At around three in the morning, a cock sounded the first crow following it up with a second one at five and a third at six. This constituted an effective way of time telling so that if people wanted to set off before dawn (*mabwibwi*), they agreed to leave *mutaywa yakhabili* (literally: second cock crow but means at 5:00 a.m.). An important element of this time keeping is the call to duty of procreation. Most Luyia believe that sexual intercourse early morning (*mabwibwi*) has higher chances of producing babies than earlier in the evening. Because both man and woman are tired after day's work, evening intimacy is dubbed recreational while the morning one is procreational. Among Abanyole, the early morning sexual intercourse is called *okhukulikha* (literally: to name).

Although chicken is the principal gifting item in Luyia society, the gifts are laden with symbolism. For instance a chick given to a child is not just to form the nucleus of the child's wealth creation in livestock. Rather, it is supposed to chart the fate of that child. If the chick grows into a hen that lays many eggs that produce more chicks that grow into chickens, this is a powerful symbol that the child will grow up to become successful in his life. If it dies or is eaten by vultures, the fate of that child as an adult becomes a source of mystical speculation by the family. If the chick turns out to be a male, it has to be returned to the benefactor and exchanged for a hen. Among the Bukusu, the crow of such a gift in the recipient's homestead brings misfortune.[34] Similarly, the chickens' circumcision initiates collect as gifts upon graduation are subject to the same ritual treatment. If these chickens die are stolen or are eaten by wild animals, this is interpreted to mean the initiate will face a challenging time in his endeavors as an adult.

C. Origins of the Luyia

(i) Egyptian and Congolese links

A detailed history of the Luyia is beyond the scope of this book as it has been chronicled by two scholars—Prof. Gideon Saulo Were (1967) and Dr. John Bwire Osogo (1966). Any attempt at exploring origins of the Luyia without proffering original historical

---

[34]. Feature article on *Westfm* website on March 30, 2012 entitled, "Chicken as an ancient reading material for Bukusu and other Luyia communities of Western Kenya" written by Timothy Makokha.

research material would be duplicitous of the excellent work by the two scholars indigenous to the region under study. Nonetheless, just as it is debatable whether Luyia as a tribe exists, so also is the story about their origin. In this regard, we find two schools of thought. Prof. Were chronicles from his fieldwork that most respondents gave conflicting accounts of their origin. Nearly all said they came from somewhere in the north while others referred to a big river, presumably River Nile or Congo. Others were more specific and said they came from a place called *Misri* (Egypt). They fled, in part, largely due to wars, pestilences, and famine. Due to lack of linguistic or artifactual proof at the time Prof. Were conducted his research, he concluded that the Egyptian theory was probably too farfetched, and the "somewhere in the north" probably referred to Uganda or the Congo. Prof. Were's conclusion resonated with other scholars of which the work of Englishman, Malcolm Guthrie[35] is best known. Although the name Niger-Congo was introduced in 1955 by Joseph Harold Greenberg,[36] the American linguist and anthropologist, it is Guthrie's 1971 classification of Bantu languages which, although slightly outdated, is still widely used to identify Africa's largest phylum. According to Guthrie, Luyia are part of the larger Niger-Congo Bantoid stalk whose migration started circa 3000 BC somewhere in what is present-day Nigeria and moved southward through Cameroon, Congo, etc. While the Were-Guthrie school of thought is credible, recent research by Bantu Egyptologists and other scholars has unveiled linguistic as well as historical evidence that make the Egyptian link quite compelling as well. I will examine both theories in detail shortly, but first just who are the Bantu?

---

[35] Malcolm Guthrie (10 Feb 1903-22 Nov 1972) is known primarily for his classification of Bantu languages. His model is still the most widely used.

[36] Joseph Harold Greenberg (28 May 1915-7 May 2001) was an American linguist famous for his work in two areas: Linguistic typology and the genetic classification of languages.

The term Bantu was first used by German philologist, Wilhelm Heinrich Immanuel Bleek,[37] whose doctoral thesis at the University of Bonn in 1851 featured an attempt to link North African and Khoikhoi (then called Hottentot but now largely pejorative) languages—the thinking at the time being that all African languages were connected. The Bantu constitute a large cluster of African languages sharing common lexical ancestry. The etymology of the root word *ntu* or *ndu* (meaning person) is the common thread that binds all proto Bantu. For instance Luyia call a human being *omundu*, Kikuyu *andu*, Swahili *mtu*, Kongo *muntu*, Zulu *buntu*, to mention but a few. Although common linguistic ancestry is not in doubt, over centuries, diachronic phonology of Bantu languages as we know them today raises doubt on whether certain languages are indeed Bantu. Still some languages are close-knit while others are as far apart as Cape Town and Cairo. Detailed comparative studies carried out by Bantu scholars like Meinhof, Meeussen, and Guthrie have made it possible to reconstruct Bantu phonology, morphology, and lexicon.[38]

(ii) Bantu in the context of African languages

To understand Bantu languages, we shall first briefly examine the context in which they are categorized among African languages. African languages can be classified into four distinct categories: Afro-Asiatic, Nilo-Saharan, Khoisan, and Niger-Congo.

[37.] Wilhelm Heinrich Immanuel Bleek (8 March 1827-17 August 1875) was a German linguist whose best work is *A Comparative Grammar of South African Languages*.

[38.] Patrick R. Bennett, *Patterns in Linguistic Geography and the Bantu Origins Controversy: History in Africa*, Vol. 10 (1983), pp. 35-51, Published by African Studies Association.

a. Afro-Asiatic languages

These constitute a language family with about 375 active languages (SIL[39] estimate) and more than 350 million speakers spread throughout North Africa, the Horn of Africa, and Southwest Asia, as well as parts of the Sahel, West Africa, and East Africa. The most widely spoken Afro-Asiatic language is Arabic, with over 280 million native speakers. In addition to active languages, this family includes several ancient languages, such as Ancient Egyptian, biblical Hebrew, and Akkadian.

b. Nilo-Saharan languages

These are spoken mainly in the upper parts of rivers Chari (Shari) and Nile (hence Nilotic), including historic Nubia. The languages are spoken in seventeen nations in the northern half of Africa—from Algeria and Mali in the northwest: to Benin, Nigeria, and the Democratic Republic of the Congo in the south and Sudan to Tanzania in the east.

c. Khoisan languages

Also known as the Khoesan or Khoesaan, these are the click tongues of Africa. Most are southern and eastern Africa though some, such as Khoi languages, appear to have moved to their current locations not long before the Bantu expansion. In southern Africa, speakers are Khoi and Bushmen (Saan), in Tanzania the Sandawe and Hadza. The Khoisan language was popularized by actor N!xau in the 1980 film *The Gods Must Be Crazy*. Prior to Bantu expansion, it is likely that Khoisan languages were spread throughout southern and eastern Africa. They are currently

---

[39.] SIL International is a faith-based nonprofit organization committed to serving language communities worldwide as they build capacity for sustainable language development. Founded in 1934, SIL has grown from a small summer linguistics training program with two students to a staff of over 5,500 from over sixty countries.

restricted to the Kalahari Desert, primarily in Namibia and Botswana, and to the Rift Valley in central Tanzania. Most of the languages are endangered, and several are moribund or extinct with no written record. The only widespread Khoisan language is Nama of Namibia, with a quarter of a million speakers, Sandawe in Tanzania is second in number with about forty thousand.

d. Niger-Congo languages

This is by far the largest family of African languages consisting of some 1,514 tongues spoken by about 85 percent of Africans—from Dakar, Senegal, in the west to Mombasa, Kenya, in the east and south to Cape Town, South Africa. As understood today, Niger-Congo has nine branches: Mande, Kordofanian, Atlantic (formerly West Atlantic), Kru, Gur, Kwa, Ijoid, Adamawa-Ubangi (formerly Adamawa-Eastern), and Benue-Congo. As mentioned earlier, the Luyia belong to the Benue-Congo branch.

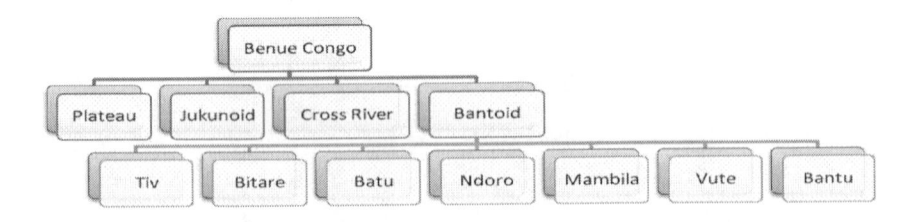

Chart 1: Greenberg's original classification of Benue-Congo languages.

(iii) Benue-Congo languages

This is by far the largest branch of the Niger-Congo language family, both in the number of languages spoken (an estimated 900) and speakers (at least 500 million). Its major divisions are the following:

- Defoid of which Yoruba with more than 20 million speakers is the largest.
- Edoid of which the best known example is Edo (also called Benin or Bini—no relationship with the Republic of Benin, formerly Dahomey) spoken primarily in Edo state of southern Nigeria. An Edo script is writing based on different color combinations and graphs.
- Nupoid: spoken mainly in central Nigerian cities like Kaduna and Abuja and includes Nupe, Ebira, and Gbagyi.
- Idomoid: found in central Nigeria of which the best known is Idoma.
- Igboid: a branch of Niger-Volta which includes many dialects of populous Igbo.
- Kainji: sixty or so Kainji languages are spoken by about nine hundred thousand people in Nigeria of which the largest four are Tsuvadi, Cishingini, Tsishingini, and Clela.
- Platoid: a congeries of fifty languages spoken in Jos Plateau and include Jju or Kaje, Birom, and Tarok.
- Cross River or Delta Cross: a group of about sixty languages spoken in southeastern Nigeria with some overspill into Cameroon and include Ogoni, Khana, Lokaa, Ibibio-Efik, among the larger ones.
- Jukunoid: a group of languages spoken by Jukun and related peoples of Nigeria and Cameroon and include the nearly extinct Bete found in Taraba State.
- Bantoid: This is the category in which the Luyia and related dialects are classified as we shall discuss in the next section.

(iv) Bantoid languages

Bantoid is by far the largest category of languages spoken on the African continent. With an estimated 680 languages, speakers straddle nearly two thirds of the continent—from eastern Nigeria across central, eastern, and southern Africa. The Bantoid languages are divided into a northern group and a southern group.[40] Northern Bantoid consists of fifteen small languages spoken in eastern Nigeria and central Cameroon. Southern Bantoid comprises eleven subgroups, of which Narrow Bantu is the largest.[41] Language experts under the auspices of Benue-Congo Working Group coined the term Narrow Bantu to differentiate between groups not recognized by Malcolm Guthrie in his seminal 1948 classification as Bantu. Although the specificity of Narrow Bantu vis-a-vis Southern Bantoid groups was thrown in doubt by phylogenetic scholars like P. Piron (1995), the terminology is still widely relevant. Southern Bantoid comprises 643 languages according to *Ethnologue*, making it one of the largest language subfamilies.

Narrow Bantu

This is a group of some five hundred languages belonging to the Southern Bantoid subgroup of the Benue-Congo branch of the Niger-Congo language family. The Narrow Bantu languages are spoken from southern Cameroon eastward to Kenya and southward to the southernmost tip of the continent. It is in this group that the

---

[40]. Greenberg in his 1963 book, *The Languages of Africa,* defined Bantoid as the group to which (Narrow) Bantu belongs together with its closest relatives. This is the sense in which the term is understood and used today. The division into North and South Bantoid was introduced by Kay Williamson (1989), building from a hypothesis first expounded by Roger Blench (1987). In this proposal, Mambiloid and Dakoid languages are grouped as North Bantoid while all else are placed under South Bantoid—a classification which *Ethnologue* uses. Although the legitimacy of the North Bantoid group was questioned by ethno-linguistic scholars like P. Piron (1995), the work did establish southern Bantoid as a valid phylogenetic unit.

[41]. According to Williamson and Blench (2000), Southern Bantoid is divided into Narrow Bantu, Jarawan, Tivoid, Beboid, Mamfe (Nyang), Grassfields, and Ekoid families.

Luyia and related dialects belong. The International Encyclopaedia of Linguistics has classified Narrow Bantu languages into sixteen alphabetical groups: A-S. The Luyia are in Group J of the southern Bantu.[42] I have so far attempted to trace origin of the Luyia as seen through the prism of ethnolinguistic scholars. Although scholarly evidence of the Benue-Congo origin is compelling it is by no means conclusive or agreeable to all. Most Luyia people, especially the Bukusu, still lay strong claims to *Misri* (Egypt) as the place from whence their ancestors came.

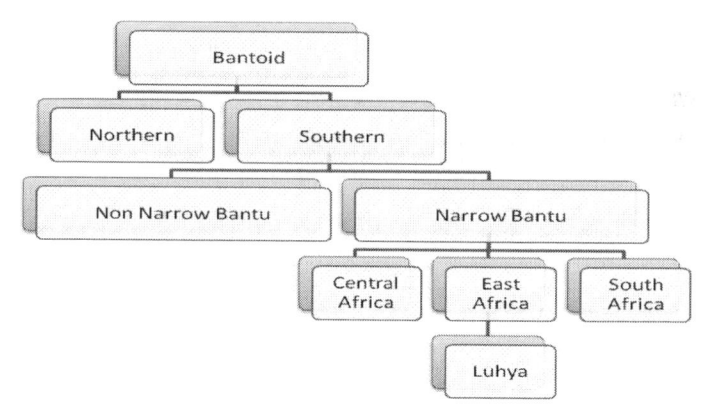

Chart 2: Watters (1989) compromise Bantoid model.

(v)   Luyia in ancient Egypt

While the Luyia story of origin seems firmly established in the Niger-Congo academic trail, the Pharaonic grail is far too holy to dismiss as apocryphal. I have made reference to oral narratives recorded by scholars like Prof. Gideon Were (1967) in which some Luyia respondents pointed to *Misri* (Egypt) as their ancestral land. Although Prof. Were's own conclusion was premised on the

---

42.   A subgroup of Bantu languages spoken in most of Uganda, northwestern Kenya, northeastern Democratic Republic of Congo, all of Rwanda and Burundi, and northwestern Tanzania.

Niger-Congo-Uganda trail, recent historico-linguistic evidence has resurrected the *Egyptian* descent from intellectual debris. Ongoing research by Kiswahili-Bantu Research Unit for the Advancement of the Ancient Egyptian Language, led by Ferg Somo,[43] has adduced compelling evidence to link Bantu languages to ancient Egyptian hieroglyphics.

Somo's research spanning twelve years so far has revolutionized the field of Afro-linguistic Egyptology, and while it has not invalidated Guthrie and Greenberg's Niger-Congo model, it certainly has unsettled it and a reevaluation of earlier theories of Bantu migrations must be undertaken. He has so far researched on 150 Bantu words using Kiswahili, Shona, Bemba, Zulu, etc., and traced their origin to the ancient Egyptian language of hieroglyphics. Each word he has analyzed, he dubs Rosetta Stone and the total collection of his study is entitled *The Bantu Rosetta Stones*. Among words he has studied include the very word Bantu (people) whose hieroglyphic equivalent is *Batu* (variations: *watu, andu, bantu, atho, atu, bandu, acho, bot, banu, banhu, adu*).

The ancient Egyptian language has long been classified as belonging to the Afro-Asiatic group of languages. However, Somo's team has established that hieroglyphics contains substantial amounts of vocabulary derived from the Proto-Bantu group of languages, especially the Niger-Congo family. According to Somo, ancestral languages of all human beings may be anywhere between ten thousand to fifteen thousand years old. Merrit Ruhlen[44]

[43.] Ferg Somo's research is ongoing. His findings are published on his portal: http://www.kaa-umati.co.uk accessed on March 2, 2010.

[44.] Born in 1944, Prof. Merritt Ruhlen is an American linguist known for his work on the classification of languages and what this reveals about the origin and evolution of modern humans. His work stands within the mainstream of standard comparative-historical linguistics. As a principal advocate and defender of Joseph Greenberg's approach to language classification, he was subjected to withering attacks none of which made him shift positions.

has even proposed that a common language once spanned the entire world. He calls this language Proto-Global. Furthermore, mitochondrial DNA evidence carried out by Bryan Sykes[45] has shown that modern human beings originated in central or southern Africa and spread across the rest of Africa and along the Arabian Peninsula carrying and diffusing languages. The findings of the oldest prehistoric human fossils in East Africa by palaeontologists Louis Leakey and Richard Leakey are internationally recognized in scholarly pantheon that eastern Africa, especially Kenya or Ethiopia is where the first man walked the earth.

According to this school of thought fronted by Sykes, it was only at a later stage that human beings spread north into Egypt. It is from this body of evidence that a vast vocabulary of words of common origin between ancient Egyptians and Proto-Bantu were compiled by Somo's research unit. Besides Somo, another socioanthropologist, James Brunson (2004) has studied ancient Egyptian art and noticed that black imagery is linked with gods. He argues that Osiris is not only depicted as black, but he was in fact black; his origins traced to somewhere in Central Africa (Brunson 2004: 57). He says that during the most important dynasties (1-4, 6, 11-13, 17-18, and 25), the pharaohs in power were black or Africoid. And during rivalry between the English and French for world domination (culminating in the Battle of Waterloo of 1815), scores of scholars, scientists, and freebooters descended on Egypt heralding the discovery of a long-forgotten ancient civilization. When Britain invaded Egypt in 1801, the mission was to seize French collection of Egyptian artifacts, he posits. One of the artifacts the British succeeded in seizing was the famous Rosetta stone; the symbolism Ferg Somo has used to anchor his linguistic research.

---

[45]. Bryan Sykes (born 9 Sept 1947) is professor of human genetics at the University of Oxford. Sykes is best known for his bestselling books on the investigation of human history and prehistory through studies of mitochondrial DNA. He is also the founder of Oxford Ancestors, a genealogical DNA testing firm.

The Luyia are not the only Bantu tribe claiming links with Egypt. Scores of Bantu tribes in Kenya and elsewhere also stake a claim to Pharaonic Egypt in their oral migratory history. One such tribe is the Ameru (Meru) of Mt. Kenya region. In his book, *Restatement of Bantu Origin and Meru History*, Alfred M M'Imanyara quotes an ex-chief who says that they came from a place called *Ruteere rwa Urio*, which he equated with *Misri* (Egypt). M'Imanyara demonstrates that the Ameru came originally from the ancient Nilotic empire of Meroe (circa 300BC-AD100), which is sometimes referred to as an island as it was bounded by both the White and Blue Niles and swamps in the south. Notice the linguistic similarity between the words "Meru" and "Meroe," which, while tempting as credible evidence, is far from conclusive. Still oral stories from elders suggest at least that Ameru were at some point in contact with civilizations from farther north. Whether or not this ties in with Meroe is subject to further anthropological research.

Another powerful voice in the study of Bantu Egyptology is Asar Imhotep,[46] the U.S.-based independent researcher and historian. In a lecture paper entitled: *Cosmology and the Origins of Egyptian Civilisation*,[47] Imhotep quotes renowned Ghanaian writer, Ayi Kwei Armah:

> Now I had grown to adulthood; inside our larger house, I was understanding life journeys of my own, and although I had imagined other paths,

---

[46] Asar Imhotep is an independent historian and researcher focusing on African culture, languages, philosophy and spiritual symbolism. His comparative study of ancient Nile Valley civilizations and their cultural connections to Bantu helped him develop a comparative methodology he called philosophical cognancy (the comparison of signs, symbols and ritual practices across African nations similar to analysing cognates in linguistics).

[47] Lecture was delivered at the SHAPE Community Center, Houston, Texas, on 15 December 2007.

I was moving into the future as a writer. The more I learned about our history, the clearer it seemed to me that if I wanted to write, I would have to study more seriously since all available evidence indicated that the narrative of our social history was at the center of the art of poets, storytellers and spokespersons. I followed the trail of evidence backwards in time. It led me to the oral traditions. These traditions, beginning with acknowledgement of places reached by groups travelling under pressure too extreme to adapt to, referred to an earlier place of departure. Sometimes the reference was simply to the Great River or Great Waters. More frequently, the traditions of migration mentioned *Misri, Misiri* or *Luti*. Those are just other names for the area known as Egypt; though in ancient times it went by other indigenous names: Ta Meri, Beloved Land, Tawi, Two Lands and more often, Kemet, the Black Nation.

According to Imhotep, the above excerpt from Armah's research into the oral history of his people is supportive of the Egyptian ancestry theory because Ghanaian languages belong to the Niger-Congo phylum of which Bantu is part. Moreover, it is not just the oral—ancient Egyptian rock art on display at various museums contains traces of Bantu. Imhotep gives another example from lecture notes by Babuidi entitled "Bantu Migration and Settlement" in which he quotes 1914 Karl Lehmann's *Kongo (Congo) Collection*.[48] "A long time ago in antiquity, people did not exist in this lower Kongo; they came from the north of the country.

---

[48] Karl Lehmann's *Kongo Cultural Collection* (20,000pp microfilm, Lidingo, Sweden, 1914, Film No.1, Cahier XVIII/13).

There also, in the north, people came from far off North, the very north of Kayinga. Kayinga is the name of the country (region) where lived our ancestors in antiquity." Kayinga is the Congolese name for the Sahara. This, argues Imhotep, is another example that the Bantu came from Egypt or, at any rate, somewhere north of Sahara Desert.

(vi) Ancient Egyptians were black

a. Evidence of Negros in predynastic Egypt

One of Africa's preeminent historians in human race's origins and precolonial African culture, Cheikh Anta Diop,[49] says that despite disagreements by anthropological researchers, all the evidence adduced is unanimous of the existence of a Negro race from the most distant ages of prehistory down to the dynastic period in Egypt.[50] Researchers like Ms. Fawcett found that the Negadah skulls seemed close to Germanic peoples. It is worth noting that the nasal indices of Ethiopians and Dravidians (Indians) seem to approximate them to Germanic peoples though both are black races. Another group of anthropologists led by Thompson and Randall MacIver set out to determine more precisely the importance of the Negroid element in the series of skulls from El'Amrah, Abydos and Hou. They found that 24 percent of men

---

[49] Cheikh Anta Diop (29 Dec 1923-7 Feb 1986) was a Senegalese historian and anthropologist whose study of human race's origins and precolonial African culture has had a profound impact on modern genealogical understanding of the human race. Regarded as one of the greatest African historians of the twentieth century, he was honored at the World Festival of the Arts held in Dakar in 1966 jointly with the late W. E. B. DuBois with an award as the writer who had exerted the greatest influence on Negro thought in the twentieth century.

[50] Details are summarized in Chapter X of Dr. Emile Massoulard's *Histoire et protohistoire d'Egypt* (Institut d'Ethnologix, Paris, 1949).

and 19 percent of women in the early predynastic Egypt and 25 percent and 28 percent, respectively in the late predynastic were black.

However, Arthur Keith[51] disputed the findings of Thompson and MacIver on the grounds that any research on contemporary English skulls using the same methodology would yield at least 30 percent Negroid skulls. Frédéric Falkenburger (1890-1965) reopened the anthropological study of the Egyptian population, and using a sample of 1,787 predynastic skulls, he arrived at the following four results: 36 percent Negroid, 33 percent Mediterranean, 11 percent Cro-Magnoid,[52] and 20 percent not specific to any of these groups but closely related to either Cro-Magnoid or Negroid (Diop 2004: 11).

If we accept Falkenburger's figures, it would appear that contrary to Elliot-Smith's[53] theory, the predynastic Egyptian population was not purebred, but a rich mix of at least three distinct races—Negroid, Mediterranean, Cro-Magnoids, and a hotchpotch of mixed races. Despite discrepancies, most Egyptologists agree that the predynastic Egyptian epoch was populated by a Negroid race rather than coming on to the scene at a postdynasty period. According to Diop, evidence from hieroglyphics suggests that

---

[51.] Sir Arthur Keith (5 Feb 1866-7 Jan 1955) was a leading figure in the study of human fossils. As the president of the Royal Anthropological Institute, he published *A New Theory of Human Evolution*, in which he supported the hypothesis of group selection and introduced the idea of cultural differences as providing a mental barrier. Writing just after World War II, he particularly emphasized the racial origins of anti-Semitism, and in *A New Theory of Evolution,* he devoted a chapter to anti-Semitism and Zionism in which he argued that Jews live by a 'dual code'.

[52.] First discovered in 1868 at the Cro-Magnon rock shelter in the Dordogne region in southern France, the human skeletons that came to be called Cro-Magnon are now considered representative of humans at that time.

[53.] Grafton Elliot Smith (1871-1937), the Australian-born British anatomist published his study on Egyptian mummies in 1912.

ancient Egyptians considered themselves black. They called themselves *kamit* which, in pharaonic lingo, simply means black (Diop 2004: 20). Furthermore, another comprehensive study by Diop in 1977 of ancient Egyptian language and Walaf, a Senegalese tongue, shows convincing lexical affinity between the two even though they are geographically miles apart.

Another powerful argument about black Egyptians comes from Basil Davidson,[54] the Africanist historian who supports Martin Bernal's *Black Athena* thesis.[55] He argues that Greek civilisation was influenced by or at least respected, Egyptians. The names of Greek gods for example came from Egypt. Great Greek mathematicians and philosophers were in awe of Egyptian civilization. Pythagoras (he of Pythagoras Theorem) spent no fewer than twenty-one years in Egypt. Aristotle said that "Egypt was the cradle of mathematics"; Aristotle's teacher, Exodus, had studied in Egypt before returning to Greece. Ancient philosophers like Socrates and Plato were influenced by Egyptian philosophy and did not doubt Egypt's supremacy; how could they? After all the pyramids were not built by guesswork but by accurate geometry which Egyptians had discovered, perfected, and proven. Herodotus, acclaimed as the father of Greek history, acknowledged the mathematical marvel of the great pyramids of Giza. Greeks of Classical Age went further to reaffirm that the Pharaonic civilization had derived from inner Africa: from the lands of "long lived Ethiopians," i.e., blacks (Davidson 2004: 44).

[54.] Basil Risbridger Davidson (9 Nov 1914-9 July 2010) was a British journalist and historian who wrote several books on Africa becoming an authority on the continent's history from 1951 onward.

[55.] *Black Athena: The Afroasiatic Roots of Classical Civilization* is a three-volume work by Martin Bernal whose thesis is that ancient Greek civilisation was influenced by Egyptian (African) and Phoenician (Asian) cultures rather than a purebred Aryan affair.

b. Black African Jews

Although several African tribes claim their ancestors came from Egypt and are somehow related to Jews, so far there are only two distinct groups which have certified provenance to African Jewry—Falasha[56] of Ethiopia and Lemba of South Africa. In fact some scholars hold the view that ancient Jews were Negroid rather than Caucasoid or Semitic. The Igbo of Nigeria consider themselves Jews and are said to have migrated from Syrian, Portuguese, and Libyan Israelites into West Africa. Historical records show that this migration started circa 740 CE. According to U.S.-based Nigerian Judaic historian, Chinedu Nwabunwanne, who has researched this subject extensively, "The migration started when Caliph Mohammed, the last leader of the Umayyads, defeated Syrian Yamani-Arab Umayyads in 744 CE." The Syrian-Jewish migrant tribes Dan, Naphtali, Gad, and Asher resettled in Nigeria where they became known as Sambatyon Jews. In 1484 and 1667, Judeans and Zebulonians from Portugal and Libya, respectively joined Sambatyon Jews of Nigeria, he says. He concludes that Nigerian Jews originated from the following six Israelite tribes: Judah, Dan, Naphtali, Gad, Asher and Zebulon, which are the six tribes Moses twice mentioned when blessing the Children of Israel. Between 2004 and 2008, Rabbi Yaacov Behrman made numerous trips to Nigeria to assess the Igbo Jews and although they practice *kosher* laws and observe other Jewish traditions, the rabbinate

---

[56.] Falasha is an Amharic word meaning exiled. It is nowadays largely a pejorative term. They prefer to be called Beta Israel (House of Israel). Probably descended from local Agew peoples converted by Jews in southern Arabia, they remained faithful to Judaism after Abyssinia (Ethiopia) was converted to Christianity in the AD fourth century. Persecuted by Christians, they settled in the area around Lake Tana in northern Ethiopia. Though ignorant of the Talmud (collection of ancient Rabbinic writings, constituting the basis of religious authority in Orthodox Judaism), members adhered strictly to Mosaic Law and observed Judaic festivals.

concluded there was not enough evidence to declare Igbo Jews truly Semitic like the Falasha and Lemba.

In Kenya, a group of about three thousand Kikuyu tribesmen claim to have lived as Jews for sixty years in the sprawling plains of Laikipia district.[57] Their rural synagogue is situated at Mairo Inya location about four kilometers from Nyahururu town and doubles up as their Kenyan headquarters. It is here they congregate to observe all Judaic festivals including Passover, the annual ritual observed by all Jews worldwide in remembrance of their liberation from slavery in Egypt. Like all those claiming Jewish ancestry, the Mairo Inya Jews ambition is to eventually relocate to the Promised Land (Israel) although there is no evidence the Israel rabbinate has received any application from them. The discovery of black Kenyan Jews is somewhat a historical irony. In 1902, Joseph Chamberlain, the then colonial secretary in England, wanted to settle Jews in Uasin Gishu District in Kenya to escape the persecution they faced in Europe. Coded Operation Samson, the Nairobi Plan was accepted by Theodore Herzel, father of the Zionist movement, that sought to unite Jews in exile, but some groups especially the Russian Jews rejected it, wanting nothing short of Israel. When the plan was put to vote at the seventh Zionist Congress in Basil, Switzerland in 1905, Operation Samson was rejected. In retrospect, some Jews regret they did not take up the offer and muse quietly how things could have been so different in the context of Adolf Hitler's holocaust.

c. Falasha

So far, we have seen the Bantu-Egyptian link through the prism of scholarly evidence in oral traditions, linguistics, and art. While the evidence is compelling, it is not conclusive enough to explain the varying strands cutting across several Bantu tribes or even

---

[57] News story in the *Daily Nation* newspaper by Joseph Kabia published on Wednesday, May 5, 2010, headlined: Longing for the Promised Land.

Nilotic ones claiming Egyptian ancestry. Judaic history perhaps explains the most significant link to Pharaohs. Jewish bondage in Egypt as slaves of pharaohs is amply documented. That they emigrated out of Egypt to the *Promised Land* is also not in doubt whether through the biblical version of Moses and the splitting of the Red Sea or otherwise. What is clear is that the exodus was a slow, confused, and lengthy process spanning over forty years. Biblical scriptures say that God appointed Moses to lead his people (Jews) out of slavery in Egypt to Canaan (Promised Land). Less known is that another band of Jews moved in a southerly direction of which the Ethiopian Falasha are well known. The Falasha call themselves Beta Israel (House of Israel) and claim descent from Menelik I,[58] son of King Solomon and the Queen of Sheba. In 1975, the Israeli rabbinate affirmed that Falasha were Jews, and from 1980 to 1992, some forty-five thousand Ethiopian Jews were airlifted to Israel to escape the great famine that ravaged Ethiopia (formerly Abyssinia). Strikingly, the Hausa and Fulani of Nigeria who speak Afro-Asiatic language, claim they are related to Ethiopians.

d. Lemba

While the Ethiopian Jews are well documented, less known is another group of black Jews found mainly in South Africa.[59] Like the Israel Jews, they consider themselves descendants of Abraham, Isaac, and Jacob. These are the Lemba, otherwise known as the lost tribe of Israel. Although Bantu and mainly Christian, their Jewish link is found in religious practices and beliefs similar to Judaism and which they say were transmitted orally from generation to another. According to Lemba oral history, their ancestors left

---

[58.] As we shall see in chapter four, one of the key figures mentioned in Bukusu migratory traditions is Maina, thought to be the same person as Menelik.

[59.] The Lemba live in the Venda, Louis Trichardt, and Pietersburg regions of Limpopo province, South Africa.

Judea about 2,500 years ago and settled at a place called Senna, later migrating farther into East Africa. A British researcher, Tudor Parfitt,[60] located Senna in Yemen, specifically, in the village of Sanāw[61] in eastern Hadhramaut. It was once a thriving Jewish city during the Babylonian empire around 500 BC and is believed to have been dominated by Israelites who had fled Jerusalem during the Babylonian invasion. Today it is largely deserted and occupied only five days a year by pilgrims.

After entering Africa, the Lemba split into two groups, with one staying in Ethiopia, the other travelling farther south, along the east coast with some settling in Tanzania and Kenya where they are best known as Ba Mwenye (lords of the land), according to Dr. Rudo Mathivha,[62] daughter of the founder of Lemba Cultural Association, Prof. G. E. R. Mathivha. Dr. Mathivha says Lemba were known in Yemen as Basenna, in Zimbabwe and Malawi Balemba and Mozambique Basenna as well. Among the Luyia clans, the word Omumenya refers to someone allowed to settle on land belonging to a different clan from his. In Bukhayo, there is a clan known as Bamenya, but I have been unable to establish whether Omumenya and Bamenya have any relationship with the Ba Mwenye referred to by Dr. Mathivha. Lemba even claim to have constructed the Great Zimbabwe, a claim that the Shona dispute. According to Lemba oral tradition, they left Zimbabwe for South Africa after committing a culinary sin—eating a rat (*imbeba*).

[60.] Tudor Parfitt (born 1944) is a British professor of Modern Jewish Studies at the University of London's School of Oriental and African Studies (SOAS), where he is the founding director of the Center for Jewish Studies.

[61.] Sometimes spelt Senna, Sena, or Sanā, it is an abandoned ancient town in Yemen located in the eastern Hadramaut valley. This village should not be confused with the capital of Yemen, Sana'a, or the town of Sanāw in Oman.

[62.] Speech to Zionist Lunch Club, Johannesburg, 15 October 1999, by Dr. Rudo Mathivha entitled, "Story of the Lemba People."

Fiction or fact: the great DNA proof

The question must be asked: Is Lemba's pitch to be regarded as God's chosen people fact or fiction? The answer to this question can be found in a groundbreaking genetic study by Prof. Parfitt who, in 1996, found out that more than 50 percent of the Lemba Y chromosomes are Semitic in origin. A subsequent study in 2000 reported more specifically that a substantial number of Lemba men carry a particular polymorphism on the Y chromosome known as the Cohen modal haplotype (CMH), which is indicative of Y-DNA Haplogroup J found among some Jews and in other populations across the Middle East.

One particular subclan, Buba, is considered as the priestly clan while among Jews, Kohanim are the rabbinical clan. The Buba carried most of the CMH found in Lemba. The same marker is also most prevalent among Jewish Kohanim (priests). The Lemba oral tradition attributes their coming to southern Africa to the Buba clan.

e. *Jewish rites found among the Luyia*

- *Circumcision:* Although Jews circumcise only a few days after birth and Luyia during or after teenagehood, the principal is the same. They both consider circumcision a rite of passage. The uncircumcised is called a gentile in Jewish culture while among the Luyia he is called *omusinde*.

- *Widow inheritance:* According to ancient Jewish law, *Halakha*,[63] a man must marry the widow of his childless brother to maintain the brother's line. This levirate marriage has subtle similarities with Luyia custom of widow inheritance.

[63.] *Halakha* also transliterated *Halocho* (Yiddish pronunciation) and *Halacha*—is the collective body of Jewish religious law, including biblical law (613 *mitzvot*) and later Talmudic and Rabbinic law as well as customs and traditions.

- *Sacrificial offerings:* The Jewish preferred sacrificial animal is sheep (*likondi*; *likhese* in Lubukusu) which is also the one used mainly by the Luyia in various ancestral sacrifices.
- *Birth rituals:* In Jewish culture it is forbidden to prepare for birth of a child before it is born, e.g., buy cots, clothes, etc. The same custom is observed by the Luyia.
- *Dietary prohibitions:* Although *kashrut* (*kosher*) dietary laws forbid the eating of certain animals and seafood of which the pig (swine) is the most famous, it is notable that among the Luyia, pigs are an alien animal. Although the Luyia nowadays eat pork, the pig is not one of the animals you'll find in a traditional Luyia stable. Like Jews, the Luyia also do not eat birds of prey such as vultures, night owls, hawks, etc. nor do they mix milk with meat.

f. Cush (Kush) Kingdom

The origins of Cush Kingdom can be traced to biblical times, specifically after floods that destroyed the entire world except those on Noah's Ark said to have perched atop Mt. Ararat straddling Turkish and Armenian frontier. According to these accounts, Noah's three sons—Shem, Ham, and Japheth—represent the three main races in the world today (Negroid, Caucasian, and Asiatic—including Mongoloid, Semitic, and Akkadian). These sons were to spread and each to have their own tongues (Genesis 10:5). It is generally believed that Ham was the ancestor of the Negroid race; and his sons are given as Cush, Mizraim, Phut, and Canaan. It is from the biblical script that we trace Cush, an ancient region in Ethiopia where the descendants of Cush settled. It is one of the biblical lands associated with Jews. Isaiah 11:11-12 mentions Cush as one of the places where God will recover the remnants of his people.[64] It is often identified as the ancient kingdom of Nubia, but in the second millennium BC, it was under Egyptian jurisdiction. In the eighth century BC Kushite King, Piye invaded and conquered Egypt. It was ruled from 719 BC by Piye's brother Shabaka, who also invaded Egypt and set up the twenty-fifth dynasty. Around midseventh century BC, the Kushite kingdom's capital was transferred to Meroë where the Kushites (Cushites) ruled for another a thousand years.

Luo as founders of the Cush dynasty

I make reference to the Cush Kingdom only because certain scholarly reports have suggested that Luyia neighbors, the Nilotic Luo whose Sudanic origin is not in doubt, are the founders of the ancient Cush dynasty. This is a significant find, bits of which can inform the Luyia migratory history. It is also illustrative to note that another neighboring tribe, the Kalenjin[65] also claim their ancestors came from Egypt.

As we shall see later, the Luo arrived in Uganda after Bantu tribes living there were settled with an organized system of political rule. Although they later founded the Babiito Dynasty from the ruins of what was Bunyoro-Kitara Kingdom (Were & Wilson 1968: 50), they had no experience as rulers and, to a large extent, had to rely on the Chwezi to show them what to do. What does this

---

[64] Isaiah 11.11-12: Then it will happen on that day that the Lord will again recover the second time with His hand the remnant of His people, who will remain, from Assyria, Egypt, Pathros, Cush, Elam, Shinar, Hamath, and from the islands of the sea. And he will lift up a standard for the nations, and will assemble the banished ones of Israel, and will gather the dispersed of Judah from the four corners of the earth.

[65] A cluster of highland Nilotic tribes numbering about ten found mainly in Kenya and Uganda and includes Keiyo, Nandi, Kipsigis, Tugen, Marakwet, Pokot, Ogiek, Terik, Sabaot, or Sebei (Kony, Bok, Bongomek), and Ndorobo. Kalenjin means "I tell you" in reference to uniting all subgroups.

say about their founding of the Cush Dynasty? The lead scholar on this subject is Dr. Terence Okello Paito whose research has concluded that the Luo not only once sojourned in Egypt but were the founders of the ancient Cush Kingdom.[66] Dr. Paito is advancing studies by postwar researchers, especially Henri Frankfort,[67] an eminent Egyptologist, whose research concluded that there are distinct groups of Africans surviving today, whose ancestry can be traced to ancient Egyptians.

Frankfort's hypothesis lay dormant until a couple of decades later at a symposium on the peopling of ancient Egypt and the deciphering of the Meroitic script, Cheikh Anta Diop (1923-1986) delivered a linguistic comparison of ancient Egyptian languages and those of contemporary Africa. Both Diop and Frankfort believed that there are people alive today in Africa who speak a language similar or very close to that spoken in ancient Egypt. The hard task was to identify that language. Dr. Paito supports both Diop and Frankfort but goes further to identify these people as the Luo (Lwoo). He argues that the Luo were the founders of the ancient Koch or Cushitic kingdom at Napata, an ancient city-state on the west bank of River Nile, some 400 km north of Khartoum built around 1345 BC by Nubians. By 750 BC, Napata was a developed city while Egypt had been seriously weakened by Assyrian conquest. King Kashta added to the Egyptian woes by attacking and occupying Upper Egypt. His policy was pursued by his successors Piye and Shabaka (721-707 BC), who eventually brought the whole Nile Valley under Kushitic control in the second year of his reign. Overall, the Kushite kings ruled Upper Egypt for approximately one century and the whole Egypt for approximately

---

[66]. Dr. Terence Okello Paito: "Luo Origins of Civilisation: Towards a Positive Identification of the Civilization of the Itiyo-pi-anu Peoples"—an abstract paper.

[67]. Henri "Hans" Frankfort (Feb. 24, 1897-July 16, 1954) was a Dutch Egyptologist, archaeologist, and orientalist.

fifty-seven years. While in Egypt, the Luo worshipped god Anu[68] and were the very *Itiyo-pi-anu* (people who dedicated services to god Anu—not to be confused with Ethiopian), argues Paito. Later bands of Luo people migrated farther south into Sudan, Uganda, Kenya, and Tanzania.

D. Growth of Interlacustrine Kingdoms

(i) The Luo factor

Although the history of major kingdoms in East Africa is rooted in oral mythology, it is widely believed that the Luo arrived in East Africa to find Bantu tribes settled. And just like the Luyia name is derived from "hearth" so also is the word Luo (Lwoo, Luu) which some scholars say originated from "fireplace." Another meaning assigned to Luo is *luwo* which means "to follow" as in River Nile. To understand the Luo-Luyia migration story properly, let us first examine the growth of kingdoms in East Africa. The first such kingdom, Kitara, is attributed to the mythical Batembuzi (means harbingers or pioneers) whose dynasty lasted for four or five reigns during the Bronze Age period. Batembuzi were succeeded by Bachwezi (Chwezi). Little is known about the Batembuzi and Bachwezi or when they established Kitara except that the kingdom spread over a vast area covering present-day central, western, and southern Uganda; northern Tanzania, western Kenya, and eastern Congo. Much of what is known is based on mythology and oral tradition with a number of current Great Lakes inhabitants claiming inheritance from the ancient Kitara Empire. The reign of Bachwezi is shrouded in mystery and legend, so much so that

---

68. In Sumerian mythology and later for Assyrians and Babylonians, Anu was a sky-god, the god of heaven, lord of constellations, king of gods, spirits, and demons, and dwelt in the highest heavenly regions.

many traditional gods in Toro, Bunyoro, and Buganda have names associated with Bachwezi kings. Archaeological discoveries at Bigo bya Mugenyi, capital of the Chwezi Empire, and Ntusi in Mubende District, Uganda, reveal rich deposits of an urban center thought to be Chwezi ruins.

According to Were and Wilson (1968), oral evidence throughout Bunyoro, Ankole, Toro, Rwanda, Burundi, Bukoba in Tanzania, and Wanga in Kenya indicates that a pastoral people dominated these territories. These people were variously called Chwezi, Hima, Huma, Tutsi, and Bahinda. Although accounts differ from one territory to another, all are agreed that the Chwezi loved their cows, especially the long-horned type presently known as Ankole cattle. The Chwezi origin is also mysterious with some people believing they were descendants of Portuguese, Greek, or Egyptians while others suggest they were of Galla or Cushitic origin. As we shall see later, members of a Wanga clan, Abamuhima were the original founders of the Wanga kingdom at Imanga (presently in Marama) and are believed to be descendants of the Chwezi or Hima. Ugandan President, Yoweri Kaguta Museveni, comes from the Bahima clan of Banyankole.

(ii) Kingdom of Bunyoro Kitara

The Kitara Empire finally broke up in early sixteenth century at the hands of invading Luo led by Chief Labongo of the Biito clan. The Luo apparently received little resistance largely because Bunyoro[69] as a kingdom was on the verge of breaking up anyway due to internal feuds, misfortunes, epidemics, and revolts. Other oral traditions say the departure of Kitara rulers was precipitated

---

[69.] Luyia call the Luo Abanyolo or Abab'bo; the former so named after Bunyoro where they founded the Babiito dynasty of Bunyoro-Kitara while the latter simply means people of the West (*imbo*).

by sudden death of Bihogo, the darling cow of royal princess which divination interpreted as ominous and a sign that they should leave.

These happenstances gave the Luo an uncontested entry, and Labongo established the Babiito Dynasty known as Bunyoro-Kitara consisting of Toro and Kooki kingdoms and some chiefdoms of Busoga. His official title was Isingoma Mpuga Rukidi I, the first in line of Babiito kings of which there are twenty-seven so far. It is said that the Luo rulers abandoned their own language and adopted the Bantu one. In fact they had to be instructed in the Chwezi rituals of kingship before they exercised full authority (Were and Wilson 1968: 45).

From the ashes of Chwezi kingdom arose several independent fiefdoms such as Bunyoro, Ankole, Buganda, and Karagwe, among the most important. The foundation of the predominantly Hima (Yima) state at Imanga, nucleus of the future Kingdom of Wanga, is largely associated with these developments. The Luo immigrants founded a number of related dynasties and subdynasties of which the Babiito of Bunyoro was jewel in the crown. Similar dynasties were established in Bukoli, Bugwere, Bulamogi, and Bugabula in Busoga and in Kiziba in Tanzania's Bukoba District. This happened probably around 1490-1733. That Bukoba District in Tanzania was for a long time part of the cultural hegemony of western Uganda is beyond doubt. Many clans of the Haya (inhabitants of Bukoba) assert that their ancestors originally came from Bunyoro Kitara, and their language is very close to some Luyia dialects.

(iii) Origin of Wanga Kingdom

NABONGO

WANGA

1050 - 1140

This structure and epitaph (inset) at king's tombs at Matungu marks the spot where remains of Nabongo Wanga, the eponymous founder of Wanga Kindom and subnation lie in repose.

Early history of the Wanga is somewhat confusing if not downright contradictory. There are two versions regarding the creation of Wanga Kingdom. We have seen that Wanga Kingdom is an offshoot of the interlacustrine kingdoms in Uganda. It was created by the ancestors of Hima, Mulembwa, Nashieni, Leka, and Tobe clans at Imanga in present-day Marama anywhere between 1598 and 1625 (Were and Wilson 1968: 59). Whereas the Hima are related to pastoral Hima of Western Uganda, the Leka (Abaleka) are an offshoot of Balega of Toro and neighboring Congo. The Hima (Abamuima) were the dominant group and rulers of the small kingdom at Imanga. However, extant records at the Nabongo Cultural Center in Matungu indicate that Wanga Kingdom was established more than one thousand years ago around AD 1100 by Nabongo Wanga who died in 1140 (see p.111 footnote 71).

a. Fall of Muhima and rise of Wanga

There are two versions regarding Wanga's settlement at Imanga. The first is documented by Prof. Gideon Were and DA Wilson (1968) and posits that Wanga led his people to Imanga between 1544 and 1652 bringing with him a new group of settlers consisting of Abashitsetse, Abakolwe, Abashikawa, Abakalibo, Ababuka, and Abarunga clansmen. Wanga oral history chronicled by these authors says they arrived in Uganda at around 1382-1571 (Were and Wilson 1968: 58). After the breakup of Chwezi dynasty, the group split into three. One went to Busoga, another to Western Kenya, while the third remained in Buganda. The group that moved into Kenya eventually settled in present day Tiriki among Abalukhoba (Balukhova) clan and was led by Wamoyi, a descendant of Muwanga I seemingly without any resistance from aboriginal inhabitants. Another historian, Dr. John Osogo (1966) goes further and traces Wanga ancestry to Mutesa who emigrated from Egypt. According to Dr. Osogo, Mutesa's three sons Muwanga (Mwanga), Mukoya, and Kamaanya founded Buganda, Busoga and Wanga kingdoms, respectively (Osogo 1966: 64). Kamaanya's offspring, Mbwoli, sired a son whom he named Muwanga I, after his uncle who remained in Buganda. Osogo writes that it is Muwanga I who later came to Tiriki where his inheritors lived for two generations before moving to Wanga. He begat two sons while in Tiriki—Wamoyi and Khabiakala. In turn, Wamoyi sired Muwanga II who begat five sons—Khabiakala, Wamoyi, Wanga,

Mukoya, and Mutende. It is this Wanga, who founded the Wanga Kingdom, according to Osogo`s expose.

Oral tradition has it that one day, Wanga and Khabiakala quarrelled after the latter's wife stole Wanga's bananas. Angered by this incident, Wanga ran away and found himself at Imanga. Here he met Muhima, the local ruler, who hired him as a herdsboy. However, according to records I obtained from Nabongo Cultural Center,[70] Wamoyi had three brothers—Mukoya, Wanga, and Wekhoba. Wanga quickly established himself in Tiriki, but Wamoyi and Mukoya decided to explore or conquer the vast lands in the neighborhood. The result of this adventure was that Wamoyi settled in Tachoni and Mukoya in Siaya. Wanga surprised everyone when he too decided to move and came to Imanga. This is the second version.

His aristocratic lineage entitled Wanga to wear *omukasa* (copper bracelet), the ultimate symbol of royalty, but because it was a big taboo for a royal to work as a commoner especially for another aristocrat, he made a conscious effort to conceal it. Bwino, the wife of King Muhima, pondered at the esoteric way the stranger behaved as if he was hiding something. Curiosity got the better of her and one day she set out to find out. She bored a tiny hole in the wall of a hut where he stayed. Then she personally served him food and left to spy through the hole in the wall. As he washed his hands to eat, she was amazed at what she saw. The stranger wore *omukasa* on the hand which was always hidden under the skin cloak. Stunned beyond belief, she dashed to relay her discovery to King Muhima. The discovery of a royal stranger among them was quite sensational and jolted the monarchy. Was he a spy? Had he been sent to overthrow the kingdom of Muhima? As the king pondered what to do with the stranger in light of this finding, royal courtiers and clan elders called for his death or expulsion. However, King

---

[70.] An unpublished manuscript entitled *History of the Wanga Kingdom 1000-2010* by Nabongo Peter Mumia II.

Muhima dismissed this option and decreed that since the stranger had already been welcomed into his kingdom, no harm should befall him. Instead, he made a lamb offering to cleanse any ritual dangers this situation posed to an otherwise peaceful chieftaincy.

As fate would have it, this discovery coincided with the arrival of Wanga's relatives from Tiriki out searching for him. They consisted of his son Murono and maternal uncle, Mukolwe and clan members of Abashikawa, Abakalibo, Ababuka, and Abakhami. They not only confirmed Wanga's royal status but also narrated the circumstances of his flight from Tiriki. The unravelling situation called for quick decisions. Although Wanga had been spared from eviction and granted full rights of abode as *omumenya* (stranger settled in another clan territory), his relatives were not. Abamuhima elders asked him if he wanted to return to Tiriki with his kinsmen. Wanga, however, refused and pleaded with King Muhima to be allowed to stay with his family. The kindhearted king agreed and allocated him land at Eshikulu near River Lusumu, Ebuchirinya, Tingale, Ebutende, Indangalasia, and Elusibo in South Wanga and Ekonjero in Buholo.

Grateful, Wanga and his relatives went back to Tiriki to fetch the rest of their families. Wanga migrated with his five sons: Murono, Muniafu, Namangwa, Mutende, and Wabala but according to an unpublished manuscript authored by the reigning monarch, Peter Mumia II, the sons were Wabala, Murono, Namangwa, Muniafu, and Wambatsa. What little royalty was left in Tiriki could not sustain the institution of *obunango* and that is how the Tiriki lost out. Settling initially at Eshikulu, Wanga quickly expanded his reach by acquiring more land for his sons and relatives who founded the various clans in Wanga bearing their names except Wabala who continued Abashitsetse dynasty that dominates *obunabongo* todate. After the death of Wanga,[71] Murono

---

[71.] According to *History of the Wanga Kingdom 1000-2010* (op cit), Nabongo Wanga died in 1140, a date engraved on his tombstone at Matungu King's (eldest son) and Wabala (chosen heir) fought over who was the rightful successor to the kingdom. In the event, Wabala was killed in Bukhayo and Murono saw another chance to seize power by outmanoeuvring Wabala's young son, Musui. In the ensuing battle, Murono was defeated and fled to Ekhatola with royal regalia where he established a rival kingdom.

The third version advanced by Simon Kenyanchui (1992) says that when the search party from Tiriki arrived at Muhima's Court, they requested to take Wanga with them which Muhima granted. However, back at Kaimosi, the family feud broke out afresh, forcing Wanga and his family to migrate to Imanga and settle permanently. The two brothers Khabiakala and Wamoyi remained at Kaimosi (Eshisiru) while Mutende migrated to South Nyanza and is thought to be the progenitor of Abatende (Kuria). Other half brothers went to Nandi.

b. The rise of Abashitsetse Dynasty

There are two versions regarding the fall of Muhima and rise of Abashitsetse dynasty. Historian Prof. Gideon Were (1967) argues that Muhima's generosity was to return later to haunt him. Now settled with his large family, Wanga fought and defeated Muhima, and in a reversal of fortunes, Muhima became Wanga's subject. This was the beginning of Abashitsetse dynasty and inhabitants of his chiefdom became known as Abawanga. As population increased, the state expanded to Musanda in the south and Elureko and Matungu in the north.

However, Kenyanchui (1992) says this interpretation is not convincing. He argues that Wanga's people were few and could not possibly have marshalled military power to conquer Muhima.

---

tombs. However, these dates contradict those advanced by eminent historians like Prof. Gideon Were who give dates of Wanga's death as 1652 (Were 1967: 119).

According to him, the most probable reason for the fall of Muhima was that through intrigue and collaboration with Abamuhima, Wanga gained popularity and was elected to succeed Muhima. If any conquest happened at all, it was probably inflicted on Abamuhima subclans which opposed Wanga's succession.

Whatever the case, historians agree this transition marked the beginning of Abashitsetse dynasty that has ruled Wanga to this day. A succession of intrigues, jealousies, and conspiracies saw the kingdom split into two in the eighteenth century—Wanga Mukulu and Wanga Elureko. The reign of Nabongo Chitechi II (died 1688) was short-lived following a rebellion against his leadership. The council of elders ordered his dethronement and replaced him with his younger brother Osundwa (died 1710).

c. Reign of Nabongo Netia and Osundwa

Nabongo Wamukoya Netia (died 1621)[72] is credited with uniting the Wanga at a time when the kingdom was under constant attack from the Teso, Luo, Bukusu, Idakho, and Abanyala. Galvanized by this sense of unity and helped by Uasin Gishu Maasai (Abakwabi), Nabongo Netia expanded the kingdom by acquiring conquered lands. Due to Maasai role in this conquest, Nabongo Netia retained Abakwabi as his personal bodyguards and with time they became a major factor in Wanga polity. It was at the hands of Abakwabi that Nabongo Netia died. According to oral legend, the king used to entertain his courtiers with alcohol parties, but Abakwabi had a rebarbative habit of urinating in the palace when drunk which made the monarch queasy. One day he threw a tantrum and ordered them killed. For this sanguineous act, Nabongo Netia attracted brutal

---

72. I have derived dates of death of various kings dating from Nabongo Wanga through to Nabongo Shitawa (thirteen dynasties in total) from the unpublished manuscript, *History of Wanga Kingdom AD 1000-2010* by Nabongo Peter Mumia II, the reigning monarch which is available at the Nabongo Cultural Center in Matungu, Mumias.

and swift revenge from the Masaai who invaded the palace and slaughtered him.

Another version of Nabongo Netia's death is told by Prof. Were (1967) and corroborated by Kenyanchui (1992). According to this version, Nabongo Netia was getting concerned at the increasing influence the Maasai wielded in his palace. Consequently he set up a scheme to kill them one by one. He employed a killer who, sitting outside the palace, held a long rope like that of a hangman. The loop was hung around the neck of a drunken Maasai, and at a signal, the hangman pulled the rope killing him. The Maasai became alarmed at the circumstances of their colleagues' death. One day, they pretended to be drunk, and when the killer set to work, the lid was blown. The angry Maasai thereby killed Nabongo Netia in revenge.

Following the regicide, Netia was succeeded by his firstborn son Chitechi II whose reign was cut short following a revolt by his subjects. He was replaced by his younger brother Osundwa toward the end of seventeenth century. Nabongo Osundwa's first task was to restore loyalty of the Maasai and proceeded to consolidate his power by befriending neighboring Batsotso. He is best remembered for halting advance of the Luo and launching a remarkable attempt to stamp out witchcraft. Nabongo Osundwa's sons, Kweyu and Wamukoya, rivaled each other over succession to the throne. As Osundwa ailed and death approached, he summoned his two sons. As the eldest, Kweyu was given a spear to symbolize the ritual transitioning of power while Wamukoya was handed a rope to signify that he would be second in command.

When Osundwa died in 1710, Wamukoya, supported by some elders, decided to organize a mutiny against his brother. He secretly stole the remains of his father and carried out burial ceremonies associated with royal succession rituals. When Kweyu discovered this trick, he seized four of the ten sacred spears, ten copper bracelets, and the royal ancestral stones and established the separate state of Wanga Mukulu while Wamukoya remained at Wanga Elureko. For several years the two brothers continued their usual intrigues, conspiracies, and intermittent civil war. It was not until they died that peace returned to the kingdom but the two polities operated separately even today.

Another version adumbrated by Dr. John Osogo (1966) says palace courtiers hatched a conspiracy to deny Kweyu inheritance because he was haughty. As Nabongo Osundwa lay dying, he sent for his elder son, Kweyu, but servant after servant returned the news that either he didn't want to come was not at home or said he will come later (Osogo 1966: 74). Fed up waiting, Osundwa handed the royal heirlooms to Wamukoya including a spear with which he speared the bull in a ritual marking the royal succession. When Kweyu learnt of this conspiracy it was too late; the king was dead and *obunabongo* (kingship) bequeathed to his younger brother. Like a wounded bull, he palpably flew into a rage and took hold of his father's body for burial at Eshimuli near his home rather than at *Eshiembekho* in Matungu, the royal burial grounds. He declared himself ruler of Wanga Mukulu (means north but is actually in East Wanga).

Shiundu succeeded his father at Elureko while his cousin Sakwa inherited the secessionist Wanga Mukulu at Eshimuli. Apparently Wanga Mukulu chieftainship impressed the German explorer, Dr. Carl Peters[73] who signed a treaty with Sakwa in which the Germans promised to offer protection to the chieftaincy. However, the accord was overtaken by the Berlin Treaty of 1885 which lulled the infamous Scramble for Africa with European powers (principally Britain, France, Germany, Belgium, and Portugal) formally partitioning the continent among themselves.

[73.] Carl Peters (27 Sept. 1856-10 Sept. 1918), one of the founders of German East Africa (Tanzania), was born near Hannover, the son of a Lutheran clergyman.

The current borders in Africa are a result of this colonial conspiracy in which Africans had no say. In the event, Kenya and Uganda were acquired by Great Britain while neighboring Tanzania was annexed by Germany.[74]

Although the two kingdoms exist to this day, it is Wanga Elureko that enjoys local, national, and international recognition. However, a 1988 visit to the home of ex-paramount chief, Japheth Wambani Rapando of Emulambo village, Mumias by former British premier, Mrs. Margaret Thatcher ignited passions of a lost kingdom. The rival kingdom relied heavily for its security on Abanyala ba Ndombi and Abatsotso who temporarily overran the state and exiled Sakwa to Kabras where he was reduced to work as a laborer in the village of a local ruler, Tsifwandayi. It was the intervention of Abamarama that rescued the kingdom from permanent foreign annexation and paved way for his return. Sakwa was succeeded by Lutomia then Rapando who died in 1936. His successor, Japheth Wambani Rapando (1921-2012), had to wait for seventy-three years before being crowned *nabongo* on nineteenth June 2009 at a ripe age of eighty-eight after his father's bones were exhumed for reburial at Eshimuli shrine according to royal custom. The two kingdoms have separate burial grounds (*eshiembekho*) with Wanga Mukulu kings reposing at Eshimuli which is within the nucleus of Mumias Sugar Company and Wanga Elureko at Matungu where the regnant Nabongo, Peter Mumia II runs a cultural resource center.

---

[74] Germany later lost all her overseas dominions after the First World War under terms of the Treaty of Versailles signed in 1919 and enforced by League of Nations, the precursor to United Nations. Besides Tanzania (Germany East Africa), she also lost Namibia (Germany South West Africa), Cameroon, Togo (Germany West Africa), and various South Pacific islands.

www.abeingo.org

The current king (*nabongo*) of Wanga Elureko,
Peter Mumia II during his investiture in 2010.

Nabongo Shiundu (died 1880) is credited with establishing effective and respectable authority, and it was during his reign that the Wanga Kingdom reached its peak. His reign marked the end of an era and the beginning of another. He allied with the Marama of Butere who helped him conquer Kisa and Buholo whose armies he later conscripted into his own. However, the Ugenya Luo regrouped and defeated Shiundu's allies and threatened to invade the capital at Elureko. To save the kingdom from total collapse at the hands of invading Luo, a truce was signed and sealed by the handover of Shiundu's daughter as a trade-off (Were 1967: 126). As we shall see later, the peace treaty was broken by Shiundu's successor, Nabongo Mumia, whose collaboration with Maasai and later British colonialists helped him conquer Luo lands in Ugenya, especially the Umira Kager clandom. The war with Jougenya Luo, however, had one positive outcome on the polity—it helped unite Abashitsetse and Abamuhima clansmen who had been on a collision course since the former's overthrow of the latter's kingdom. It was in both clans' interest to unite against a common enemy.

d.   Arrival of Swahili traders

It was during Nabongo Shiundu's reign that Swahili traders from Mombasa first arrived in Wanga. As well as carrying out ivory trade, they also engaged in slave raids especially against Babukusu and Luo of Ugenya. In return they gave Shiundu firearms the acquisition of which revolutionized local warfare to his advantage. At the same time, the establishment of a trading center at Elureko (Mumias) gave his kingdom extra glitter and attracted customers and visitors from faraway lands. Some of the early Swahili traders were Mkuta, Sudi wa Pangani, and Abdulla bin Hamid. When the Bukusu massacred five Arab slave and ivory merchants, a column of 1,500 soldiers stationed at Mumias (Kwa Sundu) invaded Bukusu territory and launched a savage attack. One report by Joseph Thomson, the first Whiteman to pass through Luyialand in 1883, chronicles inhuman atrocities visited on the Bukusu by Swahili slave traders. It included total destruction of fortified homesteads, ripping pregnant women apart and throwing children in huge bonfires that burned across villages (Were 1967: 145). It was during Shiundu's reign that the Luo permanently occupied their present settlements in southern Wanga at Tingare, Madungi, Ulema, Umala, Musanda, and Ebukaya. Shiundu died around 1882 and was succeeded by his son, Mumia. Mumia was born to Amanya, one of Shiundu's wives following a succession of infant mortalities. Soon after birth, he was abandoned by the roadside as rubbish (*makokha*) in an apotropaic ritual to confuse evil spirits out to harm him. Such children are normally named Makokha to denote the birth status. His birth coincided with a bruising war with Abamia (single Omumia) as the Luyia then called the Teso. In memory of the war, he was given a second name Omumia which later became simply Mumia. Sudi of Pangani, reputedly the most avaricious slaver later baptized him Mohamed Mumia but Nabongo Mumia's conversion to Islam was more of a convenient dalliance bereft of any deep-rooted spiritual profundity.

e.   Contact with Europeans

The first European to come into contact with the Luyia is probably Sir Henry Morton Stanley[75] in 1875 as he voyaged around Lake Victoria on his way to Uganda. But the first European known to have passed through Buluyia on foot was Joseph Thomson in 1883 where he met Nabongo Mumia in whom the British found a perfect vehicle for their grand imperial designs. They immediately recognized his authority and later elevated him to a paramount

---

[75.]   Sir HM Stanley, born in Denbigh Wales on 28 January 1841, was a Welsh explorer, journalist, and MP who coined the infamous Dark Continent epithet for Africa. First sent to Africa to look for Dr. David Livingstone, the Scottish explorer, he was known for his brutality to African porters, hanging and whipping them at the slightest provocation. He died on 10 May 1904 and was buried at Pirbright in Surrey, England. He is recorded as a bastard on his birth certificate because his mother, then 19, was not sure who the father was. An attempt to build a statue in his home town of Denbigh, Wales, in 2010 was opposed by a coalition of university academics from around the world (BBC, 26 August 2010).

chief of Kavirondo (a colonial pejorative word that included Luyia, Luo, Kisii, Kuria, Suba, Teso, and Nandi). Charles William Hobley (nicknamed Obilo), the first colonial administrator in Luyialand, wrote, "I have often made enquiries into the origin of the name of Kavirondo, and the Kisumu elders inform me that it is the name which the people of the south side of Kavirondo Gulf (renamed Winam Gulf) apply to the people of the north side; it is, however, a term only used when they meet at a dance and smoke bhang and sing about old times. They call the people of the north side Kavirondo, because they were vanquished by the latter and driven across to the south side of the bay; it was thus, originally, more or less an epithet of reproach."[76] During colonial days, the term was pejorative, and Africans loathed being called Kavirondo. Today, it is largely extinct except in historical records. *Kavirondo* is widely thought to have been first used by Swahili and Arab traders. The etymology and meaning of *kavirondo* is still shrouded in mystery with at least five different interpretations in colonial and independent literature. One version of the meaning of *kavirondo* is taken from local young warriors who, armed with spears, bows, arrows and clubs, sat on their heels, presumably translated in Kiswahili as *kaa virondo*. Similarly, when white explorers accompanied by their Swahili guides came to this part of the country, they encountered women crouching as they winnowed grains. The Swahili guides cried: "*Lo! Waangalie hao wanawake wamekalia virondo vyao*! (Lo! look at the way those women are sitting on their heels!). The explorers diarized the name *wakaa virondo* as descriptive of the natives. Thus the region became Kavirondo, the inhabitants pejoratively called Wakavirondo (people who sit on their heels). But this meaning rings hollow when it is considered that the Swahili word for heels is *visigino* not *virondo*

---

[76]   C. W. Hobley: The Journal of the Anthropological Institute of Great Britain and Ireland, Vol. 33 (Jul-Dec., 1903), pp. 325-359.

(Osogo 1966: 9). Neither is *virondo* an Arabic word. The Arabic word for heels is *ka'ab*.

Another probable meaning relates to the corruption of Wakwavi (Uasin Gishu Maasai) and *murondo* (gun) hence *Wakwavi-rondo* to distinguish between Maasai and rest of the inhabitants of western Kenya. Another version presumably from Uganda combines two words to form *kaba-londo*. In Buganda two unusual words related to royalty were combined, kabaka and *namu-londo*, the stool used as a throne on which the king is crowned.

Yet another version associated with Luo folklore says *kavirondo* comes from the word *orondo* which means demented. According to this folklore, Orondo was a powerful Luo elder statesman who settled around Maseno. When his first wife died, Orondo is said to have become demented and married a chimpanzee from neighboring Bunyore. His act sent shockwaves to the community but while still in his lonely and confused stupor, the primate killed him. For the price of bringing shame on the community, his body was tossed to sea and his memory erased from people's psyche. Accordingly, Orondo is a taboo subject among the Luo even though the patriarch was in the same league as early tribal forefathers like Owiny, Sakwa, Ger, etc and many people, especially from Siaya County bear Orondo as their surname. When missionaries came to this part of the world to christianize natives they preached confessions as the first step in inheriting the Kingdom of God. Fearing the white God, locals decided to reveal secrets of their dark past. They told missionaries that Orondo was from (*kar Orondo*) Maseno which whites mispronounced and documented as *kavirondo*.

More credibly, *kavirondo* is probably a corruption of the words *kaffir* (disbeliever in Arabic) and *rondo*, which means to smear the body with mud (Lloyd 1921: 101), a ritual practiced by indigenes during certain festive activities. The Swahili and Arabs called anyone who was not a Muslim *Kaffir*, a term adopted by white supremacists in South Africa as an instrument of racial oppression (apartheid). Although the "kaffir" part seems credible, I have been unable to corroborate "rondo" in the context in which Ven. Albert Lloyd (1921) implied among my Luo and Luyia informers. An online Swahili-English dictionary though, describes *rondo* as a leg of an animal. Whether this *rondo* (animal leg) fits the *Wakaa virondo* (people who sit on heels) explanation as is popularly intimated is purely conjectural and so the search for a conclusive meaning of *kavirondo* continues.

f. Nabongo Mumia and extent of Wanga Kingdom

Born in 1849, Nabongo Mumia is perhaps the best known and influential of all Wanga kings. He ascended the throne by a combination of circumstances, not least manipulation by his mother, Amanya. He was not the firstborn of Shiundu nor did his father have a high regard for him. Moreover he was born as *Makokha* which means a child apotropaically abandoned by the roadside as rubbish. Despite that, Nabongo Mumia proved to be a brave and shrewd king. He was the supreme authority—king, chief justice, and commander in chief of his kingdom. He played a big role in the establishment of British colonial rule in western Kenya. The British acknowledged Mumia's authority and on 15 November 1909 appointed him paramount chief of North Kavirondo district covering Luyia and sections of Luo territories, especially Ugenya and Gem. However, in the official gazette notice of 1 February 1913 by LG Bowring, the deputy governor, his title was "official headman" as paramount chief had no constitutional basis under colonial laws.

His suzerainty covered a huge swathe of western Kenya and extended as far as Naivasha in Rift Valley and Jinja in Uganda. He appointed chiefs in various locations to help him govern as follows: In Busoga (Jinja) he appointed Chief Chabasinga; Bugisu (Mbale), Chief Wanyera; Bunyala (Navakholo), Chief Ndombi; Bukusu, Sudi Namachanja; Samia, Chief Mukudi; Bukhayo, Chief Otunga;

Marachi, Chief Ndubi; Butsotso, Chief Mung'oye; Kabras, Chief Shitanda; Idakho; Chief Shivachi; Isukha, Chief Milimo; Tiriki, Chief Obuyoywa; Maragoli, Chief Agoi; Bunyore, Chief Nganyi;[77] Maasailand, Chief Lenana Talal; and Luo Nyanza, Chief Odera Akang'o (Mumia II 2010: 8). It is instructive to note that these local chiefs were appointed only after Wanga agents failed to win confidence of local people (see p.384). However, Kenyanchui (1992) disputes this version of Wanga's geographical suzerainty. He argues that Wanga Kingdom was limited to North Kavirondo (Western Province). Even then, it is notable that North Kavirondo chieftaincy included large elements of Luo, Teso, and Kalenjin tribes.

In 1901, Mumia was invited to England to witness the coronation of King Edward VII, but when he reached Mombasa to board a ship, his aides, Khachina wa Lukuru and Kaabeyi wa Shiro developed cold feet when they saw the vast waters of Indian Ocean. One Swahili trader recognized Mumia and upon learning the monarch was headed for England, the trader persuaded him to abandon the trip on the basis it was a plot by the British to disinherit him of his kingdom. His Ugandan counterpart, Kabaka Mutesa sent Regent Apolo Kagwa and historians attribute the elevation of Kabaka's status to this visit. Mumia was retired in 1926 amid protestation that a king never retires, and it was only threat of imprisonment that cooled him down. Although deprived of raw power, he was nevertheless still recognized as *nabongo* by his Wanga subjects. He died on 24 April 1949 aged one hundred years to be succeeded by his son Shitawa (died in 1974). He married sixty-two wives and sired 162 children—102 sons and sixty daughters.

[77.] Although Mumia had appointed Nganyi to be his representative in Bunyore, Nganyi nominated Munala but on coronation day, Abamutete tricked Munala by giving him so much alcohol, he missed the ceremony. In his place, Otieno Ndale, an Omutete replaced Nganyi's nominee (Olumwullah 2000).

Nabongo Mumia is also credited with facilitating the voyage to Uganda of the early Christian martyr, Bishop James Hannington.[78] He warned Hannington against undertaking this trip as not too long ago two missionaries had been murdered on the shores of Lake Victoria. And true to Mumia's prophetic words, days after entering Uganda, Bishop Hannington was killed in Busoga on the orders of King Mwanga II in October 1885 alongside, Joseph Mukasa, the Ugandan Catholic priest who tried to defend him. His remains were removed to Wanga where he was interred.

Mumia's successor, Nabongo Shitawa, saw the rising clamor for independence as an opportunity to revive traditional leadership which the colonial government had weakened. He attended courses at Government Training Institute (GTI), Maseno, and travelled widely within Buluyia to sensitize people about the incipient political order. Although he played a leading role in identifying representatives to sit in the first Parliament in 1963, Nabongo Shitawa maintained a neutral position in the KANU / KADU politics. He hosted leaders from both parties including Jaramogi Odinga Odinga and Tom Mboya from KANU and Ronald Ngala and Masinde Muliro from KADU. His coronation took place in April 1971 when the remains of his father, Nabongo Mumia were excavated from Itokho for reburial at the Kings Tombs (*Eshiembekho*) at Matungu. Nabongo Shitawa was succeeded by his firstborn son, Peter Mumia II, upon his death on April 9, 1974. Mumia II's investiture took place in April 2010 and was witnessed by dignitaries from Kenya, Uganda, and Libya.

---

[78]. James Hannington (3 Sept 1847-29 Oct 1885) was an English Anglican missionary, saint, and martyr. As he died on the orders of King Mwanga II, his alleged last words to the soldiers who killed him were: "Go, tell Mwanga I have purchased the road to Uganda with my blood."

g. Structure of Wanga kingdom

Wanga Kingdom was a confederation of clans divided into *tsihanga* (singular *lihanga*) which were in turn divided into *tsimbia* (singular *oluyia*). *Tsimbia* were divided into *ebikongo* (singular *olukongo*, literally: ridge). Although each village had a headman (*likuru*), the common denominator of administration at all levels except the family was the council of elders reporting directly to *nabongo* (king). At the royal court, *nabongo* appointed *Abakali belitokho* (courtiers), *Weyengo* (Chief Judge) and *Eshiabusi* (Judge). He was head of the legislative and executive bodies assisted by courtiers who were experts in military matters, foreign affairs, and rainmaking.

This arrangement served the kingdom and its subjects well and reduced chances of a civil war with power struggle restricted among members of Abashitsetse Dynasty. As the custodian of traditions and customs of the land, *nabongo* guarded the royal regalia of *omukasa* (copper bracelet), sacred spears, *likutusi* (leopard skin), and *lishimbishira* (head gear) which the British colonial administrators, in their ignorance or arrogance, saw as superstitious and primitive. Traditional royal greetings started with the king hollering: "Kualulukha! Kualulukha!" to which the subjects responded, *Kulama*, which means, a tree will survive even when it shades its leaves.

Historians believe the first people to settle in western Kenya were Nandi, Kony, Bongomek, and Uasin Gishu Maasai. The Luyia arrived second after fleeing invading Luo from lands around Lake Victoria and Uganda. Luyia clans share a lot in their migratory stories with some clans assimilated into Luo and vice versa. Abasonga who originally came from Busoga in Uganda are now completely assimilated by Luo and live at Alego Usonga in Siaya County after fleeing Abakhoone wars in Bunyala. There was also considerable assimilation between Nandi, Maasai, and Luyia people. Many clans in Kabras, Tachoni, and Bukusu for example are of Nandi origin while some septs in Idakho and Isukha, e.g., Abashimuli are of Maasai stalk. In fact Bungoma, currently inhabited primarily by the Bukusu, is derived from Bongomek, a Kalenjin subtribe and so is Tiriki which is a derivative of Terik, a Kalenjin subtribe related to Sabaot (Sebei). As we shall see in chapter 5, some clans in Tachoni, Kabras, Marama, and Bukusu are of Kalenjin origin. Significantly, Abanyala were originally one people but split during Abakhoone wars circa 1700. One group remained in Busia and another fled to Kakamega where they adopted customs of neighboring clans. You find a similar situation among the Kisa (Abashisa) whose tribal ancestor Muchisa migrated from Samia in Busia.

Besides extraneous migration, as recently as one hundred years ago there was considerable movement of clans within Buluyia. For example between 1870 and 1915 clans such as Ababere from Marachi, Abamutiru from Bugisu, Abashieni and their cousins Abalaku (of Nandi origin), and Abanatsiri settled in Wanga. British colonial administration reported in 1911 that Abisukha and Abidakho were settling in Kabras and Butsotso which implies that migration was still ongoing even during the colonial period.

E. Factors of Social Transformation

(i) Imperialism and religion

There are two major forces of social transformation in Buluyia—foreign religions (Islam and Christianity) and colonial administration including spinoffs in education and waged employment away from ancestral territory. Islam was brought to Wanga by Swahili and Arab traders around the third quarter of nineteenth century. Even today, there is still a thriving Muslim community in Wanga. Beyond Wanga, there seems to have been little success in spreading Islam to rest of Luyialand. Although a mosque was built at Mbale, Maragoli, in the 1930s, few Maragoli ever became Muslims. In Bukusu where the Swahili raided for slaves, they met stiff resistance and hence few, if any, Bukusu converted to Islam.

The limited penetration of Islam is largely attributed to the reputation with which the Swahili were associated while in Mumias. Between 1902 and 1907, they occupied an envious position in Nabongo Mumia's court and in the colonial administration. They were employed as tax collectors and gave favorable reports to the DC about chiefs who bribed them. When this was discovered, John Ainsworth, PC from 1907 to 1917, sacked them. However, they remained advisers and medicine men to Nabongo Mumia as well as circumcisers of Wanga Muslims despite being associated with cunning and corrupt practices. Even today, most Luyia people jokingly refer to Abawanga as *abaswahili* (implying cunning, untrustworthy people).

But where Islam as a religion lost, Christianity gained. The main Christian denominations before the First World War were Protestants and Catholics which came to Buluyia from Buganda. The Church Missionary Society (CMS) started operating near Mount Elgon in 1894 and at Maseno in 1905 while the Mill Hill Roman Catholics started their work in in 1895 at Shianda, Mumias. The Friends Africa Mission (FAM), popularly known as Quakers arrived in 1902 and started work in Tiriki and Maragoli. To avoid the rivalry which had caused suffering and death in Buganda in the 1880s, Protestants and Catholics demarcated their respective areas of evangelisation. They agreed that no mission station should be located within a radius of ten miles from each other. After the First World War, other denominations entered Buluyia in particular, the Salvation Army and Pentecostal Assemblies of God (PAG). It was because of this memorandum of understanding that the CMS decamped from Maragoli to missionize among the Luo.

The two missionaries who led this drive—J. J. Willis and Hugh Saville arrived at Maseno[79] in 1905 and set up the CMS Center. The colonial government was to later expropriate more land from the local Abahando community and gazette Maseno as belonging to Luo Nyanza despite protestations from Abahando, Abasakami, and Abamutsa clansmen. Abahando, in particular, were banished to Bunyore Rockies, and to this day, the issue of Maseno remains a sticking point in Luyia-Luo relations.

Although Christianity was accepted in most parts of Buluyia, sections of Abaluyia opposed it and formed their own independent churches. A notable case in point is *Dini ya Musambwa* associated with Elijah Masinde[80] and predominant in Bukusu but with a substantial following in Wanga, Tiriki, Kabras, Tachoni, and West Pokot. It will be recalled that the Bukusu had opposed British colonial rule and had been massacred at the War of Chetambe in 1895. Masinde continued this opposition against the British and *Dini ya Musambwa* was a perfect vehicle to demonstrate defiance and emphasize African traditional value systems. *Dini ya Musambwa* adherents pray to *Wele* (God; also spelt *Were*) who can be reached through the medium of ancestral spirits. Unlike Christianity, *Dini ya Musambwa* professed and encouraged polygamy as an essential aspect of traditional African value system.

[79.] Maseno is derived from *omuseno* (*carya ovalis*), a red hickory tree under which the first CMS church was built. Later, missionaries and government built Maseno School, a veterinary center, a Government Training Institute (GTI), Siriba Teachers College, a detention center, and an agricultural demonstration farm. Siriba and GTI merged in 1991 to form Maseno University.

[80.] Elijah Masinde (1910-1987) was born in Kimilili, Bungoma. He played football for the national team in Gossage Cup and was detained by the colonial government in Kapenguria alongside Kenyatta and after independence by the Kenyatta government. He was an anticolonial advocate of African values who founded *Dini ya Musambwa* (Religion of Ancestral Spirits) as a protest movement against orthodox Christianity. The Bukusu revere him as a prophet (*omung'osi*).

Although proscribed at one time and its founder long dead, *Dini ya Musambwa* still has a sizeable following and in 2007 started a school—its first education venture

(ii) The railway and British rule

Uganda Railway which arrived at Kisumu (christened Port Florence[81]) in 1901 was originally meant to pass through Mumias and terminate at Port Victoria on the eastern fringes of Berkeley Bay (formerly Manyala) in Busia. Although construction of a pier had already started in preparation for the railway terminus, this plan was abandoned in 1899 when a shorter route was found round Nyando Valley to Kisumu. The First World War delayed construction of further railway lines and rail links to Mumias were abandoned completely. It was argued that the Nakuru-Kampala line served Elgon Nyanza well from the stations at Broderick Falls (Webuye) and Bungoma. Furthermore it was found to be more economical to extend the line from Kisumu to Butere rather than Mumias, and in 1928 construction of Kisumu-Butere line commenced reaching Butere in 1932. Kisumu-Butere Line with stations at Kisiani, Lela, Maseno, Luanda, and Yala was the only line that did not serve exclusive settler interests and was to prove pivotal in transportation of local produce and laborers to towns and cities.

The colonial administration used chiefs to indirectly rule over the Luyia. Although Nabongo Mumia commanded influence beyond Wanga, his agents and especially the Swahili tax collectors were despised. The agitation was channelled through Kavirondo Taxpayers' Welfare Association (KTWA), initiated by Archdeacon Walter Owen of CMS in 1923. In their typical divide and rule

---

[81.] Kisumu is derived from the word *suma* (*sumo* in Dholuo) which means solicit, a place where people go to buy and sell. It was named Port Florence, in honor of Florence Preston, the wife of Uganda Railway's chief foreman, Ronald Preston in 1901.

style, colonial officers engineered a schism that split KTWA into Luyia and Luo camps. In 1925 the Luyia formed North Kavirondo Taxpayers' Welfare Association (NKTWA) while the Luo established South Kavirondo Taxpayers' Welfare Association (SKTWA). NKTWA insisted on the paramountcy of Mumia while SKTWA wanted a Paramount Chief from Central Kavirondo. Catholics spotted an opportunity to compete with CMS; they founded the Native Catholic Union (NCU) in 1924 which supported SKTWA.

People educated in mission schools did not join NKTWA, SKTWA, and NCU. They instead formed Kavirondo Central Association (KCA). However, KCA split along ethnic lines just like KTWA before it. Nabongo Mumia did not play any role in the formation of KCA; his younger brother, Joseph Mulama, did. In 1940, Mumia joined chiefs in North Kavirondo and formed the Buluyia Welfare Association (BWA) because NKTWA had voluntarily dissolved itself. His was an act of defiance because the colonial government had proscribed any political activity following outbreak of the Second World War in 1939. Members of BWA supported or joined Kenya African Study Union (KASU), later renamed Kenya African Union (KAU). Jomo Kenyatta visited Nabongo Mumia in late 1940s to solicit his help in fighting colonialists. Mumia thought that Kenyatta was joking; how could a Whiteman who flew in the sky get thrown out of Kenya? Instead, Nabongo Mumia advocated moderation of political agitation against the British.

(iii) Christianity and Education

Although Christianity set foot in Buluyia in 1894, it was not until the arrival of American Quakers in 1902 that it became a major force of social transformation. Otherwise known as Society of Friends, Quaker missionaries established a mission at Kaimosi on a site overlooking a hill dubbed "Hill of Vision" but indigenes call it Javujiluachi and remain a source of mythical fascination and a major tourist attraction. The Quaker vision was premised on four-policy areas: education, medicine, industry, and evangelism. Although evangelism was their first priority, the Quaker approach marked a radical departure from earlier evangelists who only preached the gospel without investing in vocational and educational infrastructure. Roman Catholic missionaries, for instance, who settled among the Idakho, and Wanga did not sponsor education programmes until after the First World War.

When FAM established its mission at Kaimosi, there was little resistance from the Tiriki, and in fact, they initially welcomed and enjoyed the facilities brought by the Americans, particularly health care. Things took a turn for the worse when Quakers began to question traditional way of life of Abatiriki. The ensuing animus was so pullulative that by 1910, there were only eleven Tiriki Christian converts. With time things began to change powered by the combined forces of Western civilization—Christianity, the colonial administration, infrastructure, waged labor, taxation, new property laws, and growth of urban centers. Over time these instruments of colonial control eroded the sociocultural fabric of traditional societies (Kay 1979: 68) and propitiated imperial conquest.

During the First World War, the British recruited strong Luyia men to fight against Germany and her allies. This disrupted traditional life considerably affecting key institutions like circumcision and marriage. Disruption of traditional social order by missionaries and events of the First World War which saw whole segments of culture uprooted, or at any rate, seriously disrupted, meant that by early 1920s the Luyia offered little resistance to Christianity. The rate of social change, however, varied significantly among different subnations. A study among the Idakho, Isukha, Maragoli, and Tiriki (Kay 1979: 66-81) reveals that the decline of traditional systems was a function of the growth of schooling.

In early days, the Tiriki were like cultural warriors and resisted both the mission and its schools. The Tiriki were particularly angered when the mission seemed to encroach on their land holdings, reaching a crescendo when the colonial administration burned houses in forceful eviction. The bad blood meant that for years, Tiriki tribesmen and missionaries coexisted as uneasy neighbors. This antagonism got worse when Kaimosi became a refuge for people who had violated traditional customs including girls who sought protection from the mission rather than be married off to undesirable suitors. Another sticking point was the presence of many non-Tiriki, especially Maragoli, in FAM's workforce which fostered a feeling that the mission favored people from other regions. Further, they disliked Friends' missionaries for their intractable stand on polygamy and traditional culture.

But it was the issue of male circumcision that generated outright anger and hatred between Friends' missionaries and the Tiriki. The Tiriki historically initiated strangers by the most elaborate and secretive circumcision rituals comparable only to Babukusu and Tachoni. When non-Tiriki who settled at Kaimosi failed to undergo Tiriki initiation ritual known as *idumi* with missionaries agitating for its abolition, locals became increasingly incensed toward the mission and all it stood for including schools (Bulimo 2013: 358).

Among the Idakho, Isukha, and Maragoli, the initiation ceremonies were less secretive and so the missionaries found a way of modifying the custom without eliminating it completely once they realized its importance in traditional society. The few Tiriki youths who sided with missionaries and got circumcised by mission doctors became outcasts with a pariah status. And those who participated in secretive *idumi* rituals were forced to discontinue education in FAM schools by parents who feared their sons will be forced to reveal the secrets of *idumi* which is taboo (*omusiro*). Worse still, the few who returned to class were harassed by teachers, mainly Maragoli, thus ostracising the society further. FAM monopolized education in Tiriki for nearly three decades which shut out a large segment of the community who did not subscribe to its charter. The few who persisted like Simani Sangale,[82] the first lawyer from Tiriki, had to walk for several kilometers to schools in other regions. The conflict between modernity and traditionalism undermined educational development and robbed the Tiriki of trained manpower to compete in the emerging colonial socio-economic order.

But where Tiriki lost, Maragoli gained. Demographic pressures forced many Maragoli to migrate to various places among them Tiriki so that during the colonial era, they had become a sizeable minority in Tiriki. Like Kikuyu in central Kenya, the Maragoli took advantage of the new economic and social opportunities presented by colonialism. As early as 1904 Maragoli made up majority of labor force at Kaimosi, a trend that has continued to this day. The Maragoli were among the first group of Luyia to appreciate the value of education in the early colonial era. Because it was easier to work with them than the Tiriki, Quakers established a center at Vihiga at which the missionary, Emory Rees, and his wife Deborah carried out extensive translation work in Lulogooli in a period spanning two decades (1903-1926). He arrived from South Africa and immediately embarked on learning Lulogooli and was able to translate the Bible and school texts which made missionizing among the Maragoli much easier.

The Maragoli easily compromised on issues of customary traditions and beliefs holding their last traditional circumcision ceremony in 1910. After that Maragoli purview of customary belief systems changed dramatically. Unlike Tiriki, conversion to

---

[82.] Simani Sangale, the first lawyer from Tiriki, was expelled from the local FAM school and had to trek ten kilometers to Goibei just to earn an education. He is the author of *Tiriki Customs and Traditions* 2005.

Christianity or adoption of Western values was not greeted with any social backlash among the Maragoli.

The response of Abidakho and Abisukha to the Quaker influence falls somewhere between the compliant Maragoli and recalcitrant Tiriki. The youths accepted modified circumcision ceremonies in 1917 even though other traditional rituals and religious beliefs persisted until the end of the Second World War. Unlike the Maragoli, Isukha and Idakho did not have demographic pressures and were farther removed from urban influences of Kisumu and centers with strong mission activity like Kaimosi and Vihiga. The Quakers did not push energy into evangelical work among Abidakho and Abisukha until after a Catholic mission was established at Mukumu in 1906 and Eregi in 1914. For instance their outstation at Lirhanda, Isukha did not have a full time resident missionary.

Moreover, Catholics tolerated local customs like polygamy, drinking, and dancing while friends sternly insisted that all converts must relinquish these pursuits. This attitude led to further alienation of locals who found refuge among the complaisant Catholics. But when Catholics tried to replicate their success in Isukha and Idakho among the Maragoli, they encountered resistance. The Maragoli were already firmly wedded to FAM and were benefitting from the educational system. The only Catholic presence in Maragoli arrived in the form of Maragoli Girls Secondary School at Mbale set up by Mill Hill missionaries in 1971.

But where Catholics and Quakers tussled, it is the education system that suffered with both religious orders trying to outdo each other to win hearts and souls of natives and in most cases ending up spreading thin or duplicating resources. This rivalry played into the hands of the Isukha and Idakho who ripped benefits of Christianity without giving up their traditions.

(iv) Education versus evangelism

For many years the only denomination with serious educational projects in Luyialand was FAM. Others like Pentecostal Assemblies of God (PAG) at Nyang'ori and Church of God at Kima in Bunyore initially focussed more on evangelism than education until much later. Meanwhile, although Catholics also promoted schools, the brand of education at their missions at Mukumu and Eregi was at loggerheads with central government which disapproved of catechumenical instruction. That is why most of the leading schools in Luyialand were either established by or affiliated to FAM—such as Musingu, Lugulu, Kaimosi, etc. The first government school was built in Kakamega in 1932 (now Kakamega High School) thus breaking the monopoly of FAM in the provision of educational services.

The man credited with bringing *obulafu* (literally light but figurative for development) among the Tiriki was Chief Paul Amiani of Abamuli clan. Among other things, he joined a rival denomination, *Jeshi la Wokovu* (Salvation Army), a new entrant in the evangelical market in 1932 and, by sheer force of his personality, built strong congregations that offered an alternative to the much hated FAM. When a respected *idumi* elder, Nuhu Sakwa, converted to Christianity and joined *Jeshi la Wokovu* (Bulimo 2013: 359), it was a major coup for Amiani and the beginning of a new era in Tiriki. Through him *idumi* elders accepted that Tiriki boys could choose between Christian-type *idumi* and the traditional one without being stigmatized or victimized. And with that the Tiriki finally broke with the past and embraced education as an engine for personal and economic development.

Bunyore Girls High School now a national school was started by
Church of God missionary, Mrs Twyla Ludwig in 1931.

F. Luyia Diaspora

(i) Luyia colonies

Like most Kenyans, the Luyia were uprooted from tribal
territory and settled in other parts of the country and beyond in
recent migratory processes primarily attributable to forces of
colonial rule. While a few have moved permanently, majority
maintain a close link with the ancestral land where they still have
deep kinship ties. The major reason for migration is to seek waged
employment in urban areas, a movement originally triggered by
imposition of Poll Tax in 1910. However, an increasing trend
is emerging where the Luyia, especially the professional and
business types, opt to settle in urban areas and raise families. A
large proportion, however, still observes tribal customs and when

they die; bodies are transported back to ancestral lands in western Kenya. Within Kenya, most Luyia are to be found in all towns and cities with large proportions[83] in the capital city, Nairobi and principal towns such as Mombasa, Kisumu, Nakuru, and Eldoret. But there is also a large proportion of Luyia in the Rift Valley especially in Trans Nzoia and Mount Elgon Districts. In fact, two parliamentary constituencies in Rift Valley, Kwanza and Saboti have always been represented by Luyia individuals—Saboti (since independence in 1963) and Kwanza (created in 1988).[84] Trans Nzoia was allocated two new constituencies in 2011 (Kiminini and Endebess) and following the 2013 general elections, Chris Wamalwa won in Kiminini while Robert Bukofe took Endebess.

Perhaps the most daring migratory story is that of the Maragoli who besides settlement in Rift Valley and Tiriki, have ventured deeply into South Nyanza, Uganda, and Tanzania. In South Nyanza districts of Migori, Ndhiwa, Kanyamkago, and Uriri, there are sizeable numbers of Maragoli families. During 2007 elections for instance, seven thousand registered voters in Uriri Constituency were of Maragoli origin, representing more than 20 percent of the total voter register of thirty-four thousand. A Maragoli candidate, George Kivanga, stood for elections, and although he did not win, the Maragoli are firmly established as a strong political force sought after by the dominant Luo as tie breakers. *Ethnologue*, the international language listing encyclopaedia (Issue 16) now lists Maragoli as a tribe in Tanzania. This is not surprising because in

---

[83] As early as 1969, the population of Luyia from Kakamega alone was 47,394 or 9.3 percent of Nairobi's total population, the third largest after Murang'a (Kikuyu). Source: Kenya Population Census 1969, Vol 3.

[84] Saboti (known as Kitale West until 1988): William Wamalwa, Wafula Wabuge (two terms), Michael Kijana Wamalwa (six terms), Captain Davies Wafula Nakitare (won in a by election of 2003 following Wamalwa's death), Eugene Ludovic Wamalwa (2007); Kwanza: Dr. Noah Wekesa (three terms) and George Welime Kapten (two terms).

the Bukoba region of northern Tanzania live a Bantu tribe closely related to Luyia called Haya whose descendants claim their origin in Uganda with several of their clans related to Banyankole and in particular the Hima. Suffice it to say, the Hima were founders of the original kingdom at Imanga in present day Marama, and they are known by their clan name Abamuhima.

A contingent of Maragoli immigrants settled in Bunyoro, Uganda in 1958 following an agreement between the British colonial government and the kingdom of Bunyoro Kitara. Now estimated at thirty thousand, the Maragoli were initially allocated land at Kigumba in Kiryandongo district but have now spread to neighboring distrits of Ntoma and Masindi. A pressure group under the leadership of Eliakimu Adola is pushing for official recognition of Maragoli as a fully fledged Ugandan tribe having lived here for more than five decades.

Nonetheless, there are several tribes in Uganda that are Luyia in all but name. Among these are Bagisu (brothers to Babukusu), Bagweru, Abanyole, Abasoga, not to mention Abasamia and Abanyala who straddle the colonial frontiers of Kenya and Uganda. In addition to Migori, the Luyia are also said to have migrated to other parts of Luoland. In fact an area in Siaya called Sakwa derived its name from Sakwa, cousin of Kweyu, founder of the rival kingdom at Eshimuli in East Wanga. Here they are called *kawango* (Wanga) by the indigenous Luo but are completely assimilated into the Luo culture. Another oral account explaining the large number of Luyia in Sakwa, relates to the custom of circumcision. A long time ago, a boy who freaked from circumcision was teased into fleeing the land to seek refuge in *imbo* (Luoland) where they typically do not circumcise. Another Luyia subtribe, the Songa (Abasonga) lives in Luoland at a place called Alego (hence Alego Usonga), but again this was acculturated by the Luo, the same way the Suba of Mfangano and Rusinga islands to which the late Tom Mboya belonged were assimilated by Nilotic Luo. In Gem, clans like Jo-Ujimbe, Jo-Uhoware and Jo-Urewe were actually Luyia before they got Luonised around midnineteenth century.

Increasingly, nowadays, you find many Luyia people settling in faraway lands across continents, especially in the United States, United Kingdom, South Africa, and Australia.

(ii) Detribalisation and retribalisation of the Luyia

Among the Luyia, it is significant to note that wherever they live, they tend to sustain the kinship arrangements inherited from ancestral lands. A study by Motoji Matsuda[85] in 1984 among the Maragoli in Kangemi, Nairobi established that kinship structures have not been abandoned but adapted to suit the community in their new spatial setting.

Abner Cohen (1921-2001)[86] first introduced the twin concepts of detribalization and retribalization as emerging in independent Africa simultaneously. Cohen carried out his research among the Hausa of Nigeria who had immigrated to Ibadan in the heart of the populous Yoruba. Against the view of some anthropological predecessors and contemporaries that ethnic identity was somehow primeval, Cohen took the view that mobilization of ethnic solidarity was situational and a strategy to achieve specific economic or political goals. He found out that although the Hausa lived among the Yoruba, they spoke their own language, wore their own clothes, loathed marriage outside their own community, and clung to their customs. He termed it retribalisation of the Hausa.

---

[85] Motoji Matsuda, department of Sociology, Osaka City University: African Study Monographs 5: 1-48, December 1984 titled: Urbanization and Adaptation: A Reorganization Process of Social Relations among the Maragoli Migrants in their Urban Colony, Kangemi, Nairobi, Kenya. Mr. Matsuda did his study as part of MA thesis at the University of Nairobi.

[86] *Custom and Politics in Urban Africa*, 1969: 186.

Further research into the phenomenon of retribalization reveals that it is not cultural stagnation but a dynamic process of social change adapting to a whole new urban environment characterized by competing or even conflicting priorities. In the case of Luyia urban migrants, they tend to remain just that rather than transform into townsmen or lose their identity. Often it is the men who leave the farmlands to find paid work while wives remain to till the land in rural areas and occasionally join their spouses during off season. When on annual leave, husbands return to rural homes to see their families and help in farm chores or other communal activities. In towns and cities, there is never an inclination to own property as most consider themselves transitory rather than permanent residents even though they may live a better part of their lifetime working in urban areas.

They are usually waged laborers whose earnings are barely adequate to sustain decent livelihoods and kinship obligations. The bulk of their income goes on rent and only a small percentage is sent back to support their wives and parents in rural areas. Only professionals can afford taking out a mortgage or building their own homes in urban centers. As a result, most Luyia people live in urban slum areas. In Nairobi the majority live in Kawangware, Riruta Satellite and Kangemi with sizeable chunks in Kibera, Dandora, and Mathare slums as well. Kangemi in particular, a sprawling shanty town to the west of Nairobi, is like a Luyia village. Here almost everyone speaks Oluluyia.[87] They are so numerous; they have become a political force sending one of their own, Fredrick Fidelis Gumo four times to Parliament in Westlands Constituency, Nairobi. Gumo has since retired from active politics and was succeeded as Westlands MP by lawyer, Timothy Wanyonyi, a brother to Moses Wetang'ula, the Bungoma County senator.

[87.] Feature article in *Kenya Times* headlined, "In Kangemi, Luyia is the official language" by Godfrey Miheso, Nairobi July 17, 2007.

Confronted with new problems in urban areas such as unemployment, security, crime, and discrimination, they are forced to form new social networks to safeguard their interests. This explains why several welfare organizations sprung up as defence mechanisms. Such organizations often take the form of kinship or geophysical relationships, e.g., lineage, sublocational, etc. The purpose is to reengineer traditional mode of cultural exclusivism, to reorganize kinship relations and create new relational patterns to ensure survival in the new environment.

Although these organizations also serve the same purpose as *oluyia* (in the context of village common or fireplace) did in the traditional system, they are most visible during funerals. When a clansman dies, members quickly assemble to raise funds to transport the body back to his ancestral village. This activity which takes the form of daily gatherings at the home of the deceased or an appointed venue in town, often takes anything from two days to several weeks depending on the social standing of the decedent. Other activities that bring the Luyia Diaspora together include weddings, birth, and disease or when a member is involved in crime. A few groups of tribesmen try to leverage communal energies in economic projects principally in the form of merry-go-round or pyramid schemes. Still another visible sign of tribal solidarity can be found in churches where members often go to worship in a church led by a pastor from their own community. One such church run by evangelist Mary Akatsa from Ebusiralo, Bunyore in Nairobi's Kawangware slum gained national notoriety in 1990s for its professed miracles including one tawdry appearance by "Jesus."

Outside Kenya, a large number of Luyia have settled in Europe and America. Here too they continue to organize themselves in ethnic outfits to preserve and promote their culture. Such organizations include the U.S.-based Halala and Abeingo Community Network in both UK and Canada. The Diaspora

Luyia are racing against time—living and raising their families so far away from ancestral homeland they are at great risk of losing their culture. A cursory look at these organizations' objectives reveals that Luyia Diaspora is concerned with erosion of culture and by extension, loss of identity. The formation of sociocultural groups is an atavistic attempt to create a bridge between the past and present and hopefully bequeath the ways of Luyia ancestors to their offspring born, raised, and educated in foreign lands. This is consistent with other Diaspora communities such as the Kikuyu, Luo, Kalenjin, Kisii (from Kenya) as well as Nigerian, Ghanaian, Ugandan, Zimbabwean tribes, to mention but a few.

(iii) Luyia unity

Luyia unity is a nettlesome issue that has eluded the community since formation of the super-ethnic polity more than seventy years ago. To understand why Luyia unity is an elusive subject, we must take a trip down memory lane to the genesis of Luyia as a tribal bloc. Luyia ethnicity did not exist prior to 1943 (see p.70). Instead, there lived in close proximity, a phalanx of closely related tribes sharing common linguistic and cultural traits. Most of these groups were exiguous and acephalous; besides Abawanga, they did not have a centralized system of traditional governance. For many, authority lay with appointed or hereditary clan heads who determined political and social affairs of the particular clan including foreign policy with other clandoms. However, around the time of Second World War most clan heads had realized that political parameters had shifted dramatically and only organized societies with a definite ethnic identity could hope to reap political benefits associated with economies of scale.

The seeds that grew into the Luyia nation were inadvertently sown by British politico-ethnographers who lumped all tribes to the west of Kenya as Wakavirondo to the annoyance of people so different in linguistic and cultural orientation. The fight to redeem ethnic pride was somewhat achieved when the name *kavirondo* was expunged from official use and replaced by Nyanza. Administratively, what was then North Kavirondo became North Nyanza under which most Bantu tribes belonged.

A relic from the past, this Uganda Railway bell with "Kavirondo" inscription captures the early colonial zeitgeist.

The interwar period witnessed an unprecedented growth in groupings fighting or asserting their rights vis-à-vis the colonial administration. In 1923 Young Kavirondo Association was formed to agitate for the rights of both Nilotic Luo and Bantu in an inceptive effort at confecting a united front against a common "enemy." This was later changed to Kavirondo Tax Payers Welfare Association (KTWA) when natives realized that if they must pay tax, they might as well have some say in how the tax is collected and managed. In 1925, KTWA was divided into two with North Kavirondo Tax Payers Welfare Association being predominantly for Bantu tribes while South Kavirondo Tax Payers Association covered the Nilotic Luo. These associations primarily dealt with welfare issues, but in 1934 North Kavirondo Central Association was founded to agitate for indigenous political rights. The same year, natives were allowed representation on district education boards for the first time. In 1940, Abaluyia Welfare Association was born to, among other things, popularize the name Abaluyia as a first step in creating a super-ethnic identity. Shortly afterward a language committee was formed and following its recommendations in 1943, the Luyia tribe was formally born. Other efforts at Luyia unity were discernible through the formation of associations such as Luyia union which Abaluyia living in big cities such as Nairobi, Mombasa, and Kampala identified with. There were also regional organizations such as South Nyanza and Kisii District Abaluyia Union (East Africa) which looked after the interests of the community in this part of the country with a significant number of Maragoli settlements.

Midwifing the super tribe was the easy bit, nurturing and development of sociocultural institutions to anchor a system of impregnable national ethos of the child has evaded Abaluyia tribesmen for three generations. Talk of Luyia unity has waxed and waned over the years depending on the political temperatures prevailing in a cyclical pattern that continues even today. Luyia unity is a favorite subject among politicians whenever elections are looming, but the same leaders are unwilling to jump into one political vehicle to drive the region's socio-economic interests. In this regard politicians, important opinion leaders in any society, are rather like vultures preying on dead matter and caring less about unity of purpose as a long-term goal that can potentially secure the region's political, social, and economic empowerment.

In 2005, a community organization, Luhya Elders Forum otherwise known as Luhya Council of Elders was formed to bind together community leaders from all Luyia subnations as a common front in the fight against HIV/Aids, poverty, and ignorance. The organization's leading lights were Burudi Nabwera (Tachoni) as chairman with Martin Shikuku (Marama) and Ibrahim Ambwere (Maragoli) as founding members. Politicians, principally Cyrus Jirongo noticed the organization's potential and offered to finance its activities. However, when the elders refused to endorse his candidature for presidency, he lost interest and abandoned the group. Nonetheless, Luhya Council of Elders soldiered on and elected a new chairman, Patrick Wangamati (Bukusu), with branches cropping up in Idakho, Tachoni, Bukhayo, Trans Nzoia, among other places. The organization which is part of a wave of ethnic chauvinism across Kenyan tribes has the potential to marshal support of the community and become a vehicle to drive unity and development in Western.

Luyia unity in the Diaspora is fronted by organizations like Halala in USA (2005) and Abeingo Community Network in UK (2006) and Canada (2004). Although nascent, these organizations have passed the five-year threshold which means they deserve a mention, if not a commendation for trying to advance the Luyia cause. Some have launched outreach activities in Buluyia and together with the Luhya Council of Elders are vital adjuncts in fostering purposeful Luyia unity. Just like the Luo Union (East Africa) and Iteso Cultural Union unites, their respective tribesmen across borders, unity among Luyia tribes in Kenya and Uganda can potentially change the socio-political dynamics of the community as a dominant force worthy of respect.

While Luyia unity cannot be achieved overnight, it is a process that can benefit from a four-pronged approach. A three dimensional (3D) look at the Luyia reveals at least four clusters of subnations which already have very close sociolinguistic links that can form vital building blocks in the unity drive. In the first cluster the dominant subnation is the populous Bukusu under whose stable one finds Tachoni, Kabras, and Abanyala ba Ndombi. The friendship between these groups is interwoven by history, geography, linguistic similarities as well as cross border clans. The second cluster is dominated by Maragoli, who share Vihiga County with Abatiriki and Abanyole. Their tongues are not only mutually intelligible, but the relationship between these three is historical and characterized by widespread intermarriages. In cluster three which the imperious Wanga dominate, you find the largest grouping including Isukha, Idakho, Kisa, Batsotso, and Marama. In fact Oluwanga is considered the standard Luyia with phonology that comes close to being understood by all Luyia subnations. Finally, cluster four is ruled by Abanyala and includes Abasamia, Abakhayo, and Abamarachi—the so-called Busia tribes. These tribes, especially Abasamia and Abanyala, have sizeable presence in Uganda. They share common linguistic and cultural values with a strong dose of Luo influence.

The Wanga, who had the best organized system of government (*obunabongo*) in the pre-European era, acted as the natural leaders across Buluyia, but attempts to rule the whole of Western through Wanga agents by colonialists backfired after Nabongo Mumia's representatives proved uncultured, greedy and arrogant. By early 1930s, all Wanga agents had been replaced by local rulers in most of Buluyia. The first person to represent the Luyia in national politics was Wycliffe Works Wasya Awori (Omusamia) as the representative of North Nyanza in the Legco in 1951. WWW Awori is historically more significant than even his more famous brother, Moody Awori who was named vice president following death of the incumbent, Kijana Wamalwa in 2003. As the first Luyia in Legco, WWW Awori became not only the embodiment of Luyia political aspirations but also towered as a symbol of Luyia unity. Piggybacking on WWW Awori was Musa Amalemba

(Omwidakho), the first indigenous minister (housing) from Luyialand in the joint colonial-African administration. Amalemba, who founded the Abaluyia Political Union as a political vehicle for Luyia to bargain for a stake in the preindependence negotiations, is immortalized by a housing estate in Kakamega (Amalemba Estate).

In 1957 Henry Pius Masinde Muliro (Bukusu) was elected to represent the Luyia in an expanded Legco after trouncing WWW Awori. Then in 1961, Priscilla Ingasiani Abwao (1924-2009), a Maragoli, was nominated to Legco by colonial governor, Sir Patrick M. Renison as the first Kenyan woman legislator. Muliro proved a principled and fair leader who earned respect across the community. He was easily the quintessential Luyia leader and is immortalized by an institution of higher learning (Masinde Muliro University of Science and Technology) in Kakamega. When he died, Moses Substone Budamba Mudavadi (Omulogooli), a colossal political casuist, stepped into his large shoes. By virtue of his close association with President Daniel arap Moi, he wielded immense political power that reverberated across Buluyia and beyond. While he commanded respect and helped Luyia gain employment, he made sure people who did not sing his tune were crashed. Typical of his brutal casuistry was when, as a kingpin of KANU politics in Western, he rigged Martin Shikuku, another outspoken Luyia leader out of Parliament during the 1988 *mlolongo* (queuing) elections in open daylight. After Mudavadi, another leader who came close to earning respect across the tribe was Michael Kijana Wamalwa, a Bukusu.[88] As Kenya's vice president, Wamalwa died only months into his prefecture before he could leverage power

---

[88.] Although raised as a Bukusu, Wamalwa's father, Senator William Chemayyek Ngeywo, was a Sabaot who had changed his name to Wamalwa to get education as Sabaot suffered discrimination in those days. His mother, Esther Nekesa (died 27 May 2009) was a Bukusu from the Baengele clan. His Sabaot roots did not matter as Luyia nation is a congeries of Kalenjin, Maasai, Luo and Bantu tribes.

tools in his office to expand his influence in Western as a whole. Since his death, Wycliffe Musalia Mudavadi (Omulogooli) became the titular Luyia leader, but his gentlemanly mien has attracted barbs from detractors coveting the title notably Cyrus Jirongo (Omutiriki) and Eugene Wamalwa, the youthful brother of the late Kijana Wamalwa. Perhaps Mudavadi's major achievement so far was the deliverance of eighteen seats out of a possible twenty-four during the 2007 general elections as the torch bearer of ODM party in Western. In April 2012, Mudavadi finally cut the apron strings that tied him to political supremo, Raila Odinga to launch an independent bid at the presidency of the Republic of Kenya in elections held March 2013. Mudavadi came a distant third with his Amani Coalition (KANU, UDF and New Ford Kenya) winning a paltry 18 seats in a 290 member legislature.

While political unity remains a slippery path, the most astounding success in Luyia unity occurred in a field far away from politics. This was the birth of Abaluyia United Football Club in March 1964. After months of negotiations disparate clubs from Western playing under subtribal banners unanimously agreed to merge and form one team. Except for Maragoli F. C., which remained outside the orbit until later, this amalgamation brought together teams like Marama F. C., Samia United, Bunyore, Kisa, Tiriki, Bukusu Brotherhood, Busamia, Lurambi, Butsotso, Bushibungo, and Eshirotsa. The main driver of this initiative was Jafred Ambani with Edward Kidoyo taking helmsmanship as the first chairman. The club renamed AFC Leopards after tribal names were criminalized by the Moi regime in 1981, remains the only veritable symbol of Luyia unity. It is notable that leading Luyia leaders have always sought to be elected chairmen of AFC Leopards. Among past holders of this office include Moses Mudavadi, Elijah Mwangale, Alfred Sambu, and Cyrus Jirongo. Other past chairmen include Joseph Akoya, Christopher Omufira (1966), Peter Shiyukah (1971), James Wamiya (1975), Paul Eliud

Nakitare (1977), Dr. Walter Masiga (1980), among others. Another sports team that attempted to emulate the feat achieved by AFC Leopards was Abeingo Football Club of Nakuru which in its heyday was a unifying force to be reckoned with but sadly petered into oblivion. What was achieved in sports has so far eluded the political class who preach Luyia unity by day and Luyia disunity at night. Nevertheless, the Luyia have adequate social tools to unify them into one coherent political force; not least, presence of several clans across assorted tribal polities, intermarriages, love of *ingokho* (chicken), and *esikuti* dance and transnational identification with *ingwe* (leopard) as a tribal totem.

Face of Luyia unity: AFC Leopards team of 1985. The team achieved glowing success as champions in East and Central Africa. However, the players' unity and exploits on the soccer pitch have eluded the political class.

CHAPTER 4
Family, Clan, and Kinship

A. Family

(i) Elements of a Luyia family

In Buluyia, the family[89] is a micro social group consisting of husband, wife or wives and unmarried children. A newly married son lives with his parents (*abebuli*) until he sets up his own household usually after birth of the first or second child. Because of this patrilocal arrangement, his wife is regarded as part of the family until the young couple moves out. Children sleep in their parent's house until they are about six years old. The second phase

---

[89] Family here is used in its generic sense to mean man, his wife or wives and offspring. In a more pronounced context, family is sometimes extended to include lineage (*esilibwa*).

of childhood is marked by removal of lower incisors and a change in sleeping arrangements. They temporarily sleep in the hut of a widowed grandparent and two years later the son moves into *isimba* (bachelor's hut) in the neighborhood while the daughter goes to a girl's hut (*eshibinze*). This is usually the hut of an old widow whose duty is to chaperon girls on matters of moral conduct, courtships and betrothals. But although they sleep away from home, the youngsters are still under parental control.

Economically, every household is self sufficient growing its own grains, beans and vegetables and keeping livestock. Unless beset by calamities, a family does not depend on anyone else for food. Each man and woman is able to make a few items of craftsmanship that the family needs, e.g., handless basket (*eshimwero*, variation: *esimwero, ekimwelo*), tray (*oluteru*) and wooden implements like knives (*embano*, variation: *embalu, omubano*), and hoes (*amachembe*, variation: *tsimbago*).

There is an organized system of work and division of labor so that tasks that are traditionally done by a certain sex or age group cannot be undertaken by someone outside this context. For instance it is the wife's duty to sweep, grind grain, cook, wash, fetch water, gather firewood and till fields for planting. Young uncircumcised boys (*abasinde*) take cattle to pasture, while a husband clears bushes, repairs the house, builds granaries and goes on hunting expeditions to procure meat for his family. Cross gender and joint activities include planting, weeding and harvesting.

From an early age, children are trained in certain household chores. At six years old, boys are introduced to herding livestock beginning with small ruminants like goats and sheep before graduating to cattle. Girls, on the other hand, assist their mothers with *feminine* chores, especially fetching water and firewood, gathering vegetables and grinding grain. Preparing the family's meal is a mother's job with daughters keeping a close eye as apprentices. Family meals are segregated; mother, girls and small boys eat together in the kitchen area (*mumaika*) while father and sons eat either in the living room (*mbweru*) or in the yard (*mukichi*, variation: *mulwanyi*) around a fireplace.

(ii) Starting a household

Soon after birth of the first or second child, a young couple prepares to start their own household. Both sets of parents help them procure the necessary utensils and furniture. For the first meal, they invite both their relatives in a ritual ceremony known as *okhwalikha* (variation: *olutekho, sitekho* in Lubukusu). With this meal, the man now qualifies as a husband (*omusatsa*) and woman as a wife (*omukhaye*). These are titles of social honor which bestow specific roles, duties, and expectations to holders. Before begetting children and starting a household, the wife is *omukhasi* (ordinary wife) which title restricts her role in tribal life. From now onward, they are free to welcome parents and offer hospitality to other socially correct persons. Similarly, husband and wife may now call each other by their respective ancestral names[90] and kinsmen from both sides can now call themselves *abikho* (relatives). The first child therefore lays a foundation for the establishment of strong kinship ties between relatives on both sides of the marital divide and galvanizes a wife's position in the matrimony (Bulimo 2013: 105).

In the olden days, a wife's fecundity bestowed her venerable status in the community, commanding more respect from her husband and his kinsmen than she who suffered barrenness. The respectability gauge grew higher for a wife with more sons than that with only daughters. The issue of children or lack of them is

---

[90]. These are names which every infant is given soon after birth and stand in stark contrast to names given in later years by playmates or circumcision age mates. As a rule, ancestral names may be used by near clansmen only.

often the main cause for divorce (Bulimo 2013: 447). Under Luyia customary law, a woman has no legal status; she cannot take legal action nor can she be sued. While still a girl, her father acts as her legal guardian, and when she gets married, this role is shared between the father and husband.

(iii) Children as stock of wealth

In traditional Luyia society, people desire to have many children, their hunger for numerous offspring informed by four considerations:

1. A large family is seen as prestigious and enhances a man's social status.
2. A man with numerous offspring commands respect, is feared, and can obtain justice if people try to steal or take his property by force.
3. Where there are many children, there is always plenty of food as many sons are likely to procure meat through hunting or raiding expeditions and work on farms.
4. If some children die, there is a good chance of others surviving to carry on the lineage.

While this is the standard justification, a large family in itself does not always produce the desired result where children are undisciplined because of or, in spite of, paternal authority. Although an even distribution of male and female offspring is appreciated, it is considered a misfortune (*esibi*, variation: *eshibi*) if a wife begets daughters only. The Luyia equate girls to birds; when they fly off (i.e. get married), they leave the nest empty. The parents lose not just their daughter but her contribution to the domestic economy.

It is a father's responsibility to provide his sons with bridewealth (cattle), at least for the first wives. During the first few years of marriage, son and wife are dependent on his parents for their livelihood. This dependence is reciprocated by the couple undertaking various household and agricultural duties. However, after *okhwalikha* ceremony, a father apportions the son his own garden (*omukunda*; variation: *omulimi*) and gives him the so-called *eng'ombe yamabeele* (milk cow). This is the beginning of his independence as a man, father, and husband. Although his wife may now till her own crops, a father-in-law is still the legal owner of the land—a role he asserts by planting the first seeds in the field. In the first few years of marriage, a daughter makes frequent visits to her parent's homestead to help her mother with various tasks. Apart from nostalgia (*amaofu*), these visits avail an opportunity to get gifts which are necessary, even desirable, to enhance her social status among her husband's kindred. A wife who brings no goodies from her parents is often looked down upon. Besides, should her marriage hit the rocks, she always knows that she can seek refuge and protection from her family.

Although all sons ultimately receive equal or near equal share in their father's estate of land and cattle, the first- and last-born sons enjoy certain exclusive privileges. As a rule, a father must first provide bridewealth to his firstborn son. His homestead is usually virilocal because he is like a "brother to his father" responsible for, among other duties, looking after his younger siblings. Middle-born sons are like free spirits and usually live in distant locations away from close paternal scrutiny. The last-born son (*omukokoti*, variation: *omukhokosi*) inherits his father's house plus the adjoining garden, and it his duty to look after his mother if she survives the husband. Junior siblings are expected to obey orders from their father and firstborn son in equal measure. However, the senior sibling's authority becomes more pronounced after he marries and further still, after the father's death. He holds property in trust for his junior brothers apportioning to each accordingly as they come of age (i.e., establish their own households). Over time, this relationship gradually changes to one of equalness once property (*emiandu*) is evenly distributed.

As adults, the relationship between brothers and sisters is characterized by reciprocity and mutual benefit. Brothers depend on sisters for marriage cattle while the latter look to the former for protection. Where there is even distribution of brothers and sisters, they pair up so that each brother receives his bridewealth from the sister corresponding to him in age. In return, they establish a closer bonding than with other siblings.

(iv) Structure of a polygamous family

In traditional Luyia society, a man can acquire as many wives as he possibly can support. He starts off with one wife and sets up a household, the characteristics of which we have seen above. With time he acquires an extra wife or wives, the frequency depending entirely on his tastes and whims. In a polygynous homestead where the man has his own hut (usually at the center), the elder wife's hut is constructed on the right, the second wife on the left, third wife next to the elder wife, fourth wife next to the third wife, etc., usually in a semicircular pattern. If the man does not have his own hut, the elder wife usually occupies the central position, the second wife on the right, third wife on the left, fourth wife on the right of the second wife, etc.

Huts and granaries of various wives are built only yards away from each other within the same enclosure forming a mini *litala* (a collection of houses in close proximity). A man who owns land in various parts of the village can choose to build huts for his wives on these plots. This arrangement is preferable because it reduces tensions resulting from spousal jealousy (*imbalikha*, variation: *imbotokha*).

A polygamous husband is expected to confer equal congenial and economic rights to all his wives. In practice, though, one wife acquires the "favored wife" status—a matter that is frequently a source of friction and jealousy from other wives. Irrespective of who the favored wife is, it is the elder wife (*omukhaye mukhulundu*) who enjoys a higher social status. Her house stands out in the homestead, and if the husband does not have his own hut, it is here he keeps all his tools, weapons, and heirlooms. The bond between husband and his elder wife is stronger than that with subsequent wives. And although he may have a favored wife, her status has no formal privileges and fluctuates according to his sexual whims.

Because of this relational strength, the elder wife is revered by her cowives, especially during the first few years of marriage and certainly before they have established their own households. Where the husband's mother is deceased or infirm, *omukhaye mukhulundu* (elder wife) plays the role of "mother-in-law" to the new wives. Among other roles, she houses the young wife and shares meals; but in return the newcomer takes on mundane duties of fetching water, gathering firewood, and grinding grain. This authority, however, diminishes but does not disappear entirely once the young wife moves to her new household.

Although children belong to the father, in a polygynous homestead, they are identified with their mother's household. They help their respective mothers with domestic as well and farm duties. And although they are technically one large family, they often append their mother's household to their identity. In Bunyore, for instance, the mother's clan becomes the name of the household. A boy might introduce himself as son of so and so (father). But an inquirer who knows the family rather well might ask: And from which house do you belong? (*Orulanga munyumba sina?*), to which the boy will reply: Isiralo (Ebusiralo being the clan of his mother).

The first claim to a girl's bridewealth is limited to her full brothers but where none exist, a father reserves the right to apportion the dowry to his other sons who may be ready for marriage. Among the Bukusu, bridewealth is pooled in the family stock and apportioned to whichever son is in line for marriage regardless of which household he comes from. The firstborn son from whichever wife occupies a preferential position with regard to the father's wealth in cattle (discounting cattle from bridewealth). Such cattle are always kept by the elder wife although all spouses are entitled to a share of the milk and meat that may accrue from them.

The sons must accord the same respect to the father's other wives as their own mothers. A manifestation of such deference is not to call stepmothers by name; instead they refer to them as *mama* with small *m*. However, while not disrespectful, an elder son of an elder wife is under no such obligation. This is because after his father's death, he is free to inherit his junior wife or wives. Therefore copulating with a woman he calls "mother" is tantamount to committing incest. We have already seen that a firstborn son of the elder wife is like a "brother" to his father. In exercise of this authority, he becomes like a father to his junior brothers, a relationship reinforced by marrying his junior "mother." Be that as it may, a junior wife's son cannot marry his father's senior wife.

(v) Luyia homestead

A typical Luyia homestead (*litala*) consists of several huts depending on the number of wives and adult male children who have built their own huts called *itsisimba* (bachelor huts, singular: *isimba*). Each wife lives in her own hut which she shares with her children. Although the husband sleeps with his wives in turn, he also has his own hut usually centered in the yard where he keeps his tools and weapons. In pre-European days, several families in some parts of Luyialand like Bukusu, Wanga, Kabras, and Tachoni lived in fortified villages known as *tsingoba* (singular: *olukoba*) because of insecurity. *Tsingoba* (*chingoba*) had several gates manned by sentries who warned villagers of impending attack by cattle raiders from Teso, Kalenjin, and Maasai tribesmen.

The most famous of these forts are Lumboka and Chetambe, which the British raided in 1894 and 1895, respectively, in an effort to subdue the recalcitrant Bukusu. These raids which came to be referred to as War of Lumboka and Chetambe are historically important as they not only marked decline of Bukusu military power but also an end to villagisation under a central command in *olukoba*. The Bukusu who suffered heavy casualties resolved to abandon living in forts so that never again should they die like chickens if attacked. To this day Chetambe conjures up memories of betrayal, massacre, and the danger of living in collectivised homes (see p.21). Other important forts included Nalondo, Kitingia, Bukokholo, Bitonge, Kolani, Lwandayi, Napara, Esiuma, Namatotoa, Kuywa, Namweela, Teremi, Watoya, Namawanga, and Esicheyi. At the time of Chetambe War in 1895, the Bukusu had an estimated five hundred forts, and although Chetambe and Lumboka acquired fame, the largest was Nalondo (Florence 2005: 26 and 240).

Most homesteads (*amatala*) are fenced by euphorbia (*ebikhoni*)[91] or thorny bushes which offer rudimentary protection from wild animals or thieves (*abeebi*, variation: *abefi*) and act as expressions of territorial boundaries. Simple gates made of poles complete the enclosure of a Luyia homestead. No *litala* is complete without a banana grove usually planted in the kitchen garden which acts as a shrine for various family rites. In former times people used bushes as toilets, urinated behind huts, and bathed in nearby streams or rivers. Nowadays, every *litala* (homestead) has a pit latrine in the backyard which is sometimes partitioned to double up as a bathroom.

The toilet (*echoo*)[92] is a hole in the ground dug up to thirty feet deep in a rectangular or rounded shape about three to four feet wide.

[91.] The expression *musikhoni* is frequently used to denote rural ancestral home among Luyia people.

[92.] *Echoo* is derived from a Swahili word *Choo* which means latrine. The Luyia terminology for toilet is *mubulimo* (bush) because a built up toilet was not part of traditional homestead infrastructure in the pre-European days.

It is constructed using poles and sticks with walls either covered by dried banana leaves (*amaru*) which need frequent replacement or mudded. Except in few cases, majority of homesteads nowadays have either mud or brick walled toilets. Fetching water from a nearby spring well (*esitaho*, variation: *ekitaho*) is still a principal undertaking in a family's daily routine. This task as well as gathering firewood, grinding flour, and cooking is still considered a woman's domain. The women carry water in rounded pots (*tsisiongo*) which they artistically balance on their heads beneath a ringlike support known as *ingara*. Laundry is done at the stream once a week in a day-long affair that involves washing and drying clothes and other garments. In between washing and drying, girls engage in traditional sport like *okhuruka omukoye* (skipping) or simply catch up with gossip. Meanwhile boys shepherding cattle to water springs get an opportunity to practice seduction lines or demonstrate showmanship in sports like *omuswelekha* (luging) or *okhulasa indika* (throwing the hoop). The spring well is therefore an important rendezvous in village life which provides boys and girls an opportunity for social engagement.

A traditional Luyia hut with a protruding rod at the apex that symbolizes manhood. The rod is affixed atop a king post that acts as an internal shrine where family sacrifices are offered.

B. Kinship

(i) Kinship features

The commanding features of clandom are solidarity of members, observance of exogamy, and dwelling on common ancestral land. It is the duty of every clansman to know his relatives and to observe appropriate rules of conduct in social interaction with different sets of clan relations. Big ceremonies like weddings, funerals, births, and circumcision where all clan members are expected to attend offer ample opportunities for enhancement of kinship ties.

One of the unique features of clan solidarity in Buluyia is the use of kinship terminology to refer to various categories of both affinal and consanguineous relatives. Traditionally it is rude to call people who are socially senior by their real names. Only people of the same age group (*likhula*, variation: *imbaka*) may call each other by their real or nicknames. Through kinship nomenclature we get a glimpse into another Luyia cultural trait—the emphasis on communal ownership rather than individualism. Hence names like father, mother, brother, sister, son, uncle, etc., refer not just to the biological relatives but also to vicarious individuals within the clan society. In addition to his biological father, a child will use the term *papa wanje* (my father) to refer to all married clansmen of his father's generation. When referring to a man from an unrelated clan, the child simply calls him *papa*, dropping the possessive *wanje* (my). In this sense, the term *papa* has a respectability ring about it.

On the other hand, when addressing his uncles or all men whom his mother regards as brothers, he calls them *khotsa* (uncle). *Senje* (aunt) refers to all those women the father regards as sisters—biological or clan. The Maragoli use the term *amitu* loosely in reference to both real and clan brothers. However, if specifically referring to a biological brother they use *amwavo* (sisters also refer to biological sister as *amwavo*). *Mbotswa* refers to the biological sister of a man (or the full brother of a woman, respectively).

In Bukusu, the term *wanda yase* means my brother or my sister. When referring to half brother, they call him *wanda yase owe khuluyia* (literally: my homestead brother) while a full brother is called *omwana wa mayi* (child of my mother) and a half or clan brother, *omwana wa papa* (child of the father). Clansmen of the same generation (*olubaka*) call each other *owase*, a cross-gender term which denotes deep friendship.

Other kinship terms refer to more than one category of individuals. For instance, the term *guga* or *kuka* refers to both paternal and maternal grandfathers, and *omwitsukhulu* refers to the children of one's son (same clan) or children of one's daughter (belonging to a different clan). Infants and newborn babies are sometimes variously called *kuka*, *kukhu*, *mama*, *papa*, *senje*, and *khotsa* depending on their sex. These are endearment terms used as alternatives to the person after whom they are named.

The use of kinship terms is not merely a formality; it implies specific roles, duties, and obligations for the individuals concerned. If a child calls a clansman *papa*, he behaves the same way he would behave toward his biological father. That means he accords the individual the same respect, obeys his orders, and accepts any sanctions which might arise in the course of social interaction. However, this social behavior is not fixed in absolute terms but varies according to how close the relationship is. For instance a child would be humbled in front of his father's brothers than, say, a neighbor or a distant clansman even though he calls him *papa* as well.

This relationship is one of the most enduring features of clanship (*obuleebe*) in Buluyia. By defining roles for everyone, the system offers some kind of social insurance ensuring no individual suffers social or economic privation. With an army of people to call on for help, the individual feels protected from various vagaries and misfortunes that loom frequently. For example if a child's father dies, the father's brothers step in; if they are all dead, half brothers take over, and after them the clan fathers ensuring a continuation of clanship.

(ii) Kinship terminology

Table 6: Consanguineous relatives

Term	Plural	English
Papa, Dada, Baba (So)	*Abapapa, Vadada*	Real father and his brothers
Mama, Nyina (Mao)	*Abamama, Abanyina*	Real mother or stepmother
Omwibuli, Mwivuli	*Abebuli, Vevuli*	Parent
Omusiani	*Abasiani*	Boy
Omukhana, Omukana	*Abakhana, Vakana*	Girl
Omwana	*Abaana*	Child
Omukhokoro, Omukogoti	*Amakhokoro, Vakogoti*	Last-born child
Mbotswa, Mbozua	*Abambotswa, Vambotswa*	Brother to sister or sister to brother. Never same sex
Amitu (Maragoli), *Amweru* (Tiriki*)*, *Amwa*bo	*Vamitu, Bamweru, Bamwabo*	Brother to brother or sister to sister. Never cross gender.
Mufiala, Musiala (Tiriki)	*Abafiala, Vafiala, Basiala*	Cousin
Omwiwa, Mwihwa, Omwifa	*Abewa, Biihwa, Vifa*	Man's nephew or niece
Khotsa, Koza	*Abakhotsa, Vakoza*	Mother's brother—maternal uncle
Senje, Senge	*Abasenje, Vasenge*	Father's or mother's sister—aunt

Kuka, Guga	*Abakuka, Vaguga*	Grandfather—paternal and maternal
Kukhu, Guku	*Abakukhu, Vaguku*	Grandmother—paternal or maternal
Omwitsukhulu, omwisukulu	*Abetsukhulu, Visukulu*	Grandchild
Ekisukului, Shisukhulu	*Visukului, Bisukhulu*	Great-grandparent or child
Esisoni (Eshisoni), Ekisoni	*Ebisoni, Visoni*	Great-grandchild or grandparent
Esifutula imoni	*Ebifutula tsimoni*	Great-great-grandparent or child
Masakwa, Basagwa	*Abamasakwa, Vamasagwa*	Wife's sister's husband or husband's brother's wife.
Omukoko	*Abakoko, Vakoko*	Married daughter

Table 7: Affinal relatives

Omusatsa, Omusaza	*Abasatsa, Avasaza*	Husband, man
Omukhaye, Omukaye	*Abakhaye, abakaye*	Well-established wife with children—implies respect
Omukhasi, Omukali	*Abakhasi, abakali*	Ordinary wife
Mwalikhwa, Mwalikwa	*Bamwalikhwa, valikwa*	Cowife
Mulamwa, Mulamu	*Abamulamwa, vamulamu*	Brother's wife or sister's husband
Nyakhufiala, Nabisala, Navisala	*Banyakhufiala, Banabisala, Vanabisala*	Father or mother-in-law or son-/daughter-in-law
Nabaana, Namunenwa, Basanje, Bamwayi (Tiriki)	*Banabaana, Namunenwa, Basanje, Bamwayi*	Parents of a married couple call each other *nabaana, basanje or namunenwa*

Masakwa, Basagwa	*Masakwa, Basagwa. Singular and plural are same*	Men married to two sisters call each other *masakwa*
Omukhwe, omukwe[93]	*Abakhwe, Vakwe*	Wife's brother
Owalekhwa	*Abalekhwa*	Widow
Nashikoko	*Abashikoko*	Divorcee

Table 8: Bukusu and Tachoni kinship terms

Term	**Plural**	**English**
Mayi (Mao)	*Bamayi*	Mother
Omusasi	*Basasi*	Parents
Omusinde	*Basinde*	Uncircumcised boy
Koko (Tachoni)	*Abakoko*	Grandmother
Omubele	*Babele*	Firstborn child
Omutua	*Batua*	Last-born child
Omuti	*Batiti*	Youngest
Wanda yase	*Bawanda yase*	My brother or sister
Omusolili wefu (Tachoni)	*Abasolili befu*	Brother
Omwiwana	*Abewana*	Man's nephew or niece
Yindume (Tachoni)	*Chindume*	Son
Omwisengechana	*Basengechana*	Woman's brother's child—aunt
Sianang'ina	*Banang'ina*	Child of mother's sister
Omwichukhulu	*Bechukhulu*	Grandchild
Sisoni	*Bisoni*	Great-grandchild
Simiila	*Bimiila*	Great-great-grandchild
Sinamunda	*Binamunda*	Great-great-great-grandchild

---

[93]. *Omukhwe* is derived from *ikhwe* or *vukhwi* (bridewealth). Traditionally *ikhwe* is paid so that the wife's brother can use it to marry his wife.

Sisingukhu	*Bisingukhu*	Great-great-great-great-grandchild
Sisakha malalu	*Bisakha malalu*	Great-great-great-great-great-grandchild
Omukhulu	*Bakhulu*	Oldest wife
Wango yase	*Bawango yase*	Cowife
Mukhwasi	*Bakhwasi*	Wife's brother or sister
Wambalikha	*Bambalikha*	Husband's brother's wife
Masala	*Bamasala*	Mother or father-in-law
Basakwa wase	*Basakwa base*	Men married to two sisters call each other *basakwa*. The term also applies to parents of married couples.
Owase	*Base*	Mine (brother or sister)
Namulekhwa	*Bamulekhwa*	Widow
Nasikoko	*Basikoko*	Divorcee

C. Clan and Lineage

So far we have seen that a family is the smallest unit in the kinship structure. Where a family is polygamous or consists of several married sons and their families, it is referred to as *esilibwa* (literally: gate; plural *ebilibwa*) or *inzu* (house). Several *ebilibwa* form a lineage; members of whom are descended from an apical ancestor usually great-great-great-grandfather. In turn several lineages amalgamate into an even larger social unit called a clan and hundreds of clans give way to tribe or, in our case, nation. The glue that binds all these social units is their claim to common agnatic ancestry.

(i)   Clan attributes

A clan is a community of shared interests characterized by distinct features and rules to which all members must conform. First and foremost, a clan is an exogamous unit which means marriage between clan members is forbidden. Clansmen inhabit common ancestral land, undertake clan duties, and participate in various clan rites and ceremonies. Each clan is named after its agnatic founder and, in rare and exceptional cases, women whose sons seceded from their original clans. In Idakho for example, Abamanyisi are named after Anyisi, a woman and so are Abashimuli (Shimuli) and Abakhulunya of Isukha. Such women were of exceptional character and unusual influence. In Bukusu, clans spawned by Bakitwika are named after Tukwika's wives hence Basakha (Nasakha), Bakitang'a (Nakitang'a), Bakuleti (Nakuleti), Bakwangwa (Nabukwangwa), Baluchekhe (Naluchekhe), and Bambombi (Nambombi). And just like the original nine clans of the Agikuyu[94] were founded by women, men quickly overturned the matrilineal order and Kikuyu society, like Luyia, is largely patrilineal.

Few clans derive names from certain characteristics or oddities, e.g., Banayoka in Bukusu and Abamayoka, a subclan of Abasikhale in Bunyore were so named because of noisemaking (*obuyoka*) habits. Theoretically, all clan members ought to establish an unbroken genealogical connection with an apical ancestor. However, due to lack of record keeping, seamless footprints of ancestral roots are possible only for younger clans whose family tree goes up to eight generations. According to historian Dr. John

---

[94.]   The original daughters of Mumbi and Agikuyu (the Kikuyu tribal ancestor) are Achera, Agachiko, Airimo, Amboi, Angare, Anjiro, Angoi, Aithaga, and Aitherandu. Historians say the daughters were actually ten but apparently the number ten is, according to Kikuyu mythology, an unlucky one and therefore tabooed.

Osogo (1966), some older clans claim to trace their ancestry up to thirty generations for example Abasali in Maragoli.

Each subnation is named after the tribal ancestor who, due to lack of proper genealogical records, may either be real or mythical. Hence, Babukusu trace their tribal ancestry to Mubukusu, Abanyole to Anyole, Maragoli to Omulogoli, Abawanga to Wanga, etc. Some tribes were established by brothers such as Bukusu and Gisu of eastern Uganda. Also Idakho and Isukha ancestors are said to have been brothers, but their respective names were not eponymous. Instead, Idakho means those to the south while Isukha means those to the north of River Lukose (Yala). A similar legend obtains among the Maragoli and Kisii (Gusii). Although currently living in separate geographical locations, their tribal ancestors, Omulogoli and Omugusii, are believed to have been brothers. Another striking example is Abanyala which was originally one tribe but split into two living miles apart in Busia and Kakamega. To distinguish the two groups, the name Abanyala principally refers to those in Buongo, Busia County while those in Navakholo, Kakamega are generally known as Abanyala ba Ndombi, named after their once powerful colonial chief, Ndombi wa Namusia.

Similarly, as we shall see in chapter 5, some clans are *ex situ* and spread across different subnations. Such clans include Abakhoone[95] (Bunyala, Bukhayo, Marachi, Marama, Samia, Tachoni, and Bukusu); Abamulembo (Wanga, Samia, Marachi, Bukusu, and Bunyala); Abamang'ali (Bukusu, Butsotso, Tachoni, Kabras, Samia and Bunyore), Ababulugi (Tiriki, Wanga and Maragoli); Abachero (Wanga and Kisa); Abamuli (Bunyore, Tiriki, Kisa, and Bunyala); Abatura (Wanga, Marachi, Bukusu, Tiriki, Isukha, and Bukhayo); Ababere (Marachi, Samia, Wanga, Bukhayo, Uganda, and Buhaya in Tanzania), etc. Despite historical genealogy

---

[95.] Abakhoone are also found in Mfangano Islands among Abasuba and in Uganda among Abanyole and Samia Bugwe.

pointing to a common origin, most of these clanal septs consider themselves independent exogamous units.

As population increased, so also did the number of people belonging to different social units. Inevitably, this spatial growth led to a split of the original sept into subclans which eventually metamorphosed into full-fledged clans in their own right. Various clanal septs formed territorial units and lived on clan land (*lusomo* in Tiriki, *chikholo* in Lubukusu). However, occasionally, non clan members (*abamenya*, singular: *omumenya*) were permitted to settle on clan land where there were reasonable grounds to offer such concessions, for example, if they were victims of calamities. The most common group of *abamenya* included *abewa* (sister's sons, singular: *omwiwa*) and cousins (*abafiala*, singular: *mufiala*). Any clansman reserved the right to grant the right of residence to such persons or friends and relatives from other tribes. Although these rights were initially temporary, some *abamenya* eventually became assimilated in the host clan to a point where they lost their original clan identity.

Technically, although *abamenya* may live for several generations in host clans, they do not become members but retain affiliations to their original clan and continue to be bound by rules of that sept. Socially though, the longer they lived in the host clan, the more their status began to resemble that of the autochthonous hosts provided they identified themselves with aboriginal interests. Foremost among these interests is observance of rules of exogamy, especially for boys. While an *omumenya* boy cannot marry a girl from his host clan, an *omumenya* girl can be married by a boy from the host clan (Ochwada 2007: 58). Adoption into the clan was rare and limited only to orphans or war captives from other tribes who had lost all contact with their own clans. However, special concessions were made to *abamenya* who had lived long enough and wished to be assimilated into the host clan. Usually that happened after two or three generations (fifty to seventy-five years) in which case they ceased being *abamenya* and became known as *abamilikha*, meaning absorbed or merged (Shilaro 2000: 16). In some cases, the newcomers, if they were several, formed their own clan. Such is the case with a clan known eponymously as Abamenya found among Abakhayo and Abanyala. No special ceremonies are staged or any ritual sacrifices offered in this transition. *Abamenya* children are raised as members of the family and enjoy the same social and legal status as the foster father's own children. Married women (*abakoko*), though, always remain members of the clan into which they were born regardless of how many generations they live among the husband's clan community.

(ii) New clan formation

Formation of new clans in Buluyia is a slow process that often takes several generations. Although a new clan evolved in various ways, the most common cause was a quarrel between sons of a prominent clan elder or a grievous clash between ordinary clansmen. The combatants drew support from sympathisers and if, despite intervention by clan elders the antagonism continued or exploded into open warfare, one party, usually the weaker one, fled from clan territory. Because of the strained relations, they immediately embarked on a process to exorcise all demons connected with former clan territory including the name. For at least a generation or two, they retain the old clan name while popularizing their new name, especially among the offspring which they beget in the new territory. As old people die, the old clan name expires with them until it finally fades into obscurity. The two sides consciously avoid each other's paths so long as the feud continues and bitterness prevails. They see each other as enemies; they do not maintain relations of any kind not even attending funerals of relatives from the opposite camps. If they meet at a third party's house, they do not talk to each other, exchange pleasantries, or eat and drink together. In extreme cases, one party may even walk away once he discovers the presence of an "enemy" within the precincts.

Be that as it may, sooner or later a rapprochement is attempted to bring the parties together and bury the hatchet through a ritual reconciliation ceremony known as *okhulia imbwa* (literally: to eat a dog).[96] This applies when tempers have cooled off and both parties feel it is pointless to wage war against each other especially if they live within a reasonable distance and can't avoid crossing paths. Despite the reconciliation, they continue to exist independently but observe all common clan taboos and prohibitions, particularly marriage. The status quo is maintained so long as there are still alive members of the original clan. After three generations when all elders have died and the bitterness of the conflict has faded into obscurity, the two sides may now finally pronounce themselves as truly independent and free of exogamous strictures.

The repudiation of exogamy between the two clans is expressed initially through the marriage of a girl whose mother came from another lineage of the clan (Wagner 1970: 67). If this marriage flourishes without evil consequences, it means the ancestral spirits have blessed it and such marriages are then repeated, and after a generation or so, this then becomes normal. The exact number of generations that have to elapse before rules of exogamy are relaxed depends upon the strength of clan traditions. Famous clans proud of their clan traditions, tend to hold out longer before dénouement anchored by strong memory the clan ancestor wields on his progeny. For less pompous clans, however, the breakaway subclans tend to exert their independence after two or three generations following death of the last member of the former clan.

[96.] *Okhulia imbwa* is an ancient ritual ceremony in which quarrelling brothers, families, or clans are reconciled, renounce animosity toward each other and pledge to remain on peaceful terms. It does not mean they literally eat a dog.

An illustration of these clan feuds is found among Maragoli clans of Avayonga and Avakizungu. Two brothers, Yonga and Kizungu, quarrelled over their sister's bridewealth during which the former killed the latter leading to prolonged bloodletting within the family. The supporters of Kizungu fled into what is now known as North Maragoli and Yonga and clans affiliated to him remained in what we know as South Maragoli. Another example is the quarrel between two subclans of Avayonga—the Avayose and Avagimuhia. Over a beer party, Yose boasted that he was superior to Gimuhia by virtue of being the son of Yonga's elder wife and Gimuhia that of a junior wife. Tempers flared, and the two subclans moved in opposite directions, but unlike Avayonga and Avakizungu, they have since reconciled and continue to observe rules of exogamy (Wagner 1970: 68).

In Marama, Butere, two sons of Mukhula (the progenitor of Abamukhula, the largest clan in Marama)—Mukolwe and Mumbia—had a serious quarrel during which Mukolwe not only destroyed Mumbia's village but killed many of his children as well. To demonstrate his anger against his brother, he declared that he did not wish to share the same burial grounds with him and when he died; his body should be buried at Ebulambalo where his wife came from (*ebukhwe*)—something of a taboo for a Luyia man. After his death, Mukolwe's family suffered ill fortune in warfare and hunting. To ward off the misfortunes, a diviner advised him to dig up Mumbia's bones, make a sacrificial offering, and bury the bones in their rightful place according to tradition. After this ritual, Abamumbia and Abakolwe renounced their hostilities and resumed friendly relations. This blot on the sociocultural relations of the two clan communities was to later serve as a deterrent to any future conflicts. Today, whenever clan members pick a quarrel, they are quickly reminded of the Mukolwe-Mumbia incident and cautioned to avoid anything that can split and destroy the clan community.

We find another example of how a clan can split among the Bukusu and Tachoni. The Bameywa originally lived in Tororo, Uganda. One of the wives of the clan progenitor, Meywa, was a Tachoni and her son migrated to Tachoni territory. As we have seen, it was customary for *omwiwa* (sister's son) to be welcomed by his uncle and granted right of abode. His descendants adopted his name and became known as Abameywa (Wagner 1970: 69). In another twist of fate, Meywa clansmen in Uganda separated following the murder of a member of a junior house by a senior house clansman. The junior had challenged the senior to a tree-climbing competition in which the latter lost and to avenge the defeat, he speared his stepbrother in anger. The ensuing clan feud and bloodletting caused the two sides to move with their supporters and sympathizers settling in two different parts of Bungoma. Those settling in the lowlands of East Bukusu became known as Bameywa Bamwalo (lower Bameywa) and those setting in the highlands Bameywa Bengaki (upper Bameywa). While the Bukusu Bameywa are endogamous, the Tachoni brethren consider themselves independent enough to marry from any of the two Bukusu Bameywa groups.

We have seen how quarrelling between brothers of a leading family can split a clan community as in the case of Yonga and Kizungu in Maragoli or Mukolwe and Mumbia in Marama. The two social occasions which provide fodder for disagreements are alcohol parties (*mumalwa*) and funerals (*masika*). A calumnious remark blurted under influence of a substance often triggers tongue-lashing and implosion of pent-up anger over some family or personal matter. If the quarrelling degenerates into fistfights and despite intervention by clan elders, the two combatants continue to stalk each other, one or both may decide to leave the clan territory and settle somewhere else. However, the most serious quarrels which flare into open conflict occur during funerals when relatives openly accuse a clansman of having bewitched the deceased. These are serious accusations which cause great emotional discomfort and often lead to revenge and witch hunting. When the situation reaches unbearable proportions, one party walks out in protest to settle in far flung places.

Another reason clans split is illustrated by the case of Bameywa which we have described above. It was customary for nonclan members to settle in host territories as *abamenya* (strangers). In the main, right of abode was granted to *abewa* (nephews) or friends (*abalina*, variation: *abetsa*) and relatives (*abikho*) from other clans or tribes. Although in most cases this arrangement was temporary, if *omumenya* stayed long enough, started a family and was at peace in his new environment that marked the beginning of an independent clan. That is why we have clans living permanently *ex situ* across a number of subnations, e.g., Avasagala in Maragoli.[97] When they establish permanent residence, they are now called *abamilikha*. Some of these clans have become completely autonomous while others are still affiliated to the "mother" clan and continue to observe rules of exogamy. Some even adopted *abamenya* nomenclature as their new clan name (Ebukhayo and Ebunyala Busia). An *omumenya* sought refuge for various reasons. If he was orphaned at an early age and there was no one among his clansmen capable of looking after him, his uncle stepped in and offered sanctuary. Other contributory factors to *obumenya* (seeking refuge) include natural calamities, famine, outbreak of epidemics, and threats or fear of evil magic in the neighborhood. If a large number of clansmen take refuge in a foreign territory, they are known as *abarende* (neighbors), e.g., Ab'biba clansmen in Emuli, Bunyore.

By far the main reason clans split is through population growth. With each new generation, it becomes impractical to maintain clan

---

[97.] Avasagala are found in Bukusu (Basakali) and Isukha (Abasakala). They originally came from Busoga, Uganda. There is a railway station in Busoga known as Namasakali believed to be their original home.

solidarity and observe all the elements of cultural tradition. Where clan rights and duties involved the whole clan, gradually these tend to be limited to groups of families or lineages and with time, these evolve into subclans. Over a few generations, the various subclans begin to assert themselves as independent units with regard to economic, political, and legal issues. But although they may be sovereign in these departments, it takes a few generations before the umbilical cord that ties them to the mother clan is excised to set them free from the tough rules of exogamy.

If after marriage husband and wife discover that they are remotely related, they must undergo a cleansing rite to forestall ritual dangers that may afflict their offspring. Their matrimony is contaminated by a ritual danger known as *oluswa* which is righted by a customary rite of lustration. A typical example of such remote affinity may be traced to their mothers' subclans which although semiautonomous, nonetheless, still observe rules of exogamy. The lustration procedure involves a sacrificial offering of an animal (sheep, goat, or cow). The couple is then smeared with the animal's chyme (*obuse, ovose* in Logooli) by a clan elder who chants an incantation as he does so and the meat roasted and eaten by relatives and neighbors. Then at dusk, the woman's brother climbs the matrimonial hut and on top of the rod (*eshisuli*) that protrudes from traditional huts hangs upside down a cracked pot that had fallen into disuse through frequent use. The pot's orifice represents the female cervix and the body, the womb while the *eshisuli* denotes the phallus, a symbol of manhood. The symbolism of placing the pot upside down onto the *eshisuli* is to create a reversal of sexual intercourse between the couple, the cracks in the pot allowing the escape of harmful semen (*butiu*). After this ceremony, not only has *oluswa* danger been cured, from now on, the two subclans become independent clans.

At other times, a group of clansmen may flee to distant lands and form new septs in the wake of natural calamities, wars, famine, epidemics, or witchcraft. Bands of fleeing clansmen carry twigs to signify their intentions as peaceful refugees rather than as invading forces. If they are deemed genuine, they are disarmed and allocated the status of *bamenywa* (*abamenya*) and allowed settlement as a subclan of the host clandom. If following a serious altercation part of a clan emigrated and settled in a neighboring tribe, the newcomers maintained their original name but considered themselves socially independent from their original clan. Similarly, a person who is in serious breach of taboo including killing a clansman may be expelled from clan land along with his family often to distant lands. With time, their lineages grew and formed a clan or subclan.

Another factor which caused clans to scatter and settle away from clan territory was tribal or clan warfare. The victorious clan or tribe settled its people on the conquered land to assert ownership and protect it from invaders. War captives or those given shelter on account of indigence sometimes created their own lineages and with time subclans or clans. However, before being adopted in the clanship, clansmen first made serious inquiries into the identity of the forsaken or orphaned child. Using what information they gathered from the child, they asked neighbors, strangers at marketplaces, etc., if they knew of anyone whose child was lost. Only after all inquiries returned no positive clues could adoption be formalized through a public proclamation at the village common (*oluyia*). These inquiries were informed by the need to forestall infiltration by enemies who used children as spies.

It was taboo in Luyialand for a family in a position of leadership to hire someone of royal pedigree as a servant. We find two examples in Wanga and Bukusu where royals disguised their nobility to gain refuge and employment. The classic case of Nabongo Wanga is well documented (see p.111). Less known is the case of a Maasai leader known as Tolometi who arrived one evening looking destitute in the court of Mukhwana, the leader of

Bakimweyi clan. Tolometi was hired as a general laborer, but as time passed by, Mukhwana`s wife noticed that the Maasai was wearing items of nobility such as *enjabasi* (rectangular ivory armband) and *lichabe* (circular ivory armband). Ordinarily, such a discovery should have been followed by instant dismissal and a cleansing rite as otherwise a curse would befall the hosts. But in this case, Tolometi owned up and said he was fleeing persecution from Uasin Gishu and was genuinely grateful for Mukhwana`s kindness.

His sincerity touched Mukhwana's heart who allowed Tolometi to bring his family and livestock for settlement. A big feast was staged to mark the bond of brotherhood not only between Mukhwana and Tolometi but also between their respective consanguineous relations who would now observe rules of exogamy. In the event, one of Mukhwana's sons impregnated Tolometi's daughter and eloped with her creating animosity and polluting ritual tranquility. To avoid an escalation of hostilities between the two families, a rapprochement was worked out in such a way that Tolometi was allocated territory in another village. The mother of the boy at the center of elopement was Omunesoba clanswoman and so he was referred to as Omukimweyi Omunesoba. Children from Mukhwana's other wife were noisy, so they were called Bakimweyi Banayoka while the rest were called Bakimweyi Bamukhwana. The family of Tolometi came to be known as Bakimweyi Batolometi (Makila 1978: 86).

Different clans pooled resources to wage warfar,e and if victorious in their pursuits, the conquered land was divided equally among the victors. Various clans settling on annexed dominion inevitably caused a radical realignment of clan territory and sociocultural relationships. Although common ancestry is often the pillar upon which clans are built, there are certain exceptions to this rule. Such is the case for instance with heterogeneous clans with assimilated immigrants from different backgrounds. The immigrants are free to retain aspects of their culture that are not inimical to the clanship and in that case they become a subclan of the main clan cluster.

In large polygamous families, it was customary for children to be known by their mother's clan. Over time when sons start their own families, especially after death of the patriarch, some of these names grew into popular use and came to characterize the sons and their children. Such is the case with the following Bakitwika clans in Bukusu which are named after wives of Tukwika, the eponymous clan founder: Bambombi (Nambombi), Bakitang'a (Nakitang'a), Basakha (Nasakha), Bakuleti (Nakuleti), Bakwangwa (Nabukwangwa), Baluchekhe (Naluchekhe). Sometimes, a household may be associated with certain characteristics, abilities, or peculiarities. A good example is the Abamayoka subclan of Abasikhale of Bunyore, Kenya, and Banayoka, a subclan of Bakimweyi of Bukusu. These subclans are named after *obuyoka* (noise), apparently due to their noisemaking characteristic. Another example is the nickname of Bakhanyama given to Bayemba of Bukusu famed for their love of meat (*enyama*) or the lineages of Bakhami (milkers) and Basaya (cheekbone carriers). In such cases, the names describing these elements may grow in usage until they become formally adopted as a clan or subclan name. Although most clans are named after ancestors, there are some that derive their name from place names, e.g., Balugulu (higher grounds).

Finally, clans may split when certain subclans feel snubbed by fellow clansmen either for reasons of pride or protest against certain antisocial characteristics (*tsifwo*). A good example is Avagivagi, formerly a subclan of Avayose who were forced to become an independent clan following an incident in which Omuyose failed to carry out clan obligations toward Omugivagi. Avagivagi found in South Maragoli are stigmatized as *abalosi* (witches) and that might explain why they were cold-shouldered (Wagner 1970: 71).

The evolvement of clans is a dynamic process; while new clans are created, others disappear altogether swallowed by larger ones. Examples of extinct clans include Abahunia, Abamulukuyu, and Abaluchera from Marama where they are known collectively as *emikuru* (scaffolding poles) because they support large clans. The difference between a full-fledged clan, subclan, or lineage is sometimes blurred as the latter two may be at various stages of attaining sovereignty. An average lineage is two hundred, subclan five hundred while a clan may be anything up to twenty thousand as is the case of Abamironje (they prefer to be called Abasoyi) in Isukha.

The political interaction between various clans or subnations is largely a function of linguistic, geographical, and ethno-cultural relationship. Although tensions exist even among closely related clans, subclans, and subnations, an analysis of historical factors reveals a clear distinction between clans or subtribes that are friendly and those that are outright enemies. Occasional clan feuds are settled by certain rituals or following death of the last person to remember the altercation. However, sanguineous animosity between certain tribes may continue for several generations implying that all forms of social interaction including marriage are strictly forbidden. Such was the case between Babukusu and Wanga, Teso (Wamia),[98] Maasai, and Sabaot (Sebei) while they regarded the Tachoni, Abanyala ba Ndombi, and Kabras as friendly. In postcolonial era, Babukusu added Maragoli who settled in large numbers in Trans Nzoia to their nemesis' list because the newcomers had a perception of haughtiness and ethnocentrism. On the other hand, Maragoli were on friendly terms with Abanyole, Abatiriki, and Abidakho but sworn enemies with Terik, Nandi, and Luo. The Isukha and Idakho regard each other as brothers and are friendly with the Kisa, Marama, and Batsotso. The Busia subnations—Samia, Abanyala,

---

[98.] Hostilities between Iteso and Babukusu ended after the two tribes agreed to participate in a reconciliation ritual known as *okhulia imbwa* (dog eating) which took place just before the colonial era (see p.351).

Abakhayo, and Abamarachi—maintain close relations among themselves and the Luo, sharing many cultural traits. Abakhayo are particularly friendly with Nilotic Iteso.

(iii) Clan taboos and superstitions

All clans have certain taboos (*emisiro*, variation: *emisilo, emigilu* in Logooli) which they observe and totems which they consider sacrosanct. For some clans it is taboo to eat certain plants, meat of certain animals, or drink milk of cows of a certain color. Among the Bukusu, it is taboo for women in menstrual circle to go to a quarry (Nangendo 1986: 69) which according to legend symbolizes the place where *Wele* (God) took the clay to make the first man on earth. Other taboos prohibit the killing of certain animals like python, birds, lizards, and frogs. The following are some of the more common taboos, superstitions, and peculiarities prevalent in Buluyia:

a. If while on an important journey a. woodpecker sings on your left, you must call off the safari and return home at once. Conversely if the wood pecker sings on the right side of the road, the omens are auspicious and the journey will be successful.

b. While on a journey, you must inquire gender of the first child of the first person you meet. If it is the same sex, the omens are good; if the opposite sex, you must either cancel the journey or take your chances. If your firstborn is a son and you meet two boys walking either together or in quick succession, the omens are particularly auspicious and vice versa.

c. Although stumbling is a bad omen among the Maragoli, it is worse to stumble with one's left foot than with the right. In the latter case one returns home only if it happens twice in succession. If one stumbles with both feet in quick succession, it means two different troubles lie ahead. Among the Wanga, however, it is considered lucky to stumble with the left foot when going out on a journey but unlucky to stumble with the right. But when returning home from a journey the opposite prevails, i.e., lucky to stumble with the right foot and unlucky for the left foot.

d. Meeting a type of rat called *elivengi* among the Maragoli is considered a bad omen, but a small antelope called *ekisunu* is a very good sign and so is a silver squirrel with a long bushy tail.

e. Meeting *esimindwa* (red hawk) is a bad omen, and if the *enyiru* bird crosses a person's path twice and whistles, he must return home at once.

f. If an owl (*elikure*) cries near a homestead, this is a sign that someone in that home will soon die. To avert danger the owl portents, it must be driven away with a firebrand lit from a hearth of the targeted household.

g. If a jackal (*libwe*; variation: *esibwe, ekivwe*) is heard crying, this means that someone important in the tribe or clan is about to die.

h. Among the Bukusu, if one comes across *nafusi* ants, this means one will receive good hospitality if he is visiting or something pleasant is in store for him.

i. Sneezing is generally considered a bad omen and if a person sneezes repeatedly before taking up an important assignment, he puts it off for some time if possible. However, among the Wanga, if someone sets off to visit a friend who is sick and dying and sneezes before he starts the journey, this is an indication the friend will recover from his illness.

j. If an antelope crosses a road in front of marriage cattle while being taken to the bride's father, it is a bad omen indicating that the animals will die.

k. It is a taboo to cut nails or hair at night because doing so is tantamount to wanting to kill your parents.

l. It is taboo to sweep the house or take rubbish out at night. It is said that by doing so, you are throwing your luck out (*ofubanga tsikhabi*).

m. It is taboo to kill a python (*ivaka*) among the Maragoli while the Wanga may not kill a bushbuck (*imbongo*) as it is a tribal totem.

n. If you spot a snake, you must clasp your left arm with the right (man) and vice versa for a woman. By this act you are "tying" the serpent on the spot as you summon someone to come and kill it.

o. It is taboo to wash hands with soap after a meal of chicken. Anyone who does so is admonished that he will never rear poultry.

p. It is taboo to mix meat and milk (especially fermented) at the same time while eating *obusuma* (ugali). The Luyia believe anyone who does so will not be lucky in rearing cattle.

q. It is taboo to kill a frog and a chameleon as the amphibian and reptile are associated with luck.

r. It is taboo to go to the spring well to fetch water after sunset. If it cannot be avoided, a woman must be escorted by a man and a purification rite staged. This involves pouring some water from the pot to the ground while uttering an incantation. A woman who breaches this rule is punished by miscarriages.

Clan taboos act as a form of social sanction violation of which is punishable by ritual consequences. They are part of the mystical belief system that characterizes Luyia society. If one's skin turns pale or peels off or the hair begins to fall off, one of the foremost interpretations is that the individual has engaged in acts that violated *emisiro* (taboos, singular: *omusiro*). Infringement of any kind of customary prohibitions pose ritual danger to either the individual concerned, those with whom he interacts, or both.

The origins of clan taboos is a matter of conjecture but one way in which they originated was through an edict from an influential clan elder. If after consulting a diviner, a serious illness or epidemic is attributed to consumption of a certain dish, the clan elder forbade his children from eating that particular dish. To ensure his edict was enforced, he pronounced a curse on anyone who defied him. The same formula was applied to objects, animals, and plants that were deemed the cause of a particular misfortune to any clan member (Wagner 1970: 74). The degree to which taboos are observed depends on the potency with which clansmen associate them. Hence a taboo imposed by a clan elder survives only as long as the elder's curse is still perceived to be potent and consequences of violation definite. In any case, cleansing rites offer a safety net for transgressors rendering infraction of most taboos innocuous.

(iv) Clan reputation

All clans have certain unique physical characteristics, peculiarities, and social reputations which come to the fore in the course of interaction with other clans. Some clans are said to be made of tall (*abarambi*) or short people (*abembikiti*), light skinned (*abalafu*) or dark skinned (*abamwamu*, variation: *abamali*), pretty faced (*abamakondo*) or ugly faced (*okubi*). Some have a reputation of being greedy or preposterous (*amanani*);[99] others easily irritable or quarrelsome (*abasololi*), others have "loose" women (*abayeyi*)

---

[99] *Amanani* (singular: *linani*) is a mythical animal (ogre) known for its callousness in Luyia folklore. The term is used to describe a greedy or indifferent person.

and others are cunning (*abachanja* or *abaswahili*[100]). Other clans are known by their vocation, e.g., rainmakers (*abakimba*), diviners (*abafumu*), circumcision surgeons (*abashebi*, variation: *abasebi, bakhebi*), or blacksmiths (*aberanyi*). Besides, some clans have a reputation of practicing witchcraft (*obulosi*) which is socially opprobrious while others are great warriors (*abelihe*). The reputation of *obulosi* or any of the other characteristic peculiarities mentioned above is merely a latent disposition which can lie dormant for generations only to break forth without warning following certain triggers (Wagner 1970: 76). Ordinarily this reputation does not prejudice interclan interaction, but it is something other clans take into account on important social discourses like marriage. A girl whose family is stigmatized as *abalosi* faces difficulties in securing a local groom and often has to seek matrimony in faraway lands where little is known about her family background.

(v) Leadership of the clan

The office of a clan elder (*omwami* or *omukasa*)[101] was bestowed upon someone with a strong personality whose opinion was respected among his contemporaries by virtue of his knowledge of clan history, traditions, and customs. Theoretically such an individual was the seniormost member of the clan community in accordance with the principle of age grade seniority governing

---

[100.] Abaswahili are coastal people, mainly from Mombasa. Upcountry, they have a reputation of cunningness (*obuchanja*), and the term *omuswahili* is used interchangeably to refer to the people as well to their characteristics.

[101.] *Omukasa* also means the copper bracelet which is the ultimate symbol of *ubunabongo* (kingship) among the Luyia. In Maragoli, the clan head was sometimes called *Wengoma* (literally: of the drum) because as an item of totemic symbolism, the drum was kept only by the most venerable among the Maragoli.

all family and clan relations. It must be noted, however, that a clan elder was never an elective office. It merely drifted toward an individual with a forceful personality who was welcoming and commanded respect. Although age was an important consideration, it was by no means the only criterion through which an individual acceded to the office of a clan elder. If no particular individual exhibited leadership qualities, the clandom was ruled by a council of elders until a single individual emerged. Lack of central authority, however, exposed the clan community to schisms and intrigues which placed the social unit at a military disadvantage. Because of need to consult before decisions are made, such acephalous clans tended to have weak structures of command and became easy targets for cattle raiders or conquest by enemy clans and tribes. If elders feuded and disagreed, clan solidarity weakened leading to disintegration of the clan community.

Clan leadership often gravitates toward an older individual powered by the sheer size of his kinship network. In old age, a man sits atop a huge family tree that may include several wives, children, grandchildren, great-grandchildren, and other relations acquired by virtue of his son's and daughter's marriages. Among other things, he acquires a venerable social stature and with it more duties and obligations. His authority is called upon to resolve conflicts between clan members or with other clans.

Unlike *ubunabongo* (kingship), office of a clan elder is not hereditary. When the patriarch dies, his authority is not automatically inherited by his eldest son but passes on to his eldest living brother in accordance with the principle of seniority. Ancestral belief systems exert an enormous influence in traditional Luyia society (Bulimo 2013: 175). An old person is usually respected and feared in equal measure because he is potentially a troublesome spirit when he passes on. The power inherent in old age is manifested in the fear of a dying curse or possibility of his spirit playing the role of a guardian angel against evil forces. For these reasons, most people normally accord the elderly respect and obey their authority.

In chapter 3, we saw how elders congregated around an evening fire (*oluyia*) to discuss events of the day, plan for the future, tell stories of warfare or simply gossip. While this sitting was largely an adult affair, boys who had undergone circumcision or distinguished themselves as natural leaders during various daily or seasonal activities such as herding cattle, playing games or farm work, were welcome to join elders. It is from this pool of boys that future *abami* (leaders) or *abakasa* (chiefs) emerged. Courageous and fearless individuals who organized successful cattle raids were also in line to succeed to the office of a clan elder. Such individuals were seen as strategists and clever and their opinions held sway in social discourse.

By far the greatest asset in the armory of a clan leader is economic wealth (*emiandu*). In a traditional setting he was rich he who owned a large herd of cattle and huge tracts of acreage, whose granaries were always full and who had several wives and children. Such an individual always had people milling around his homestead including relatives, loafers, and layabouts who were ready to work for him, sing his praises, laugh at his jokes, and defend him in return for hospitality. Moreover, it was expected of the wealthiest clansman to stage feasts and lend some of his livestock to the needy. Recipients of this benefaction naturally became beholden to him, which amplified his social standing and authority. For all the respect and influence, clan leadership was not without drawbacks, not least, loss of privacy as his homestead became the center of social life in the clan community.

In addition to being the central authority in a clan community, a clan elder sometimes doubles up as the link with the paranormal. He presides over sacrificial offerings as *omusalisi* (sacrificial priest) in addition to or, on behalf of, the oldest living member of a family or lineage that is offering the sacrifice (*omusango*). During funerals, he acts as *omuseni* (comforter) whose duty it is to help the bereaved cope with emotions of death, calming tempers that often flare when accusations of witchcraft arise and apportioning estate of the deceased. The qualifications for the offices of *omuseni* and *omusalisi* involve a little more than that of *omukasa* (chief). In addition to being well versed in customary law and clan traditions, the occupant is often an individual of exemplary personal character, almost stoic and famed for his kindness, honesty, and fairness. He simply must be beyond reproach and past the age of sexual desire.

Although a clan head can potentially act as an arbitrator, a sacrificial priest and political leader, it is not always the case that all three functions are carried out by one individual. Of course some clans produce exemplary individuals who combine all these roles, but in most cases, these functions are split among elders who have distinguished themselves in a particular area of expertise.

We have seen that the office of a clan head is neither hereditary nor elective but merely oscillates toward an individual who commands the highest respect from the clan community. Although his role is well understood and tied to specific clan functions, a clan elder does not otherwise wield any real power over his "subjects." Apart from his immediate family, he can neither interfere in other families' affairs nor demand tribute or favors from them although it is customary to render him some meat and alcohol whenever a sacrificial feast is offered. Although his powers are seemingly limited and his role largely ceremonial, his presence at family or clan feasts is often actively sought because it gives the ceremony an "official" seal of approval or blessings. This realization grants clan heads the privilege of attending any feasts staged in a clan community with or without invitation. And if *obuinda* (wealth) propels him to this office, several gifts that he receives from the functions he attends only serve to increase his stock of wealth.

Despite lacking judicial authority, during certain occasions, a clan head is empowered to summon clansmen to undertake communal tasks, especially during calamities like crop failure. Yields from joint communal activity are shared equally among all clansmen. Other areas where a clan head can issue a rallying call include clearing bush land to make a road, building a bridge across a river or in the olden days, building *olukoba* (fort). In all cases, the whole community stands to benefit from these labors—a clan head cannot use these powers for private gain.

In most Luyia subnations, a clan head is never formally appointed or installed in this office. His office merely evolves due to a combination of circumstances, not least his personal character and certainly his wealth. The only exception is Bunyore where investiture of a clan head was formerly a three-year process during which three types of insignia were bestowed (Wagner 1970: 82). He was first given *indabusi* (club) followed by leopard skin (*lisero lie ingwe*) in the second year finally capping his bestowal as clan head with *olusimbi* (fur cap) in the third year. The most recent coronation took place on July 24, 2009, among Abamanyinya clansmen of Central Bunyore. The clan head, Josphat Tindi, dreamt about this role in 1993, but it was not until 2007 that the prophecy came to pass.[102] In addition to *indabusi, lisero lie ingwe* and *olusimbi*, Tindi also inherited *omukasa* (copper bracelet), the ultimate symbol of kingship among the Luyia which makes him not just a clan head but a *nabongo* (king) among his Abamukuti subclan.

[102.] Josphat Tindi told me during an interview in Nairobi that his grandfather, Hezron Tindi, dreamt about *obunabongo* (kingship) in his homestead in 1948.

Josphat Tindi dons full regalia of a Bunyore clan head
following his coronation as head of Abamukuti clansmen of
Ebutongoi in July 2009.

The office of a clan headman is not always occupied. If after his death no one suitable has emerged or identified, the official insignia is kept by the deceased's eldest son or a clansman of his lineage. No one else is allowed to keep the insignia or wear the leopard skin in public. The formal coronation takes place at the village common (*oluyia*) and is accompanied by a big feast to which everyone contributes. The official investiture involves one clan elder handing over *indabusi* to the new appointee while another elder gives a short speech highlighting merits of the office and expectations of the people with regard to headman's role in maintaining clan solidarity and security.

Formerly in Maragoli only the most celebrated clan warrior was bestowed special insignia in a public ceremony. He was first shaved and anointed with ghee before an old warrior who had been decorated in his time presented him with a headdress made of cowrie shells,[103] a ribbon of colobus monkey skin and a skin cloak confected from various animals (Wagner 1970: 82). He was also given assorted paraphernalia including finger rings, rare feathers, wristlets, ivory armlets, and spears which were entrusted in his care and could only pass onto his eldest son when he became old or to his successor.

(vi) Role of paternal and maternal kinsmen

We have seen that clan genealogy is largely patrilineal, i.e., an individual can only trace his ancestry through his paternal line. That is not to say that the maternal relatives are not important. In the course of an individual's life, the maternal uncles, aunts, and grandparents play specific roles. The maternal uncle (*khotsa*) in particular maintains effective kinship relations with his nephew, fulfilling specific customary duties toward him especially with regard to ceremonies like circumcision and weddings. The maternal aunts too play an important role in the lives of their nieces, imparting certain lessons in girlhood which their mother would not ordinarily talk about directly, e.g., sexual relations. The only other relative free to talk about sex with young girls is their grandmother because under Luyia ethnography, grandparents and grandchildren are like equals.

[103.] Cowrie shells were introduced to Luyialand by Arab and Swahili traders circa 1875 and quickly gained currency as symbols of power, wealth, and mysticism. Their unique shape is pregnant with notions of spirituality and creation across several cultures around the world. The front represents female genitalia while the back shape symbolizes pregnancy and fertility. Long before notes and coins were used as money, cowrie shells were an accepted form of legal tender across many parts of the world.

Although paternal and maternal relations are in theory maintained in equal measure, in reality, paternal relatives tend to overshadow those on the maternal side. This is largely due to an accident of geography rather than a systematic attempt to cut off links with maternal kinsmen. In a traditional setting, children grow up in their father's homestead where majority of relatives are paternal. In rare cases where parents live uxorilocally, children will grow closer to relatives from the mother's side. Either way, the various ceremonies staged by a family provides ample opportunity to foster close kinship relations with relatives from both sides.

Traditional Luyia society was functional upon specific tasks, duties and obligations of clan members. Although tribesmen are no longer bonded by these traditions, they are nevertheless important in any ethno-cultural analysis of the Luyia. The magico-religious ceremonies and sacrifices could not possibly take place without all relatives attending. Anyone who stays away is deemed to have ulterior motives and is blamed if ancestors refuse to accept the offering. Rite of passage ceremonies are milestones in the life of an individual and all relatives are expected to attend. The following are some of the most common ceremonies and rituals which all relatives are required to honor.

- *Okhwalikha*: All relatives are expected to attend the *okhwalika (olutekho, sitekho)* rite when man and wife first establish their household after the birth of their first or second child (Bulimo 2013: 105).
- Circumcision (*sikhebo*): The feast following the graduation from a circumcision hut (Bulimo 2013: 328)
- Weddings: A wedding (*Eshiserero*, variation: *esiselero*) is a major milestone in the life of two individuals coming together in matrimony.

- Funerals (*amasika*): All relatives must pay last respects to the deceased. Anyone who stays away attracts suspicion that he may have killed the decedent (Bulimo 2013: 479)
- Ancestral sacrifice (*omusango*): Relatives are obligated to attend the various cleansing rites resulting from real or imagined ritual dangers. Absence of a clan relative renders the offering ineffective and a clan member who has absented himself is blamed or suspected of having caused the ill fortune which has attacked the victim.

(vi) Peopling of Buluyia

The peopling of Luyialand is a phenomenon that occurred from late fifteenth century onward and continued beyond eighteenth century so that by midnineteenth century, all subnations, as we know them today, were settled in their present localities. Historical evidence, however, suggests that western Kenya was inhabited by a certain people during the Stone Age. The discovery of dimple-based pottery by Archdeacon Walter Owen, one of the early missionaries at Maseno CMS in 1920s at Yala suggests a thriving Sangoan industry dating back to prehistoric Stone Age, about ten thousand to a hundred thousand years ago (Were 1967: 57). But who exactly Sangoans were is beyond the scope of this book. Suffice it to say that Bantu arrival in the fifteenth century was preceded by Kalenjin tribes but the Luo followed much later. Other sources trace Luyia settlement to eleventh century at least going by death records of Wanga kings. The tribal founder, Nabongo Wanga, was born in 1050 and died 1140, according to records obtained at Nabongo Cultural Center, Matungu.

As late as the eighteenth century, the Bukusu displaced Bongomek (Abangoma) from Bungoma and banished them to Mt. Elgon where they settled among the Sabaot. The huge movement of people, war captives, and intertribal marriages caused a realignment of tribes with new clans created and others assimilated. This process of tribal or clanal realignment was both ways—some Bantu clans got assimilated into Nilotic tribes and vice versa. Some of the earliest arrivals are either extinct or exiguous. Among these are Abaongo,[104] Abakhwana, Abayengere, Abangoma, Abasiyemba, Abakuba, Abayeko, Ababubi, Abamalenge, Abaloba, Abalemesi, Ababiitsi, Abagosa, and Abanguili (Osogo 1966: 30). It is notable that most of these clans still exist either in Congo or Cameroon. Early arrivals that still have a dominant presence include Abasang'alo (in Bukusu, Kabras and Tachoni), Abakokho (Bukusu and Marama), Ababotso (Bunyala), and Abasonge or Abasonga (Bukusu, Tiriki, Kabras and Abanyala ba Ndombi).

In terms of language, Oluwanga is considered the standard Luyia perhaps because the Wanga neighbor Luyia subnations on the extreme end of the language pole, i.e., the Bukusu and Busia subnations. Geographically, Wanga is strategically located; the only polity at the center of the three main counties of Luyialand (Kakamega, Bungoma, and Busia). A linguistic analysis reveals the following four patterns of lexical adaptability and relationship:

- Wanga—Marama, Kisa, Tsotso, Isukha, and Idakho
- Bukusu—Tachoni, Kabras, Bunyala (Kakamega), and Gisu (Uganda)
- Maragoli—Tiriki, Bunyore
- Samia—Marachi, Bunyala (Busia), and Bukhayo

[104.] Abaongo are a cluster of clans that lived in an area known as Buongo which is sandwiched between River Nzoia and River Ndekwe, a tributary of Nzoia. The area to the east on the mouth of River Ndekwe is known as Bunambo where Abakhoone first settled after expelling autochthonous clans.

CHAPTER 5

Luyia Subnations and Clans

In the following section, I shall give a brief outline of major clans and list the various known clans per subnation indicating in brackets the clan which is found in more than one territorial polity or country. Although I mentioned in chapter 3 that there are at least four to five tribes in Uganda which qualify to be called Luyia, the scope of this book is limited to Kenyan Luyia with cursory references to Ugandan *Luyia*, especially the Samia and Banyala. Besides these two cross border groups, most Luyia subnations passed through Bunyoro, Buganda, and Busoga in Uganda before settling in their current locales. As a result, you will find clans in these places that are duplicitous in Buluyia. For example, the following clans in Bunyoro are also found among the Luyia and Luo—Abasonga (Bukusu, Abanyala ba Ndombi, and Tiriki) where they are variously called Abasonge, Basonge, or Abasonje and are also found in Congo;[105] Abarega (Wanga, Samia, and Bunyala) where they are variously known as Abaleka or Abaleke, and also in Congo (Baleka); Abachaki (Bunyala); Ababoro (Samia, Marachi, Bunyala), etc. What the reader ought to bear in mind is that clans existing in parallel polities assume the nomenclature of a particular subnation where they live. Hence Abatura and Abang'ale which are spread in more than six subnations are classified independently as belonging to the separate polities. Altogether, I have found 863 clans in Buluyia (discounting Songa) which compares favorably with Osogo's (1966) estimated 750.

1. Abakhayo (Khayo)

Table 9: Abakhayo clans (brackets indicate alternative spelling or where else clan members are found)

Abachabe	Abachimo (Abakimo)
Abadiru (Abamudiru)	Abaguri (Marachi)
Abakhamani	Abakangala (Samia, Bukhayo, Bunyala Kakamega, Kabras, Marachi, Bukusu, Uganda, Congo)
Abakhabi (Bukusu)	Abakhadonyi
Abakhauka	Abakhibe (Abashibe)
Abakholo (Kisa)	Abakhoone (Bukusu, Marama, Tachoni, Marachi, Abanyala, Samia, Abanyole Uganda)
Abamakunda	Abamenya (Abanyala)
Abamudiru (Abamutiru)	Abamukwe
Abamwaka (Marachi)	Abarunga (Wanga, Marachi)

---

105. We use Congo here to refer to two countries—the Democratic Republic of the Congo (formerly Zaire) and Republic of Congo (formerly Congo Brazzaville). The two countries are populated by people of similar ethnography and are only separated by River Congo.

Abatsohe (Abatsoye)

Abatura (Bukusu, Wanga, Tiriki, Isukha, Marachi)

Abafofoyo (Marachi, Samia, Ugenya)

Abadumbe

Abade (Samia, Bunyala, Uganda)

Ababere (Samia, Wanga, Haya, Marachi, Uganda)

Abakhero

Abakhala (Bunyala)

Abasubo (Marachi, Samia, Usonga, Busoga)

Abadepu

Abasikula

Abalakayi (Kisa)

Abakimo

Abatulu

Abakwete

Abameywa (Bukusu, Samia, Abanyala ba Ndombi, Tachoni, Uganda)

a. Brief migrational history

Abakhayo are one of the four Luyia subnations living in the wider Busia region. They are the most populous numbering 179,489 (Kenya Census 2009). The people are referred to as Abakhayo (Bakhayo);,their geographical location, Ebukhayo (Bukhayo), and their language, Olukhayo. They share linguistic, cultural, and historical value systems with Abamarachi, Abasamia, and Abanyala neighbors. Beginning with immigration, the clans of Abamenya, Abachimo, Abaguri,[106] and the Abachabe came from Busoga in Uganda where they still have clan relatives. Original Abakhayo are descendants of Khayo who led them from Egypt, according to their oral history (Osogo 1966: 105) although he did not reach the Promised Land. Unrelated clans settled among them are collectively known as Abakhayo without deep emotions attached as witnessed in Samia and Marama.

[106.] Abaguri perhaps derive their name from Akuru who is presumably the son of God from whom *abandu* (people) are descended (Osogo 1966: 17).

The major clans in Bukhayo are Abaguri, Abakhoone,[107] and Abakhabi. Abaguri (Abaguuri) are by far the dominant clan spreading their reach as far as Marachi. The clan has three main subclans—Abatsami, Abambomere, and Abakadia of which the latter constitutes the ruling lineage. Abakangala (also in Samia, Marachi, Bukusu, Kabras, Bunyala Kakamega, Uganda, and Congo) and Abamudiru were originally Gisu from Mount Elgon while Abakhadonyi came from Bunyala. On the other hand, Abakhabi are of Kalenjin origin and first lived at Sang'alo in present-day Bungoma. Due to clan warfare and cattle raids, they migrated together with Abamukunda (literally: those of the land also of Nandi origin) to settle in Bukhayo. Some of their relatives are found among the Bakiyabi of Bukusu. Abamenya (means immigrants) are also found among Abanyala while Abakhoone, the former dominant clan in Buluyia is now split across several polities (Bukusu, Tachoni, Marama, Marachi, Bunyala, Samia Bugwe and Abanyole of Uganda). Some Abakhoone clansmen fled to Mfangano Island where they live among Abasuba. Besides the ironsmith clan of Abamang'ali (Bang'ale), the other most widespread clan in Buluyia is Abatura (Abadura or Batura) who are found among six subnations—Abawanga, Babukusu, Abatiriki, Abisukha, Abamarachi, and Abakhayo.

Abatura and Abarunga (Kalenjin origin) first lived in Tiriki before fleeing to Wanga and onward to Bukhayo although Prof. Were says Abatura came from Bukhayo (Were 1967: 118). In fact some texts refer to Abatura as a Luyia subnation. This could be because they spawned a large number of clans including Abatsohe (Abatsoye), Abakhibe (Abashibe), Abamwaka, Abadiru (Abamudiru), Abasikula, Abalakayi, Abatulu,

---

[107] Abakhoone is a large clan that is dominant not only in Bukhayo but also in Bunyala (Busia). They used to be the dominant clan in Luyialand until they were defeated circa 1770 through trickery by smaller clans.

Abakwete, Abameywa, and Abamukwe. Most of these clans are autonomous and can intermarry. Abasikula, in turn, gave rise to two subclans—Abakhauka and Abakimo—which later became independent but continue to observe rules of exogamy between themselves as well as with the mother clan.

The clan of Abakholo is also found among Abashisa (Kisa) while Abafofoyo is the dominant clan in Marachi but a minority in both Bukhayo and Samia. While nearly all clans in western Buluyia did not practice circumcision as a rite of passage, the only exception was Abachabe (Barebe) and clans of Kalenjin origin which imported their culture.

Table 10: Bakhayo population distribution by administrative unit, surface area, and density

Admin Unit	Total	Area (sq km)	Density
Busia	205,982	681	481
Township	35,663	22.3	1,597
Mjini	26,493	7.7	3,434
Mayenje	9,170	14.6	628
Matayos	75,682	173.9	435
Nangoma	12,258	28.4	431
Muyafwa	3,881	8	487
Murende	3,877	11.3	342
Nagoma	4,500	9.1	494
Lwanya	8,753	18.3	478
Busende	3,116	7.7	407
Igero	3,147	5.6	559
Luliba	2,490	5	494
Bukhayo West	33,480	72.8	460
Bugegi	11,262	27.8	405
Mundika	9,966	23.4	426
Esikulu	12,252	21.6	568
Busibwabo	11,328	32.5	349

Nasira	4,542	12.5	364
Alungoli	3,145	7	449
Nakhakina	3,641	13	280
Nasewa	**9,863**	**21.8**	**452**
Mabunge	3,592	6.3	575
Buyama	2,881	7.4	391
Lunga	3,390	8.2	413
Nambale	**94,637**	**237.8**	**398**
Nambale Township	**32,293**	**68.7**	**470**
Nambale Township	15,793	33.6	469
Kisoko	8,937	21.7	412
Siekunya	7,563	13.3	568
Bukhayo East	**21,696**	**58.6**	**371**
Siringa	5,746	15	382
Madibo	5,782	12.4	465
Buyofu	3,922	11.5	341
Mungatsi	6,246	19.6	319
Bukhayo Central	**18,189**	**48**	**379**
Malanga	6,629	19.2	345
Sidende	7,579	18	421
Lwanyange	3,981	10.7	371
Bukhayo North	**10,954**	**27.5**	**398**
Lupida	5,128	14.3	359
Kapina	5,826	13.2	440
Walatsi	**11,505**	**35**	**329**
Musokoto	4,753	12.5	379
Khwirale	6,752	22.5	300

Adapted from Kenya Census 2009, *Kenya National Bureau of Statistics, Nairobi, August 2010.*

b. *Political leadership and notable clansmen*

Like other Luyia groups, Abakhayo are a patrilineal society with lineage derived exclusively from agnatic ancestors. Clan elders determined the political and social organization in Ebukhayo until this system was disrupted by colonial chiefs. With Kenyan independence in 1963, political leadership changed to direct representation in the Legislative Assembly in Nairobi. In the beginning, Abakhayo and Abamarachi shared one constituency known as Elgon South West with Abamarachi dominating the polity. The first MP was Christopher Crowther Makokha (1927-2011), Omukhayo, who lost the seat barely three years later in 1966 in a by-election triggered by his decampment to Jaramogi Odinga's Kenya People's Union (KPU). The beneficiary was Charles Eliseus Asiba (born 1935) on a KANU ticket, but he too lost the seat now renamed Busia East to Gerald F. Masbayi, Omumarachi, who won two terms (1969-74 and 1974-79).

In the Fourth Parliament, Dr. Mukasa Apollinary Mango, another Omumarachi won and he was to rule over both Abamarachi and Abakhayo until the constituency was renamed Nambale in 1987. The first MP in the newly named constituency was Philip Wanyama Masinde (Omukhayo from Abakhani sept) who rose to become minister for Labor and ruled Nambale for two terms until 1997 when Butula was hived off Nambale as a political riding for Abamarachi. He was replaced by Chrysanthus "Chris" Okemo (Omuguri clansman) in the Seventh Parliament during the 1997 elections who dominated the political landscape in Bukhayo since winning in 1997-2002, 2002-2007, and the Tenth Parliament (2007-2013). The highlight of Mr. Okemo's political career was when he served as finance minister, one of the choicest portfolios in executive governance. Reputedly one of the top five richest Luyia of his time, Okemo's low moment came in May 2011 when the UK principality of Jersey sought his extradition to face charges on money laundering. Okemo was charged alongside former Kenya Power and Lighting Company managing director, Samuel Kariuki Gichuru. Okemo was fell by former attorney general, Amos Sitswila Wako (Omukhabi; 1946-) in his attempt to become the first senator of Busia in a devolved government. His former constituency of Nambale was won by a former World Bank executive, John Bunyasi (Omuguri). Nambale was split to create an additional constituency called Matayos with inaugural competition for political office occurring during the 2013 General Elections. Matayos is one of eighty new constituencies created nationwide following Parliament's adoption of the Ligale Report in June 2011. The first Matayos MP following the 2013 general elections is educationist, Geoffrey Makokha Odanga.

Wako, the son of educationist and author, the late Daniel Wako, was Kenya's longest serving attorney general (1991-2011), a record for the volatile office. His brother Charles Wako was a senior civil servant whose last known posting was chairman of the Kenya Civil Aviation Authority. Other famous personalities in Ebukhayo include the late Dr. Yonah Otsyula (Omutura), one of the earliest indigenous doctors in Kenya famous for pioneering the establishment of Alupe Leprosy Research Hospital, Dennis Afande, the ex-diplomat; Peter Kubebea (Omukhabi), the hotelier; Ernest Bunyasi, the parastatal chief (KTDA); Martin Kunguru (Omukhoone), ex-Managing Director, NSSF; Kenneth Akide (Omuguri), chairman of Kenya Law Society; Brigadier Ken Dindi Okoki (Omuguri), armed forces chief legal officer and lawyer Akhavi Gevase, an East African Assembly member in Arusha, Tanzania.

Map 3: BAKHAYO

Map 3 Map of Bakhayo tribesmen showing major locations.

2. Abanyala (Banyala or Nyala)

Table 11: Banyala clans (brackets indicate alternative spelling or where else clan members are found)

Ababamba	Ababongo (Wanga, Samia)
Ababono	Ababoro (Marachi, Samia, Bunyoro)
Ababotso	Abadebo (Abadepu)
Abadiera	Abayineki
Abakhabala	Abakhabotsa (Bakhabocha)
Abakhala (Bukhayo)	Abakhoone (Bukusu, Tachoni, Marama, Bukhayo, Marachi, Samia Bugwe, Bunyole Uganda)
Abakhumatsi	Abakhunza
Abakhwanga	Abaleke (Samia, Wanga, Uganda)
Abalodo	Abalubanga

Abaluo	Abalwani (subclan of Haya, Tanzania)
Abamakhiya	Abamatseke
Abamenya (Bukhayo)	Abamulembo (Wanga, Samia, Bukusu, Marachi)
Abamuli (Bunyore, Tiriki, Kisa, Idakho, Luo)	Abamuripo
Abamwakwe	Abangineki
Abang'oma	Abanyekera
Abanyifwa	Abasinyama
Abayobo (Samia, Abanyala ba Ndombi)	Abasirwa
Abasitwoki	Abasora
Abayaya (Bukusu, Abanyala ba Ndombi)	Abaye (Bukusu, Bunyore, Congo)
Abapunyi (Marachi)	Abamaaba
Abawiri	Abamalunga
Abamayindi	Abamanzaba
Ababulwa	Abatsabwa
Abasibinga	Abade (Samia, Bukhayo, Samia Uganda)
Abakholo	Abagwang'a

a.   One people three nations

Abanyala (Manyala, Banyala) provide us with an insight into how clans split, migrated, and eventually became a subnation in their own right. They were originally one people living on the shores of Lake Victoria with large pockets also found in Uganda, but they are now largely exogamous. Due to various wars circa 1750-1770 in what is now Bunyala (Buongo) between invading Abakhoone and Abasamia, a large contingent of Abanyala fled to safety in Kakamega. A century later during the great famine of *Lumala* (destruction, circa 1840), more clans emigrated and in the recent past, the frequent flooding of River Nzoia caused even further migration.

In Kenya, Abanyala reside in two (some say three)[108] territorial units—Kakamega and Busia. The two subnations still share common linguistic and customary traits although the Olunyala spoken by Kakamega brethren is somewhat transliterated due to influence from neighboring Bukusu, Kabras, Isukha, and Tsotso tongues. To distinguish between the two groups, Abanyala technically refers to those in Buongo, Busia County, while those residing in Navakholo District are called Abanyala ba Ndombi, so named after a powerful chief who ruled over the chieftaincy during colonial era—Ndombi wa Namasia.[109] When referring to their language (Olunyala) one has to make a clear distinction and so is their physical territory (Ebunyala). Despite the spatial spread, Abanyala call each other *omwikho* (relative) and often use the term *olwikho* when referring to their complex kinship networks.

Although officially classified as Luyia, Abanyala of Busia (population 66,723 according to Kenya Census 2009) are halfway between Luo and Luyia in terms of cultural orientation. Starting from linguistics, most are bilingual, comfortable in both Olunyala and Olunyolo (Luo). Then there is the critical question of culture, especially circumcision rituals. While most Luyia subnations outside Busia practice circumcision as a rite of passage, Abanyala, like Luo didn't as a matter of custom. Instead, they removed six lower teeth like the Luo. Several names are also of Luo origin. They are bound with the Luo in a common geographical destiny. Living along Lake Victoria bays, their chief economic preoccupation is fishing. It is little wonder, Abanyala identify themselves with both cultures dipping in and out when it suits their circumstances. Long

---

[108]. Abakabras also consider themselves Abanyala, but their language and culture is influenced greatly by the neighboring Nandi (see p.240).

[109]. In other contexts they are also referred to as Abanyala ba Mayero, another powerful chief who preceded Ndombi and ruled over both Abanyala as well as southern Bukusu. The colonial government called them Kakalelwa, a Nandi nickname.

before the Luyia as a tribe was born (see p.144), many Abanyala had migrated to Mombasa in the 1930s; settling around Kongowea and Magongo suburbs on the mainland and working mainly at Kilindini harbor as porters.

Administratively, the colonial government first lumped Western and Nyanza under one polity—Kavirondo; later splitting it into South Kavirondo (Nyanza) and North Kavirondo (Western). When the pejorative Kavirondo was expunged, the colonials created South, Central, North and Elgon Nyanza. Samia location which grouped Abanyala, Abakhayo, Abamarachi and Abasamia under one administrative unit was first under Central Nyanza (predominantly Luo territory); hence Abanyala at the time regarded themselves Luo. At independence in 1963, North Nyanza became Kakamega District, while Elgon Nyanza was split into Bungoma and Busia districts. Samia location moved to Busia district in Western Province and it was at this point that Abanyala and Abasamia began to see themselves as more Luyia than Luo.

Map 4 shows the major administrative locations in
Bunyala, Busia County

b. Role of Abakhoone in clan realignment and migration

Abakhoone (Bakhoone) whose military power was legendary
first arrived in Bunyala circa AD 1500 from Bunyoro and found
Abalanda (Abatiera) and Abalusere. Their earliest known ancestor
is Namada, but it is his great-grandson, Khobi who is credited
with establishing Bakhoone settlement in Buluyia where they
carried out warfare against aboriginal clans. Abakhoone reign
of terror and conquest lasted at least two hundred years. To
counteract Abakhoone imperialism, the smaller clans led by
Abalwani (Bakhoyo and Bamakhanga subclans) hatched a plot in

which they tricked Abakhoone warriors into eating poisoned meat occasioning severe diarrhoea. Physically emaciated, Abakhoone suffered heavy defeat in the ensuing clan warfare meeting their Waterloo when Mufulu, their most vaunted warrior, was killed. The death of indefatigable Mufulu finally crashed what little resistance remained among Bakhoone ranks unleashing a wave of panic that saw clansmen flee in all manner of directions. Some fled to Butere, Bukusu, Bukhayo, Bugwe, and the islands of Mfangano, Rusinga, Sigulu and Lolwe in Lake Victoria. Those who hid in thickets and swamps were pursued and speared to death after cries of children and cackling of chickens gave them away. Among things Abakhoone blame for the fate which befell them are chickens. Consequently, surviving clansmen vowed not to eat *ingokho* (chicken), a favorite dish among the Luyia (Osogo 1966: 47).

Although vanquished and no longer a vaunted warrior class, Abakhoone are still a dominant clan in Bunyala alongside Abamulembo whose clan totem is a palm (*olukhindu*, variation: *lishindu*). The overall impact of Abakhoone on Luyia society is the realignment and movement of clans around tribal territory and beyond. Although pockets of Abanyala had settled in Kakamega directly from Uganda during the Teso wars, significant peopling of Navakholo and Kabras is a direct consequence of Abakhoone territorial expansionism which expelled many clans from western Bunyala in what came to be known as *Eshiatikho* (emigration).

Abakhoone were followed to Bunyala by Abamatseke, Abang'oma (Bongomek), Ababoro (also in Bunyoro, Samia and Marachi), Abamulembo, Abangineki, Abakhunza, and Abalubanga. The clans of Abamatseke, Abanyifwa, Abawiri, Abangineki, Abamalunga, Abapunyi, and Ababoro are of Luo origin. Alongside Abanyekera, Abamulembo originally came from Tiriki under the leadership of Masinde, their earliest known ancestor who is said to have been a brother or cousin of Wanga, the founder of Wanga Kingdom. Abamulembo also live in Ugenya, Siaya. Apparently "omumulembo" means one that is endlessly changing homes. Today, Abamulembo are the largest clan in Bunyala followed by Abakhoone, Abanyekera, and Abasinyama. Abamulembo arrived in Bunyala led by Saywa (Osogo 1966: 42), and although they were welcomed by ordinary villagers, the chief of Buongo location sensed danger. Saywa arrived during a period of famine and promised to bring rain from his *abakimba* (rain magicians) friends. Within days, it started raining to a huge relief of the people who immediately planted crops. That year, they had a bumper harvest and to reward their savior, they dethroned a helpless leader and ennobled Saywa as the new chief.

Saywa's descendants have dominated Bunyala polity ever since and are largely credited with organizing battles that finally vanquished the dreaded Abakhoone (Osogo 1966: 43). Some of the major subclans of Abamulembo include Abalwang'a, Abapondi, Abamukwambo, and Abagongo. Abanyekera originally lived in Bumogera in Buganda. Their earliest known ancestor is Ramogi whose grandson Murwa progenitated the subclans of Abasisalia, Abalianda, Abasibala, and Abamwoya.

The warlike Abasinyama are related to Abamurono of Wanga and are said to be descendants of Sirima, the father of Murono, the father of Wanga (not the founder of Wanga Empire). This Wanga left Butura to settle in Bunyala circa 1690 at a place called Munani where his descendants dominated local clans even renaming the local landmark Wanga Hill (old name Nanjuku named after Abayuku clan). They became powerful allies of Abaongo and drove away smaller clans into Samia, Ugenya, and beyond (Osogo 1966: 43). Later Abasinyama and Abakhoone warriors raided Luo territory of Alego and annexed Usonga and Kadenge. The social disruption occasioned by this war caused further clan migrations with the result that some clans fled to Bunyore, Kisa, Marama, and Idakho. Examples of these clans include Abamuli of Bunyore, Abamukhula of Marama, Abanyama, Abasakala, Abanyikhu, and Abamakambe of Idakho (Osogo 1966: 44).

c. Meaning of Abanyala

Abanyala have a reputation of being strong fighters, and every year they mark this custom by holding traditional wrestling (*amabwi*) festival. The fighting tradition stems from fierce battles waged against them by Abakhoone warriors who drove huge sections of Abanyala into exile to Kakamega and Bugwe in Uganda.

In fact some scholars have suggested that the name Abanyala derives from the Luyia word *khunyala* (we can), a war cry that eventually defeated Abakhoone and scattered them to four winds of the earth. Since then they are referred to as *abanyala* (those who can).[110] Clans driven away by Abakhoone include Abatecho, Abatabani, Abasagwa, Abasia,[111] Abamuswa, Abalemesi, Abasiriisi, Abakaabwe, Ababotso, Abamayingo, Ababiitsi, Abakhangabwe, Abamunyu, Abayabwe, Abakweri, and Abakhala. Although some of these clans settled in Kakamega, others found refuge in Wanga while others crossed back to Uganda and another section migrated to Luoland where they got assimilated (Abamuswa) and are generally known by a Luo rendition, Joumuswa. A subclan of Abamuswa remained in Bunyala and is known as Abauma. The clan of Abasirwa spawned fifteen subclans, some of which have become autonomous. These are Abadubusi, Abakoma, Abakhwaya, Abamwakala, Ababembwe, Abayofu, Abang'ang'a, Abaolo, Abadimba, Abakhokosi, Abayimini, Abakhatibo, Abakhulang'u, and Abalobokha.

[110.] Although it is tempting to assume the name Abanyala began with defeat of Abakhoone, it ought to be born in mind that Abanyala came from Uganda and significant numbers still live within Buganda polity in Bugerere, Kayunga District where they are called Abanyala.

[111.] The name Busia derives from Abasia (Abasya) said to be the earliest known aboriginals of this area before being expelled by Abakhoone. Remnants of this clan are today found among Abanyala ba Ndombi in Kakamega and Bugisu in Uganda.

d.   Ugandan Abanyala

In Uganda, Abanyala live in Kayunga District situated within the Buganda Kingdom's old county of Bugerere. In September 2009, their leader, Captain Baker Kimeze publicly petitioned Pres. Yoweri Museveni for autonomy from Buganda. Museveni's response was ambivalent, carefully calculated to please both sides. On one hand, he assured Baganda that Kayunga will not be allowed to break away and, on the other hand, ruled that Abanyala have a right to practice their culture. The issue of Abanyala autonomy remains potentially explosive politically with the Baganda taking the view that Museveni was behind the propping up of separatist chiefdoms in Buganda to weaken Kabaka (Buganda king). These tensions culminated in riots in Kampala at which at least ten people died after the Kabaka of Buganda, Ronald, Muwenda Mutebi II was blocked from visiting Kayunga in September 2009. Interestingly, when Martin Luther Nsibirwa, the most prominent Omunyala in history was the county chief of Bugerere in the 1920s later becoming the *Katikiro* (prime minister) of Buganda, Abanyala were proud to be a part of Buganda but today they claim to be marginalized as a cultural community and want autonomy. The Banyala and Baluli became part of Buganda in 1900, but failure to incorporate their clan systems into the kingdom's ethos remains a source of searing fulmination.

e.   Banyala legends

Fig tree legend

A girl from Abamakhiya clan called Nakhabuka was touted as the most beautiful girl in the land and her fame spread far and wide. She was the Banyala equivalent of Cleopatra whose ineffable beauty has beguiled societies for centuries. Abakhekhe of Samia heard about her fame and plotted to abduct her. They found her bathing at Burungasi near Makunda School on the banks of

River Nzoia. First they enticed her, but when she flatly rejected their enchantment, they shot her with an arrow and ran away. Bleeding profusely, she trudged home with the arrow wedged in her body. Just yards away from her homestead, she fell down and died. According to Abanyala mythology, a fig tree sprang up at every spot her blood dropped. In honor of her memory, an annual festival consisting of wrestling, dancing, and feasting is held in nearby Bukhwanga up to the present day. It is a calendar event that formerly lasted eight days during which other communal activities were suspended. Held just before the planting season, Nakhabuka cultural festival is a major rallying call to farmers to prepare their gardens in advance. Besides being a lasting memorial to the spirit of Nakhabuka, the festival is a symbol of unity among Abamakhiya clansmen in particular and Abanyala tribesmen in general. The centennial anniversary of the festival was held in August 2012 at Budalang'i grounds, Busia County.

Sumba festival

Sumba of Abakhabotsa clan is said to have performed miracles, and when he died, a religious festival consisting of dancing, wrestling, sacrifices, and feasting was observed annually on Sumba Island in Lake Victoria. Generations later a Nabakhabotsa (a girl from Sumba's clan) married a Mukhone boy. A few years after marriage, the spirit of Sumba told her that the festival should henceforth be organized by her offspring. That is how the Sumba festival was moved from the hands of Abakhabotsa to Abakhoone. The festival was a great occasion lasting several days and attracted people from as far away as Samia and Alego. It was equivalent to present-day Maragoli cultural festival held every year on December 26 and 27. It involved the whole community with people from across Bunyala contributing food and alcohol as a matter of custom. Although tributes were voluntary, there was a veiled ritual sanction to underscore its magico-religious importance. Abanyala believed that gods would withhold rain if people did not participate in this sacrifice and no one wanted to be blamed. Such belief systems caused conflict with early missionaries who forbade Christian converts from attending the festival leading to unwelcome cultural tensions between the new and old ways. To avoid mistakes early Christian evangelists made in Tiriki (see p.132), the missionaries learnt to coexist with traditional practices.

Table 12: Banyala population distribution by administrative units, surface area, and density

Admin Unit	Total	Area (sq km)	Density
Bunyala	**66,723**	**188.3**	**354**
Budalang'i	**66,723**	**188.3**	**354**
Bunyala West	**14,427**	**14.6**	**992**
Bukani	6,561	3	2,217
Siginga	3,531	2.5	1,400
Bukoma	4,335	9.1	478
Bunyala North	**13,015**	**27.3**	**477**
Bulemia	6,810	12	569
Sisenye	4,540	9.4	482
Mundere	1,665	5.9	282
Bunyala East	**14,743**	**41.9**	**352**
Budalang'i	5,608	15.9	354
Mudembi	4,113	13.4	307
Ruambwa	5,022	12.6	399
Bunyala Central	**10,381**	**47.7**	**218**
Magombe West	4,344	21.2	205
Magombe East	2,579	7.6	340
Magombe Central	3,438	18.9	183
Khajula	**7,776**	**20.1**	**387**
Mabinju Mabusi	3,225	7	462
Lugare	2,333	5.2	450
Rugunga	2,218	7.9	280

Bunyala South	6,381	36.8	173
Rukala	3,071	10.5	294
Ebulwani	1,211	11	110
Obaro	2,099	15.3	137

Adapted from Kenya Census 2009, *Kenya National Bureau of Statistics, Nairobi, August 2010.*

f.   Political leadership and notable clansmen

The earliest known political organization in Bunyala was centered on *omwami* (leader) of which Nasokho[112] is the earliest best known. In those days, a ruler was like a supreme being capable of offering solutions to all sorts of problems including natural calamities. He had to be either a rain magician (*omukimba*), a diviner (*omufumu*), or a herbalist. If not, like Wanga kings, *omwami* had to have these experts either as part of his courtiers or at his beck and call. Nasokho had none of these and was helpless when a massive drought enveloped his chieftaincy leading to starvation and death. Meanwhile, a Maasai rainmaker called Masiribayi told people to prepare land ready for planting, and within days, it rained. By public acclamation, he dethroned Nasokho and was declared the new *omwami* (Akong'a 1987: 72).

Early postindependence politics in Bunyala revolved around one man, James Nakhwanga Osogo, from the populous Abamulembo clan who straddled the political landscape in Bunyala like a colossus. Not only was he the first MP in 1963, he went on to capture the seat, first known as Ruambwa then Busia South for a record four consecutive terms (1963-69, 1969-74, 1974-79, and 1979-1983) rising to become minister for commerce and industry.

[112.]   According to Prof. Gideon Were, Nasokho was the leader of local inhabitants of Buyemba which was part of Abanyole territory in eastern Uganda. Besides Abayemba, other people who lived here included Babuya who were later joined by Abasonge (Were 1967: 93).

However, his victory in 1979 was short-lived. He lost an election petition filed by a new kid on the block, one Peter Habenga Okondo from Abamakhiya clan and in the ensuing by elections of 1980, Okondo stepped into Osogo's shoes. The flamboyant Okondo, the first African to enter big-time real estate business in Nairobi (Tyson and Habenga) was to prove more than equally sized to fit into Osogo's big shoes.

In 1988, the constituency was renamed Bunyala and naturally Okondo recaptured the new riding as the undisputed king of Bunyala politics. In 1997, it was renamed Budalang'i, name of the divisional headquarters to the chagrin of Abanyala chauvinists. At the height of the push for plural politics in Kenya in late 1980s and early 1990s, Okondo, now a labor minister in the Moi government, became a supercilious KANU[113] hawk *par excellence* and was prone to defending Moi's tyrannical government even where it was indefensible. He engaged in verbal clashes with leading human rights campaigners of the day such as Bishop John Henry Okulu (1929-1999) of Maseno Catholic Diocese, Bishop Alexander Kipsang Muge (1948-1990) of Eldoret and Reverend Timothy Njoya (born 1941) of Nairobi besides opposition politicians and civil society earning the label "loose tongue." In those days, politicians were given to zoning certain parts of the country as their fiefdoms and dictated who could come in and who couldn't. On his part Okondo declared Busia out of bounds for anyone opposed to KANU.

At the height of this game of political and moral brinkmanship, Bishop Muge announced a visit to Okondo's constituency but vintage Okondo warned him that if he dared go to Busia, he would not return alive. Muge defied Okondo's fiat and three days later travelled to Busia for a big rally but in a strange twist

---

[113.] KANU stands for Kenya National African Union. The party enjoyed authoritarian power in Kenya for forty years first under Mzee Jomo Kenyatta then Daniel arap Moi before being swept out of power in 2002 in plural elections.

of fate, he perished in a fatal road accident on his way back to Eldoret. Muge's death in 1990 sent shockwaves across the land and shocked even the "loose-tongued" Okondo who immediately resigned his ministerial portfolio never to open his mouth again. And although he won the multi party elections of 1992, Okondo died a lone, desolate man in 1996 and was quickly cremated by his English wife in another departure from the cultural norm (Bulimo 2013: 521). His old rival, James Osogo, briefly returned to national politics as an MP in the by elections that followed Okondo's death. In the meantime other fire eating politicians in Bunyala were sharpening knives and in the 1997 elections in Bunyala (now renamed Budalang'i); Osogo lost to Raphael Bwire Wanjala from the minority Abasitwoki clan of Sigulu Island. Wanjala won again in 2002 but lost to flamboyant youthful lawyer, Ababu Namwamba (Omumulembo) in 2007 who rose to full ministerial portfolio in the dying days of Raila-Kibaki Grand Coalition government. Namwamba retained his seat in the 2013 general elections.

In Nairobi's Westlands constituency, Fredrick Fidelis Gumo (Omumakhiya) dominated the polity since winning the by-election of 1994 following death of the incumbent, Amin Walji, a son of immigrant Indian railway collies. Since then Gumo (born 1946) won in three consecutive elections (1997-2002, 2002-2007, and 2007-2013) rising to become a full minister. Prior to his entry into Nairobi's political arena, Gumo had been mayor of Kitale and MP for Kitale East (now Cherengany). He beat the reverential Masinde Muliro in 1979 amid accusations of heavy rigging but although he "won" again in the snap elections of 1983, Muliro successfully petitioned the results. Gumo did not contest the Kitale East by-elections of 1984 and twice in 1988 and 1992 unsuccessfully tried to capture Kwanza and Bunyala ridings before shifting political base to Nairobi in 1994. Another *ex situ* Munyala politician is the late John Onukho Mutere[114] (Omumulembo clansman) who seized Bahati seat in Nairobi from Fred Omido (a Maragoli) during the first multiparty elections in 1992. A Munyala woman from Abamulembo clan, Prof. Christine Mango (wife of late Dr. Mukasa Mango of Marachi) served as MP for Butula in Marachi in 2002-2007. John Mugabe Were, born Omumulembo was adopted by a Bukusu family in Webuye. He won the Embakasi parliamentary seat in Nairobi in 2007 but was slain shortly afterward under circumstances that are yet to be fully investigated and concluded.

Other famous Abanyala include the late Dr. John Nikola Bwire Osogo (Omumulembo), author of *History of Baluyia* and brother to James Osogo; Prof. Calestous Juma (Omumulembo) of Harvard University and founder of Nairobi-based African Center for Technology Studies (ACTS); Magdalene Anyango Odundo (Namakhiya), the international ceramic artist; Peter Onalo (Omumakhiya), the lawyer; Charles Obinga, the accountant; Benedict Makhulo, a school principal and chairman of Port Victoria Fishing Society and Mahaga brothers (Ababongo), Fabian Mudongi, founder of Port Victoria and his brother, Dr. Tuzinde Mbaga.

3. Abanyala ba Ndombi

Table 13: Abanyala ba Ndombi clans (brackets indicate alternative spelling or where else clan members are found)

Abaafu (Bukusu)	Ababeenge
Abacharia (Bukusu, Tachoni)	Abachende
Abachimba	Abadabani

[114.] His daughter, Cynthia Mutere stood as a candidate in Budalang'i in 2007 but was unsuccessful in establishing a Mutere political dynasty.

Abaengere (Tachoni, Bukusu)

Abakembe (Bukusu)
Abakoye
Abakwangwachi (Bukusu, Marachi)
Abalechia
Abamakhuli (Bukusu, Tachoni)

Abamisoho
Abamugi
Abamuruba (Bukusu)

Abangira
Abasaacha
Abasaya (Bukusu)
Abasia (Gisu)
Abasiloli (Bunyore, Bukusu)
Abasonge (Bukusu, Kabras, Tiriki, Bunyoro, Congo)
Abasuu
Abaucha
Abaumwo
Abayima (Bukusu, Wanga)
Abayisa
Abayundo (Wanga, Bukusu)

Abakangala (Samia, Bukhayo, Bukusu, Kabras, Uganda, Marachi, Congo)
Abakhubichi
Abakutenga
Abalanda (Bukusu)

Abalindo
Abamani (Marama, Wanga, Kisa, Butsotso)
Abamuchuu
Abamukhongo (Bukusu)
Abameywa (Bukusu, Bukhayo, Tachoni, Samia, Uganda)
Abaokho
Abasakwa
Abaseenya (Bukusu)
Abasihondo (Bukusu)
Abasiukhu (Bukusu)
Abasumba

Abatecho (Tachoni, Bukusu)
Abauma (Bukusu)
Abayaya (Bukusu, Abanyala)
Abayirifuma (Tachoni, Bukusu)
Abayobo (Samia, Abanyala)

a.   Brief migrational history

Abanyala ba Ndombi number 89,722 (Kenya Census 2009) and reside in Navakholo District, Kakamega where they are mostly known by their one-time powerful colonial chief Ndombi wa Namusia. Ndombi was succeeded by his son Andrea then by Paulo Udoto, Mukopi, Wanjala, Barasa Ongeti, Matayo Oyalo, and Muterwa. Some texts refer to them variously as Abanyala ba Mayero (after Chief Mayero), Abanyala ba Navakholo or simply central Abanyala. Their earliest known history begins at a place called Buyemba in Uganda (present-day territory of Abanyole). Invasion by Teso (Wamia) from Soroti drove them south with some columns settling in Bunyala Buongo[115] and others moving to Kakamega. The Kakamega folks were soon joined by other clans driven from their land by aggressive Abakhoone. Certainly, this was the case with Abalanda, Abasia, Abatabani, and Abatecho, some of whom live in Bugwe, Uganda. Abasia are among early settlers in Bunyala, and it is from this clan that the name Busia (Ebusia) is derived.

Early anthropologists like Charles Hobley (Obilo) who also became the chief architect of colonial administration in Western suggested that Abanyala were a mix of Bantu and Teso clans. Although this view was upheld by scholars like Prof. Bethuel Ogot,[116] research by Prof. Gideon Were in 1960s established that the genealogy of Abanyala pointed to Bantu and Maasai or Nandi origin (Were 1967: 94). When they arrived in Navakholo, they displaced some Kabras clans who migrated northward to settle in what is today South Kabras.

During colonial rule Abanyala were known by the Nandi word, Kakalelwa but this term has since faded into obscurity. Although they share a common ancestry with Abanyala of Busia, their culture is influenced by the neighboring subnations of Kabras, Bukusu, and Batsotso. For instance, while the Busia brethren did not circumcise as a matter of custom, Abanyala ba Ndombi adopted circumcision rituals of their immediate neighbors and even have their own circumcision surgeons (*abashebi*, variation: *abasebi, bakhebi*). As far as clan dispersal is concerned, quite a number of septs are

---

[115.] Buongo was founded by Abaongo, one of the earliest clans to populate Luyialand, but which is now largely extinct but immortalized by the place bearing its name.

[116.] BA Ogot in: "Migration and Settlement among the Southern Luo Peoples," a PhD dissertation, University of London, 1965.

duplicated in various subnations with at least twenty in Bukusu alone (see table 13 p.215). Abakangala live in Bukhayo, Bukusu, Samia, Kabras, Marachi, Uganda and Congo while Abayobo are also settled among Abasamia. Despite a common ancestry, it is surprising that Abanyala groups share only a few clans principally Abayobo and Abayaya. The largest clan is Abayirifuma which is also found among the Tachoni while Abasiloli are also in Bunyore. Abayirifuma along with Abakwangwachi (also in Bukusu and Marachi) are products of forced marriages between Bukusu women who had sought refuge in Bunyala following invasion of their Buyemba territory by the Teso. The refugees were rescued by Mukite wa Nameme's warriors who brought them to settle in their current abode (Were 1967: 136).

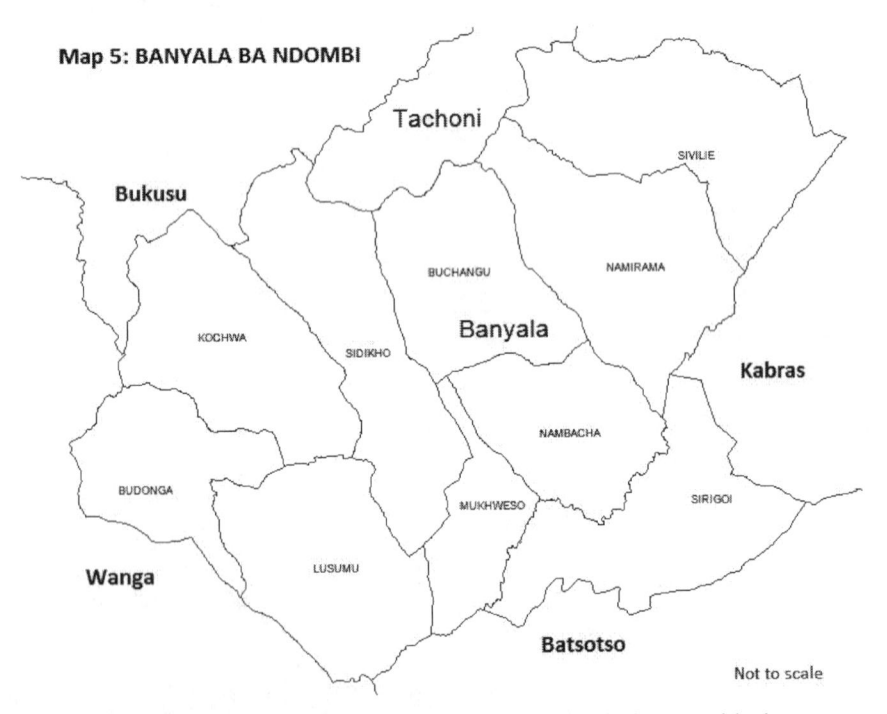

Abanyala ba Ndombi who live predominantly in Navakholo District, Kakamega County are an offshoot of Abanyala of Busia. Map 5 shows the major administrative locations.

Dr. John Osogo, however, traces the origin of Abayirifuma to Abakwabi (Uasin Gishu Maasai) specifically to a man called Masiribayi (Osogo 1966: 90). It was Masiribayi's son, Mayero who led Abanyala from Busia to settle in Kakamega—at first in Butsotso but eventually at Navakholo. That is why they are sometimes referred to as Abanyala ba Mayero. Apart from Abayirifuma, other clans that came from western Bunyala include Abatecho, Abalanda, Abasumba, Abasakwa, Abaengere, Abamukhongo, Abauma, Abasia, Abamakhuli, Abatabani, (Debani) and Abamunje (Abamugi). Mayero was succeeded by Kisauli who in turn was succeeded by Tabasi Namasia, the father of Ndombi. However, the more popular name is Abanyala ba Ndombi, so named after Ndombi wa Namasia, a grandson of Mayero who led Abanyala resistance against British rule. He organized his people into an army and fled from Butsotso to Navakholo where they predominantly live today. He was named chief on recommendation of Nabongo Mumia and died in 1940 after an eventful reign.

Table 14: Abanyala ba Ndombi population distribution by administrative unit, surface area, and density

Admin Unit	Total	Area (sq km)	Density
Navakholo	89,722	175.1	512
West Bunyala	38,407	73.3	524
Budonga	6,460	13.4	483
Lusumu	12,090	19	637
Sidikho	9,237	20.9	443
Kochwa	10,620	20.1	529
East Bunyala	22,122	45	492
Sivilie	11,787	23	513
Namirama	10,335	22.1	469
Nambacha	29,193	56.8	514
Mukhweso	5,342	8	667

Sirigoi	8,342	18.5	451
Nambacha	6,065	13.7	442
Buchangu	9,444	16.6	569

Adapted from Kenya Census 2009, *Kenya National Bureau of Statistics, Nairobi, August 2010.*

b. Current political leadership and notable clansmen

With Kenya's independence in 1963, the power of colonial chiefs became secondary to that of elected representatives. The new political dispensation started with the constituency of Lurambi South (renamed Lurambi in 1988) which pitted Abanyala ba Ndombi and Abatsotso in a battle for political supremacy. And because the constituency incorporates Kakamega Town, the largest metropolis in Buluyia, it attracts a third force, the neighboring Isukha. So although the Batsotso and Abanyala are the dominant communities, they often have to court the Isukha who possess the swing vote. Abanyala have dominated the politics of Lurambi since independence. The first MP in 1963 was a Munyala, Jonathan Welangai Masinde, who lost in 1969 elections to a Mutsotso, Brown Tsuma (Omushiibo clansman).

In the 1974 elections, another Munyala, Shadrack K Okova, represented constituents in the third Parliament only to pass the mantle to another Munyala, Wasike Ndombi in 1979. Ndombi lost to a Mutsotso, late Reuben Otutu (Omushambishi clansman) in 1983 only for Ndombi to bounce back and reclaim Abanyala dominance in 1988. In the first postindependence multiparty elections of 1992, a Mutsotso, Reverend Javan Imbululi Ommani (Omukhonya) deposed Ndombi. But Abanyala were to regroup and reclaim the seat in 1997 courtesy of a medical doctor, Newton Wanjala Kulundu (died 2010). Kulundu won again in 2002 rising to become a minister for labor but was defeated by Athanas Manyala Keya (Omwisukha) in 2007 elections. In neighboring Lugari, a Munyala politician, Apili Sifuna Waomba Wawire (1955-2012), defeated the quintessential Tachoni political godfather, Burudi Nabwera, in the 1992 multiparty elections.

Due to intratribal rivalry in Lurambi, there is a strong feeling that the constituency needs to be split to separate the two subnations. During public hearings by the Independent Interim Boundaries Review Commission (IIBRC) in Kakamega, many people submitted that Lurambi should be split into three constituencies—Lurambi (Batsotso), Navakholo (Abanyala), and Eshieywe (Kakamega Town). In the end, the Ligale-led commission recommended one additional constituency, Navakholo, carved out of Lurambi. After initially disowning the committee's recommendations to create eighty new constituencies, Parliament finally adopted the Ligale report in June 2011 increasing Kenya's parliamentary ridings from 210 to 290 for the 2013 elections. Emmanuel Wafula was elected the first MP for Navakholo in the 2013 general elections while Keya lost Lurambi to agronomist, Raphael Otalo.

Besides politicos, other famous Abanyala ba Ndombi are Prof. Wanyama Kulundu, ex-principal of Kenya School of Law and a brother of the late MP, Newton Kulundu, Prof. Judith Ndombi Waudo of Kenyatta University; Mark Udoto, a civic leader; and Prof. Canute P. M. Khamala, the insect biologist and a pioneer founder of Department of Zoology, University of Nairobi.

4. Abanyole (Banyore)

Table 15: Banyore clans (brackets indicate alternative spelling or where else clan members are found)

Ab'biba	Abahando
Abakanga (Kisa)	Abakhaya
Abalako (Bukusu)	Abalonga

Abamang'ali (Samia, Butsotso, Kabras, Bukusu, Marachi, Tachoni)

Abamukunzi

Abamuli (Tiriki, Bunyala, Idakho, Luoland)

Abamutete (Tiriki)

Abamutsa

Abanangwe

Abasaama

Abasakami (Kano)

Abasiekwe

Abasikhale

Abasilatsi (Abasiratsi)

Abasiloli (Tachoni, Bukusu, Abanyala ba Ndombi)

Abasiralo

Abasubi (Abasyubi)

Abatongoi

Abatsulia

Abayangu (related to Abamasaba of Idakho)

Abbayi (Bukusu, Tiriki)

Aberanyi

a. Question of identity

Abanyole numbering 185,069 (Kenya Census 2009) are the fourth largest Luyia subnation after the Bukusu, Maragoli, and Wanga. They emigrated to Bunyore from Uganda leaving behind their clansmen Abanyole (Abanyuli) who live around Tororo, in eastern Uganda. Before settling in Bunyore, they wandered through Kadimo, Sakwa, Bondo, Akala, and Gem leaving behind pockets of Abanyole clansmen of which Jousere of Alego are best known. Geopolitically, Bunyore used to be a division under Kakamega district at independence in 1963. Then in 1990, Bunyore became part of a new district hived off Kakamega called Vihiga which grouped Avalogooli, Abatiriki, and Abanyole. Vihiga was further split in 2007 so that Bunyore now has its own district called Emuhaya. The name Emuhaya is somewhat controversial even a misnomer and inconsistent with Bunyore worldview. Although the constituency under which Abanyole are represented in Parliament is called Emuhaya, the name is in contention because Emuhaya was originally a village in Emmutete where the first colonial chief was coronated. Kima in Emmutete is the district headquarters but Luanda in Ebusikhale is the main urban center in Bunyore.

The main street in Luanda Town, one of the earliest
outposts of Indian settlements is the most urbanized part
of Bunyore, Vihiga County.

Today, Abanyole are scattered in various parts of Kenya with large settlements in Seme and Sagam in Luoland,[117] Lugari, and Busia. In reference to this dispersal, Abanyole say *khuhilanga olubambwa lwa Anyole musibala* (we are spreading Anyole's genes in the world). They also call themselves *Anyole lichina* (literally: Anyole stone) to emphasize that they are authentic rather than an immigrant tribe or clan (*abamenya*). Incidentally, the first place Abanyole ancestor settled was *maachina* (rocks) known variously as Bunyore Hills, Esia Nganyi (Nganyi's hill), Ebuhando Hills, or Emabungo (jungle).

[117.] Abanyole who have settled in Luoland include the Kasagam (Abasakami), Nyamwalo (Abalielo), Otombolio (Abatongoi), and Kachuka (Aberanyi).

b. Rain magicians

Among other things, Abanyole are nationally acclaimed as rain magicians with Abasiekwe clan running away with a lion's share of this credit. The art of rainmaking (*obukimba*) was bestowed to Nganyi family by a wandering Nandi woman rejected by Avalogooli, according to oral mythology (Bulimo 2013: 49). Despite majority of Abanyole being Christians, they still have faith in traditional rainmaking rituals and the occult. In his formative years as a Christian convert, former head of the Anglican Church in Kenya, Archbishop Festo Olang' (Omusakami), challenged this dichotomy by purposely breaching a ritual taboo. Against his parents' wishes, he went to the family sacrificial shrine (*olusambwa*) and touched the shrine rod which only sacrificial priests are allowed to. Neither him nor his family suffered any ritual consequences, but despite that, Archbishop Olang' admitted that it required "a strong faith in God and great courage to counter the power of the spirits of the dead" (Olumwullah 2002: 264).

Rainmaking is one of the attributes that gives Abanyole positive tribal identity as *abandu beifula* (people of rain). The art of traditional rainmaking rose to national prominence when during independence celebrations in 1963, Musungu Nganyi, the then chief *omukimba* (rainmaker), received a government invitation through Eric Khasakhala to stop rain in Nairobi so that it would not interfere with the historic events (Akong'a 1987: 81). Pres. Jomo Kenyatta, himself an anthropologist,[118] apparently believed in the power of traditional mystical crafts. When in the 1970s, it was clear the rains had failed and the country was facing starvation, Kenyatta invited Musungu Nganyi for consultations at Gatundu, his rural home in Kiambu, near Nairobi.

[118.] Kenyatta was the author of *Facing Mount Kenya*, an anthropological account of his people, the Agikuyu.

A Nganyi rainmaker demonstrating techniques of making rain.
The tradition of rainmaking gives Abanyole positive identity
and respect among other Luyia subnations. Photo: courtesy of
IDRC/DFID/Thomas Omondi.

Abanyole also have a negative identity as *abandu bomusala* (literally: people of the tree, where tree is *cannabis sativa*), so named because they smoke bhang in large quantities or *amajini ke Luanda* (genies of Luanda), so-called because they are perceived as urban thugs by other Luyia subnations. The Luo call them *jamwa* (strangers) while other Luyia groups perceive Abanyole as stubborn, a perception that is perhaps justified by the fact that some of the most feared gangs originated in Bunyore—Angola Msumbiji and Otoyo Mang'ang'a.

Within Bunyore, there is clan rivalry for supremacy as to who is a true blue-blooded Omunyole. Abamutete claim to be the quintessential Abanyole and call themselves *abangeleza* (English) and speak *olusungu* or *olufotifoti*. They call other Abanyole *Abapokoti* (Pokots) implying backward people and pride themselves as having brought *obulafu* (literally: light but means development) to Bunyore largely through their association with Church of God at Kima (Olumwullah 2002: 43). Because of rainmaking, Abasiekwe say they were the natural leaders of Abanyole until Abamutete played trickery on Munala, Nabongo Mumia's chosen representative in Bunyore. According to oral accounts, Munala from the Nganyi lineage was appointed by Mumia to represent him in Bunyore, but on the day of his coronation, Abamutete gave him so much alcohol that his investiture was a shambles. When Munala failed to turn up during the inauguration ceremony, Abamutete fished out a clansman, Otieno Andale, to complete their *coup de grace* (Olumwullah 2002: 53). Other oral accounts say Abasiekwe[119] are an immigrant clan (*abamenya*) from Bunyala (Kakamega) and hence cannot lay claim to leadership despite their pedigree credentials of *obukimba* (rainmaking).

c.   *Brief migrational history*
Abanyole cite Omwa as their earliest known ancestor. He was the father of Muhindira[120] who begat Anyole, the founder of the Abanyole. Anyole had several sons with different wives who later founded the various clans in Bunyore. According to oral history recorded by Prof. Osaak Olumwullah in 1992, sometime

---

[119.]   According to this account recorded by Prof. Osaak Olumwullah, Asieche, the clan founder came from Bunyala (Navakholo) and first settled at Emuhaya. Here he begat Nerungo who begat Amukhobu and Achetsi who begat Akanga, Abayi and Asiekwe, the progenitors of clans bearing their names (Olumwullah 2002: 53).

[120.]   Muhindira is also given as the father of Andimi who in turn begat Mulogoli, the tribal ancestor of Avalogooli. EE Barker in *A Short History of Nyanza (1958)* intimated that ancestors of Abanyole, Avalogooli and Abagusii (Kisii) were brothers but this view was dismissed by historian, Prof. Gideon Were (Were 1967: 73) as lacking any historical basis. Nevertheless, the three groups share significant lexical and cultural similarities.

around late fifteenth or early sixteenth century, a group of ten brothers arrived at a place in a valley near Kisumu and decided to split and explore the neighboring lands. One group, consisting of Muhindira, Muhando, Ngome, Musali, and Wekhomo came toward Bunyore Hills while Mugusi, Etende, Andimi, Ekongo, and Tarime went round the lake (*inyanza*). At Bunyore Hills, they received a hostile reception from Abarwa (Kalenjin) who lived in caves. In the ensuing battle, Musali was killed, and the rest retreated toward present-day Lela.

After restrategizing, they returned and smoked out Abarwa and those who escaped left behind a child whom the four brothers named Amaatsi or Amutsa (believed to be the progenitor of Abamutsa). Muhindira and Wekhomo moved farther west and settled at a place later named Wekhomo. Muhindira begat Mwenje who in turn begat Munyole who died while his wife was pregnant. She gave birth to a baby boy whom she named Anyole believed to be the progenitor of Abanyole. Anyole begat Amuli,[121] Amutete, and Asiratsi who may be referred to as *bene liloba* (owners of the land), which according to this oral account are the original clans of Abanyole (Olumwullah 2002: 49). However, these records contradict accounts chronicled by Prof. Gideon Were (1967) which posited that Muhindira was the father of Anyole who begat Amutete, Asikhale, Asiratsi, Amang'ali, Asiekwe, Atongoi, Asakami, Amuli, Mwiranyi, Amuhaya, Abayi, and Ahando. It is possible that the *bene liloba* came from Anyole's elder wife while the rest were begat by junior wives.

Although Abanyole in Uganda and Kenya share a common ancestry, they were not founded by the same ancestor, at least not directly. According to Dr. Osogo, the earliest known ancestor of both groups of Kenyan and Ugandan Abanyole is either Matiebo or

---

[121.] Other records say that Abamuli are descended from Maasai and related to Abashimuli of Idakho and Kisa and Abamuli of Bunyala (Busia).

Mwenge (Mwenje) from Bunyoro. Anyole, the founder of Abanyole (Abanyuli) of Uganda is a direct descendant of Matiebo or Mwenje but the founder of Abanyole in Kenya was a distant relative of the original Anyole of Uganda (Osogo 1966: 25). Both groups of Abanyole were originally part of a big clan known as Abenge descended from Mwenge (Mwenje) who lived in Bunyoro. The two groups separated at Ibanda with Ugandan Abanyole moving westward to settle in Bukedi District while the remaining group split into three groups formed by Aroonya's three sons—Mwenje (named after an earlier ancestor), Simuli, and Sakami and settled at Igoye and Kadenge.

Their cultural totem then was a water bird known as *namwenge* and a night owl. Mwenje's descendants continued to be called Abenge while Simuli and Sakami became Abamuli and Abasakami, respectively (Osogo 1966: 53). Further splits occurred and a section of Abamuli found their way to Bunyala while another went to Seme near Maseno. This group consisted of ten brothers and cousins, a mixture of Sakami's family and Mwenje's son, Anyole. It is this Anyole who is thought to be the progenitor of Abanyole of Kenya.

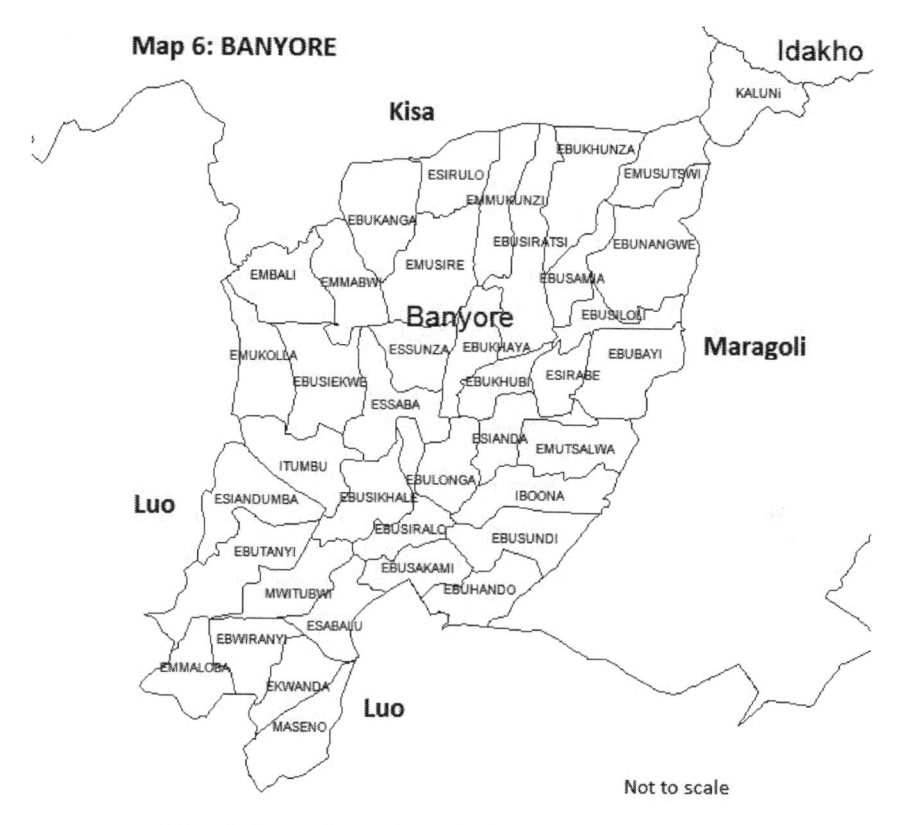

Map 6 shows the major administrative locations of
Bunyore in Vihiga County.

The largest clan is Abamutete (also found in Tiriki) followed
by Abatongoi[122] whose quintessential ruler was Sello Tuti. Under
Tuti's tutelage, Christianity and education flourished in Ebutongoi.
Abatongoi (Abatongoyi) are related to Abadongo of Samia and are
believed to have been left behind when the rest of Abasamia passed
through Bunyore to settle in Busia. Other Samia clans in Bunyore
besides Abatongoi and Aberanyi include Abbayi, Abakhaya and

[122.] There is a clan among the Haya of Tanzania known as Batongele which Dr.
John Osogo says exists (or existed) in Buluyia under the name Abatongole
(Osogo 1966: 24). Whether this has any relationship with Abatongoyi is
purely conjectural.

Abamukunzi, Abakhunza, Abasiloli (Osogo 1966: 55). The last four are collectively known as Abamang'ali and the territory which they occupy Ebusamia.

It was at Owekhomo in the village of Emuhaya[123] that the first colonial chief, Zakayo Sangolo, in East Bunyore was ordained. Not far from Owekhomo is the hamlet of Kima. It is here that the South African Compounds and Interior Mission (SACIM) first set up a Christian center in 1905 on land donated by Otieno Andale. Between 1906 and 1907, the mission established two more parishes (*ebikweng'u*) in Esibuye and Ebunangwe to act as buffer zones from the advancing army of Catholics. More *ebikweng'u* were established at Es'songolo, Essalwa, Ematsuli, and Mumboha between 1912 and 1927 with the largest being Emmutete, Ebutongoi, Emang'ali, Ebusiekwe, Ebbayi, Ebusiratsi, and Ebukhaya (Olumwullah 2002: 124).

In 1926, Kima was taken over by American evangelists from Anderson, Indiana, to become the Church of God headquarters in East Africa after SACIM ran into serious financial difficulties. The church was also instrumental in creating and expanding educational opportunities in Bunyore so that by 1937 it was running a total of seventy-eight schools.

[123.] Emuhaya is derived from the word *omuhaya*, a large tree under which coronation of the first chief in Bunyore took place (Alembi 2002: 80). It was under this tree that important communal gatherings took place.

Church of God headquarters in East Africa at Kima in
Bunyore. Founded by South African missionaries but
later taken over by Americans from Indiana, the church
has played a leading role in education in Bunyore.

The history of Abasakami is closely intertwined with the Luo
and in fact pockets of Abasakami clansmen live in Sagam, near
Kisumu, where they are known as Kasagam. As the railway line
approached Lolwe (Lake Victoria), C. W. Hobley, the colonial
administrator in Kakamega was transferred to Kisumu (Port
Florence) to establish the new headquarters of Nyanza Province.
In 1900 Hobley appointed a Luo chief, Odera Ulalo[124] to assist
him in this task. Among other things, Chief Ulalo built a huge
walled fort (*olukoba*) with eight gates at a site where present-day
Ebusakami Secondary School stands (Ogot 2006: 6). It was
called Luanda Kodera (Luanda of Odera) in recognition of Chief

---

[124.] Odera Ulalo was the equivalent of Nabongo Mumia of Buluyia. His jurisdiction
covered huge swathes of Luo territory (Luo *pinje*) including Kisumu, Sakwa,
Asembo, Gem, Uyoma, Imbo, and Seme.

Odera Ulalo's authority. The colonial government posted Nubian soldiers to protect the *olukoba* which had become an important cooling station on the caravan route to Uganda. The first shop at Ebusakami Trading Center was built by a man known as Obutundu, an Omusiratsi clansman who settled as *omumenya* (immigrant) among his mother's clan, Abasakami. He is immortalized by a hill in the neighborhood called *esikulu sio Obutundu* (Obutundu hill).

After independence, Ebusakami reverted to Buluyia, but Maseno (Emuseno) which now had a school and a mission hospital remained in Nyanza Province even though majority of inhabitants were and still are Abanyole (Abahando and Abalako). It remains an emotive subject in the relationship between the Luo and Luyia just like Kitale in Rift Valley Province also ignites passions between the Luyia (read Bukusu) and Kalenjin. Local elders petitioned the colonial government as early as the 1930s[125] seeking compensation after the Carter Land Commission of 1930 left Maseno in Nyanza. NNE Obando, the secretary of Abahando, wrote to the DC, North Nyanza on 18 April 1950 reminding him of the landlessness facing Abahando, Abamutsa, and Abasakami who at this point were languishing in the neighboring Esianganyi (hill of Nganyi; Luos called it Sanganyinya). Sixty years later in April 2010, Abahando made similar representations at IIBRC[126] chaired by former Vihiga MP, Andrew Ndooli Ligale.

---

125. In one of the correspondences retrieved from Kenya National Archives, the District Officer of North Kavirondo (Kakamega), acknowledged in a letter dated 3rd July 1934 that he thought the Abaluyia had a "reasonable claim to benefits arising out of the area from which their members have been moved." But when in 1950, Bunyore people tried farming at Maseno; they were slapped with trespass orders.

126. IIBRC mandate was to review district, divisional, and constituency boundaries in consultation with local people and make appropriate recommendations to the Kenyan government.

Abamang'ali are alien to Bunyore having emigrated here from Samia and spread as far as Bukusu, Kabras, Tachoni, and Butsotso. Their movement is partly due to clan realignment caused by Abakhoone invasion but also a result of innate intrepidity that drove them into various places in search of markets for iron implements of which they are universally acclaimed. In Bunyore they spawned a cluster of clans generally known as Abasamia which include Abasiloli, Abakhunza, and subclans of Abakube, Abanamale, and Abamuchina living in East Bunyore. In southwest Bunyore, live Aberanyi (from *okhwiranya*—tinsmithing) said to be another offshoot of Abamang'ali (from original Abang'aale clan).

Abamuli are descended from a Maasai ancestor, whose wife founded the Abashimuli ruling clan of Idakho (Were & Wilson 1968: 6). The clan is also found among Abatiriki, Abidakho, Abashisa, Abanyala, and Seme in Luoland. A long time ago, Abamuli used to eat *amasimba* (mongoose) in one of the culinary peculiarities also found among some Isukha clans who fed on monkeys (*amakhondo*). Abayangu are related to Abamasaba of Idakho while the clans of Ababayi and Abalako are also found in Bukusu (Babayi and Balako). Ababayi split from the rest of Babukusu as they fled from Iteso invasion in Ebwayi (Amukura) with some settling in Bunyore while others moved on to Tiriki. Other bands of Babukusu settled in Maragoli, Tiriki, Kisa, and Isukha where they were among the earliest Bantu settlers. The Baye or Babaye clan in Congo is thought to be a remnant of Luyia Bantu migration through central Africa. In Buluyia, this clan is probably the same as Abaye or Ababayi of Bunyore and Bukusu (Babayi). The name is derived from *okhwaya* (herd cattle) because these people were great pastoralists.

Abasikhale are known for being industrious and business minded due to their proximity to Luanda, the most urbanized center in Bunyore. Most are petty traders at Luanda market which they share with the neighboring Luo from Siaya. Luanda (means rock) is strategically located on the main Kisumu-Busia Road and intersects with a major road leading into Siaya Kogelo, Pres. Barrack Obama's ancestral homeland. Coupled with a railway station on the Kisumu-Butere line, Luanda attracts heavy traffic of traders and tourists. It is also one of the earliest settlements of Indian traders who have lived here for at least four generations; they even have their own crematorium at Mulukhoro, Itumbu, sublocation.[127]

The clan of Abasubi (Abasyubi) is perhaps the most spatially distributed across Bunyore and is said to be an offshoot of another wandering clan, Abamuli (Osogo 1966: 55). From their original home at Mundichiri, Abasubi are nestled in little islands at Essaba and Luanda between the territory of Abasikhale and Abasakami. They are famed for odd jobbing including being hired as *abayabili* (grave diggers) because, for ritual reasons, clansmen cannot bury someone who died under certain circumstances, e.g., committed suicide, was struck by lightning, etc. (Bulimo 2013: 484). The clan of Abasaama lives as *abamenya* (immigrants) among Abatongoi neighboring Abakhaya. Their original home was Emmutete and do not observe rules of exogamy with either Abatongoi or Abakhaya. They even have their own church and during competition for political office between the dominant Bunyore clans of Abamutete and Abatongoi, Abasaama always vote for an Ommutete candidate. Also living as *abamenya* among Abamutete is little known Abahingu who besides Emmutete, also reside at Emanyinya (Ebutongoi), Ekwanda, Esirabe, and in Bukoba, Tanzania. Another clan that is spread across Bunyore is Ab'biba whose descendants are found at Emmuli, Ebukhaya, and Ebulonga among other parts of East Bunyore. Ab'biba live at Esiandumba as *abarende*

[127.] The first Indian *duka* (shop) was established at Kakamega in 1903, and by 1938, there were twelve Indian centers across Buluyia including Kimilili in Bungoma, Lunyerere in Maragoli, Butere in Marama, Nambale in Bukhayo, Sio Port in Samia, Mumias in Wanga, Luanda, and Mwichio in Bunyore, etc.

(neighbors) as opposed to *abamenya* (immigrants) and are said to be an offshoot of Abamuli.

Table 16: Banyore population distribution by administrative unit, surface area, and density

Admin Unit	Total	Area (sq km)	Density
Bunyore	185,069	173.5	1,067
Emuhaya Division	76,394	74.1	1,031
East Bunyore	17,427	16.2	1,079
Ebubayi	5,503	5.6	988
Emutsalwa	3,886	4.4	893
Esianda	5,097	4	1,283
Esirabe	2,941	2.3	1,303
North Bunyore	20,256	20.1	1,007
Ebukhaya	3,920	3	1,290
Ebusubi	2,498	2.6	951
Ebulonga	3,121	3.4	918
Ebusiratsi	6,834	7.2	952
Em'mukunzi	3,883	3.9	1,004
North East Bunyore	23,157	24.4	951
Ebukhunza	5,578	6.1	914
Ebunangwe	7,371	8.2	896
Ebusama	3,409	2.7	1,251
Ebusiloli	3,523	3	1,163
Emusutswi	3,276	4.3	766
Wekhomo	15,554	13.4	1,157
Ebuhando	4,351	3.9	1,119
Ebusundi	5,842	5.1	1,138
Iboona	5,361	4.4	1,213
Luanda Division	108,675	99.4	1,093
Central Bunyore	27,551	30.3	910
Ebukanga	3,913	4.9	803
Em'mabwi	4,125	4.5	919
Emusire	6,937	7.2	996

Esirulo	3,424	4.7	731
Es'saba	5,705	5.3	1,079
Es'sunza	3,447	3.7	920
South Bunyore	**22,327**	**20.6**	**1,086**
Ebusakami	5,565	3.1	1,788
Ekwanda	4,695	3.6	1,308
Em'maloba	1,785	4.2	422
Esabalu	5,262	4.1	1,287
Maseno	5,020	5.5	906
South West Bunyore	**20,592**	**20.5**	**1,006**
Ebutanyi	6,144	7.4	831
Ebwiranyi	3,232	3.3	985
Esiandumba	6,560	5.2	1,272
Mwitubwi	4,656	4.6	1,004
West Bunyore	**38,205**	**28.1**	**1,359**
Ebusiekwe	7,327	6.1	1,195
Ebusikhale	9,680	4.4	2,179
Ebusiralo	4,723	3.4	1,387
Embali	4,643	4.9	947
Em'mukola	4,331	4.8	951
Itumbu	7,301	4.5	1,639

Adapted from Kenya Census 2009, *Kenya National Bureau of Statistics, Nairobi, August 2010.*

d.   *Most politicized subnation*

Clan authority was bestowed upon qualified individuals through a ritualized three-year process. However, with the advent of colonialism, chiefs and headmen became the center of political authority in Bunyore assisted by *amakuru* (equivalent to ward councillors) who looked after villages. Bunyore, then divided administratively into West and East Bunyore, had two chiefs. The first chief for East Bunyore was Zakayo Sangolo based at Kima, Emuhaya, while West Bunyore had Nelson Komba based at Mulukhoro, three kilometers from Luanda Township. With independence, political authority shifted to direct representation in the Legislative Assembly. The first MP in Bunyore (Emuhaya constituency) was Eric Edward Khasakhala, the son of Zakayo Kwendo (aka Daktari Kwendo). Khasakhala lost the 1969 elections to Wilson Mukuna from the Abatongoi clan who ruled for two terms (1969-74 and 1974-79). Khasakhala recaptured the seat of power in 1979 and again in 1983 but lost to trade unionist, Samuel Muhanji (Omutongoi), in the *mlolongo* (queuing) elections of 1988. Sadly Muhanji died in a road accident in 1990, and in the ensuing by election, Mukuna's son Kenneth Sande captured his father's former seat to establish a Mukuna political dynasty. In the first postindependence multiparty elections in 1992, Sande lost to former government printer, Sheldon Muchilwa (died May 2010), from Abamutete clan. Muchilwa was reelected in the 1997 elections for a second term and rose to become an assistant minister.

However, the dominance of Abamutete and Abatongoi in Bunyore politics was broken in 2002 by a Mombasa lawyer, Kenneth Otiato Marende, from the minority Abasikhale clan. Marende won a second term in 2007 but vacated the seat after his election as Speaker of the National Assembly, the highest political office any Munyore has ever held. In the by-elections following Marende's ascendancy, Dr. Wilbur Khasilwa Ottichilo,[128] originally from Ebusiekwe but living as *omumenya* among Abatongoi, took the spoils. The 2007 elections in Emuhaya attracted a record twenty-eight candidates, gaining notoriety as the most politicized constituency in Kenya after Kitutu Masaba in Gusii which had thirty-three aspirants. Perhaps thanks to the crowded field, Abanyole will from 2013 have a second constituency (Luanda) following adoption of Ligale Report by Parliament in June 2011. Dr

---

[128.] Before becoming an MP, Ottichilo was a former director of the Regional Center for Services in Surveying, Mapping, and Remote Sensing, Nairobi and also worked as a wildlife ecologist with Kenya Wildlife Services.

Ottichilo retained his seat as Emuhaya MP while the lawyer, Chris Omulele (Omuli clansman) bagged the new riding of Luanda.

e. Notable clansmen

Besides political faces, other prominent personalities in Bunyore are Justice Uniter Kidula, the magistrate (Omusiratsi); Prof. Aggrey Amwayi of Maseno University; Ambassador Franklin Esipila; Reverend Byrum Makokha (Ommutete), head of Church of God in East Africa; Prof. Aggrey Sindabi of Egerton University; Shem Tube, the musician (Omusiratsi); Kwendo Opanga (Omwiranyi), the journalist; late Hezekiah Ang'ana (Omusikhale), the footballer; late Mbalanya Omwakwe (Omusikhale), a Luanda businessman; late Javan Okwayo (Omusikhale), pastor and businessman; late Wilson Alinyo (Omuli), businessman; late Joel Mukoya (Omusiekwe), businessman; late Prof. Reuben Olembo (Ommutete), the academic; Prof. Norah Olembo (scientist); late William Melchizadek Oketch, the first black headmaster of Maseno High School (Omutongoi); late Elizabeth Semo Masiga (Omusiekwe), the permanent secretary; late Gilbert Makanga (Omusikhale), businessman; late Captain Willy Marende (Omusikhale), the Kenya airforce pilot who flew the 1982 coup plotter Hezekiah Ochuka to Tanzania; Tom Alwaka (Ommutete), the publisher; Prof. Joshua Akong'a (Omub'biba) from Esiandumba, the academic and the late academic cum entrepreneur, Dr. Ezekiel Alembi (Omwiranyi).

Others are late Williams Ngaah, the FIFA referee (Omusakami); first African archbishop of Church of the Province of Kenya, late Festo Habakkuk Olang' (Omusakami); Simeon Anabwani, former director of broadcasting, his brother Prof. Gabriel Anabwani (Abamang'ali) from Kilingili; Kenneth Opala, the journalist (Omub'bayi); Mary Akatsa (Omusiralo), the evangelist; Prof. Florida Amakobe Karani (Omukhaya); late Pastor Bernard Amayamu (Omukhaya); Davies Oyiela, the footballer (Omusiekwe);

the late Shem Chimoto (Omusikhale) associated with nurturing footballers; and his son Arthur Okwemba, a national team player.

5. Abakabras (Kabras)

Table 17: Kabras clans (brackets indicate alternative spelling or where else clan members are found)

Abachuna	Abakhusia
Abaluu	Abamachina (Marama, Bukusu, Tachoni)
Abamuchi	Abamutsembi
Abamuwande	Abashuu
Abasonje	Abatobo
Abatsikha	Abamutamia
Abatsetsi	Abamakangala (Samia, Tachoni)
Abasoko	Abatali
Abamululi	Abanzasi
Abamutsembi	Abamukhuyu
Abasang'alo (Bukusu, Tachoni)	Abashikusi
Abashibika	Abang'aale (Bunyore, Bukusu, Tachoni, Butsotso, Samia, Marachi)
Abamwambwa	

a. Abakabras are Abanyala

Abakabras live at a place eponymously called Kabras, just outside Kakamega on the way to Webuye. They are referred to variously as Abakabarasi, Abalasi, or Abakabras originally derived from the Nandi word, *Kapras*. An individual is referred to as Omulasi or Omukabarasi. Most of the recorded information about them is courtesy of Prof. Gideon Were (1967) and Dr. John Osogo (1966). During Prof. Were's research in the 1960s, he spoke to Matayo Shirenje, the community's chief spokesman at the time who traced their earliest known ancestor to Munyala whether that is a real or mythical person is subject to conjecture. According to Prof. Were, the original Abakabras lived in the area around Navakholo Forest long before the arrival of Abanyala who had split from their brethren in Busia. But according to Dr. Osogo, Abakabras consider themselves Abanyala and even fought over the name with Abanyala ba Ndombi.

The polities now occupied by the Kabras and Abanyala ba Ndombi used to be called Bunyala. It took the intervention of an administration mediator to judge who should retain the name Abanyala (Osogo 1966: 93). Under an agreed formula, the administrator gathered representatives from both sides and gave them a test in Olunyala. The Kabras mixed their version with some Swahili and Nandi words having been influenced by or intermarried with the Nandi whom they neighbor. The administrator ruled that Abanyala ba Ndombi would retain the name Abanyala while the Kabras would keep the Nandi name Kapras which later became Kabras or Kabarasi. Although some clans are from western Bunyala, the Kabras have a significant number of Nandi clans which used to circumcize girls.

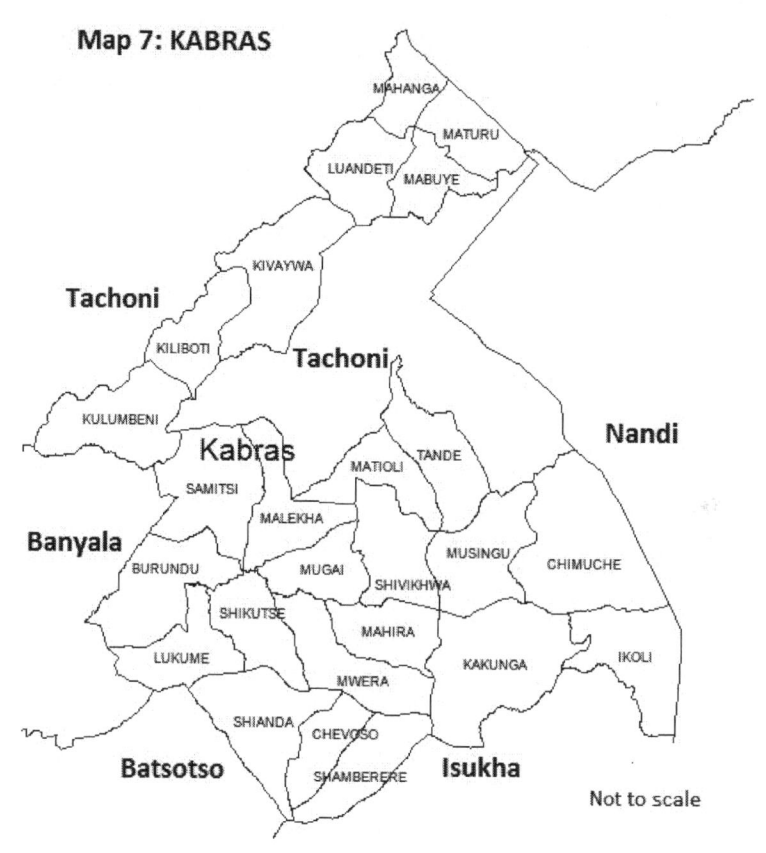

Map 7 shows the major administrative locations in
Kabras, Kakamega County.

The clan of Abakhusia originally lived in Lurambi, an offshoot
of Abanyala who migrated from Busia in 1700s. The majority of
immigrating Abanyala, however, settled to the east of Butsotso at a
place called Navakholo. Although pockets of Abakabarasi remain
in Butsotso, the majority live in South Kabras while Abatachoni
occupy North Kabras. The earliest Abakabarasi seem to have come
from Ankole in Uganda or Congo, presumably related to Bahima
who established the ancient kingdom in Wanga. Between 1679 and
1706, columns of Gisu immigrants arrived from Mbale and joined
Abakhusia in South Kabras. Abakabarasi are very closely related

to Abanyala ba Ndombi, Tachoni, and Bukusu with some clans tracing lineage to Kalenjin ancestry. They are famous warriors who, during the colonial administration, formed the bulk of Luyia recruits into the police force and Kenya African Rifles (KAR) army. Some texts say the name Abalasi is derived from *okhulasa* (throw) so-called because they were sharpshooters in warfare and hunting expeditions. The largest clans are Abasonje and Abamachina. Abamakangala are spread across Tachoni and Samia while Abamachina (those who live on stony grounds) are also found in Marama, Bukusu and Tachoni.

Table 18: Kabras population distribution by administrative units, surface area, and density

Admin Unit	Total	Area (sq km)	Density
Kakamega North	**205, 166**	**427.4**	**480**
Kabras Central	**43,427**	**94.2**	**461**
Matioli	**12,214**	**28.5**	**428**
Tande	3,928	9.1	432
Mukavakava	3,230	7.2	451
Butali	3,647	9.2	397
Shipala	1,409	3.1	456
Mugai	**8,049**	**15.7**	**514**
Lukala	2,065	4.5	455
Musungu	2,530	5.5	460
Sundulo	3,454	5.6	613
Shirugu	**14,701**	**36.3**	**405**
Malekha	5,636	14.5	388
Samitsi	4,721	12.4	382
Sheywe	4,344	9.4	461
Township	**8,463**	**13.7**	**620**
Isanjiro	1,954	2.7	736
Shivikhwa	4,204	8.6	488
Malanga	2,305	2.4	966

Kabras South	**43,373**	**73.5**	**590**
Shianda	**28,164**	**43.9**	**641**
Shamberere	4,042	4	1,016
Shamoni	6,176	8.7	706
Sasala	4,978	10	497
Ifwetere	2,465	3.7	669
Lunyinya	4,997	7.8	639
Chevoso	5,506	9.7	568
Mahira	**15,209**	**29.6**	**514**
Muting'ong'o	2,643	5.8	455
Shilongo	5,174	8.9	583
Mwera	4,185	8.2	509
Mukhonje	3,207	6.7	480
Kabras East	**40,396**	**99.6**	**406**
Chesero	**22,659**	**49.6**	**457**
Ikoli	9,698	19	511
Lwanda	4,853	12.3	395
Fuvale	1,789	9.1	196
Kakunga	6,319	9.2	685
Chemuche	**17,737**	**50**	**355**
Musingu	1,706	4.8	354
Tumbeni	2,695	8	337
Masungutsa	1,197	3.2	376
Chimoroni	5,311	14.6	363
Lukhokho	2,804	8.2	341
Kimangeti	4,024	11.1	361
Kabras North[129]	**51,856**	**113.4**	**457**
Sirungai	**15,387**	**29.6**	**520**
Tombo	6,189	12.8	483
Shiandiche	3,617	5.5	655
Manda	5,581	11.2	497
Chegulo	**19,662**	**45.1**	**436**
Namushiya	4,482	12.5	359
Mahusi	4,921	12.1	406
Matsakha	4,553	9	507

Chebwai	5,706	11.5	494
Shivanga	**16,807**	**38.8**	**434**
Cheptuli	2,122	3.8	557
Muriola	5,078	14.6	347
Teresia	4,157	7.1	584
Fuvuye	5,450	13.2	412
Kabras West	**26,114**	**46.7**	**559**
Burundu	**10,247**	**20.1**	**510**
Burundu	3,014	6.2	484
Mutsuma	2,095	4.6	458
Sawawa	3,565	6.5	547
Shimuli	1,573	2.8	568
Lukume	**15,867**	**26.6**	**597**
Lukume	5,110	7.5	684
Shikutse	6,784	12.7	532
Lukala West	3,973	6.4	623

Adapted from Kenya Census 2009, *Kenya National Bureau of Statistics, Nairobi, August 2010.*

b. Political organization and notable clansmen

In the early colonial period, the Kabras were ruled by a Wanga chief, Shiundu Sakwa, but he was so unpopular local headmen refused to obey his authority. In 1915, Nabongo Mumia sent another agent known as Sunguti to replace the unpopular Sakwa, but even this did nothing to placate growing hostility to Wanga agents who had been posted across Buluyia. Peace only returned to Kabras after a local man, Mulupi was appointed. In modern politics, the Kabras are represented in Parliament through a constituency known as Malava created in 1988. Before that, it was called Lurambi North which they shared with Tachoni. At independence in 1963, Jonathan Welangai Masinde, a Munyala represented Abalasi in the Legislative Assembly and won again

---

[129.] Majority of people in North Kabras are Tachoni.

in 1974 losing to Joshua Mulanda Angatia in 1979. Angatia, a committed Quaker from Shamoni village, won again in 1983.

In 1988, the constituency was split into two and renamed Malava and a new constituency, Lugari created. Although Mr. Angatia was declared winner in the *mlolongo* (queuing) elections of 1988, he lost an election petition and in the ensuing by-election, Nathan Anaswa, a former headmaster of Musingu High School won. Angatia recaptured the seat in the 1992 elections and was appointed minister for health. In the 1997 elections, however, he lost to Soita Shitanda who recaptured the seat two times (2002-2007, 2007-2013) making him the most successful politician from Kabras. Mr. Shitanda capped his political career with appointment to a full ministerial position (housing). He lost his bid to become the first governor of Kakamega County to former Butere MP, Wycliffe Oparanya in the 2013 general elections. Shitanda was succeeded as Malava MP by newcomer, Moses Malulu. Meanwhile, Mr. Angatia. died in 2004 without material benefits that often accompany the political class in Kenya. Like Masinde Muliro in Bukusu, Angatia stayed true to his convictions on righteousness powered by unrelenting faith in Quakerism. These convictions were at odds with a corrupt KANU government in which he served.

Outside politics, perhaps Abakabras's most famous son is the late Jonathan Niva, the indomitable national team (Harambee Stars) footballer who also played for Abaluyia Football Club. He was called *Simba wa Kenya* (Lion of Kenya) in tribute to his razzle-dazzle dribbling skills on the soccer pitch. Other famous Abalasi include former chief justice, the late Zaccheaus Chesoni and his daughter, Atsango Chesoni, who as deputy chair of Committee of Experts played a leading role in drafting Kenya's new constitution. In July 2011, Ms. Chesoni was named executive director of Kenya Human Rights Commission. Abakabrasi are also represented in the judiciary by Justice John Mwera, a senior judge of the High Court. Another famous Omulasi from historical pages is Soita Libukana Samaramarami from Lwichi village who sat on Nabongo Mumia's Council and Tatuli Mbasu, proprietor of Shieywe Guest House in Kakamega. Others include Dr. Shikuku Musima Mulamula, the university don and Chemuku Wekesa, a research scientist at KEFRI from Burundu where Niva also hailed.

Meanwhile in neighboring Lugari, a settlement scheme populated by diverse Luyia groups, the first MP in 1988 was former ambassador, Burudi Nabwera, a Tachoni who rose to become minister for information and broadcasting. However, his political career was cut shot in the first post *uhuru* multiparty elections of 1992 when Apili Sifuna Waomba Wawire (1955-2012) deposed him. In 1997, former Youth for Kanu operative, Cyrus Jirongo (Omutiriki), took over only to lose in 2002 to a medical doctor, Enock Wamalwa Kibunguchy as KANU and Moi era apparatchiks were swept away from power by a whirlwind of democratic change. Mr. Jirongo, however, recaptured the seat in 2007 under his party, KADDU which he later abandoned to die a natural death. A new constituency, Likuyani, was hived off Lugari following Parliament's adoption of the Ligale Report in June 2011 that recommended creation of eighty new ridings countrywide. Dr Kibunguchy, the former MP for Lugari, captured the new Likuyani constituency.

6. Abashisa (Kisa)

Table 19: Kisa clans (brackets indicate alternative spelling or where else clan members are found)

Ababoli (Samia, Bukusu, Marachi, Congo)

Abachero (Wanga)

Abakambuli

Abakanga (Bunyore)

Abakhatse

Abakhobole (Butsotso, Gem)

Abakutenga

Abakwabi

Abalakayi (Bukhayo)

Abalukulu (Bukusu, Gisu)

Abamaholia

Abamanyulia (Marama, Butsotso)

Abamurono (Wanga, Marachi)

Abaruli (Isukha)

Abashibungo

Abashirandu

Abashirotsa (Marama)

Abawino

Abayonga (Maragoli, Isukha)

Abamani (Marama, Butsotso, Wanga, Abanyala ba Ndombi)

Abamatundu

Abamwiru

Abasamia (Tiriki)

Abashimuli (Idakho, Bunyore, Bunyala, Tiriki)

Abashirima (Butsotso, Tiriki)

Abatayi

Abayiri

b.   Mixed tribal heritage

If any Luyia subnation is congerious that has to be Kisa or Abashisa as they also call themselves. Here you find clans with Luyia, Kalenjin, Maasai, and Luo origins. Kisa is today populated with three clandom clusters—Abashisa, Abasamia, and Abashirotsa. Long before the immigrants arrived, they found Abamaholia, Abashirandu, and Abamatundu living here. Other arliest clans include Abalukulu (also in Bukusu and Gisu), Abayiri, Abakutenga, Abamwiru, and Abakhatse. These are the original clans, but legend has it that bands of roaming tribesmen sojourned in Kisa and were offered temporary hospitality by indigenes who sympathized (*babalolera eshisa*) with them. The newcomers were called Abashisa (those sympathized with), and it is believed this is how the subnation of Kisa evolved after they outgrew aborigines, according to oral mythology.

The main column of new immigrants which came from Idakho is an offshoot of Abashimuli founded by a Maasai called Kasamu (Kasamani), but the clan toponymy is matrilineal. It derives its name from Ashimuli, one of Kasamu's wives from Butsotso (see p.332) and includes subclans of Abamase and Abakhunzulu. Abashibungo are related to Abamuima of Wanga, the original founders of the ancient kingdom at Imanga while Abakanga (also in Bunyore) came from Tiriki and are cousins of Abashitsetse. The earliest known ancestor of Abakanga is Nasitsi. The dominant clan in Kisa is Abashirotsa whose earliest known ancestor is Ebaba and are an offshoot of Abakondi of Idakho (Osogo 1966: 87). Abakambuli who have produced a disproportionate number of luminaries and high achievers call each other mnemonically as Okambo, in tribute to their founding ancestor.

The clan with the largest number of people of Nandi ancestry is Abakhobole (also found in Butsotso and Gem). At first the Kisa were friends with Luo of Gem (Abakami), but when they discovered that Abakami were also fighting Abamarama, they decided to end this friendship and support the latter. In turn Abakami sought support from Luo of Alego and Kathomo and waged successful war against Abashisa driving them from huge chunks of Kisa territory. To regain lost grounds, Abashisa turned their fire on Abanyole, Abidakho, and Abatsotso. They succeeded in annexing Abanyole territories of Eshibinga, Munjiti, Kachombero, and Enanga and drove Abidakho from Emulunya, Eshiasuli, Ekonjero, Mundaha, Mwikalikha, and Mwisero, among other places. Abatsotso lost land at Khwisero, Eluhambi, Eshisango, Mulufu, and Mulububi.

Although Abashisa claim their earliest ancestor was Kasamani[130] (said to have been a Maasai or Nandi), the core clans in Kisa are descended from a man known as Muchitsa (Mukitsa)[131] who had four sons: Achero, Andayi, Okambo, and Muyonga. These sons became the founders of the various clans bearing their names. Interestingly, Muchitsa was a clan leader who came from Samia following Abuti, founder of Aberecheya clan in Marama. When Abuti left Samia, Muchitsa is said to have posed

---

[130] Abidakho and Abisukha also claim their ancestor was Kasamu said to have been either a Maasai or Nandi.

[131] Notice the phonological similarities between Muchitsa and Abashisa or Abakisa. Whether Muchitsa is the semieponymous founder of the subnation or whether the name evolved from an act of sympathy (*eshisa*) is conjectural.

as a workman and pleaded to join him as he was not comfortable living with his clansmen in Busia. One day, Abuti's wife discovered that Muchitsa was wearing ornaments symbolizing a status of *obunabongo* (kingship). Just as Wanga had pleaded with King Muhima of Imanga once his cover had been blown (see p.110), so also did Muchitsa plead for his safety and formally requested to be accorded the status of *omumenya* (immigrant). Abuti acquiesced and gave him seven days to travel back to Samia to bring his family for permanent settlement.

Map 8 shows the major administrative locations in Kisa,
Kakamega County.

Abuti kept a record of the seven days by counting a stick every day as the sun rose and set. This phenomenon made a permanent imprint among Aberecheya, and former MP for Butere, Hon. Martin Shikuku (1933-2012), frequently made references to it during parliamentary petitions. Just on the stroke of the hour, Muchitsa's drum was heard from afar signalling his return accompanied by livestock and his entire clan including his four sons: Muyonga, Andayi, Achero, Okambo, and a nephew, Andakayi. They settled at Shiateta (Buloma) and Lukunga (Ikokwa) but later moved farther to settle at Khusurusi (Shianda) where they met resistance from Omukhula (founder of Abamukhula of Marama) who plotted to kill them. Luckily, Omuseta who was also a resident of Khusurusi sympathized and revealed the plot to Abuti who arbitrated and passed judgment that saved Muchitsa's family. Still fearful of the intrigues and clan feuds, Muchitsa moved with his sons to settle elsewhere.

Okambo settled at Ebukambuli and became the founder of Abakambuli, Muyonga (Abayonga), Andayi (Abatayi), Achero (Abachero)[132] while Muchitsa's nephew Andakayi, founded Abalakayi. Although these clans were established several generations ago, up to today Omutayi, Omuyonga, and Omukambuli cannot intermarry; but Omuchero does not have to observe any rules of exogamy. According to Kisa legend, Omuchero sexually assaulted a clanswoman by which act he became ritually contaminated (*oluswa*). His brothers cursed and excommunicated him from clan polity, and from then on, Abachero were considered "enemies" whose girls could be married by any of the other clans.[133] They are referred to as *abaana bomukoko* (children of a married clanswoman) rather derogatively in a wide conspiracy to exclude them from leadership positions.

The commoners who accompanied Muchitsa out of Samia clustered into a clan known as Abasamia and grew so big some of them migrated to Tiriki. However, Abawino from East Kisa retained clan identity because like Abamang'ali (Abang'are), they were blacksmiths renowned for purveying sought after iron

---

[132] E. E. Barker in a *Short History of Nyanza (1958)* intimated that Abachero originally came from Alego, but this was later dismissed by Prof. Gideon Were (Were 1967: 71) as lacking any historical basis.

[133] Under Luyia marriage customs, one does not marry from friendly clans but *omusuku* (enemy). Early historians like Dr. John Osogo may not have been privy to this fact and assumed that Abachero were Luo or not related to Muchitsa by ancestry (Osogo 1966: 88).

implements like hoes, machetes, spears, and knives. And so also are Abaruli, another clan associated with blacksmithing spread across two villages—in Kisa West and Khumailo. Abaruli are also found in Isukha. Collectively, Abasamia is the largest clandom in Kisa but not the most dominant; these honors held by the ubiquitous Abashirotsa. Abashimuli joined them from Idakho with another band going to Bunyore and Tiriki where they are called Abamuli. A group of Abachero settled in Wanga, and one of their main duties in the kingdom was to carry out ritual killing of Wanga kings by strangulation (*okhumika*) then burying them. Because of this unusual ritual role, they were nicknamed Abamiki (Abamichi).

Abamanyulia who live in Kisa, Butsotso, and Marama are originally from Tororo in Uganda. They first settled at Chula Yimbo (Chulaimbo) or Kadimo then moved to Alego Boro before coming to Emanyulia via Gem where some Abamanyulia still live today. The most famous Omanyulia, the publisher and journalist, Barrack Okwaro Muluka traces his ancestry to at least seventeen generations.[134] Abamanyulia migrated from Kakira near Jinja about AD 1400 under a man called Muholi (Mukholi), father of Musoka (Musoga), father of Akwenda, father of Shitindo, father of Nyulia, father of Munyu, father of Nangofia, father of Namukunda, father of Omusinde, father of Tsuma, father of Mutsotso, father of Aswani, father of Okonji, father of Muluka, father of Maina, father of Barrack Okwaro Muluka, the genealogist.

Besides Abakhobole, other clans nesting in neighboring Butsotso include Abamani, Abamanyulia, Abachero, and Abashirima. Abamani (Jouman in Dholuo) originally came from Gem are also found in Wanga, Marama, Butsotso, and Bunyala (Navakholo) while Abayonga of Namasoli live in Isukha and Maragoli as well. Abamanyulia are also found in Marama as do Abashirotsa.

[134.] Article by Barrack Muluka in the *Standard* newspaper published on February 3, 2009.

Table 20: Kisa population distribution by administrative unit, surface area, and density

Admin Unit	Total	Area (sq km)	Density
Khwisero	102,635	145.6	705
Kisa Central	19,743	24.7	799
Wambulushe	10,519	13.3	792
Mundeku	4,451	5	899
Emutsasa	4,773	6.5	736
North Kisa	16,283	26.4	617
Mundobelwa	11,160	15.9	704
Mwikalikha	5,123	10.6	485
Mulwanda	5,242	7	747
Khusiku	5,382	6.1	889
Mushiangubu	6,334	7.4	859
Shirali	5,499	8.3	660
Kisa South	11,107	20	554
Emalindi	4,306	8.6	503
Eshibinga	4,149	6.5	638
Mundaha	2,652	5	534
Kisa East	11,815	16.9	700
Emasatsi	5,648	7.8	720
Emuruba	3,017	5.1	598
Munjiti	3,150	4	788
Kisa West	11,262	17.8	633
Dudi	2,872	3.8	765
Muhaka	5,252	7.9	663
Doho	3,138	6.1	512
Shirombe	9,968	10.9	911
Ebuhala	3,636	4	903
Ekomero	6,332	6.9	916

Adapted from Kenya Census 2009, *Kenya National Bureau of Statistics, Nairobi, August 2010.*

c. *Traditional and modern power structures*

Abashisa had a traditional form of government led by a supreme ruler known as *omwirwatsi* (adjudicator) who was responsible for the smooth running of his polity adjudicating on matters of war and peace and officiating at sacrificial offerings. His regalia consisted of a calfskin adorned with small bells with a leather belt decorated with cowrie shells slung across his neck and shoulder. A headdress embellished with feathers of whydah bird, a copper bracelet (*omukasa*), on his wrist, and a spear in his right hand completed his regalia. Unlike *nabongo* of Wanga, the office of *omwirwatsi* was not strictly hereditary although in most cases, the eldest son inherited the mantle. It was not associated with mystical powers in rainmaking, divination, or herbalism. He ruled in conjunction with a council of clan elders. When he died, he was buried in a sitting position with a drinking straw (*olutsheshe,* variation: *oluchekhe, lusekhe*) in his mouth and a pot placed on his head.

Administratively, Kisa was part of the larger Kakamega District until 1999 when Butere/Mumias District was created. Then in 2009, Khwisero District was established to cater specifically for Abashisa. Traditional *obwami* (leadership) gave way to direct representation in the Legislative Assembly at independence in 1963 when Abashisa were lumped with Abamarama under one constituency, Butere. However, Khwisero constituency was created in 1997 to cater specifically for Abashisa's political interests. Before that Abamarama (read Martin Shikuku) dominated politics of the two polities save for the Sixth Parliament in the 1988 *mlolongo* (queuing) elections in which Jesse Esikhati Opembe (Omumatundu) "won" but died a year later. The first MP for Khwisero was the late Harrison Aywa Odongo who lost in 2002 to Julius Odenyo Arungah (2002-07). Mr. Arungah (Omukambuli clansman) was ousted by a businessman, Evans Bulimo Akula (Omushirotsa), in the Tenth Parliamentary elections in 2007. So far no politician has emerged as the undisputed king of Kisa politics by virtue of winning successive elections. In the 2013 general elections, Benjamin Andola dethroned Akula.

d.   Notable Kisa clansmen

Outside the political sphere, Abashisa have distinguished themselves in other fields as well, not least in entertainment and academia. Former appellate judge, Justice Emmanuel Okello O'Kubasu's (Omumatundu), long career in the judiciary came to an abrupt end in April 2012 following a judicial purge. O'Kubasu's exit from the judiciary left Justice Aggrey Otsyula Muchelule as the seniormost judicial personality from Kisa. In the world of books, three names stand out, two of which share a surname but are not siblings. These are Prof. George Eshiwani (Omukambuli), former vice chancellor of Kenyatta University and Prof. Arthur Eshiwani, a board member of KCA[135] University in Nairobi. The other big names in academia are the historian, Prof. Eric Masinde Aseka of Kenyatta University and Dr. Dickson Makanji, the Japan-based academic and entrepreneur.

In entertainment, famous artists who achieved national fame include the comedian, late Peter Shicheyo Lukoye (popularly known as Tamaa bin Tamaa), musicians David Amunga (he of the *America to Africa* fame; born 1938) from Abakumbuli clan, legendary benga crooner, Wilson Omutere aka Sukuma bin Ongaro (Omukambuli, born 1945), and late George Mukabi. From the world of sports, Abashisa have produced two dashing footballers—Mickey Weche (Omuyonga) and John Shoto Lukoye, son of the late comedian, Peter Lukoye. In boxing, they boast of the Denmark-based professional boxer, Evans Ashira Oure.

[135.]   KCA stands for Kenya College of Accountancy, precursor to KCA University, a private institution of higher learning specializing in accountancy and business management.

In the media, you find Barrack Okwaro Muluka (Omanyulia), the publisher and journalist; the late Amboka Andere and former KTN news anchor, Esther Adongo Arunga (Omukambuli).[136] Another famous name is Francis Atwoli, the trade unionist (Omuchero); John Abuko, United Nations engineer; Dickson Katibi, former director, Kenya Airways; Weboko Inyundo, the engineer (Omuchero); John Liboyi, the IT specialist; the late Hezekiah Maloba Openda, the first black principal of the East African School of Aviation (1927-2005); Dr. Henry Wamwayi, the veterinary doctor; Engr. Protus Murunga (Omuruli); chairman of Kenya Rural Roads Authority and Moses Shiroko, a businessman. The mother of Ida Odinga (wife of prime minister, Raila Odinga), Rose Ayuya is from Khwisero. She was the first African trained nurse and the first indigenous woman to open a bank account in Kakamega in 1937. As I write this book, the account is still open, and at seventy-six years old, it is possibly one of the oldest active accounts in Kenya.

7. Abamarachi (Marachi)

Table 21: Marachi clans (brackets indicate alternative spelling or where else clan members are found)

Ababere (Wanga, Samia, Bukhayo, Uganda, Haya)	Ababule
Abafofoyo (Samia, Ugenya)	Abakolwe (Marama, Wanga)
Abakwera	Abamalele

[136.] KTN stands for Kenya Television Network. Esther Arunga was a favorite news anchor, but in February 2010, she resigned from the station in a cloud of controversy over her association with a religious sect known as Finger of God founded by saxophonist Joseph Hellon. She later married one of the sect's members, QuincyTimberlake.

Abamuchama (Abamutsama)

Abamulembo (Wanga, Bunyala and Samia, Bukusu)

Abamurono (Wanga, Kisa)

Abamutu

Abang'ayo

Abapwate

Abarano

Abasimalwa

Abasumia

Abatelia

Abatura (Tiriki, Isukha, Bukusu, Wanga, Bukhayo)

Abonwe (Samia, Wanga)

Abang'aale (Kabras, Samia, Bunyore, Tachoni, Bukusu, Butsotso)

Abasubo (Bukhayo, Usonga, Samia, Busoga)

Abakangala (Kabras, Samia, Bukusu, Bukhayo, Abanyala ba Ndombi, Uganda, Congo)

Ababirangu (Samia, Usonga)

Abasireku (Samia, Uganda)

Abakhoone (Bunyala, Samia Bugwe, Abanyole of Uganda, Bukusu, Tachoni, Bukhayo, Marama)

Abageri

Abapunyi (Bunyala)

Ababoro (Bunyoro, Samia, Bunyala)

Abaliba

Abamucheka

Abamayanga

Abarunga (Wanga, Bukhayo)

Abamwaka (Bukhayo)

Abamukowa (Marama)

Ababuka (Wanga, Tiriki)

Ababukachi

Abakwangachi (Bukusu, Abanyala ba Ndombi)

a. Early settlements

Marachi like other Luyia subnations is a patrilineal society with power revolving along a chain of clan headmen. The people are known as Abamarachi (Abamaraki) and their geophysical territory is Ebumaraki (nestled between Samia, Wanga, and Bukhayo) while their dialect is Olumaraki. The main trading centers are Butula, an eponym of the political constituency created in 1997 and Bumala. The Marachi are a cluster of clans that settled in the area from different directions including those from Nilotic Luo and Kalenjin.

They do not share a common ancestry as say Abanyole, Abawanga, Avalogooli, or Babukusu. Most clans, however, first lived in Bunyala Buongo near Lake Victoria but later moved to Ugenya. By around 1814, the Marachi started migrating south due to warfare with the Luo, and by 1841, they had all settled in their present location. Pockets of those left behind became assimilated into Luo. The tribal name derives from the Luo word *marach*, which means "bad ones" in reference to the constant tribal warfare waged against the Luo by people now clustered as Abamarachi. They prefer to be called Abamaraki, the extrapolated version which means growers in Oluluyia.

The largest clans are Abafofoyo and Abamulembo (also found in Wanga, Bunyala, Bukusu, Samia, and Ugenya). Abaguri who transcend borders with Bukhayo migrated to Marachi from Busoga first sojourning in Teso and Sirabale in Bukhayo before settling in their present abode. Abaguri, the ruling clan in Bukhayo are related to Abafofoyo, the aristocratic sept in Marachi.[137] Abafofoyo came from Bunyoro and lived in Buganda, Busoga, and Ugenya before settling in Butula. Founded by Nafoyo Mareba, Abafofoyo used to be called Abapokoyo (Babokoyo) when they lived in Busoga and spoke olupokoyo which was akin to Olunyoro (Osogo 1966: 106). Mareba established his rule among other clans and bequeathed leadership to his heirs. However, Abakwabi (Uasin Gishu Maasai) whom Mareba had engaged as soldiers turned against Mukamwanja, the chosen heir. Instead they imposed Musundi as chief, and in the ensuing civil war, some sons of Mareba fled to Samia and Ugenya. In Samia, they lived among Abakhekhe, and this is why Abafofoyo sometimes pass as one of Abakhekhe

---

[137] In Samia (Kenya and Uganda), the dominant family of Awori which has produced a vice president in Kenya (Moody Awori) and a presidential candidate in Uganda (Aggrey Awori) are Abafofoyo. Moody Awori even named one of his businesses Mareba Tiles in memory of the clan founder, Nafoyo Mareba.

cluster of clans. It is from this lineage that Canon Musungu Awori sprouted to raise his famous family of political rulers, scientists, and businessmen in Kenya and Uganda.

Abamulembo are also found among Abawanga, Babukusu, Samia, and Abanyala (Busia) while Abakolwe also live in Marama and Wanga and are descendants of Wanga's uncle, Mukolwe.[138] Abatura whose wings span six subnations are found among Abatiriki, Abisukha, Babukusu, Abawanga, and Abakhayo while Abamurono are originally from Wanga. Ababere also live in Samia, Wanga, Bugwe, and Bukhayo. Ababere, Abamalele, Abamutu, Ababule, Abamuchama, and Abang'ayo are of Kalenjin origin. Abang'ayo, in particular, trace their origin to Terik of Nyang'ori. Interestingly, Ababere are also found among the Haya of Tanzania who, like the Luyia, also claim Egyptian ancestry (Osogo 1966: 24).

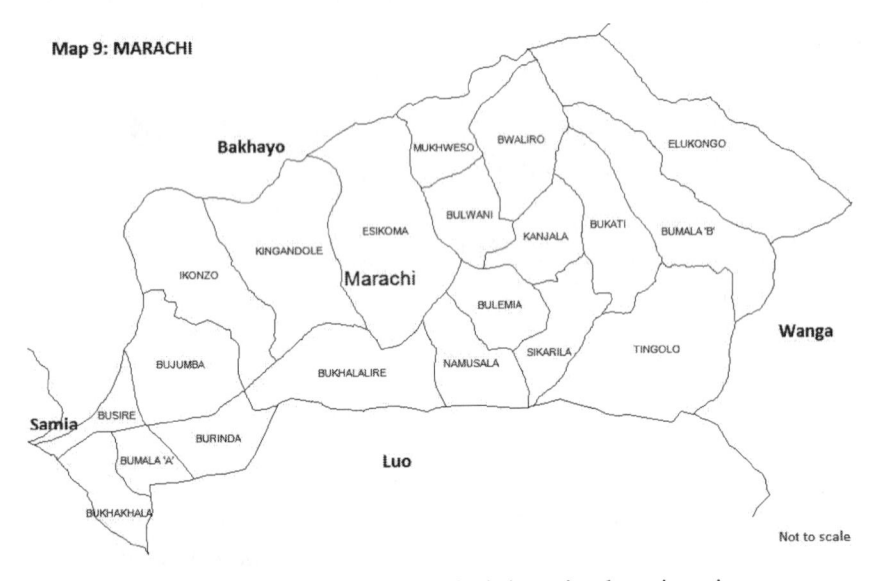

Map 9 shows the major administrative locations in
Marachi, Busia County.

---

138. Dr. John Osogo says Mukolwe, the clan founder was a Maragoli who settled among the Wanga (Osogo 1966: 72). It is instructive that Mukolwe is a popular name in Maragoli as well as Marama and Wanga.

In the nineteenth century, constant civil wars and raids from the Maasai, Kalenjin, and Teso forced Abamarachi to live in fortified villages (*tsingoba*, singular: *olukoba*), a custom they borrowed from the Tachoni, reputed as owners of most *tsingoba* in Luyialand including the famous Chetambe Fort in Webuye. Most of these forts Marachi and neighboring Ugenya Luo either inherited or annexed from the Tachoni, but with time, they learnt the art and started building their own. Abatura clansmen are said to have been masters of this craft. The Ugenya Luo invaded and took possession of some of these forts (Ogutu 1991: 77-96), which provided not just defence from invading armies but also played an important part in social engineering of the kinship system. Friendly clans laagered in the *tsingoba*, thus entrenching clan hegemony of the initial occupants.

Table 22: Marachi population distribution by administrative unit, surface area, and density

Admin Unit	Total	Area (sq km)	Density
Butula	**121,870**	**247.1**	**493**
Elukhari	**13,250**	**26.3**	**505**
Sikarira	4,896	7.8	628
Kanjala	2,747	6.9	396
Bukati	5,607	11.5	486
Marachi East	**31,669**	**68**	**466**
Tingolo	10,804	24.5	442
Bumala "B"	8,377	16.3	513
Elukongo	12,488	27.2	459
Elugulu	**18,654**	**42**	**445**
Bulemia	3,514	7	500
Emukhweso	4,230	8	531
Bwaliro	4,605	11.2	411
Bulwani	2,628	6.8	387
Namusala	3,677	9	409
Marachi Central	**30,066**	**58.1**	**518**

Esikoma	10,857	23.6	460
Bukhalalire	8,959	15.4	584
Kingandole	10,250	19.1	536
Bujumba	**18,840**	**37.7**	**500**
Bujumba	7,096	12.7	561
Ikonzo	4,623	8.6	540
Namwitsula	3,397	8.1	418
Burinda	3,724	8.4	445
Bumala	**9,391**	**15.1**	**620**
Bumala "A"	3,504	4.4	801
Busire	2,825	3.7	771
Bukhahala	3,062	7.1	431

Adapted from Kenya Census 2009, *Kenya National Bureau of Statistics, Nairobi, August 2010.*

b. *Political organization and notable clansmen*

Like other Luyia subnations, clan elders wielded power in Marachi society. With the advent of colonialism, this power was shared with colonial chiefs of whom Laurenti Ongoma was preeminent. However, after independence, the people elected their representatives directly by secret ballot. Abamarachi shared one constituency with Abakhayo (initially called Elgon Southwest then Busia East then Nambale) until 1997 when Butula was hived off Nambale to specifically serve political interests of Abamarachi leaving Nambale to Abakhayo. The first MP in 1963 was Christopher Crowther Makokha (1927-2011), Omukhayo, who lost the seat barely three years later in 1966 in a by-election triggered by his decampment to Jaramogi Odinga's Kenya People's Union (KPU). The beneficiary was Charles Eliseus Asiba (1966-69 and 1969-74) from Bukhayo. He was replaced by Gerald F Masibayi (Omumaraki) from the populous Abafofoyo clan in 1969 who also won a second term in 1974.

However, Abafofoyo stranglehold on Marachi/Bukhayo polity was cut shot in 1979, when a medical doctor, Mukasa Apollinary

Mango from Abonwe clan, won. Dr. Mango (died in 2000), who rose to become a minister for health ruled for two terms and when in 1988 it was renamed Nambale, Abamarachi lost their dominance with Philip Wanyama Masinde (Omukhayo), winning. Masinde won a second term in 1992 and was named minister for labor. However, in 1997, Butula was created specifically for Abamarachi and the first MP in the new constituency was Yekoyada Francis Omoto Masakhalia. He was appointed minister for energy and later finance, but in the multiparty elections of 2002, Dr. Mango's wife, Prof. Christine Abungu Mango (Omumulembo from Bunyala), recaptured the seat to create the Mango political dynasty.[139] In the event, Prof. Mango served one term losing to newcomer, Alfred Bwire Odhiambo in the Orange Revolution of 2007. In the 2013 general elections, the riding was won by Michael Aringo Onyura, a former Kenya Revenue Authority executive.

Besides politicians, other famous Abamarachi include Wilberforce "Maradona" Mulamba, the footballer; Prof. Nimrod Odundo Bwibo, the medical academic from Busiada village; Gabriel Mukele (Omufofoyo), the lawyer who served as vice chairman of the defunct Electoral Commission of Kenya; George Wesonga, the KNUT chairman; Dr. Chimareini Mango (late Mango's son), the chiropractor; Dominic Odipo, the journalist; Dr. Daniel A. Shikanda, the pharmacist cum footballer; Desterio Oyatsi, the lawyer; Prof. Josephat Awuor Odwako Mulimba, consultant orthopaedic; Henry Mukabi, the teacher; Casperi Ohande, the farmer and Dr. Samuel Vernanzius Obiero, the university lecturer. Others include Thomas Nobala and Yohana Koli credited with introducing the Anglican Church in Marachi.

[139.] Besides the Mango's, other political dynasties in Buluyia include Mudavadi and Akaranga in Maragoli, Khaniri and M'Maitsi in Tiriki, Wamalwa and Wetang'ula in Bukusu, Mukuna in Bunyore, Oyondi in Butere, and Awori in Samia (Kenya and Uganda).

8. Avalogooli (Maragoli)

Table 23: Maragoli clans (brackets indicate alternative spelling or where else clan members are found)

Avaanamiri
Avadegu
Avadirigi
Avagamuguywa
Avagezi
Avagimuhia
Avagiseve
Avagisiri
Avagivagi
Avagondu
Avagusui
Avaguva
Avahevi
Avahomba
Avakihayu
Avakisui
Avakivembe
(Idakho—Abashibembe)
Avakizira
Avakoyani
Avakulunya
Avalamula
Avalisungu (Idakho)
Avalogovo
Avaluga
Avalungusia
Avalwimbuli
Avama'avi
Avamagetsa

Avadamaywa
Avadidi
Avafunami
Avageyio
Avagihayo
Avagisemba
Avagisinde
Avagisunda
Avagonda
Avagumira
Avaguuga
Avaguya
Avahiahia
Avakadukire
Avakirima
Avakitagwa
Avakivuta

Avakizungu
Avakuli
Avakuvera
Avaliero
Avalitu
Avaludanya
Avalugiri
Avalwangala
Avam'mbaya
Avamadayi
Avamahovo

Avamalaha
Avamasana
Avamasanga
Avamaseero (Idakho)
Avamasingira
Avambaya
Avamboga
Avambulika
Avambunda
Avamenge
Avamigangu
Avamugetsi
Avamugoye
Avamuku
Avamwizande
Avandega
Avang'ang'a
Avangomba
Avanondi
Avanyama
Avarogovo
Avaruga
Avasaaki
Avasaali (Tiriki)
Avasacha
Avasagala (Tiriki, Idakho, Isukha, Bukusu, Luo)
Avasaina (Tiriki)
Avasalia
Avasanga (Idakho)
Avasaniaga (Bukusu, Tachoni, Tiriki)
Avasuba (Bukusu, Gisu, Suba, Tiriki)
Avasweta
Avateembuli
Avatembe
Avatiba
Avatongoli
Avavudiku
Avavurugi (Tiriki)
Avayonga (Kisa, Isukha, Bukusu)
Avayose
Avayuya
Avazalala
Avazuzu
Avigina
Avizende

a. Ancestral origins

Although Mulogoli is widely acknowledged as the tribal ancestor of Avalogooli, historians like Dr. John Osogo (1966) traced Maragoli genealogy to at least two generations before him.

Mulogoli is a progeny of Andimi[140] (circa 1500) whose ancestry is linked to Muhindira (circa 1470). Muhindira's father was called Omwa who is also cited as the father of Anyole, the eponymous progenitor of Abanyole subnation. But it is from Mulogoli the real story (both oral and documented) of Avalogooli begins. He had eight sons—two of them Ma'avi and Kirima by his elder wife and the other six by his young wife, Kaliyeza (Saali, Yonga,[141] Kizungu, Muku, Saniaga and Ng'ang'a). Ma'avi, Kirima, Saali, and Kizungu spawned the largest progeny and constitute what the Maragoli refer to as *zinyumba zinene* (big houses). The major clans under the Ma'avi cluster include: Avadidi; Avadiku; Avafunami; Avagihayu; Avagondu; Avaguva; Avaguya; Avaguya; Avakisui; Avakivuta; Avamalaha; Avamasana; Avamboga; Avamigangu; Avamugetsi; Avamuku; Avandega; Avang'ang'a; Avanondi; Avalogovo; Avasacha; Avasalia; Avasanga; Avatembe; Avatongoli and Avayonga. Under the Kirima cluster, we find clans such as Avalungusia; Avagamuguywa; Avamasingira; Avalugiri; Avizende; Avageyio; Avakuli; Avaludanya; Avalwangala; Avangomba; Avanyama; Avakuvela; Avakulunya; Avagisiri; Avasaaki, Avamaseero and Avatembuli while Saali boasts of Avakoyani; Avam'mbaya; Avamagetsa; Avasuva; Avasweta and Avazuzu. Finally, the Kizungu stable houses the following clanal septs: Avadegu; Avadidi; Avadirigi; Avagisemba; Avagiseve; Avagisunda; Avagumira; Avahomba; Avakihayu; Avakitagwa; Avakizira; Avaliero; Avamahovo; Avambulika; Avamulamula; Avamwizande; Avasagala; Avasaniaga; Avasuva and Avigina. However, according to Prof. Gideon Were (1967), Avasaniaga (also

---

140. Some sources say Andimi had three wives: Mwanzu the mother of Mulogoli; Amugovolie who had no children and Ndengu the mother of Mwenje.

141. Yonga's ancestry is somewhat uncertain or contradictory. Some oral sources say he was one of the sons of Mulogoli's younger wife while others say that his biological father was Ma'avi who, being the eldest son from his elder wife, inherited his "young mother" when Mulogoli died. In this sense Ma'avi doubled up as his half brother as well as his stepfather or father.

in Tachoni and Tiriki) were originally Babukusu who split from the mother tribe at some point in its migratory journeys. Other Maragoli clans which originated from Babukusu are Avamaseero (also in Idakho) and Avasaki.

One of the tragic chapters in the history of Maragoli was the murder of Kizungu by his brother Yonga. In the ensuing pogrom, the tribe split into North and South Maragoli and for several generations the two chieftaincies stood athwart as bitter enemies. The two brothers apparently disagreed over the distribution of bridewealth paid for one of their sisters and in the ensuing quarrel Yonga killed Kizungu. It is taboo to kill a clansman and tradition demands that the culprit and his family be banished as outcasts to remote lands as a punishment. In the case of Yonga, he took refuge in Ma'avi's homestead (his stepbrother).

Overcome with grief and unbearable pain of losing their father, sons of Kizungu decided to migrate to what is today North Maragoli. Here they formed an alliance with the neighboring Idakho and tried to avenge their father's homicide by waging war against Avayonga. Shortly after, Kirima followed Kizungu's progeny to North Maragoli. The animosity between north and south Maragoli was so intense no social relations were condoned and for several generations intermarriage outlawed. It was not until colonial rule and establishment of Christian missions about a hundred years ago that North and South Maragoli began to slowly see eye to eye again.

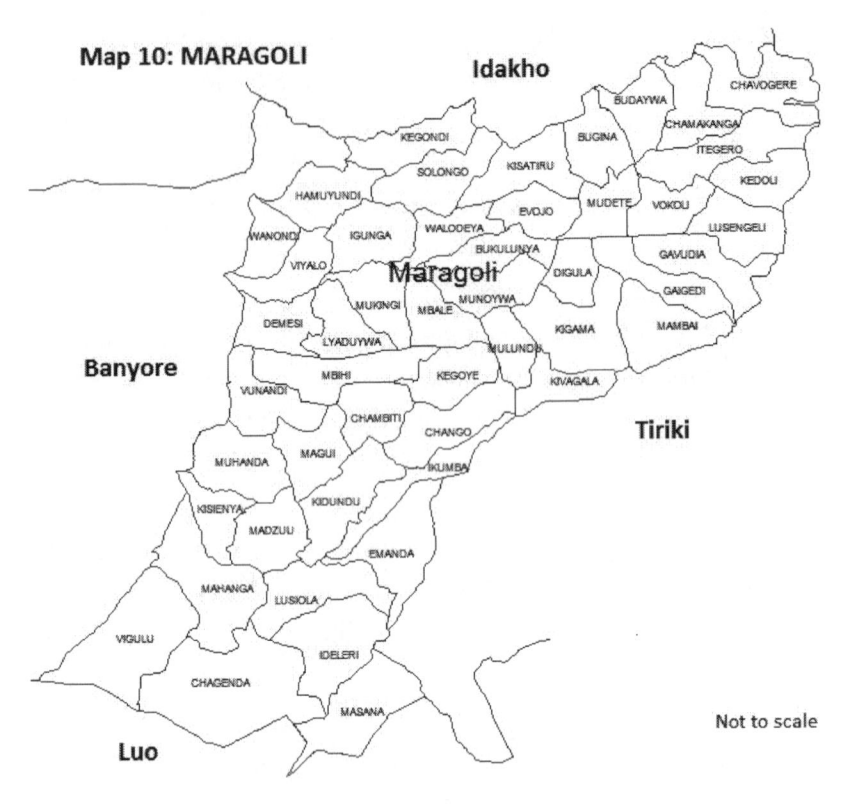

Map 10 shows the major administrative locations in
Maragoli, Vihiga County.

Besides internal strives, the Maragoli were also constantly
at war with the Nandi and Luo. While the Nandi raided Maragoli
homesteads to steal cattle, the Luo fought over land. In one famous
battle, Maragoli warriors regained some of their lost territory at a
place called Chavavo (place of Luos). The neighboring Bunyore
territory was largely insulated from Luo attacks because of their
reputation as rain magicians.

The largest clans in Maragoli are Avama'avi, Avakizungu,
Avakirima, and Avasaali. These clans spawned several lineages
that later became independent clans. For the most part, however,
the younger clans remained beholden to mother clans (*zinyumba
zinene*) both in times of peace and war and continued to observe

rules of exogamy. Although members of *zinyumba zinene* can intermarry, the subclans spawned by say Avama'avi cannot even though they have become independent. The prestige of a clan depends on its age and how close it is to the tribal ancestor; hence it is common to find a Maragoli clansman suffixing his clan with *enyumba inene* (mother clan). For instance a Musweta clansman would say he is Omusweta Omusaali or Omugisemba Omukizungu, where Omusaali and Omukizungu are the *zinyumba zinene* (mother clans).

It is widely believed that Mulogoli, the tribal ancestor was a brother to Mugusi, the progenitor of Abagusii otherwise known as the Kisii (Gusii). The two groups are said to have split when the Luo invaded their territory and both are closely related to the Kuria (Abatende) and Suba. The clan of Abasuva (also in Tiriki) is living testimony of these ancient ethnocultural links. In turn the Gusii are also said to be related to Ameru (Meru) of Mt. Kenya sharing linguistic, temperamental, and cultural similarities. Wherever else these groups might have come from, one thing that is not in doubt is that they sojourned in Uganda before settling in this part of East Africa. Remnants of Abasuva (Abasuba or Abasoba) still remain in Ugenya at a place called Ukwala. Dr. John Osogo even attests that Avalogooli, Abasuba and Abagusii are offshoots of an ancient clan known as Abasoba (Osogo 1966: 35) which is also found among Babukusu and Bagisu. Whatever the case, it is instructive that Logooli and Luganda languages share up to 40 percent lexical similarities and both hold *eng'oma* (drum) as a cultural totem. The Maragoli emigration to South Nyanza that started circa 1927 was rather like retracing footsteps of their ancestors. Today significant colonies of Maragoli exist in Kanyamkago, Migori, and Uriri and across the border in Tanzania and Uganda especially at a place called Kigumba in Bunyoro Kitara kingdom.

b. Serpent mythology in Maragoli cosmology

The serpent is a highly venerated symbol of phallism and mystery of the cycles of life and death in Maragoli society. Besides *eng'oma* (drum), the serpent especially the puff adder and python are revered as items of totemic symbolism with power to accord or deny life (see p.181). The Maragoli believe that the tribal ancestor, Mulogoli received a message from the gods that he should migrate to a fertile place where he can grow crops to raise his family. These gods are represented through the medium of ancestor worship and the serpent. We have seen how twice every year, the Maragoli organized *ovwali* sacrifices to honor the spirit of Mulogoli at Mungoma Caves in South Maragoli (see p.272). These offerings were conducted by specially anointed sacrificial priests (*avasalisi*) directly descendant from Mulogoli. It is instructive that among the heirlooms Mulogoli gave to Ma'avi, his inheritor, was a serpent. In turn, Ma'avi bequeathed the serpent to his youngest son, Nondi and that is why Avanondi clansmen have always presided over *ovwali* rituals.

People who do not understand the depths of Maragoli cosmology may misrepresent or misinterpret association of the reptile to evil pursuits and necromancy. This view is not entirely without foundation as witches (*avalogi*) often use snakes as part of witchcraft paraphernalia. The negative connotations notwithstanding, in the wider context of Maragoli ethno-cultural purview, the serpent is a symbol of fertility and rebirth. Fertility is denoted by its phallic shape which erects when ready to strike while rebirth or renewal is symbolised by the snake's constant sloughing (Kabaji 2005: 36 & 37). If one marries a woman from a family that keeps snakes, custom dictates that the bride also keeps a serpent in her new home otherwise she will not beget children.

Although majority of Maragoli have converted to Christianity, they still venerate power of the occult. It is taboo to kill a python (*ivaka*), cobra or puff adder (*irihili*) and where this has happened, a rite of lustration (*omuluka*) must be performed to pacify spirit of the serpent otherwise the killer will not beget children (Bulimo 2013: 150). The serpent belonging to the sacrificial priest of Avanondi is considered a royal snake which is not only venerated and cared for, but when it dies, it is accorded a "royal" burial with full ritual honors befitting a clan elder (Kabaji 2005: 37).

In Abrahamanic religions (Christianity, Islam and Judaism), the serpent is portrayed as the ultimate enemy of man who, by tempting Eve and Adam to eat of the forbidden fruit, brought death and misery to mankind. Across cultures, the serpent is a mysterious creature that has beguiled man since beginning of time. Ancient Greeks considered it a reincarnation of the soul while Buddhists revere cobra for having protected Siddhartha Gautama, the religion's Nepalese founder, from wild animals as he sought enlightenment (Buddhism) in the forest. Among the Ameru of Mount Kenya, the python is considered the spirit protector of rain (*ntato*) and it was taboo to kill it as it is among the Nyakach Luo who call it *omieri*. The Igbo of Nigeria address a python as "Our Father" in respect of its power, wisdom and deadliness.

c. Preservation of genealogical records

The Maragoli had a unique way of preserving genealogical records through the vehicle of folk poetry recitals, especially by youth. While sitting around a fire or at some other social gathering, youth interrogated each other to see who recited the longest lineal ancestry. Under rules of this custom, they used a definite template as the example below shows:

Question: *Dada wowo nivwaha?* (Who is your father?)
Answer: Bernard Salano
Question: *A Salano*? (Who is Salano's father?)
Answer: Epainito Mandala
Question: *A Mandala?*

Answer: Aggrey Militsa
Question: *A Militsa?*
Answer: Luvai Mudaka
Question: *A Mudaka?*

This template not only enabled Maragoli youth to know and remember their family tree, it was an ingenious method of passing vital aspects of culture and history from generation to generation. Anyone who fell short went home and consulted parents or grandparents so that next time he could win the recital contest. In between recitals, players told spicy anecdotes about achievements of their ancestors in warfare, leadership or special vocations. Because of this competition, it is little wonder that most Maragoli are able to trace their ancestry way above the tribal average of four to six generations.

Table 24: Maragoli population distribution by administrative unit, surface area, and density

Admin Unit	Total	Area (sq km)	Density
Vihiga	221,294	201	1,101
Chavakali	65,558	51.9	1,264
Chavakali	18,452	15.1	1,223
Evojo	2,854	2.8	1,016
Igunga	4,559	4.1	1,117
Walodeya	5,122	2.7	1,912
Wanondi	2,656	2.5	1,054
Viyalo	3,261	3	1,086
Izava North	11,733	9.5	1,232
Mbale	5,171	3.2	1,634
Bukulunya	2,906	2.8	1,050
Munoywa	3,656	3.6	1,018
Izava South	13,872	9.6	1,940
Demesi	3,921	3.3	1,192

Lyaduywa	4,988	3	1,648
Mukingi	4,963	3.3	1,496
West Maragoli	**21,501**	**17.6**	**1,222**
Hamuyundi	4,427	4.3	1,026
Kegondi	5,235	4.2	1,244
Kisatiru	5,318	4.4	1,209
Solongo	6,521	4.7	1,394
Sabatia	**64,120**	**59**	**1,087**
Busali East	**12,270**	**13.1**	**934**
Chavogere	4,268	5.4	795
Itegero	4,657	4.6	1,012
Kedoli	3,345	3.2	1,055
Busali West	**11,423**	**10.6**	**1,082**
Budaywa	3,583	10.6	1,082
Bugina	3,950	3.4	1,155
Chamakanga	3,890	3.6	1,078
North Maragoli	**18,487**	**16.3**	**1,134**
Digula	2,784	2.1	1,311
Kigama	6,460	6.1	1,066
Kivagala	2,727	2.4	1,117
Mudete	4,353	3.3	1,312
Mulundu	2,161	2.4	914
Wodanga	**21,940**	**19**	**1,156**
Gaigedi	3,507	3.3	1,050
Gavudia	4,154	4.1	1,026
Lusengeli	4,523	3.8	1,205
Mambai	5,110	4.8	1,064
Vokoli	4,646	3	1,529
Vihiga	**91,616**	**90.2**	**1,016**
Central Maragoli	**23,370**	**17.2**	**1,362**
Chango	5,931	4.1	1,437
Emanda	6,348	5.3	1,202
Ikumba	5,815	3	1,929
Kidundu	5,276	4.7	1,114
Lugaga	**11,809**	**12.1**	**1,092**

Magui	3,905	3.6	1,092
Muhanda	4,501	4.6	980
Vunandi	3,403	3.9	875
Mungoma	**19,800**	**21.1**	**937**
Kisienya	2,467	2.8	895
Madzuu	4,318	3.7	1,165
Mahanga	6,723	6.5	1,030
Vigulu	6,292	8.1	774
South Maragoli	**19,293**	**27.8**	**693**
Chagenda	5,321	11.1	481
Ideleri	4,967	5.7	872
Lusiola	3,481	4.6	753
Masana	5,524	6.5	857
Wamuluma	**17,344**	**12**	**1,446**
Mbihi	8,679	5.1	1,707
Chambiti	3,468	2.9	1,183
Kegoye	5,197	4	1,306

Adapted from Kenya Census 2009, *Kenya National Bureau of Statistics, Nairobi, August 2010.*

d.   Traditional and modern power structures

Avama'avi occupied the important office of *omusalisi* (sacrificial priest) who officiated at the semiannual *ovwali* (special ceremony paying tribute to the tribal ancestors) at Mungoma caves near Vigulu, South Maragoli. The only other clan to produce *avasalisi* was Avanondi (descended from Avama'avi) while Avigulu (clans from Vigulu) were famous for their pottery skills. Avasaniaga (also in Tachoni, Bukusu, and Tiriki) were famous for producing dream prophets, the last of which was Nangweya (died in 1918). Nangweya was so famous, he was consulted by Abanyole, Abatiriki and Abanyolo (Luo). These séances along with traditionalist practices crumbled to death with the advent of colonialism. Despite erosion of the power of mystics, it was a Ma'avi chief who was appointed to rule over Avalogooli in the new secular order. In preindependent Kenya, however, it was a Maragoli woman, Priscilla Ingasiani Abwao (1924-2009), who first blazed national politics. Not only was she the first Maragoli at the top political hierarchy but also the first Kenyan woman legislator following her nomination to Legco by colonial governor, Sir Patrick M. Renison, in 1961.

At independence in 1963, the two Maragoli chieftaincies (north and south) were represented in Legco by one politician, Joseph Daniel Otiende under a constituency called Vihiga. Mr. J. D. Otiende served for one term only rising to become minister for health and housing in the First Parliament. He did not seek reelection in 1969 after becoming disillusioned with the Kenyatta government's policies. Otiende (born 1918) was a principled politician who did not amass wealth that often come with political office in Kenya and leads a humdrum life in Mbale, central Maragoli. He is immortalized by a housing estate in Nairobi southlands named after him (Otiende Estate). He was succeeded by Peter Frederick Kibisu (Omukizungu)[142] who served two terms (1969-74 and 1974-79) losing the 1979 elections to Moses Substone Budamba Mudavadi (1923-1989) who died in office during his third term. In 1988 Vihiga was split into two constituencies—Sabatia (North Maragoli) and Vihiga (South Maragoli), thus putting paid historical rivalry between the two chieftaincies.

Like the proverbial substone that became the cornerstone, Moses Mudavadi, (Omukevembe) wielded political clout beyond Maragoli. He was easily the kingpin of Luyia politics of his time largely due to his close association with President Daniel arap Moi. His Mululu home became a shrine for delegations of people from across Luyialand seeking political and financial favors.

[142.] Peter Kibisu was sacked by Pres. Jomo Kenyatta as an assistant minister after supporting a parliamentary motion in 1975 adopting the JM Kariuki investigations report chaired by the then MP for Kimilili, the late Elijah Mwangale. Others sacked with him from the executive were Masinde Muliro and John Keen.

He was succeeded by his son, Wycliffe Musalia Mudavadi who, albeit for one term (2002-07) still rules the roost in Maragoli and is the preeminent Luyia politician of his time. His bid for presidency in 2013 flopped coming a distant third with a paltry three percent of votes cast. His Amani Coalition of three parties (KANU, UDF and New Ford Kenya) somewhat redeemed itself with 18 seats countrywide. Mudavadi's former Sabatia seat was won by newcomer, Alfred Agoi. Just before the 2002 parliamentary elections, Mudavadi had joined a group of leaders[143] opposed to President Moi's choice of successor (Uhuru Kenyatta). For some unexplained reason, Moi plucked Mudavadi back into KANU from the Rainbow Alliance, as the rebels called themselves, and named him vice president, a largely titular office. This defection angered his supporters across the country and, in particular, his constituents in Sabatia who taught him a lesson by electing a political nondescript, the Reverend Moses Epainitous Akaranga, a former banker. After five years in political wilderness, Akaranga bounced back to win the coveted gubernatorial seat to become the first governor of Vihiga County. His step sister, Beatrice Adagala won the women's representative seat to establish the Akaranga political dynasty in Maragoli.

Meanwhile, the new Vihiga was represented by the architect, Bahati Musira Semo (1988-92), Andrew Ndooli Ligale (1992-97 and 2002-07) and Yusuf Kifuma Chanzu (1997-2002 and 2007-13). Chanzu retained his seat in the Eleventh Parliament following the 2013 general elections. In Nairobi, an *ex situ* Maragoli politician, Fredrick Esau Omido, served Bahati constituents for three consecutive terms (1979-83, 1983-88, and 1988-92). Prof. Filemon Indire, former Kenyan ambassador to the Soviet Union, was a nominated MP between 1983 and 1988.

[143.] Key members of the Rainbow Alliance included Raila Odinga, George Saitoti, Kalonzo Musyoka, Joseph Kamotho, and Musalia Mudavadi.

e.   Notable clansmen

Other famous Avalogooli include Ibrahim Ambwere (Omasingira), the entrepreneur and reputedly the richest Luyia of his time; Henry Miyinzi Chakava,[144] the publisher; broadcasters Herman Igambi, Catherine Kasavuli, Gladys Erude and Solomon Omolo Mugera; late Paul Agoi, colonial chief; Dr. Arthur Mudogo Kemoli, the musician and university don (1947-2012); Gaylord Avedi, former permanent secretary; Francis Chahonyo, parastatal chief; Ambassador Bruce Madete, former chief of protocol; Dr. Walter Lusigi, former World Bank ecologist; Prof. Francis Davis Imbuga, the playwright (1947-2012); Paul Kelemba aka Madd (Omaavi), the cartoonist and Anthony Ambaka Kegode, the airline entrepreneur.

Others include Justice Festus Azangalala; Steve Mwenesi, the lawyer; Elly Aluvale (Omusweta) airline entrepreneur; university dons Kavetsa Adagala, Prof. Arthur Luvai and Dr. Henry Indangasi; Elmanus Angaluki Vodoti, the educationist; Prof. David Kikaya, the diplomat and university don; Saulo Chabuga, founder of African Divine Church; Aggrey Luseno, the publicist; Francis Choge, former mayor of Vihiga and ILO expert; Peter Adams Ludaava, the hotelier; George Aladwa, Nairobi mayor; Rogers Mulemi, a Kakamega businessman and Major General Gordon Kihalangwa, assistant chief of general staff.

[144.] Henry Chakava was the first African editor of Heinemann Publishing in 1972. Under his stewardship, the multinational company became 100 percent wholly Kenyan owned and changed its name to East Africa Educational Publishers. Mr. Chakava rose to become the company's chairman in one of the longest running career pathways spanning more than forty years.

9. Abamarama (Marama)

Table 25: Marama clans (brackets indicate alternative spelling or where else clan members are found)

Ababoko (Cameroon, Haya)

Abacheya

Abakara

Abakharo

Abakhongo

Abakhuli

Abakokho (Bukusu, Gisu, Cameroon)

Abakolwe (Wanga, Marachi)

Abakotse

Abalafu

Abalukhoba (Tiriki)

Abalukokho

Abamachina (Kabras, Tachoni, Bukusu)

Abamakambo

Abamakhaya (Isukha)

Abamakoya

Abamamu (Tsotso)

Abamani (Kisa, Butsotso, Wanga, Abanyala ba Ndombi)

Abamanyulia (Kisa, Butsotso)

Abamatundu

Abamukhula

Abamukhuyu

Abamukowa (Marachi)

Abamulole

Abamunali

Abamureko

Abamuyira

Abamwende (Wanga and Butsotso)

Abanyukhu

Abaseta

Abashiambitsi

Abashiana

Abashianda (Butsotso)

Abashibanga

Abashieni (Wanga)

Abashihaka

Abashihongo

Abashiibo (Butsotso, Tiriki)

Abashikalie

Abashikanda

Abashikulusi

Abashikunga

Abashinyula

Abashirotsa (Kisa)

Abashitsaha

Abasikairi

Abatamanyini (Butsotso)

Abatere

Abatita

Abatsotse

Abebokono

Aberecheya

Abekalie	Abakhoone (Bunyala, Samia,
	Abanyole Uganda, Bukusu,
	Bukhayo, Tachoni, Marachi)
Abamumbia	Abamabuusi

a.   Strong sense of clan identity

If a strong sense of clan identity exists anywhere, it is in Marama, Butere. Here you find a confederation of over fifty clans proud of their history who loath being lumped together as Abamarama. Locally the dominant clan, Abamukhula[145] and their subclans (constitute up to 40 percent of Marama population) are the ones generally referred to as Abamarama and other clans feel offended if called Abamarama. Why the place was named Marama in the first place is an open question; perhaps even a misnomer, but the ethnonym is characteristic of the insensitivity of the colonial and later independent governments to local feelings, traditions, and history. Marama is sometimes erroneously used synonymously with Butere (derived from Abatere clan who initially came from Tiriki), but actually Butere is a small town made famous when the railway was extended from Kisumu to the township in 1932. Among the Tiriki, there is an independent clan known as Abamarama whether this is a coefficient of clans common between Tiriki and Marama requires further anthropological research. However, Abatere are related to Abalukhoba and Abashitsetse, the former ruling clans in both Tiriki and Wanga who revere bushbuck (*imbongo*) as a totem. Despite these local differences, Abamarama are united under their cultural totem, *ikhulo* (waterbuck). The clan of Ababoko also found among the Haya of Bukoba in Tanzania and in Congo holds *imboko* (buffalo) as a sacred animal.

[145.]   Although some scholars say Omukhula is the progenitor of the clan, others say the name means "flowing stream" after clan founders won a competition of pouring milk so that it flowed from the ridge to the valleys. The founders cheated by mixing milk with water and won the contest (Osogo 1966: 88).

Map 11 shows the major administrative locations in
Marama, Kakamega County.

Besides Abamukhula, other big clans include Abashirotsa
(came from Idakho or Isukha),[146] Abatere, Abashieni (related to
Bongomek), Abamanyulia, and Abalukhoba who are also found
in Tiriki and are related to Abashitsetse of Wanga. Interclan
rivalry and warfare was common in the pre-European days. At one
time, Abamarama (or associated clans) drove Abamanyulia and
Abatamanyini as far as Butsotso but these expelled clans gradually
returned to their former lands following further quarrels among

---

[146] The founder of Abashirotsa is said to have been a son of Chibololi of Isukha
known as Shirotsa who later emigrated to Butere area. Chibololi was said
to have been a Maasai or Nandi by the name of Chiproot (transliterated to
Chibololi) whose father, Naswayi is believed to have been the founder of
Abamironje, the dominant clan in Isukha.

themselves. However, a sizeable number of their respective clans still reside as independent septs in Butsotso to this day.

The clan of Abalafu is a hybrid cross incorporating Luyia, Luo, and Kalenjin ancestries. Some Abalafu (means light-skinned) clansmen claim to be related to Abashieni whom, as we saw above, are of Kalenjin origin while others, especially Abachenya subclan, claim Luo ancestry (Were 1967: 70). The genesis of Abalafu is traceable to intermarriages between Abashieni and Kalenjin, particularly the Tugen (Lihraw 2010: 52). Abamabuusi are related to Abakhoone and came to Marama during the *Esiatikho* wars of circa 1750 (see p.205). It's worth noting that some clans were swallowed by larger septs and are, to all intents and purposes, extinct. Examples of such clans include Abahunia, Abamulukuyu, and Abaluchera. In local lingo, the swallowed clans are known as *emikuru* (poles) because they support bigger clans. Others are offshoots of Abawanga (Abamuyira), Abamarachi (Abashitsaha), Abatsotso (Abashikunga) while others such as Abakotse are offshoots of Abashirotsa.

b.   Brief migrational history

Marama, as we know it today, was populated by clans that came from different directions. Following the collapse of the Chwezi Empire in Uganda, Wamoyi migrated to Tiriki with his three sons, Wanga, Khabiakala, and Eshifumbi according to Prof. Gideon Were (1967). While Wanga migrated to Imanga following family feuds, Eshifumbi moved farther north to Emahondo where he became the ancestor of Abamuyira and Abamakoya. Angulu, Wanga's nephew, emigrated to Butere where his descendants founded the following clans: Abakhuli, Abashiambitsi, Abakhongo and Abaseta.

There are two versions about Aberecheya, whose most famous son is Martin Shikuku (1933-2012), the maverick politician otherwise known as the "people's watchman" in tribute to his rhapsodized stand against corruption and bad governance. Using records from Regeya Progressive Society, Prof. Gideon Were says that Sechere, son of Sumba came from the Bagweru of Uganda and first settled at Jinja where he begot a son called Musoga who became the ancestor of Abasoga. When he migrated from Busoga he settled at Busia where he sired Samia who became the ancestor of Abasamia. Then he moved on once more to Ebusinga near Mundika where he begat Musonga, the ancestor of the Abasonga.

However, an independent study sponsored by Shabanji Opukah[147] traces their ancestry to Sumba as their earliest known ancestor. He had three sons—Soga the forefather of the Abasoga of Jinja, Uganda and Sechere and Mugweru (founder of Bagweru tribe in Mbale, Uganda). Sechere moved to settle at Odiado hills in Samia where he sired Regeya (founder of Aberecheya) who, in turn, begat Abuti who settled in Marama. In Samia, Sechere's family neighbored Amukhula (founder of Abamukhula). Other oral traditions indicate that Abasoga originally came from Bunyoro Kingdom in western Uganda, and because they arrived at their present locality after swimming (*khusoga*) across River Nile, local people said *betsa ni basoga* (they came while swimming) and this became the genesis of Abasoga tribe from which many clans in Luyia land are either descendant or related.

Table 26: Marama population distribution by admimistrative unit, surface area, and density

Admin Unit	Total	Area (sq km)	Density
Butere	139,780	210.5	664
Township	20,335	22.5	904
Shirotsa	8,244	6.8	1,208

[147.] The study is entitled *Aberecheya's History and Growth, 2nd edition (2009)*. Shabanji Opukah, the sponsor is a public relations personality and a Kakamega businessman who worked for many years for BAT in London.

Shirembe	4,536	4.8	942
Shinamwinyuli	7,555	10.9	695
Marama Central	**24,382**	**38.5**	**633**
Ibokolo	7,144	11.5	621
Mutoma	6,107	6.5	940
Imanga	11,131	20.5	543
Marama North	**20,796**	**32.9**	**632**
Lukoye	4,791	7.8	616
Shiraha	6,237	11.6	539
Inaya	3,346	6.1	548
Bushitinji	6,422	7.4	836
South Marama	**12,023**	**18**	**670**
Shibembe	4,956	5	988
Shiatsala	3,155	4.2	748
Masaba	3,912	8.7	449
Shianda	**11,157**	**13.4**	**835**
Shianda	3,304	3.7	885
Mabole	4,695	5.6	834
Bubala	3,158	4	788
Lunza	**31,250**	**51.3**	**609**
Lunza	**9,873**	**19.4**	**508**
Buchenya	6,825	7.7	887
Shitari	8,824	16.4	540
Bumamu	5,728	7.8	731
Marenyo	**11,308**	**18.5**	**644**
Muyundi	6,365	8.8	724
Shikunga	2,393	4.9	607
Buboko	2,550	4.8	536
Manyala	**7,929**	**15.5**	**511**
Bushieni	3,256	7.1	458
Eshihenjera	4,673	8.4	556

Adapted from Kenya Census 2009, *Kenya National Bureau of Statistics, Nairobi, August 2010.*

c. Traditional and modern political system

Although each clan had its own independent ruler and war leader, the subnation was under the jurisdiction of *omwami* (leader) who was assisted in discharging his duties by clan elders. Unlike other Luyia subnations, *omwami* in Marama did not necessarily have to be a medicine man, rainmaker, or sacrificial priest. These offices were adequately covered by other people. His job was purely administrative and he presided over serious cases that affected the subnation leaving minor ones to various clan elders. He wore special insignia which included *ikutusi* (skin cloak), a copper bracelet (*omukasa*) on the wrist, and a headdress adorned with cowrie shells and whydah bird's feathers.

When he died, a suitable individual was elected by clan elders to replace him. The body of *omwami* was wrapped in a fresh bull hide (*esikhoba*) and buried in a sitting position. His drinking straw (*olutseshe*) was put in the mouth and his head covered by a pot into which two holes were drilled. The pot was placed in such a way that the two holes aligned with the eyes so that he could "see" what was going on. After the corpse had decomposed sufficiently, a goat (*imbusi*) was slaughtered for the final death rituals before his head was finally pushed into the grave (Bulimo 2013: 519).

After independence, politics in Butere reverted to direct rule whereby natives elected their own representative at the Legislative Assembly in Nairobi. The post colonial politics in Marama was dominated by one individual, ex-seminarian, Joseph Martin Shikuku (1933-2012). Shikuku from the minority Aberecheya clan bestrode the Marama political landscape like a colossus for a period spanning thirty years. Out of ten parliaments since independence to 2007-2013, Shikuku sat in six of them. When he was detained in 1975 by Jomo Kenyatta after declaring that KANU was dead, his seat was filled by Richard Litunya (Omukambuli). He was released by President Daniel arap Moi upon Kenyatta's death in 1978 and easily recaptured Butere riding in the 1979 elections and again in 1983.

However, in the *mlolongo* (queuing) elections of 1988, Shikuku was rigged out despite having the longest queue in one of the most blatant abuses of the electoral process in Kenya. As fate would have it, the "winner" Jesse Eshikhati Opembe (Omushisa) died a year later and in the ensuing by-election, John Okwara (deceased) became the MP, again after Shikuku was openly rigged out. Shikuku recaptured Butere in the multiparty elections of 1992 but lost in 1997 to Dr. Amukowa Anangwe who ruled for one term only losing to Wycliffe Ambetsa Oparanya in 2002. Oparanya won again in 2007 and was named minister for planning and national development. Oparanya's political fortunes blossomed when he won the 2013 gubernatorial contest for Kakamega, Kenya's second most populated county after Nairobi. His former fiefdom of Butere was captured by newcomer, Andrew Toboso Anyanga. Meanwhile in Nakuru, Shikuku's younger brother, Dr. Lwali Oyondi captured the Nakuru Town seat in 1992 to establish another political dynasty in Luyialand.[148] However, unlike his brother who dominated Butere politics, the veterinary doctor ruled for only one term losing the seat in 1997.

Other notable people from Marama include the late Prof. Gideon Saulo Were,[149] historian and author of *A History of Abaluyia of Western Kenya*; brothers Dan and Ben Musuku, footballers;

[148.] There are ten political dynasties in Luyialand: Mudavadi in Maragoli (father and son), Awori in Samia (brothers in Kenya and Uganda), Khaniri in Tiriki (father and son), M'Maitsi in Tiriki (father and son), Mango in Marachi (husband and wife), Oyondi in Marama (brothers—Shikuku and Lwali), Wamalwa in Bukusu (father and two brothers), Mukuna in Bunyore (father and son), Wetang'ula (brothers) in Bukusu, and Akaranga (brother and sister) in Maragoli.

[149.] Prof. Were, an acclaimed historian and university professor, died in a car crash in July 1995 on Kericho-Kisumu road. Besides *A History of Abaluyia*

Shabanji Opukah, public relations consultant (Omurecheya); Alfred Richard Tsalwa, first senator for Kakamega; Harry Wamubeyi, former DC; Rev. Tim Wambunya; Moses Mutuli, the actuarist; Dr. Mutakha Kangu, lawyer and academic; Mohamed Khamis Munyanya, ex-Kenya Architectural Society chairman; and Dr. Jedidah Enoch Onchere (Omushirotsa), former lecturer at Egerton University resident in UK.

10. Abasamia (Samia)

Table 27: Samia clans (brackets indicate alternative spelling or where else clan members are found)

Ababeebo

Ababirangu (Usonga, Marachi)
Ababongo (Abanyala, Wanga, Uganda)
Ababuri
Abachaki (Uganda)
Abadde (Bunyala, Bukhayo, Uganda)
Abadipa (Busoga)
Abadongo
Abafofoyo (Marachi, Bukhayo)
Abagemi
Abahanga (Uganda)
Abaini (Uganda)
Abakamondo

Ababere (Wanga, Marachi, Haya, Khayo, Bugwe)
Ababoli (Kisa, Uganda, Congo)
Ababoro (Marachi, Bunyala, Bunyoro)
Ababwala (Uganda)
Abadayirwa (Uganda)
Abadepi (Busoga)

Abadira (Uganda)
Abadwing'i (Uganda)
Abafuta (Uganda, Busoga)
Abagwanga (Uganda)
Abahauli (Uganda)
Abajabi (Abakabi)
Abakangala (Kabras, Samia, Bukusu, Bukhayo, Abanyala ba Ndombi, Uganda, Congo)

---

of Western Kenya, he also coauthored *East Africa through a Thousand Years* with D. A. Wilson.

Abakemo (Uganda)
Abakhasokho (Busoga)
Abakhoba (Uganda, Haya)

Abakhulo
Abakhwi (Uganda)
Abakukhu (Uganda)
Abaleke (Abanyala, Wanga, Uganda, Congo)
Abaliani (Busoga)
Abalucha (Uganda)
Abalundu (Cameroon, Uganda)

Abamakondo (Uganda)
Abamanyi (Uganda, Ugenya)

Abamulimba (Uganda)
Abang'aale (Bunyore, Bukusu, Marachi, Tachoni, Kabras, Butsotso, Uganda)
Abanyideti (Uganda)
Abanyimoti
Abasiirwa (Uganda)
Abasiralire
Abasiye (Uganda)
Abasubo (Marachi, Bukhayo, Usonga, Busoga)
Abataboona (Uganda)
Abenge (Uganda)

Abakhabukaki (Usonga)
Abakhekhe (Bukusu)
Abakhoone (Bukusu, Tachoni, Samia, Marama, Abanyala, Marachi, Abanyole Uganda)
Abakhumachi (Uganda)
Abakombe (Uganda)
Abalanda (Uganda)
Abalemesi (Busoga)

Abalindo (Uganda)
Abalumbi (Uganda, Congo)
Abalyali (Usonga, Uganda, Busoga)
Abamakwe (Uganda)
Abamulembo (Bunyala, Wanga, Bukusu, Marachi)Abameywa (Bukusu, Bukhayo, Abanyala ba Ndombi, Tachoni, Uganda)
Abanapa
Abanyanga (Uganda)

Abanyikhodo (Uganda, Busoga)
Abapodi
Abasinywa (Uganda)
Abasireku (Marachi, Uganda)
Abasota
Abasyakhuba (Uganda)

Abayobo (Abanyala)
Abonwe (Marachi)

a. Geographical spread

The people of Samia straddle two countries—Kenya and Uganda. In modern era, they are famed as high achievers in academia but in ancient times were largely associated with iron smithing and forging. The spread of Samia people across several Luyia subnations (especially Bunyore, Kisa, Butsotso, Tachoni, and Bukusu) is largely a product of mercantile intrepidity as they crisscrossed Buluyia in search of markets for iron implements. They speak Olusamia and their geophysical territory is known as Ebusamia. An important factor to note about Abasamia (Abasaamia) is the gender differential when referring to a clan member. Hence while a man from the Abachaki clan is called Omuchaki, a woman is a Nachaki. This nomenclature is typical of all Luyia subnations in the wider Busia region—Marachi, Bukhayo, Bunyala, and Samia.

While in Kenya Abasamia are grouped under Luyia, in Uganda they are listed as an independent tribe domiciled in two districts (Busia and Namayingo) with four political constituencies. The major clans in Samia are Abadongo, Abamanyi, Abataboona, Ababuri, and Ababirangu cluster of clans. Although Abakhekhe are listed under the Samia, they tend to consider themselves different from the rest of Abasamia. Some scholars consider Abakhekhe as a subnation of the Luyia even linking them to the Hehe of Iringa, Tanzania (Osogo 1966: 101). They are said to be of a Hamitic origin, part of the eastern Cushites found in Ethiopia and Sudan. They are closely related to Abasoga and Abanyankole of Uganda and speak Olukhekhe dialect which has subtle nuances to Olusaamia. Clans allied to Abakhekhe whose earliest known ancestor is Akeki are Abakhulo, Abanyanga, Abanyideti, Abakolo, Abakobe, Abakhala, and Abakweri (from Abagweru of Uganda). Abakhekhe and allied clans detest being called Abasamia just like some Butere septs resent being called Abamarama (see p.74).

Some clans claim both lineages, e.g., Abang'aale, Abamenya, Abaliali, Abasota, Abonwe (also in Marachi), and Ababere (also in Wanga, Bukhayo, Samia Bugwe and Bukoba, Tanzania) and are neutral in the bitter rivalry between the two clandoms. Another clan found in Tanzania is Abakhoba who are said to be an offshoot of the people who gave their name to the town of Bukoba in Tanzania (Osogo 1966: 11). Among Abakhekhe clandom, the largest clan is Abakhulo which has three major subclans—Abeidokho (rulers), Abadera, and Abasitumba.

Samia settlement in Busia (named after Abasia clansmen who still exist in Bugisu and Bunyala in Kakamega) occurred in three waves beginning circa 1500. The first group to arrive includes Ababirangu who spawned Abadebu, Abajabi, Abamaripo, Abayingi, Abaliro, Abade (Abadde), and Abanyibomi, among the major clans. This group was led by Siranga, an Omubirangu clan head and established settlements as far as Alego and Ugenya.[150]

The major clans in the second wave, which occurred circa 1600 included Abakhoba, Abamaindi, Abayuku, Abadunyi, Abaliali, and Abamaakwe. They came from Ibanda in Busoga, Uganda. Like the first lot, these too have left a mark represented by names of places bearing their names such as Budunyi, Bukhoba, Buyuku, etc. But it is the third group which arrived circa 1700 that has evolved as a dominant force in Samia polity today. This includes Abadongo, Abatabona, Abamanyi and Ababuri who all trace their ancestry to a man called Tebino (Osogo 1966: 97).

Not much is known about Abakangala except that they speak olukangala, a dialect of Olusaamia. Historical accounts suggest that they came from Sigulu Island in Lake Victoria but moved and sojourned in the territory around Mt. Elgon before spreading in various directions to settle among Abakhayo, Abakabras, Bukusu, Abanyala ba Ndombi, and in Samia with some columns moving northward to Uganda. They had a system of government similar to that of Abasamia and Abakhekhe. Other accounts indicate that they originally came from Congo where they are called Makangala.

---

[150] Although some clans later left Ugenya following Luo invasion or got assimilated, their presence is immortalised by names such as Siranga, Uranga, Ukwala, Sifuyo, Umina, Simenya, etc.

Because of shifting, their positions on issues and places, Abakangala, acquired a reputation of being unreliable, giving rise to a new word in local lingo *okhwekangala* (saying something one minute and arbitrarily denying it the next).

Abamakondo means the beautiful ones which imply that the clan is famed for its beautiful people. Abang'aale (Abang'are, Abamang'ali) are specialists in the craft of iron smithing making implements like hoes and spears and are also found in Bunyore (Abamang'ali), Bukusu (Bang'ale), Butsotso (Abamang'ale), Marachi, and Kabras (Abang'aale). Ababongo clansmen, who are spread across Wanga and Bunyala, are of Luo ancestry.

Map 12 shows the major administrative locations in Samia, Busia County.

Ababoli is a small clan also found in Samia Bugwe in Uganda and Kisa. The same clan is found in Congo (Ababooli). A male clansman is referred to as Omuboli and a woman as Naboli. Ababoli clan derives its name from *okhubola* (talkative) found in Samia mythology about *omukhasi omuboli* (talkative wife). They currently live in Ebumulimba village sandwiched between Sigalame High School and Sio Port (Bujwang'a). Abakhoba are also found among Samia of Uganda living around Bukhasaba Township while another cluster lives in Budimo and Bwimini chieftaincies in Uganda. The most famous Omukhobe is the chief justice of Uganda, Benjamin Odoki.

Samia is one of those communities that suffered administrative injustices under colonial border demarcations. The community is split almost equally between Kenya and Uganda with relatives on both sides of the border forced to seek clearance to visit clansmen. This anomaly continues even today, but it was worse during the military dictatorship of Idi Amin. A good example is the Awori family whose dilemma was popularized by two brothers holding senior positions in both countries (see p.292). The Awori dilemma is by no means isolated. Several clans in Samia Kenya have branches in Samia Bugwe, Uganda, as well as Busoga. Some Samia clans found in Busoga include Abadepi, Abaliali (Abalyali, also in Usonga), Abakhasokho, Abadiba, Abafuta, Abaliani (Abalyani), Abanyikhondo, Abalamesi, etc. They live mainly in Buswale county, eastern Uganda, and although they still speak Olusaamia, their language is influenced by Olusoga, the dominant tongue in the county.

Like other subnations in Buluyia, precolonial Samia society was patrilineal. Perhaps because of Luo influence, Abasamia like Abamarachi, Abakhayo and Abanyala did not ordinarily circumcise their boys. Instead, they adopted another rite of passage borrowed from the Luo—removal of six or four lower teeth.[151] Like traditional circumcision this operation was undertaken without any anaesthesia. It was a painful experience which tested the courage of the individual and his ability to become a man. Any signs of flinching earned one derogatory epithets.

According to a Luo anthropologist, Dan Omondi K'Aoko (1986), extraction of the lower teeth was never the equivalent of circumcision among the southern Luo. He argues that even among the Kipsigis, Teso, and Maasai, the removal of teeth did not replace ritual circumcision.[152] The extraction of the lower teeth served three purposes: during tetanus attacks, it provided a convenient way of feeding the patient with liquid foods, administering liquid medicinal herbs, and as a mark of tribal identity. Some Bunyore clans also removed six lower teeth due to Luo influence.

---

[151] In his book titled *Luo Circumcision Rites (1986)*, the author Dan Omondi K'Aoko explains that teeth removal was never meant to act as THE rite of passage for Luo men. It was a completely independent ritual serving specific socio-hygienic purposes. The book sets out to debunk the myth that Luo did not traditionally circumcise and gives an elaborate account of various forms of circumcision undertaken in Luoland. The only difference is that unlike Bantu Luyia, circumcision candidates did not engage in any elaborate ceremonies nor stay in a secluded hut.

[152] Maasai men and women remove two middle teeth on the lower jaw for oral delivery of traditional medicine while some Kalenjin tribes remove one or two lower teeth as a mark of tribal identity. Former Kenyan president Daniel arap Moi of the Tugen subtribe had one lower tooth removed.

Table 28: Samia population distribution by administrative unit, surface area, and density

Admin Unit	Total	Area (sq km)	Density
Funyula	**93,500**	**265.1**	**353**
Nambuku	**11,890**	**32.7**	**364**
Lugala	1,953	5.6	351
Mango	1,899	4.5	420
Sibinga	2,969	7.1	419
Ganjala	2,267	7.5	302
Ludacho	2,802	8	350
Namboboto	**16,253**	**37.3**	**436**
Luanda	4,221	9.5	444
Buloma	3,457	8.2	424
Namboboto	2,424	4.8	507
Mudoma	2,986	5.2	578
Nyakhobi	3,165	9.7	327
Odiado	**9,584**	**22.6**	**425**
Kabwodo	1,349	4.1	331
Odiado	3,003	8.5	354
Budalanga	1,171	3.4	349
Wakhungu	4,061	6.7	610
Nangosia	**10,609**	**27.5**	**385**
Luchululo	1,657	4.6	358
Sirekeresi	2,695	6.1	443
Bukhulungu	3,364	9.1	370
Sigulu	2,893	7.7	378
Agenga	**13,946**	**44.5**	**313**
Sigalame	3,960	12.6	315
Agenga	4,383	12.5	352
Ojibo	3,662	10.9	335
Bukiri	1,941	8.6	226
Nanguba	**11,432**	**36.3**	**315**
Bujwanga	5,696	14.5	394
Nanderema	3,117	12	260

Rumbiye	2,619	9.8	267
Bwiri	**19,786**	**64.3**	**308**
Busembe	4,347	11.9	366
Busijo	4,274	11.1	384
Hakati	5,668	20	283
Namuduru	5,497	21.2	259

Adapted from Kenya Census 2009, *Kenya National Bureau of Statistics, Nairobi, August 2010.*

b.   Political organization and the Awori factor

Leadership in Samia revolved around village elders. In Samia Bugwe, each village was ruled by an elder known as *nalundiho*, who among other qualities had to be a rainmaker (*omukimba*). He was responsible for law and order and resolved clan disputes. When a *nalundiho* died, his office was inherited by his eldest son. The most famous family in Samia is the Awori's. Although originally Marachi (Omufoyoyo), ancestors of the patriarch, Canon Jeremiah Musungu Awori settled in Ebusamia. He sired eighteen children from one wife, Maria and apart from the firstborn who died of a snake bite aged seven, others went on to become high achievers in politics, business, academic, and medical fields. The most famous of the Aworis is perhaps Dr. Arthur Moody Awori, who represented Abasamia in Parliament for five consecutive terms (between 1983 and 2002) rising to become Kenya's vice president when the incumbent, Michael Wamalwa Kijana died in office in August 2003. His brother Aggrey Siryoyi Awori, another politician in Uganda, rose to become a minister and challenged Pres. Yoweri Kaguta Museveni for Ugandan presidency in 2001 (he came third). Their elder brother, the late Wycliffe Works Wasya Awori represented what was then North Nyanza in the Legislative Council from 1951-57. WWW Awori, as he was popularly known was also the first known Luyia journalist. In 1945, he started a newspaper called *Omuluhya* which lasted for two years and in 1948 launched *Radio Posta*, first as a weekly and later a daily. Other high achievers from the Awori stalk include the late Hannington Awori (1930-2010), the entrepreneur, Dr. Mary Okelo, the founder of prestigious Makini schools in Nairobi, and the late Nelson Awori, the renal transplant pioneer.

The first politician to represent Samia in Parliament was Arthur Aggrey Ochwada (Omukhulo) while James Machio was a senator for Busia district. Ochwada (1926-2013) lost the 1967 by election to Habil Wilson Kanani (Omukhulo) in what was then called Busia Central Constituency. Ochwada, a former trade unionist and detainee, recaptured the riding in 1969 but was trounced in 1974 by Prof. Julia Auma Ojiambo, a Nadongo (first Kenyan woman to join the executive). The constituency changed its name in 1988 to Funyula. The reigning MP is Dr. Paul Nyongesa Otuoma (Omunyanga), elected in 2007 and appointed full minister. The veterinarian retained his seat in the 2013 elections.

c.   *Notable clansmen*

Apart from Awori's, other notable personalities in Samia include the late Prof. Hillary Ojiambo, the first cardiologist in sub-Saharan Africa; Dr. Smokin Wanjala,[153] the supreme court judge; Fred Ojiambo, the lawyer (Omubukhaki); Joe Masiga, the footballer and dentist (Omudongo); Dr. Majale, Kenya's first orthopaedic surgeon; Hillary Ng'weno (Omutabona), the media baron[154] and his son, Amolo Ng'weno, founder of Africa online, the continent's first Internet service provider; Prof. Sylvester

---

[153.]   Dr. Wanjala, a law academic from Sifuyo village also served as deputy director of the Kenya Anti Corruption Commission. He resigned in September 2009 after Parliament disagreed with President Kibaki's extension of the tenure of his boss, Justice Aaron Ringera but was in 2011 appointed Supreme Court judge.

[154.]   Mr. Ng'weno, a nuclear scientist from Harvard, was the first African editor of *Daily Nation* aged only twenty-six. He established one of the most successful

Namuye, the ICT specialist; senior chief Mukudi Namwonza, colonial-era administrator; John Khakhudu Agunda, the journalist (Omuburi); Lawrence Majale, the teacher's trade unionist; Dr. Walter N. Masiga, the veterinarian; Steve Oundo, the architect (Omutabona); Dr. Mathias Wanyama Oggema, the first Kenyan geneticist (Omutabona); footballers Noah Wanyama and his son McDonald Mariga (Abatabona) from Namboboto village, the most successful footballer from East Africa to play in top flight European league.[155]

In Uganda, famous Abasamia include Benjamin Joseph Odoki—Uganda's Chief Justice; James Munange Ogoola, a judge; Simon Mayende, former minister for higher education; Gabriel Opio, Minister of Gender, Culture and Labor; the late Alikipo Ochunju Ouma, a judge of the high court and first lawyer from Samia; Prof. Patrick Mangeni, a mathematician; Prof. Fred Wabwire-Mangeni, an epidemiologist at Makerere University's School of Public Health; James Aryada, the first Ugandan to get a first class degree in mathematics from Oxford University, one of a handful of distinguished centers of academic excellence in the world. Others include Moses Mapesa Wafula, executive director, Uganda Wildlife Authority; John Wejuli Wafula, Managing Director, Uganda Clays Limited; Amos Dayan Ngolobe, deputy director of Public Prosecutions; Chango Macho W'Obanda, a senior presidential adviser; Raphael Bwire Ouma, the educationist; Philip Were Mangeni, former Commissioner, Ministry of Finance; Dr. George William Nasinyama, deputy director, School of Graduate Studies, Makerere University; Denis Masinde Onyango, the footballer; Charles Wandera Nalyaali, founder of Uganda

---

weekly publications in Kenya, *Weekly Review*, and also ventured into TV and radio productions under his media empire, Stellagraphics.

[155.] Donald Mariga played for the Italian champions AC Milan and his crowning moment was when the club won the European Club Championship Cup (Uefa) in May 2010 after beating Bayern Munich of Germany in Madrid, Spain.

Microfinance (now Equity Bank); and the late Major General Francis Nyangweso (1939-2011), a former Olympic boxing champion, chief of general staff and minister for defense.[156]

11. Abatachoni (Tachoni)

Table 29: Tachoni clans (brackets indicate alternative spelling or where else clan members are found)

Ababichu (Bukusu)
Abacharia (Bukusu)
Abacheo
Abaechalo

Abahabiya (Bukusu)
Abakafisi (Abamatili)
Abakamutebi (Bukusu)

Abakhumaya
Abakuusi (Bukusu)
Abamachina (Bukusu, Kabras, Marama)
Abamakhanga (Bukusu)

Abamalicha
Abameywa (Bukusu, Bukhayo, Samia, Abanyala ba Ndombi)
Abamwongo

Abachambai (Bukusu)
Abachemai
Abachika
Abaengele (Bukusu, Abanyala ba Ndombi)
Abakabini
Abakamukongi
Abakhoone (Bukusu, Marama, Bukhayo, Bunyala)
Abakobolo
Abaluu
Abamakangala

Abamakhuli (Bukusu, Abanyala ba Ndombi)
Abamarakalu (Bukusu)
Abamurumba

Abang'aale (Bukusu, Bunyore, Marachi, Butsotso, Samia, Kabras)

[156.] Information about Abasamia in Uganda was adapted from Wikipedia, accessed on March 29, 2011.

Abangaachi (Bukusu)
Abarefu (Bukusu)
Abasamo
Abasaniaka (Bukusu, Maragoli, Tiriki)
Abasioya (Bukusu)

Abawayila
Abayirifuma (Abanyala ba Ndombi)

Abanyangali
Abasamba
Abasang'alo (Bukusu, Kabras)
Abasefu (Bukusu)

Abatecho (Abanyala ba Ndombi)
Abawele
Abayumbu (Bukusu)

a. The lost tribe

Abatachoni (Tachoni) provide a unique study into how tribes evolve through the process of ethnic assimilation and amalgamation. Thought to have originated from Egypt, the Tachoni, originally Nilotic, were once the dominant tribe in the territory around present-day Bungoma, Trans Nzoia and Uasin Gishu. The history of Abatachoni has always baffled, even eluded Luyia historians like Prof. Gideon Were (1967) and Dr. John Osogo (1966) whose accounts have now been enhanced by a new study, *Tachon Peoples—History, Culture and Economy* by Demmahom Olovodes Lihraw. According to Lihraw (2010), the Tachoni were the original Kitoki (corrupted to Kitosh) people who took in, as herdsboys, roaming bands of people that later evolved as Bukusu.[157] Through a complex process of ethno-social evolution, the Tachoni lost their language and adopted Bantu dialects beginning circa 1230 and over sixteen generations (circa 1730) became completely

---

[157.] Conventional understanding before Lihraw's extrapolative take associated *Kitosh* with the Bukusu, a term first recorded by Joseph Thomson, the first Whiteman to travel through Luyialand on foot in 1883. *Kitosh*, which the Kalenjin used to describe the Bukusu, means the "terrible ones." It was an offensive word which Babukusu detested before being officially outlawed in 1940s.

bantuised. Olutachoni, language of the Tachoni, is a cross breed between Olubukusu, Olunyala and Olukabras with nuances of Nandi. Although now completely bantuised as Luyia the Tachoni retain key aspects of culture that are distinctly Kalenjin especially female circumcision and ancient religious rituals.

Earlier historians identified Abatachoni as a product of the intertribal marriages between Bukusu and Abangoma (Bongomek), a Nilotic Kalenjin tribe from whose name Bungoma is derived. According to this line of historical thought, the Bukusu intermarried in large numbers with the Kalenjin or Maasai when they lived at Ebwayi (present day Amukura) and Mwalie in Malakisi. They called the offspring from these intertribal unions Yumbu (Wolf 1980: 308), believed to be the ancestors of Abatachoni. With time, Kalenjin language of the Yumbu disappeared and was replaced with a Bukusu dialect which later evolved into Olutachoni. The Yumbu theory is challenged by Lihraw (2010) who says Abayumbu was merely a clan among the Mwalie cluster rather than the *pater familias* of Abatachoni. Besides intermarriages, Bukusu and Elgon Maasai (as they are sometimes called) lived as uneasy neighbors frequently raiding each other. While the warlike Elgon Maasai, especially the Sebei (Sabaot), captured boys to enlist as warriors, the Bukusu seized women who later became wives (*babeche mung'abo*). It is thought that the Tachoni, as a subnation, originated from this symbiosis. The populous clandom of Bakitwika (Bakitiika) which has spawned several clans among Bamasaaba (Bukusu, Gisu) was originally Kalenjin or Maasai which underwent bantuisation between 1230 and 1308 following intertribal matrimonies (Lihraw 2010: 7).[158]

---

[158] Major clans descendant from Bakitwika include Basibende, Batilu, Bamuki, Babichachi, Babambo, Babulo, Bakipemuli, Basitui, Bakimweyi, and Bakiyabi.

b. Evolution of the Tachoni

Since evolution and migration from Egypt, the Tachoni were known by various names. Toli and Temwa are cited as the Tachoni equivalent of biblical Adam and Eve. They are said to be part of the Azania group of Nilotes that trekked southward along the Nile. In Egypt they were called Matur while in Sudan they were divided into two groups—the Lamek and Kabini which later reunited under a paramount chief (*letia*) Kaptaijon Kitoki. It was from this reunion that they were called *El Kitoki* (people of Kitoki), the name they carried through into Kenya and Uganda. When they sojourned at Sirikwa, they were called *Chesirikwet* (easterners) and it is here they first met Bamasaaba and Maasai communities. In the ensuing battles for territorial supremacy, a major dispersal occurred with one group heading into Mt. Elgon while another settled in Kitale (Koitalel). The third group, comprising eight clans headed for Mbaiyek on the eastern slopes of Mt. Elgon in Uganda. The Mt. Elgon group intermarried with the indigenous Ateker people to found the Sabeweiny (Elgon Maasai) of which the Sabaot (Sebei) are best known and from which the clan of Abashieni in Marama is descendant. At Sirikwa, the clanal system that exists today was already in place with major clans established including Songiek (Abasonge), Kamkong'i, Kapchu (Ababichu), Kapkenda (Kipkendiek), Kapchiruk (Chimuluku), Terik (Tiriki), Kapsioya (Abasioya), Ngachi (Abangachi), Kiborit (Abakiboriti), Kimwei (Abakimweyi), Kiptuk (Abakitwika), and Kapsinayi (Lihraw 2010: 13-14).

Abatachoni live in the newly created district of Bungoma East, especially in the localities of Webuye, Sitikho, Bokoli, Misikhu, Ndivisi, Namarambi, and Chetambe. Although Lugari District, a major postcolonial settlement scheme, is a hotchpotch of several subnations, the majority of people are Tachoni as well as residents of North Kabras in Kakamega North District. Pockets of Tachoni enclaves nest among other communities such as Abakiboriti and

Kabyonek (Sabaot) while several clans are transnational living among Bukusu, Kabras, Wanga, Marama, Bakhayo, Marachi, Maragoli and Banyore (see relevant clan tables). The Tachoni also interacted and intermarried with the Gusii; some of the mixed offspring settling in northern Tanzanian region of Kagera and believed to be descendants of some Haya and Ziba clans.

Map 13 shows the major administrative locations in Tachoni, Kakamega County.

c. Fighting for recognition and territorial rights

Tachoni, which in Kalenjin means "those who went or left" was first used in 1917 and adopted as a name to define closely related clanal septs during mid 1940s, around the same time the Luyia nation was born. During registration of persons over eighteen for purposes of tax collection by British colonists, the Tachoni protested being registered as Bukusu. To resolve the question of tribal names, the colonial government convened a conference of all tribes in the region at which related clans resolved to adopt the name Tachoni as a tribal identity. The origin of the name Tachoni is a controversial subject to which various theories are advanced. One school of thought posits the name was chosen in honor of their unifying leaders, Kaptaijon and Lentoijon, while another links them to an incident in which the Sabaot described them as *Ta cho nü* (we are going but shall return). The third theory links Tachoni to baptismal (*marich*) and initiation rites (*khulicha*) at a sacred place known as *stapchon* said to be a corruption of Sang'alo (*Tacho*) and Bokoli (*Stapcha*). The place at a river where these ceremonies took place is known as *musitabicha* (all season water). Theory four which is closely linked with three, traces Tachoni to *tacho*, meaning a place of rich vegetation believed to be present-day Sang'alo. Their Wanga and Kabras neighbors referred to them as *abandu be tacho* (people of Tacho) or simply *orutatsone* (Lihraw 2010: 17-25).

The Tachoni, spelt variously as Tachon, Tajon, Taijoin, Tachonü, Tojon, Toijon, Tatsone, and Abatachoni revere *likhanga* (guinea fowl) as their tribal totem. It is a sacred symbol associated with creation mythology, adroitness, and spirituality. Whatever the merits of these theories, the Tachoni are not less Luyia, any more than other Luyia subnations because the Luyia nation is a hybrid mix of original Bantu and Nilotic Luo, Kalenjin, and Maasai people who have undergone a process of bantuisation. The Tachoni lost their Nilotic tongue owing largely to intermarriages with Bantu tribes, especially Bamasaaba (Bukusu and Bagisu). Except for circumcision and baptismal rites, the Bantu women married by Tachoni men dominated in all other aspects of acculturation while Tachoni women married by Bantu men adopted the language and traditions of their husbands. Luyia wives retained key aspects of their culture especially language and naming system which Tachoni men adopted or learnt willy-nilly.

Moreover, many Bantu boys were hired as shepherds or farm help and lived within Tachoni homesteads practicing their culture without interference. Like the Tiriki (Terik), the only condition of social integration was induction into initiation rites of *khulicha* (circumcision) and *marich* (baptism). Over sixteen generations (four hundred years), the Tachoni had lost their Nilotic tongue and become assimilated into Bantu linguistic phylum with a distinct dialect, Olutachoni, a cross between Olubukusu, Olunyala and Olukabras. Language was therefore a vital vehicle in ethnocultural transformation from Nilotes to Bantu of the once dominant Tachoni.

Loss of identity is not something the Tachoni lost sleep about. They embraced new identity with vigour and attempts by the colonial government to subjugate them were met with fury. As early as 1924, they founded institutions to fight for their rights in a judicious and organized way. First they fought for a distinct identity (see p.299) by resisting their numbers being registered as Bukusu or Kabras for tax purposes. To resolve the searing question of identity, the colonial government convened an Area Councils and Names Conference in 1947 at which several related clans adopted Tachoni as their new ethnocultural identity. Earlier in 1937, they hired a British QC, Mr. Mylchreest to represent them against a colonial agent, Chief Amutallah who was interfering with their push for territorial sovereignty. In 1956, through Patel Advocates of Eldoret, they petitioned the colonial government which had imposed the teaching curriculum and Common Entrance Examinations (standard six) in Olubukusu (Lihraw 2010: 108-109). The struggle for recognition and separate territorial rights continued at the Lancaster House conferences achieving some success when Kimilili location was divided into three in 1960 with Ndivisi predominantly lageered by Tachoni.

d. Fiercely ritualistic

Besides being fiercely ritualistic, the Tachoni are skilled craftsmen famous for building fortified homes (*tsingoba*) across Wanga, Marachi, and Bukusu the most famous of which are Lumboka and Chetambe near Webuye. The Tachoni surrendered Chetambe to Bukusu warriors fleeing colonial assault following the fall of their previous holdout, Lumboka, named after a Tachoni army commander, Lumboka Sibionei. Chetambe was the last bastion of Bukusu resistance to colonial rule. Like Lumboka the previous year, columns of British, Sudanese, and Ugandan soldiers invaded the fort in 1895 to flash out the stubborn Bukusu in what came to be known as the War of Chetambe.

The Tachoni are still very traditionalist with some clans practicing female circumcision, the only Luyia subnation to do so. They also practice ancient burial customs. In March 2010, a ninety-year-old Tachoni elder, Mavachi Mandira from Luvusi village, grabbed national headlines when he was given a traditional burial last practiced more than fifty years ago.[159] Instead of a coffin, he was wrapped in a shroud of fresh cow skin before being interred in a ritual that must not be witnessed by women and children. For the all important rituals such as circumcision (*khulicha*), baptism (*marich*) and burial, Tachoni clansmen face east in accordance with notions about good and evil. The east (*ebukwe*) where the sun rises represents energy and good tidings while the west (*mumbo*) is associated with darkness and evil where bad spirits live. Just like *olusiola* (*markhamia platycalyx*) and *munanyezo* trees play a sacred role among Abanyole and Abatiriki, respectively, it is notable that among Abatachoni, *omutoto* (peepul) is a sacred tree. It is a type of fig tree which Buddhists also hold as a sacred shrine. Whenever the Tachoni lived or sojourned throughout their migratory history, they planted *omutoto* under whose shade they performed cleansing rituals.

[159.] Article by Denis Odunga headlined "Village treated to rare traditional burial," published in the *Daily Nation* of March 17, 2010.

e. Clan clusters and specialist vocations

Tachoni subnation has about fifty clans clustered into eight main clanal septs (Lihraw 2010: 29-31):

1. Abachika (Kapchikhen), found mainly in Kakamega and Bungoma consists of six clans—Abamwongo, Abachambai, Abakabini, Abakobolo, Abamakhanga, and Abacharia.

2. Chimuluku (Chipruk) which evolved from intermarriages between Tachoni and Purko Maasai has five exogamous clans—Moitek, Mandoli, Ababwoba, Chepkwabi (Abakwabi), and Kapsimisi (Abasimisi).

3. Abamwalie, the largest clandom has seventeen major clans—Ababichu, Abaengele, Abakamutebi, Abakamukong, Abakuusi, Abalukulu, Abaluu, Abatasama, Abamakhuli, Abamalicha, Abameywa, Abanyangali, Abarefu, Abasamo, Abasaniaka, Abasonge, and Abayumbu. Most of these clans have, in turn, spawned several independent subclans. For instance Ababichu have generated three subclans—Abakaliuba, Abalusaka, and Abamuyi; all of whom live at Webuye, Lugari and Malaba. Abamakhuli have produded four subclans—Abaking'asi, Abalunza, Ababwele, and Abamayakali while Abayumbu have two subclans—Abakhaya and Abanjabasi. Abasonge has spawned four clans—Abatawai, Abakibande, Ababitelia, and Abawandekiti while Abasamo have three—Abasimaolia, Abakhusia, and Abalimo. Abasaniaka, who also live in Maragoli and Tiriki have three subclans—Abakisila, Abisimo, and Abamusali.

4. Kabyonek Group which is famed for producing *abashebi* (circumcision surgeons) and baptismal priests has five clans—Abahabiya, Kabyonek, Abakafusi (Abamatili),

Abameywa, and Abasioya. Abahabiya have three subclans—Abachikolati, Abamuumbwa, and Abamuruli.

5. Tambach Group, the majority of whom live in Tambach, Nandi country, has three clans—Abakimweyi, Abasangale, and Abamangeti.

6. Grates Group, skilled in the art of rainmaking and iron smithing, consists of twelve clans—Abachewa (Kapchewa), Abachemwile, Abahabichwa (Kapchwa), Abahambi (Abakhambi), Abamutama, Abakubwayi (Kipchebwai), Abaleke (Kaplekei), Abamarakalu, Abamuchembi, Abamukhuyu, Abasamba, and Abawande

7. El Kony Group consists of six clans of which two—Abakitwika and Abashieni—have spawned several major clans among the Bukusu, Gisu, and Marama. The other four include Abangachi, Abacheo, Abakiboriti, and Abasang'alo. In turn Abangachi, one of the dominant clans in Tachoni, has produced three subclans namely, Abawaila, Abakhumaya, and Abawele found mainly around Webuye, Kimilili, Lugari, Sirisia, and Kapsengei. Abasang'alo have spawned five subclans—Abamwinami, Abatamwoya, Abaholela, Abaleka (Wanga and Marama), and Abakhaabi (Bukhayo). Abakitwika (Abakitiika) is the largest single clan among Babukusu and has spawned ten independent subclans—Abasibende, Ababichachi, Ababambo, Abakiyabi, Abamuki, Abasitui, Abakipemuli, Ababuulo, Abamatilu, and Abakimweyi.

8. Relievers Group comprises seven clans transferred by Chief Chitere of Kabras to *Letia* Nyikuri (Sifuma), the Tachoni ruler during the 1870 war with Abanyala. These clans include Abamachina, Abamuchi, Abasiu (abasihu), Abamakangala, Abasoko, Abatobo, and Abanjasi. Abasoko and Abatobo have since gone back and reclassified themselves as Kabras.

Quite clearly not all clans are of Nilotic origin. The Tachoni, like Tiriki, observed assimilation policy in which war captives, destitutes, or clans that simply wanted to settle among Abatachoni got acculturated into the tribe. The newcomers had a choice to be adopted into one of the existing Tachoni clans or continue with their original identity. The largest clan is Abangachi while Abasaniaka are also found in Bukusu, Tiriki, and Maragoli. Abatecho, Abaengele (Abahengele) and Abayirifuma are common clans with Abanyala ba Ndombi while at least twenty clans are shared with the Bukusu (see table 13 p.215 and table 39 p.344). The majority of Abaengele were originally Teso war captives captured during the Teso War of 1596-1600. Abawayira and Abangachi are closely related and observe rules of exogamy (Osogo 1966: 94). As we have seen, a few clans were renowned as specialists in certain arts and crafts. As far as apiculture is concerned, only a few clans successfully produced honey from beehives. These included Abahabiya, Abamatili, Abanyangali, and Abachika. The prized product was used in alcohol brewing, as medicine and as wedding gift (Lihraw 2010: 277).

Table 30: Tachoni[160] population distribution by administrative unit, surface area, ad density

Admin Unit	Total	Area (sq km)	Density
Lugari	292,151	668.9	437
Matete	60,891	101.2	601
Chevaywa	33,145	57	581
Kivaywa	14,462	23.7	609
Kiliboti	7,320	13.2	554
Kulumbeni	11,363	20.1	565

[160.] Tachoni people are spread across three main districts: Kakamega North, Lugari, and Bungoma East. Consequently, the total population given is not strictly for Tachoni alone but a congeries of tribes living in the Lugari settlement scheme.

Luandeti	**27,746**	**44.2**	**628**
Luandeti	8,162	14.5	565
Mahanga	5,787	8.5	682
Maturu	7,625	11.7	653
Mabunye	6,172	9.6	644
Lugari	**106,123**	**265.8**	**399**
Mautuma	**25,082**	**83.8**	**299**
Mukuyu	11,147	23.8	469
Mbagara	13,935	60	232
Lugari	**31,381**	**81.3**	**386**
Lugari	12,593	43.5	289
Marakusi	18,788	37.8	498
Lumakanda	**29,955**	**59**	**507**
Munyuki	15,417	26	593
Mwamba	14,538	33	440
Chekalini	**19,705**	**41.7**	**473**
Koromaiti	9,532	19.8	483
Musembe	10,173	21.9	464
Likuyani	**125,137**	**301.8**	**415**
Likuyani	27,243	97.2	280
Seregeya	15,704	56.3	279
Soy	11,539	40.9	282
Kongoni	**46,554**	**99.7**	**467**
Sango	10,724	32.1	334
Mawetatu	12,129	24.3	499
Kongoni	23,701	43.3	548
Nzoia	**30,321**	**54.9**	**552**
Vinyenya	5,361	10.1	530
Musemwa	5,049	19.4	261
Moi's Bridge	7,569	15.6	486
Matunda	12,342	9.9	1,250
Sinoko	**21,019**	**50.1**	**420**
Nzoia	4,148	16.1	258
Mwiba	3,256	16.6	196
Namunyiri	7,080	9.9	718

| Milimani | 6,535 | 7.6 | 864 |

Adapted from Kenya Census 2009, *Kenya National Bureau of Statistics, Nairobi, August 2010.*

f. System of traditional and modern government

The smallest political unit was a clan headed by a clan elder (*omwami*) who ruled with the assistance of three council members known as *masis* (messengers). Traditionally, each clan lived in a fort (*olukoba*) which defined extent of the jurisdiction of a clan elder. The *omwami* and his assistants were responsible for internal affairs and management of foreign policy. Sitting atop the tribal hierarchy was *Letia* (leader) who ruled through an advisory council comprising various clan heads. In addition to the advisory council, *Letia* also kept an independent board of elders known as *mal'mayiet* revered for their deep knowledge of tribal laws and customs. The *mal'mayiet* board was composed of five departments—*Laitarian* (defence), *Marichobiti* (spiritualism), *O'muliuli* (magic buster), *Omung'osi* (seer), and *O'komuse* or *Metainik* (sage). The first recorded *Letia* is Kapchikhen el Maturu, *Laitarian* is Nechemsri, *Omung'osi* is Loiboiben el Nalo, *Marichobiti* is Kabin el Ter, and *O'komuse* is Bel Set Nemsri, a brother to the first *Letia* (Lihraw 2010: 38). The last great *Letia* of Abatachoni was Nyikuri Iyeya Wamukune aka Sifuma (famous) who died in 1902.

The *Letia* wore special insignia that included a colobus monkey skin cloak (*ekutusi*), a copper bracelet (*omukasa*) and ivory ornaments on the wrist (*lichabe* and *injabasi*) in addition to donning a cowrie shell. The *Letia* had a royal sceptre (*yindabusi*) made from a rhino horn, *lebweni* headdress decorated with palm leaves and ostrich feathers, a three-legged royal stool (*esitiena*) made from *omurembe* (*erythrina abyssinica*) or *omukhuyu* (fig) tree. A fully kitted *Letia* donned a royal spear and shield as well as a flywhisk among other regalia. These emblems, symbols, and paraphernalia were visible tools of authority passed from one *Letia* to the next. Succession to the office of *Letia* was through a system where an incumbent nominated his son to succeed him on the basis of his personal qualities rather than on the principle of seniority.

The heir-apparent planted a peepul tree (*omutoto*) and constructed a shrine at its foot then rested a beer pot on *esibo*, a clay tray for serving royal meals during coronation ceremonies. The swearing in ceremony was presided over by a specialist known as *omung'osi* (seer) assisted by another ritualist called *ombiti*. He stood on an animal skin facing east. First he was dressed with *injabasi* followed by *lichabe, omukasa, ekutusi,* and *lebweni* before being handed *yindabusi*. He then sat on the royal stool, *esitiena* to receive final instructions and blessings. After this he stood up and walked straight to the hut of his elder wife without looking back or sideways. Here he sat on another skin mat stretching his legs toward the front door to be anointed with ghee and cleansed with herbs before returning to sit on *esitiena* and officially pronounced *Letia* (Lihraw 2010: 252-253). If the named heir was a minor, one of the elders became his guardian until he came of age and ready to take up leadership duties. On inauguration day, he sat on the royal stool then fresh milk was poured onto his head before being shaved to complete the succession ritual.

Although the struggle for Tachoni rights began as early as 1924, it was not until the founding of Tachon Union in 1945 (registered in 1955) that the subnation sent a clear political message. They dispatched delegates across the country to seek support in finding solutions to their problems. Alarmed at activities of the union, the colonial government dubbed Tachoni Mau Mau sympathisers, an excuse to isolate them from the Luyia and launch an attack. Even though Burudi Nabwera, the shining Tachoni politician at the time was in KADU, a party the colonial government tacitly supported, he was dubbed communist and therefore antigovernment. This label derived primarily from Mr. Nabwera's Eastern bloc training and his association with Jaramogi Oginga Odinga.

At Kenya's independence in 1963, the Tachoni were placed in one constituency known as Lurambi North, a large riding that spanned Trans Nzoia, Uasin Gishu, Bungoma, and Kakamega districts. Politically, there is no constituency which is predominantly Tachoni although Lugari, created in 1988, comes close. The riding came into existence when the larger Lurambi North was abolished, and in its place three constituencies created—Webuye, Malava, and Lugari. The first MP in the newly created Lugari constituency was former diplomat, Burudi Nabwera (1988-92),[161] a Tachoni who had also previously represented Lurambi North twice before in 1969-74 and 1974-79. Burudi, however, lost the seat to Apili Waomba Wawire (1955-2012) in the 1992 multiparty elections. Mr. Wawire ruled for one term before being swept away by the well-oiled machinery of Cyrus Shakhalaga Jirongo from Tiriki in 1997.

Jirongo's Youth for Kanu '92 movement played a pivotal role in Moi's reelection following the reintroduction of multiparty elections in 1992. Despite his charm and wealth, the flamboyant Jirongo lost the seat to a medical doctor, Enock Wamalwa Kibunguchy, as Moi era apparatchiks were swept away by a tidal wave of radical political change. Jirongo, however, quickly recovered to recapture the seat in 2007 under his party, KADDU, a corruption of the preindependence party, KADU. In 2013, Jirongo contested and lost Kakamega senate seat under a new party he founded called Federal Party of Kenya (FPK). His Lugari constituency was inherited by former journalist, Ayub Savula. In neighboring Webuye, another Tachoni, Alfred Wekesa Sambu, beat Musikari Kombo as the

---

[161.] Burudi Nabwera, 97 in 2013, was briefly the chairman of the Luyia Council of Elders in the run up to the 2007 elections. Other board members included veteran politician Martin Shikuku (ex-MP for Butere) and businessman, Ibrahim Ambwere. Nabwera was succeeded by Joseph Daniel Otiende, 94 in 2013, Kenya's first minister for education (later health and housing) from Maragoli. The current chairman as of 2013 is Patrick Wangamati, a Bukusu.

Orange revolution made inroads into Bukusuland. Another Tachoni political heavyweight is veterinary doctor, Noah Muhalangángá Wekesa, who has dominated Kwanza constituency in Rift Valley since its creation in 1988. Dr. Wekesa's political fortunes are largely due to the early demise of George Welime Kapten, the charismatic Kitale lawyer who defeated him in 1992 but died under mysterious circumstances in 1998 shortly after winning his second term in 1997. Since then Dr. Wekesa consolidated his power in Kwanza winning all subsequent elections but lost his bid to become the first governor of Trans Nzoia County to former PS, Patrick Khaemba in the 2013 general elections. His former Kwanza riding was captured by newcomer, Ferdinand Wanyonyi.

Besides politicians, other notable Tachoni personalities include Prof. Richard Musangi, the former vice chancellor of Egerton University; Everett Shitanda, the secretary to the Commission for Higher Education; Vitalis Musebe, the journalist; and colonial era chief, Namutala khwa Mayeku.

12. Abatiriki (Tiriki)

Table 31: Tiriki clans (brackets indicate alternative spelling or where else clan members are found)

Ababala (Wanga)	Ababuka (Wanga, Marachi)
Ababulugi (Maragoli)	Abakhadiri
Abakhuvera	Abakisiki
Abakisindi	Abakove
Abalukhoba (Marama)	Abalukhombe
Abamaavi (Maragoli)	Abamalaba (Bukusu)
Abamarama (Marama)	Abambo (Bukusu, Cameroon)
Abamuhia	Abamukombero
Abamuli (Bunyore, Bunyala, Idakho, Kisa and Seme)	Abamutete (Bunyore)

Abanatsiri (Wanga)   Abarimbuli (Isukha, Maragoli)
Abasaali (Maragoli)   Abasalia
Abasamia (Kisa, Bunyore)   Abasanga
Abashibo (Marama, Butsotso)   Abashirika (Idakho)

a.   Meaning of Tiriki

Tiriki derives from Terik (Terikeek), a Nilotic Kalenjin tribe closely related to Sabaot of Mt. Elgon. Their oral migratory history indicates that they migrated from Mt. Elgon and their lingo-cultural tradition is similar to the Bongomek group. They are called Tiriki all those communities who came to this area and adopted circumcision rituals of the Terik. However, the Luyia Bantu could not correctly pronounce the name Terikeek without adding a vowel after the consonant *k*, so they started calling themselves Tiriki. Besides people, the Luyia also either mispronounced or misspelt Terikeek place names. Thus Kibsambaay became Gisambayi, Cheebkaay became Jepkoyai, Kiboochi became Givogi; Taambooyoo became Tambua and Keribwa became Iriva to mention but a few. The Terik also live at Nyang'ori[162] and have to a large extent been assimilated into the populous Luyia or Luo tribes. In explanation of this, Terik scholars say that a long time ago during wrestling matches, the vanquished took the moniker of the victor to symbolise total defeat. That is how some Terik people have Luyia and Luo names.

The Terikeek are sandwiched between the Luyia, Nandi and Luo with majority living in Vihiga and Nandi districts. UNESCO lists Terik and Olusuba as endangered languages. There are no

---

[162.] The Terik are sometimes also referred to as the Nyang'ori. However, it is largely a disparaging term which they detest. Its exogenesis dates to pre colonial era when the pastoral Terikeek helped themselves to cowpeas (*ng'or*) in Luo gardens on their way back home from pastures. Because of this the Luo called them *Nyang'or* (cow pea thieves) and the name stuck when the colonial administration formally adopted it to describe the place and the people.

written materials in Terik and most young Terik speak Nandi. In an effort to preserve their language and culture, Terik Council of Elders petitioned the UN Commission on Human Rights in 2005 on what they saw as an encroachment on their ancestral land and cultural annihilation by the populous Luyia. The most ambitious project to resuscitate the language was launched in 2011 in which pupils from nursery up to Class Three take lessons in Terik three days a week. This initiative is driven by Terik Essential Programmes Agency for Development in partnership with University of Manitoba, Canada.

Although various communities live side by side in harmony, searing friction remains a reality occasionally exploding into open conflict; the most fatal of which occurred in early 1990s. Administratively, Tiriki was originally part of Kakamega District. In 1990, Vihiga District was hived off the larger Kakamega to administer the chieftainces of Tiriki, Bunyore and Maragoli. However, in 2007, Vihiga was split to create two new districts of Hamisi (Tiriki) and Emuhaya (Bunyore) while Vihiga remained for Maragoli. The main centers in Tiriki are Hamisi, Shamakhokho, Serem, Nyang'ori, Gambogi, Kiboswa and Cheptul.

b. Brief migrational history

Unlike other Luyia subnations, clan authority as a form of tribal administration was inferior to the age grade system (*likhula*) in Tiriki. Leadership among the Tiriki was determined by seniority in the *likhula* system irrespective of clan strength, history or origin. Most inhabitants of Tiriki were migrant clans from various Luyia subnations with the neighboring Maragoli constituting the largest contingent. The two largest clans (*zimbamba*, singular: *luvamba*), Abalukhoba and Abambo (also in Cameroon—Mbo) are also the earliest Bantu arrivals in Tiriki. Abambo were originally Babukusu who split from the main tribe as it fled from Teso enemies at Buyemba in Uganda and Lulitsi is putatively their earliest known ancestor (Osogo 1966: 56). Abalukhoba came to Tiriki under the leadership of Khoba who later spawned several other clans including Abamumbo, Abalukhombe Abikhaba and Abashitsutsa. Khoba's other son; Alulitsi was the father of Kisienya, Ameyo and Wanga whose descendants also formed several clans and subclans.

Other early arrivals were Abamuli, Abatura, Abakhatiri and Abasanga. Abasamia came from Busia and are also found among Abashisa (Kisa) and Abanyole (Abamang'ali) while Abamarama, a clan in Tiriki, is a whole subnation in Butere area. This link requires further anthropological research to establish whether Tiriki Abaramama are the founders of several clans known as Abamarama in Butere.

Abamuli and Abamutete came from Bunyore while Abarimbuli (Avatembuli), Abakisindi (Avagisindi), Abasaali (Avasaali), Abamaavi (Avama'avi), Abasanga (Avasanga), Abasaniaga (Avasaniaga), Abasuba (Avasuba), and Abakirima (Avakirima) came from Maragoli. Abatura are thought to have come from Bukhayo while another band of Abatura settled in Mumias among the Wanga and in Isukha, Bukusu and Marachi. Besides straddling other Luyia subnations, three clans are also scattered among the Kalenjin and Luo. These are Abakuka who besides Wanga are also found in Kalenjin (Kapiinjoy) and Luo (Kasiguga); Abasaniaga are in Maragoli, Bukusu and Tachoni. In Kalenjin they are known as Kapchepkwang while in Luo they are called Kamunara. Abasuba who are also in Maragoli are known as Kapchenjiro in Kalenjin and, of course, Abasuba among the Luo while the Bukusu call them Basoba and Gisu Abasoba.

In this context, it must be noted that Wanga, who founded Abawanga subnation in Mumias, first lived in Tiriki after his family emigrated from Uganda following breakup of the Chwezi Kingdom under the leadership of his grandfather, Wamoyi (see p.109). The ruling dynasty of Abashitsetse and Abalukhoba (Balukhova) are closely related. The kinship between these two clans is so close-knit that during important ritual ceremonies, they always invite each other. A good example is during coronation or burial of Wanga kings. A delegation of Abalukhoba elders not only attends but performs a specific ritual role. During these functions, a Mulukhoba elder sits on a royal stool to symbolise the unbreakable bond of brotherhood (Were 1967: 116) between the two septs.

c. Ancestral shrines and oathing rituals

A typical Tiriki homestead had an ancestral shrine (*lusambwa*) rather like the type found among Babukusu. A family head was responsible for looking after it and, in his absence, the eldest male clansman. Additionally, head of a homestead held an inherited position of horn keeper and it was his duty to blow the horn (*oluika*) to summon help when the community was under attack by cattle rustlers.[163] Once the alarm was sounded by one horn blower, the rest joined making a sustained cacophony that rallied the community to common defence and scared off attackers. Other subnations like the Bukusu, Wanga, Marachi, Tachoni, and Kabras lived in walled villages (*tsingoba*) with sentries posted at various gates to warn villagers of any intrusive attacks.

Besides common defence, the Tiriki community also observed first fruits rituals. The elders kindled *bwali* (bonfire) at a crossroads and threw green leaves on it closely observing the direction in which the smoke billowed. The most venerable elder beseeched ancestral spirits to bless people's health, crops and cattle and to drive *abalosi* (witches) to *imbo* (Luoland). After this entreaty, the elder cast his stick in the direction of *imbo* and others followed suit

---

163. Although the position of horn keeper was through inheritance, it did not pass automatically to the next in line according to the principle of seniority practiced by other Luyia groups. The occupier of this office had to possess qualities of leadership such as bravery, wisdom and fearlessness to succeed. If no one in the immediate family fitted the bill, someone outside the family was appointed by the father or clan elders.

to signify end of the ritual. However, the bonfire was kept burning all day with every passerby throwing more leaves, grass or food on it. No farm work was allowed until the following day. Ritual supplication to ancestral spirits through *bwali* ceremonies were conducted during stressful periods such as defeat or fear of defeat in battle, epidemics or famine. Although a few elders still observe *bwali*, and pray at domestic shrines, these rituals are, to a large extent extinct, at least at the community level.

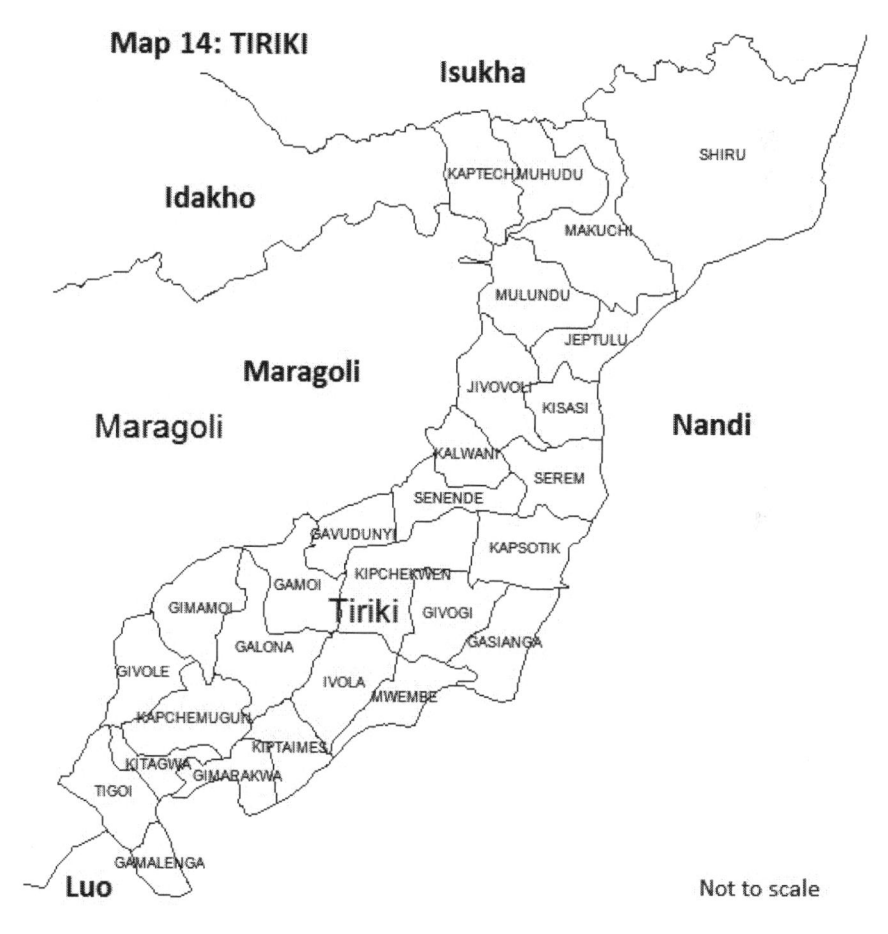

Map 14 shows the main administrative locations in Tiriki, Vihiga County.

Diehard traditionalists blame Christianity and *abasungu* (whites) for misfortunes and loss of morals in the community. By crusading against customary traditions, the Church was blamed for destroying traditional defence systems that protected the land from attack by mystical forces (Sangree 1966: 88). Under traditional justice system, elders administered certain ordeals and oathing to extract confessions especially in cases of incest and witchcraft. Although the British outlawed most of them, they saw merit in at least one ritual. Known as *omurembe*, the accused publicly pronounced his innocence by thrusting a spear into the trunk of *omurembe* tree *(erythrina abyssinica)*. If one's declaration was false, the magical powers of *omurembe* brought sickness and death to his family. In contrast, the Wanga used the magic powers of *omurembe* to cure mumps *(tsindendeyi)*. Holding the sick child in her hands, the mother circled *omurembe* tree three times chanting a spell and by this ritual her child was cured shortly afterward. In Luo mythology, *omurembe* tree was also highly venerated. The Luo believed if a sick person circled the tree eight times, he got cured and anyone cutting the magical tree down risked instant death.

Table 32: Tiriki population distribution by administrative unit, surface area, and density

Admin Unit	Total	Area (sq km)	Density
Hamisi	148,259	156.4	948
Jepkoyai	40,507	42.9	944
Gisambai	21,452	24.1	892
Galona	6,502	8.2	793
Gamoi	5,106	5.5	928
Gavudunyi	3,854	4	958
Gimomoi	5,990	6.3	947
Jepkoyai	19,055	18.9	1,009
Givole	4,937	4.7	1,054
Kapchemugung	5,565	6.5	852

Kitagwa	3,419	2.7	1,254
Tigoi	5,134	4.9	1,039
Shamakhokho	**27,535**	**25**	**100**
Senende	**7,998**	**8.3**	**965**
Kalwani	3,446	3.6	948
Senende	4,552	4.7	979
Shamakhokho	**19,537**	**16.7**	**1,167**
Jivovoli	7,072	6.6	1,069
Kisasi	5,676	4.5	1,069
Serem	6,789	5.7	1,200
Shaviringa	**38,993**	**39.5**	**988**
Muhudu	**16,659**	**19.9**	**837**
Kaptech	4,758	6.6	718
Muhudu	6,021	6	1,000
Mulundu	5,880	7.3	811
Shaviringa	**22,334**	**19.6**	**1,142**
Jeptulu	5,644	5	1,141
Makuchi	7,072	7.5	940
Shiru	9,618	7.1	1,357
Tambua	**41,224**	**49**	**841**
Banja	**22,535**	**27.3**	**826**
Gasianga	4,500	6.6	687
Givogi	4,334	5.6	770
Kapsotik	6,394	6.4	994
Kipchekwen	7,307	8.7	842
Tambua	**18,689**	**21.8**	**859**
Gamalenga	4,085	2.5	1,605
Gimarakwa	3,064	3.8	800
Ivola	4,443	6.2	718
Kiptaimes	3,049	4	757
Mwembe	4,048	5.2	785

Adapted from Kenya Census 2009, *Kenya National Bureau of Statistics, Nairobi, August 2010.*

d. Territorial and military organization

The Tiriki have territorial divisions called *tsisomo* (singular: *lusomo*) which loosely means hamlets or villages but which is used interchangeably to refer to subnations or clans (*zimbamba*). It was the duty of each *lusomo* to ensure that circumcision candidates were ready for initiation rites and to build *tsirumbi* (circumcision huts, singular: *irumbi*) in secret groves in dense forest known as *kavunyonje*. According to a recent study, there are thirty-six sacred groves in the two divisions of Tiriki still existing.[164] Each *lusomo* had an army known as *ibololi* (plural: *tsibololi*) recruited from among circumcision initiates. Membership of an *ibololi* regiment consisted of not just the active warriors and their dependants but also retired ones. The settlement of various clans from Maragoli in Tiriki over several generations upset the existing territorial arrangements. With each new wave of invading immigrants, the territory under control of a particular *ibololi* was frequently diminished and whenever the Tiriki were pushed farther east they formed a new *ibololi* (Sangree 1966: 93).

The Luyia Tiriki and Kalenjin Terik disagree as to the exact territorial jurisdiction of each *ibololi*. The Luyia claim that at any given time, each *ibololi* had its own definite territory which did not overlap with that of any other unit. However the Kalenjin say that an *ibololi* consisted of members from different territorial domains. This disagreement reflects a major difference between traditional military organizations in predominantly Nandi and Luyia areas. According to the Luyia Tiriki, each *lusomo* organized its own war raids and shared the booty among its members. When necessary, two units joined forces to mount a major joint attack.

[164.] Research paper entitled "Persistence and Loss of Cultural Values of Tiriki Sacred Groves in Hamisi District, Kenya: Implications for Management." The authors, Fredrick Nyongesa Kassilly and Harrison Mugatsia Tsingalia (2007) are lecturers at Masinde Muliro University of Science and Technology, Kakamega.

Each *lusomo* had access to a sacred grove (*kavulokosi*) at the hilltop and a *kavunyonje* (circumcision grove) in the valley. I have made reference to kindling of *bwali* fire with regard to first fruit rites. But it was on *kavulokosi* that the biggest annual *bwali* rituals were held usually in late December or early January to bless the next crop, drive away *abalosi* (witches) and pray for success in warfare. Occasionally *bwali* ceremonies were held if a specific request was made to elders; for example to pray for success of a pending cattle raid. When times were hard or misfortune struck the land, e.g., prolonged drought or livestock epidemic, people sought intervention of ancestral spirits through *bwali* offerings at the sacred groves. These were held in addition to family and *lusomo* level rituals. Rarely were community affairs conducted on a tribal basis like the Maragoli (see p.268). Most of the rituals including circumcision, marriage, birth and death were performed on a *lusomo* basis. If people came from other *tsisomo*, it was largely due to curiosity rather than a customary obligation on their part.

e. Who is a Tiriki?

Although ancestors of Wanga kings briefly sojourned among Abalukhoba, the Tiriki, like other Luyia subnations, did not have a centralized tribal authority. Each *lusomo-ibololi* unit was virtually independent. And where clan membership determined strength of kinship (*obuleebe*) in other Luyia subnations, among the Tiriki it was the sense of brotherhood enamored through initiation rites (*idumi*) that bonded the tribal community. According to Terik customs, special camaraderie established through membership of the same age group (*likhula*) was stronger than that between clansmen. It did not matter which clan or tribe you came from; so long as you participated in *idumi* circumcision rituals you automatically got assimilated into Terik community and became Omutiriki (Bulimo 2013: 285). The man generally credited with pioneering this assimilation process is a Terik elder called Diligin and the first Luyia clan to be accepted in Tiriki is Abalukhoba followed by Abambo (Sangree 1966: 6-8). The tribal totem of Abatiriki is *ingolole*, a mask won by initiates to cover their heads so that they cannot be seen by unauthorised persons especially women and the uninitiated.

Any male adult who dodged initiation rites was looked down upon and treated like a pariah; he had no social status and commanded no respect. In fact, a clitoridectomized Terik woman had more social gravitas than an adult male who was not circumcised (*omusoleli*). The Kalenjin Terik practiced clitoridectomy (female genital mutilation) and although Bantu Luyia women did not, they still recognized the social authority commanded by a woman who had undergone the ritual. Respect, social position, and nationality were acquired strictly through initiation rituals. Many Tiriki families have ties with clans in other Luyia subnations who do not practice Kalenjin-type initiation rites. These kinship ties are normally respected and honored but should a conflict of interest arise, the Tiriki families shift loyalty to their own *lusomo* or *iboli* rather than their consanguineous clansmen.

f.   Modern governance and notable personalities

In the early days of colonialism, Tiriki location was administered under Central Nyanza District along with Maragoli and Bunyore until 1939 when these localities came under North Nyanza. With independence in 1963, power politics among the Tiriki shifted from *lusomo-ibololi* to representation in the Legislative Assembly in Nairobi. Their constituency is called Hamisi, named after a trading center founded by a Mr. Hamisi, a Swahili trader. Hamisi is one of five constituencies in Luyialand characterized by dynastic rule—the others being Sabatia, Saboti, Emuhaya, and Butula. Apart from two outsiders, the politics of Tiriki are the preserve of two dynasties—M'Maitsi and Khaniri. The first MP in Hamisi was Stanley Imbanga Godia (1963-1969), a Maragoli Tiriki from Givogi followed by another Maragoli immigrant, James Harry Onamu (1969-74) who shifted his base from Nakuru West constituency where he served as the first MP in 1963. Although he lost the 1974 elections to Samson Lumbete M'Maitsi (from the populous Abalukhoba clan), Mr. Onamu recaptured the seat in 1979. Mr. M'Maitsi, however, regrouped and deposed Onamu in the Fifth Parliament in 1983. He went on to win the *mlolongo* (queuing) elections of 1988 but sadly died in office the following year and, in the ensuing by elections, his son, Vincent Sakwa M'Maitsi won to establish the M'Maitsi political dynasty. The young M'Maitsi, however, ruled for only one term. In 1992, Nicodemus Khaniri entered the scene but he too died of a heart attack just three years into his first term. His son, George Munyasa Khaniri won in a by election in 1995 and again in the 1997 general elections to firmly establish the Khaniri political dynasty. The young Khaniri won the next two subsequent elections in 2002 and 2007. His political star radiated when he became the first senator of Vihiga County following the 2013 general elections. His former Hamisi constituency was won by Charles Gimose.

Another *ex situ* Tiriki politician is Cyrus Shahalaga Jirongo who rose to fame as the chairman of the infamous Youth for Kanu '92, an influential well funded pressure group that campaigned for the reelection of President Daniel arap Moi in the multiparty elections of 1992. Jirongo went on to represent Lugari, a settlement scheme on the western flank of Buluyia neighboring Uasin Gishu in Rift Valley Province in the Eighth and Tenth parliaments, i.e., in 1997 and 2007. His bid to become the first Kakamega County senator in the 2013 general elections was thwarted by Dr Bonny Khalwale from Idakho. Lugari is peopled by various Luyia ethnic groups among whom the Tiriki, Tachoni, Maragoli and Banyore are dominant.

Beyond politics, other famous Abatiriki include musicians late Daudi Kabaka Masika (Omulukhoba), late John Mwale and

John Nzenze; Prof. George Godia, former permanent secretary; Philip Kisia, the former Nairobi Town Clerk; Simani Sangale (Omudura), the first lawyer in Tiriki and author of *Tiriki Traditions and Customs*; Nathan Adembesa, the first African Town Clerk of Mombasa; Samuel Aluda, former magistrate; colonial chief, Paul Amiani (Omuli); and Nuhu Sakwa, largely credited with modernising antiquated *idumi* circumcision rituals. Another famous Tiriki is Daudi Zakayo Kivuli (1896-1974), founder of an independent religious sect, African Israel Nineveh Church. Kivuli's ancestry is rooted in Umira Kager clan from Ugenya but was acculturated into a Tiriki after undergoing *idumi* rituals at Nyang'ori.

13. Abisukha (Isukha)

Table 33: Isukha clans (brackets indicate alternative spelling or where else clan members are found)

Abakhanyi	Abakhumbwa
Abakhulunya	Abamahalia
Abakusi	Abamilonje (Abamironje)
Abamakhaya (Marama)	Abaruli (Kisa)
Abarimbuli (Tiriki, Maragoli)	Abasalwa (Idakho)
Abasakala (Maragoli, Bukusu, Idakho, Luo)	Abashilukha
Abashikulu (Idakho)	Abashitaho (Idakho)
Abashirukha	Abasiritsa
Abasikhobu	Abasulwa
Abateheri	Abaterema
Abatsunga	Abatura (Tiriki, Bukusu, Wanga, Bukhayo, Marachi)
Abashimutu	Abayokha
Abayonga (Maragoli, Kisa)	Abichina

Abakhaywa
Abakukhumi

Abitsende
Abashisalatsi (Idakho)

a. Brotherhood with Idakho

The ancestors of Abidakho and Abisukha are believed to have been brothers just like the founders of Babukusu and Bagisu of Uganda or Maragoli and Gusii. Those who settled to the north of Lukose (River Yala) were called Isukha and Idakho those to the south. According to oral legend, the names of these ancestors are Mwisukha and Mwitakho, the former and latter being the elder and junior, respectively. Other reports dismiss the putative brotherhood linkage and point to disparate clans that populated these polities from different ancestries. According to historian, Dr. John Osogo, the connection between these two neighbors is more lexical than ancestral (Osogo 1966: 59). Isukha (means forward or first) and Idakho (means backward or lower). The Nandi called them Kakumega, the name of which was first chronicled by Joseph Thomson, the first Whiteman to come to Luyialand in 1883.

Nonetheless, Abisukha (also spelt Abesukha) are a proud people with rich customs and traditions. They have lived for centuries in the forest habitat of Kakamega, a land they fondly refer to as Eshieywe. Abisukha, Abidakho, Abatiriki and Babukusu are perhaps the last strong outposts of traditional cultural practices in modern Buluyia. They worship *isikuti* (small long drum) the beats of which they dance *lipala*, a unique style in which they rhythmically gyrate shoulders back and forth. They are largely credited with inventing *isikuti* which spread to other subnations and is now nationally associated with all Luyia.[165] Besides *isikuti* dancing ceremonies, their other love affair is bullfighting, a

---

[165] *Isikuti* was popularized in Kenya through the national schools and colleges' music festivals as well as during football matches involving AFC Leopards, the soccer club largely associated with the Luyia. Oral mythology says the name derives from an incident in which a Whiteman was entertained by

traditional sport that commands a fanatical following. An attempt in 2008 to bring the sport to the national stage in Nairobi was thwarted after spirited opposition from animal rights activists who termed it a blood sport.

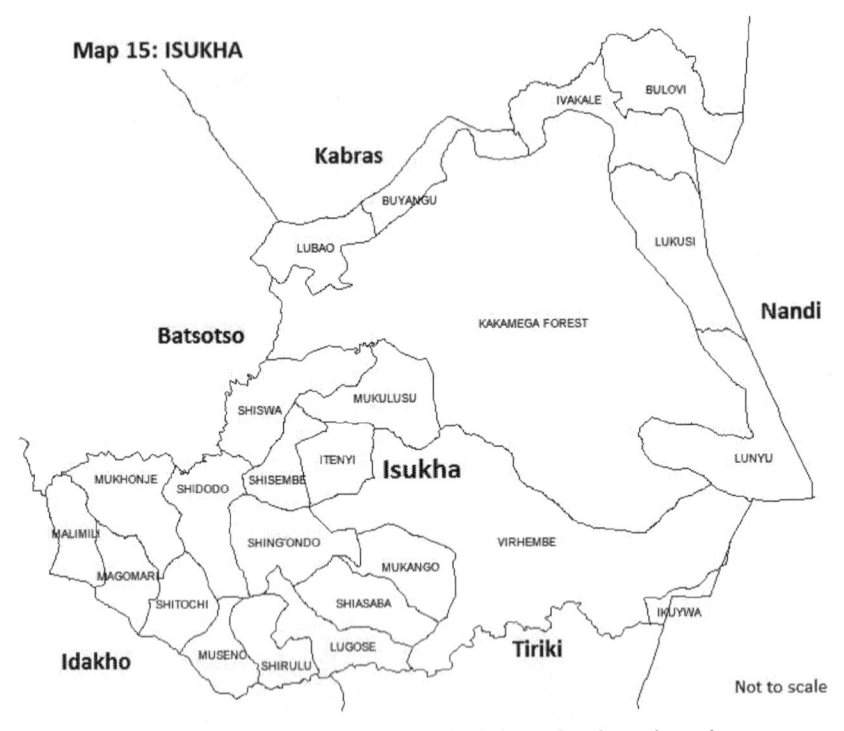

Map 15 shows the main administrative locations in Isukha, Kakamega County.

In the past some clans ate monkeys (*amakhondo,* variation: *amashene*) but this culinary heritage is now socially frowned upon and few, if any, still eat bush meat. Living on the fringes of Kakamega Forest, one of Africa's last remaining equatorial rainforests, Abisukha are strategically placed to safeguard this ecological treasure. Rich in flora and fauna, the forest is home

---

drummers and later commented "it's good" which the Luyia transliterated to *isi-kuti.*

to some of the world's rarest snakes and is a top favorite with ornithologists who troop here from all over the world to see and photograph rare birds.

Jeremiah Sichero is credited with bringing *obulafu* (literally: light but it means development) to Isukha. He was educated at Kabete (Jean's School) in 1925 and worked in the colonial administration variously as an agricultural officer, health visitor, teacher, court elder in the Local Native Council (equivalent to magistrates' court) and chief of Isukha in 1943, a position he held for 20 years.

b. Failed Eldorado

Gold was discovered on Abamahalia clan land in 1929 by a British firm, Rosterman Gold Mines Ltd. But due to dwindling deposits, the goldmines (transliterated to *ikolomani*) were closed in 1952 thus ending a controversial economic chapter that survived for at least a generation. Dubbed by scholars a "failed Eldorado," the Kakamega gold rush did little to bring real economic benefits to the Luyia. First, peasant farmers lost their land to the imperial juggernaut which undervalued it and paid them a pittance rather than the full market value. Secondly, natives provided a constant supply of cheap labor. They were not only poorly paid but suffered mining accidents and lived under unhygienic conditions. What economic spinoffs accrued were in the form of petty trade which did nothing to compensate the disruption of traditional lifestyle.

By 1952 just as a state of emergency was declared owing to Mau Mau uprising, the goldmines closed leaving a legacy of peasant mistrust for government agrarian policies that lingers to date (Shilaro 2000: 3). Since then locals have continued prospecting for gold using crude implements and risking their lives. In April 2011, three miners died after a disused goldmine collapsed on them. However, gold mining received a jolt when in 2010; the government announced it had awarded a tender to a foreign firm to prospect for gold in Kakamega and South Nyanza. If and when gold is rediscovered, I hope it will bring real economic benefits to locals and avoid the mistakes of the "failed Eldorado."

Table 34: Isukha population distribution by administrative units, surface area, and density

Admin Unit	Total	Area (sq km)	Density
Kakamega East	**159,392**	**445.5**	**358**
Shinyalu	**118,049**	**140.6**	**839**
Ilesi	**19,412**	**23.6**	**821**
Mukhonje	8,952	11.4	786
Malimili	4,786	6.1	787
Mugomari	5,674	6.2	920
Murhanda	**28,285**	**36**	**786**
Mukulusu	8,179	10.9	753
Shisembe	5,146	5.9	879
Shiswa	10,227	12.4	828
Itenyi	4,733	6.9	685
Khayega	**35,807**	**38.3**	**936**
Lugose (Lukose)	6,079	8.3	734
Sitochi	8,256	6.7	1,233
Museno	5,913	5.7	1,045
Shirulu	4,755	6.6	720
Shidodo	10,804	11	980
Shibuye	**34,545**	**42.7**	**808**
Virhembe	9,620	13.7	701
Mukango	6,416	8.8	730
Shing'ondo	11,259	11.2	1,004
Shiasaba	7,250	9	804
Ileho	**41,343**	**79.2**	**522**
Kambiri	**23,496**	**42.2**	**557**
Lubao	6,285	8.4	750
Ivakale	6,022	13.1	460

Bulovi	6,480	13.3	488
Buyangu	4,709	7.4	635
Ivihiga	**17,847**	**37.1**	**482**
Lunyu	9,606	19	505
Lukusi	6,656	15.3	436
Ikuywa	1,585	2.8	573
Kakamega Forest	**83**	**225.6**	**0**
Bukhungu	**45,577**	**30.8**	**1,478**
Shirere	33,510	17.4	1,923
Mahiakalo	12,067	13.4	900

Adapted from Kenya Census 2009, *Kenya National Bureau of Statistics, Nairobi, August 2010.*

c. Clan settlement and Maasai ancestry

The clan of Abasakala originally came from Busoga in Uganda and is a progeny of Asagala who was the father of Imbo (after whom Yimbo in Siaya is named). Abasakala clansmen moved from Yimbo following Luo invasion to settle in various parts of Buluyia. Along with Abatura, Abang'ale and Abakhoone, Abasakala (Abasagala, Avasagala) is one of the clans with a wide spatial spread in Western. It is found among Babukusu (Basakali); in Maragoli (Avasagala), Idakho and Luoland (Kibos) where they are known as Jasakala. Abasalwa are also in neighboring Idakho while Abasulwa, due to the influence of Church of God, are like a Bunyore colony. These two clans are believed to be closely related to Abasiekwe subclan of Abasalwa from Bunyore who live at a place called Essalwa. The strong links with Bunyore are symbolised by the fact that they are widely intermarried with Abanyole, use the Bunyore Bible and preach in Olunyole.

Abamilonje (Abamironje) otherwise known as Abasoyi are the largest clan in Isukha. Although the name Abamilonje stuck, it implies "strange" people who tell lies and they prefer the more endearing name of Abasoyi. The clan originated from a Maasai known as Naswayi who begat a son called Chiproot (locally corrupted to Chibololi). One of Chibololi's sons, Shirotsa emigrated to Marama and founded Abashirotsa clan. But according to Prof. Gideon Were (1967), Abamilonje along with Abakusi and Abamahalia were originally Babukusu who split from the mother tribe as they wandered to their present locale (Were 1967: 77). Today, Abamilonje clansmen live in two parts of Isukha—around Mukumu and Isukha East.

Abitsende is the second largest clan in Isukha and it is thought the founder originally came from Wanga's Abashitsetse clan. Other reports indicate they came from Kabras (Osogo 1966: 64) near Nandi country and are brave warriors. Abatsunga came from Marama and were fierce warriors against the Nandi; Mambili and Murumbutsa cited as some of their celebrated fighters. Abamakhaya are descendant from Wibalu, originally from Wanga (Osogo 1966: 64) but besides Isukha, Abamakhaya clansmen also live in Marama while Abasiritsa and Abakukhumi came from Bunyala. Abatsunga and Abichina are specialists in the art of rainmaking and circumcision, respectively while Abateheri and Abaruli are blacksmiths.

Abakhulunya trace their origin to a man known as Akahanyi believed to have fled from Funyula Hills in Samia (Mwayuuli and Nobuhiro 1989: 18). He married a woman by the moniker of Akhulunya from whom the clan derives its name in a rare matrilineal ethnonym in Buluyia. The clan lives within the municipality of Kakamega (Eshieywe) around Bukhungu and Milimani. Abayokha are related to Abamweche of Butsotso and their earliest known ancestor is Ambula son of Atsulu.

Cheche is a famous name in Isukha history because Cheche the man, begat ten beautiful daughters renowned for their fecundity so that wherever they got married they pulullated the clans into which they lived. The first person to get a degree (Bachelor of Arts) in

Isukha was Omuchina clansman, Adriano M. Shitakha from Ishienjera (Mwayuuli and Nobuhiro 1989: 8).

Located on the main Kisumu-Kakamega road, Khayega
is the main trading outpost in Isukha.

d.   Political leadership and notable clansmen

After independence, political power in Isukha shifted from chiefs to elected representatives. Some of the most famous preindependence leaders include Chief Ichibini and Chief Milimo. Isukha and Idakho shared Ikolomani constituency until 1988 when Shinyalu was created to cater specifically for Isukha political interests. The first MP at independence, Jonathan Muruli (1963-69) was Omwisukha from Abitsende clan. He was replaced by Omushimuli clansman from Idakho, Seth Lugonzo (1969-74, 1983-88, and 1988-92). Mr. Lugonzo lost the 1974 elections to Omwisukha, the late Clement Kalani Lubembe (1974-79), a trade unionist from Abayokha clan who was defeated by another Omwisukha, Jeremiah Khamati Murila (1979-83), Omukhumbwa clansman.

When Shinyalu was created in 1988, Japheth Livasia Lijoodi became the first MP but lost to lawyer, Japheth G Shamalla in 1992. Shamalla (Omukusi) was succeeded by Daniel Lyula Khamasi (Omutsunga) who served two terms (1997-2002, 2002-07). Khamasi was defeated by a businessman from Abitsango clan, Charles Lugano Lilechi who sadly died in May 2009 and in the ensuing by election, Justus Mugali Kizito of Maragoli heritage won. Mr. Kizito's grandparents migrated from Maragoli to settle at Ileho,[166] near Nandi escarpments.

Other notable Isukha personalities include Athanas Manyala Keya (Omahalia), MP for Lurambi (2007-13); Bishop Horace Etemesi, former head of Butere diocese; John Katumanga (Omukhulunya), the late KNUT chairman; footballers Josphat Murila (Omukhumbwa), Livingstone Madegwa and Patrick Shilashi (Omurimbuli); former PCs Victor Musoga (Omusalwa) and John Etemesi (later chairman of NGO Council of Kenya); Kizito lost the 2013 general elections to former director of culture, Silverse Anami Lisamula. Isaya Mwinamo (Omukhumbwa), the musician; academics Prof. Shanyisa Anota Khasiani (Omahalia), Prof. Gilbert Khadiagala and Dr. Machanja Ligabo; Antony Lubulela, the lawyer; Lady Justice Stella Munai Muketi (1962-2012); Charles Shikanga of Betting and Licensing Control; Jos Konzolo (Omusakala), the Nairobi businessman; Joshua Odanga, former diplomat and postmaster general and Prof. Miriam Khamati Were (Omukhumbwa) from Lugala village married in Marama and sister to Jeremiah Murila, the ex Shinyalu MP.

[166.] Ileho is a remote part of Isukha on the fringes of Kakamega Forest neighboring Nandi escarpments. In the distant past, Ileho was leper territory but immigrants who did not then know local history, were welcome to settle there.

14. Abidakho (Idakho)

Table 35: Idakho clans (brackets indicate alternative spelling or where else clan members are found)

Abakobero (Butsotso, Tororo)	Abakondi
Abahamani	Abamakambe
Abamanyisi	Abamasava (Bukusu, Tiriki)
Abambale	Ababuka
Abamuhali	Abangolori
Abanyikhu	Abamusali
Abasalwa (Isukha)	Abasanga (Maragoli)
Abashiangala (related to Abatere of Marama)	Abashikulu (Isukha)
Abashimuli (Tiriki, Kisa, Bunyore, Bunyala)	Abashirika (Tiriki)
Abashisira	Abashitsyula
Abakhwese	Abashisalatsi (Isukha)
Abamuhika	Abakhwang'a
Abasilikwa	Abakhobe
Abamahira	Abamusungu (Maragoli)
Abaseero (Maragoli)	Ababwanishili
Abayeemi	Abamabuusi
Abasagala (Maragoli, Isukha, Bukusu, Tiriki, Luo)	Abashitaho (Isukha)
Abanyama	

a. Peopling of Idakho and Maasai ancestry

The migratory history of Abidakho (also called Abetakho or Abitakho) is largely intertwined with the rest of Luyia subnations who point to *Misri* (Egypt) as their original land. The rest is defined by clan superiority and warfare. An interesting aspect to the genealogy of Abidakho is the link with Maasai and Nandi. Prof. Gideon Were (1967), the acclaimed historian on Abaluyia, says that the founder of dominant Abashimuli clan was Kasamu

Naluse, a Maasai immigrant. Kasamu (Chasam) first lived at Sang'alo in Bungoma before moving to Butsotso where he married a local girl, Ashimuli who bore him many sons. When Kasamu moved to Idakho, one of his sons remained behind and is believed to be the founder of Abashibuli clan in Butsotso (Osogo 1966: 59). He was welcomed to Idakho territory with his family (now known as Abashimuli)[167] by the then *omwami* (leader) called Ashisira,[168] founder of Abashisira, the aboriginal clandom. Kasamu integrated with Abidakho and gained such popularity with local people that he became ruler of the combined Abashisira and his own Abashimuli clan.

Meanwhile, his clansmen abandoned Maasai culture and language and adopted Olwisukha. The Tachoni ethnographer, Demmahom Lihraw (2010), however, says that Kasamu led his Chepruko (Abachimuluku) clansmen from Soy following a family dispute and settled in Kakamega. Here they intermarried with Abashisira the offspring of which produced the people now known as Abashimuli (Lihraw 2010: 60). Another important fact to note is that the founders of Abidakho and Abisukha are believed to have been brothers. Although some oral narrators believe these were called Omwitakho and Omwisukha, it is notable that many clans in Isukha and Idakho populated these polities from different directions. Some scholars, notably Dr. John Osogo (1966) say Isukha means "upper" while Idakho means "lower" in reference to settlement of these subnations south and north of River Yala (Lukose), respectively. Not only are they neighbors, the two share similar cultural traits not least, their love of *isikuti* dance and bullfighting.

---

[167] According to this line of reasoning, Abashimuli are among a few clans in Luyialand which derive their name from a matrilineal ancestry.

[168] Dr. John Osogo says the ruler of Abashisira at this point in time was Ndunde (Osogo 1966: 59).

Map 16 shows the main administrative locations in
Idakho, Kakamega County.

Abashimuli are, by far, the most dominant clan in Idakho
and perhaps the largest in Buluyia with an estimated population
in excess of twenty thousand.[169] Abamanyisi are probably one
of few clans in Buluyia that derive their ancestry from a woman
(Anyisi) said to have had exceptional qualities. The only other
known matrilineal clans are Abashimuli and Abakhulunya from
the neighboring Isukha and of course the Bukusu offshoots of
Bakitwika (see p.177). Abamanyisi are related to Abamanyi of
Samia with whom they parted ways in Ugenya (Osogo 1966: 62).
Most leaders in Idakho come from Abashimuli clan; the most
famous being Chief Shivachi who acceded to power in 1910 and
was succeeded by his son, William Shikali Mbolo who ruled from

---

[169.] Average clan size used to be 750 during the 1940s but this has steadily
increased due to population pressures. When clans become so large, they tend
to subdivide into subclans which eventually become independent save for
rules of exogamy.

1943 until after Kenya's independence. He is feted as the most successful Idakho leader who brought *obulafu* (literally: light but means economic development) among Abidakho (Mwayuuli and Nobuhiro 1989: 100). Other notable personalities include Kasamu, Mbukuli, Ungai, Mulongo, Butukhu, Shikomola, and Khaweri. Mulongo and Butukhu were grandsons of Kasamu who founded the subclans of Abamulongo and Ababutukhu. Chief Shivachi was a member of Ababutukhu subclan.

The second largest clan is Abamusali (related to Abang'onya from Butsotso but has no relationship with Abasaali of Maragoli and Tiriki). The clan has spawned a large number of subclans—most notable of which are Abasiahi and Abamukambi (known variously as Abolwichi, Abamatunda and Abambukuli). The third largest is Abashikunga (believed to have come from Mount Elgon) followed by Abamasaaba (came from the Bugisu). Peter Shiyuka, an ex PS and rally driver is perhaps the most famous Omasaaba. Abamasaaba subclans include Abanabuli, Abashimatse, Abayonga, Abamakole, Abamushityula, Abamukare, Abashilakaya, Abakhubi and Abatsui.

Abakondi are scattered across Buluyia mainly in Tiriki, Kabras and Isukha and revere *Munyolo* (iron chain) as their cultural totem. The totem is under custody of Munyolo *inzu* (lineage) and only a Munyolo clansman can carry the object. Other clansmen, though, can request its magical use to administer a curse on someone who has breached taboos or failed to observe customary prohibitions such as engaging in incestuous or bestial sex and theft (Bulimo 2013: 111). A number of clans came from Maragoli the best known of which are Abamusungu and Abaseero (originally from Bukusu). Abashiangala settled in Idakho from Butsotso and are probably related to Abakangala of Samia. It is one of a number of clans that fled Samia during the *Esiatikho* wars stoked by Abakhoone (see p.206).

Abamuhali originally came from Bugisu and their earliest known ancestor was Mulioto (Osogo 1966: 61). His ancestors spawned a number of subclans of which the best known are Abamulioto, Abikinwa, Abalusiola, Abamutete (not related to Abamutete of Bunyore and Tiriki). Abashisalachi are believed to have split from Abamuima, the original founders of Wanga kingdom while Abashukulu's earliest known ancestor was a Nandi from Nyang'ori called arap Kibukusyo. The clans which live along River Yala are collectively known as Abalukose and include Abashirika, Abamagambe, Abanyama, Abashikulu, and Abashitsa.

Abanyikhu are closely related to Abasakami of Bunyore and lived at Kajulu near Kisumu then Kano before settling in Idakho. Some descendants of Munyikhu, the clan ancestor live in Tiriki, Isukha, and Kisa. Abamakambe originally came from a place called Magambe in Bunyala. They were driven away by Abaongo and lived in Alego before being pushed farther into Kisa and later Idakho. The main subclans of Abamakambe are Ababwandia, Abamasaa and Abasindifu. Abamanyisi are an offshoot of Abamanyi of Samia and live around Eregi. The "si" was added to their name as a term of ridicule because they were not popular with the clans they found in Idakho (Osogo 1966: 62). Some of their major subclans include Abanasuli, Abatwehe, and Abakolooba.

Table 36: Idakho population distribution by administrative units, surface area, and density

Admin Unit	Total	Area (sq km)	Density
Kakamega South	104,669	143.6	729
Ikolomani North	61,724	86.7	712
Shisere	25,861	40.6	637
Mutaho	6,098	11.1	550
Shikulu	5,500	9.4	588
Shiseso	6,731	9.1	739

Shimanyiro	7,532	11	682
Shirumba	**17,614**	**19.3**	**914**
Shivagala	7,300	7.5	977
Malinya	5,585	5.3	1,051
Shitoli	4,729	6.5	728
Isulu	**18,249**	**26.8**	**680**
Musoli	6,161	9.4	657
Shibuname	2,697	5.9	455
Lunenere	5,681	6.4	888
Mukongolo	3,710	5.1	724
Ikolomani South	**42,945**	**56.8**	**756**
Iguhu	**22,028**	**32.9**	**670**
Lirhembe	3,139	3	1,043
Savane	4,412	8.5	521
Makhokho	4,926	6.1	806
Shiveye	3,394	5.3	646
Ivonda	6,157	10	615
Shikumu	**12,377**	**14.7**	**843**
Shabwali	3,196	4.8	668
Madivini	4,990	5.3	938
Kaluni	4,191	4.6	917
Eregi	**8,540**	**9.3**	**918**
Shisejeri	3,596	2.9	1,233
Shanjetso	2,673	3.4	782
Lukose	2,271	3	764

Adapted from Kenya Census 2009, *Kenya National Bureau of Statistics, Nairobi, August 2010.*

b.   *Power structures and notable clansmen*

The clan head, *omwami* was the center of political authority among Abidakho as with many Luyia subnations. After independence, political leadership shifted to parliamentary representation. Idakho and Isukha shared one constituency, Ikolomani until Shinyalu was hived off in 1988 to cater exclusively for Abisukha. The first MP in Ikolomani was Jonathan Muruli, a Mwisukha (1963-69). He was replaced by a Mwitakho, Seth Lugonzo (1969-74, 1983-88, and 1988-92). Mr. Lugonzo from the populous Abashimuli clan lost the 1974 elections to a Mwisukha, the trade unionist, Clement Kalani Lubembe (1974-79) who was defeated by another Mwisukha, Jeremiah Khamati Murila (1979-83) before he (Lugonzo) recaptured the seat in 1983 and won again in the *mlolongo*[170] elections of 1988.

In the first postindependence multiparty elections of 1992, Benjamin Ashoni Magwaga won but was defeated at the next elections in 1997 by Joseph Jolly Mugalla (1935-2003), the trade unionist. He too ruled for one term (1997-2002) and was replaced by the youthful medical doctor, Bonny Dixon Khalwale in 2002. Khalwale, a traditionalist bullfighter was reelected in 2007 for a second term and despite a successful election petition in 2011 by Bernard Shinali, he easily recaptured his seat after defeating the petitioner in a by election. Incidentally, the doctor's name means sickly but of course a doctor can never treat himself. In the 2013 general elections, Dr Khalwale (Omusali) contested and won the Kakamega senate seat against the combative Federal Party of Kenya leader, Cyrus Jirongo (Omutiriki). The medical doctor was succeeded as MP for Ikolomani by his erstwhile political nemesis, Bernard Shinali (Omushimuli).

The preeminent politician from Idakho, however, is Musa Amalemba who rose to become a minister for housing in the colonial administration. He is immortalised by an estate bearing his

---

[170.] *Mlolongo* literally means a queue. In 1988 at the height of one party tyranny by Daniel arap Moi's KANU party, it was decreed that parliamentary elections would be conducted by voters queuing behind pictures of the candidates they wished to elect. The system degenerated into a shambles after candidates with the shortest queues were declared winners and was abandoned as quickly as it had been sneaked in after attracting countrywide and international condemnation.

name in Kakamega (Amalemba Estate). Amalemba (Omushimuli clansman) is historically significant for pioneering attempts to foster Luyia unity. He founded Abaluyia Political Union as a political vehicle for the Luyia to bargain for a stake in the emerging political dispensation at the dawn of indepedence. His father, Stephano Shimechero, settled in Tiriki in 1914 where he became one of the earliest Christian acolytes.

Besides politicians, another notable personality in Idakho is the late musician, Jacob Luseno, originally from Tiriki but his mother married into Abamasaba clan of Mumbetsa when he was still very young and was assimilated. Others include John Mukalasinga Khaminwa, the lawyer (Omushimuli); footballer Elijah Lidonde (Omushikulu); Oliver Musila Litondo (Omushikulu), the actor; Yvonne Khamati,[171] the diplomat; the late Brigadier Wilson Shigoli (Omushimuli) who served as chairman of Nairobi City Commission; Brigadier Josphat Bukhala (Omusali), the ex military attaché in London; Zakariah Shimechero, the career civil servant; Stanley "Moneybags" Livondo (Omushiangala), the political activist who rose to fame after showering money from a helicopter in 2007; Prof. Sammy Kubasu (Omushiangala), the university academic and Justice (rtd) Effie Owuor, the first woman high court (and court of appeal) judge. Justice Owuor was also Kenya's nominee to the ICC at The Hague in 2005. Another famous son of Idakho is Father Maurice Muhatia Makumba, Head of the Catholic Diocese of Nakuru.

[171.] Yvonne married Mr. Vincent Kilonzo from Matuu in Ukambani in June 2009. She was a political youth activist who unsuccessfully vied for Makadara parliamentary seat in Nairobi in 2007.

15. Abatsotso (Batsotso, Tsotso)

Table 37: Batsotso clans (brackets indicate alternative spelling or where else clan members are found)

Abakhobole (Kisa)	Abakibiywa
Abakobero (Idakho)	Abamamu (Marama)
Abamaani (Kisa, Wanga, Marama, Abanyala ba Ndombi)	Abamanyulia (Kisa, Marama)
Abamatioli	Abamucherera
Abamukoya (Marama, Bukusu)	Abamweche
Abamwende (Marama, Wanga)	Abang'onya
Abangusi	Abanyakwaka
Abashialo	Abashiamusingili
Abashianda (Marama)	Abashibeye
Abashibimbi	Abashibuli
Abashiibo (Marama, Tiriki)	Abashimukoko
Abashirima (Kisa, Tiriki)	Abashirumba
Abashisiru	Abasumba
Abatamanyini (Marama)	Abashambishi
Abakhonya	Abangotse
Abamukhuyu	Abakhananga
Abamang'ale (Samia, Bunyore, Tachoni, Kabras, Bukusu)	Abamukhura
Ababeye	Abashiabechere

a. Peopling of Butsotso

Abatsotso live mainly in Lurambi, Kakamega District and although Mutsotso is believed to be the quintessential ancestor, he is rather mythical than a historical figure. This is because, like the Marachi and Kisa, Abatsotso are a congeries of clans of different tribal origins—Bantu, Luo and Kalenjin. The toponymy of Abatsotso is not clear and it is merely conjectural to assume the name originates from a clan head. Early settlers in Butsotso, however, trace their origins to Elubiri in Mukono District, Uganda (Were 1967: 71).

They later moved to Tororo in Jopadhola country before settling in Lurambi after wandering through various places including Sang'alo and Marama. These early settlers were Abakobero followed by Abashibuli founded by progenitors of Abashimuli of Idakho. When they arrived in Lurambi, they found the area occupied by Abakhusia (Kabras) who voluntarily moved farther east.

Abatsotso neighbor Isukha and Idakho to the South, Marama to the West, Wanga and Abanyala ba Ndombi to the North and Kabras to the East. They are very traditionalist and, besides Abanyole, Babukusu and Abamarama, Abatsotso are the only other Luyia subnation skilled in the art of rainmaking (*obukimba*). Cockfighting is a huge spectator sport among Abatsotso where teams compete on a weekly basis. They name adversarial cocks after famous personalities doing riveting political duels such as Osama bin Laden, George Bush, Raila Odinga (Agwambo), Mwai Kibaki, etc. Bukura Agricultural Institute (now a constituent college of MMUST) is within Butsotso and Ingotse was part of the Rosterman Gold Mines that collapsed in 1952.

The largest clan, Abang'oya was founded by a man called Kisumi, believed to have come from Bugwe in Uganda. Abang'oya are related to Abamusaali of Idakho and have three major subclans—Abanangabo, Abalwaminyi, and Abalusatsi. The second major clan is Abamweche which is related to Abashieni (Abanashieni) of Marama. The earliest known ancestor of Abamweche is Litsinji, the father of Mareeba (Maraba) which moniker is immortalised by a place in Kakamega. The third largest clan is Abatamanyini whose earliest known ancestor, Wesamba settled here from Uganda. Abanashisiru, another big clan, are cousins of Abashitsetse of Wanga whose earliest known ancestor is Amuhoyi believed to be a corruption of Wamoyi. Abanashisiru have spawned the subclans of Abasaalisi, Abalukala, and Abasichina.

Despite the congerious peopling of Butsotso, Abatsotso are closely related to Abawanga and Abamarama. Eight Batsotso clans are also domiciled in Marama—Abamani, Abamukoya (also in Bukusu), Abamwende, Abashianda, Abashiibo, Abatamanyini, Abamamu and Abamanyulia. Of these two are also found in Kisa—Abamani and Abamanyulia (both of Luo ancestry) while Abashiibo are also in Tiriki. Four clans are shared with Kisa—Abakhobole (Nandi origin), Abamani, Abashirima and Abamanyulia while two are in Wanga—Abamwende and Abamani and another two in Tiriki—Abashiibo and Abashirima. The art of *obukimba* (rainmaking) is largely associated with Abamwende (also found in Marama and Wanga).

Table 38: Butsotso population distribution by administrative units, surface area, and density

Admin Unit	Total	Area (sq km)	Density
Lurambi	**113,791**	**195.8**	**581**
North Butsotso	**47,443**	**82.8**	**573**
Esumeyia	8,978	19.9	452
Shinoyi	8,880	15.5	573
Ingotse	9,439	16.2	582
Matiha	12,652	18.2	696
Shikomari	7,494	13	575
South Butsotso	**17,377**	**31.2**	**557**
Matioli	6,220	9	690
Eshibeye	5,552	13.3	419
Emukaya	5,605	8.9	628
Central Butsotso	**25,744**	**48.8**	**527**
Shibuli	11,702	25.3	463
Shiyunzu	9,256	14.8	626
Eshisiru	4,786	8.8	547
East Butsotso	**23,227**	**33.1**	**703**
Indangalasia	7,431	10.8	686
Shirakalu	5,864	8	731
Murumba	9,932	14.2	700

Shieywe	48,304	17.9	2,700
Township	10,055	2.6	3,879
Sichilayi	38,249	15.3	2,500

Adapted from Kenya Census 2009, *Kenya National Bureau of Statistics, Nairobi, August 2010*

b. Political organization and notable clansmen

Traditional system of government in Butsotso was through clan elders and later by colonial chiefs. However, after independence, Abatsotso were represented by an elected member of the Legislative Assembly. Abatsotso share Lurambi constituency (originally Lurambi South) with Abanyala ba Ndombi and urban dwellers, especially Isukha in Eshieywe (Kakamega). At independence, the first person to represent them was not a Mutsotso but a Munyala, Jonathan Welangai Masinde (1963-69). Abatsotso were second time lucky in 1969 when their candidate, Brown Tsuma (Omushiibo) won. Tsuma was defeated in 1974 polls by another Munyala, Shadrack K. Okova who gave way to another Munyala, Wasike Ndombi in 1979.

In 1983, a Mutsotso, Reuben Otutu (Omushambishi) ascended the throne in Lurambi only to relinquish it again to Mr. Ndombi during the *mlolongo* (queuing) elections of 1988. In the multiparty elections of 1992, Abanyala lost to a Mutsotso, Javan Ambululi Ommani (Omukhonya). However, Abanyala regrouped and in 1997, they regained their dominance of Lurambi politics by electing Dr. Newton Wanjala Kulundu. Kulundu (died March 2010) was reelected in 2002 and rose to become minister for labor but lost the 2007 polls to Mwisukha, Athanas Keya Manyala (Omahalia), the ex financial attaché in London. Keya lost the 2013 elections to newcomer, Raphael Otalo (Omutsotso).

Outside politics other notable personalities in Butsotso include late Prof. Morris Alala, the first mathematics professor in Kenya; David Zalo Okuku, the late music maestro; Paul Olando, the former PC; Samwel Ambundo, first black chairman of Barclays Bank; Prof. Ruth Khasaya Oniang'o, a former nominated MP (from Ematioli but married in Marama); Julius Mbagaya, the evangelist; Titus Khamala (Omushisiru), founder of Cornerstone evangelical ministries; late Chief Omutsembi Nduku; Chief Frederick Andati; and Major General (rtd) Geoffrey Lukale Okanga, the airforce pilot.

Map 17 shows the main administrative locations in Butsotso, Kakamega County.

16. Babukusu (Bukusu)

Table 39: Bukusu clans (brackets indicate alternative spelling or where else clan members are found)[172]

Baabiya	Baafu (Abanyala ba Ndombi)
Baala	Baande
Baata	Babaamanga (Gisu)
Babaambocha	Babaasaba
Babambo	Babangachi (Tachoni)
Babayi (Banyore, Tiriki)	Babenge
Babeti	Babichachi
Babichu	Baboya
Baburire (Gisu)	Babuulo (Gisu)
Babuutu (Gisu)	Babuya
Babwoba	Bachambayi (Tachoni)
Bachango	Bachemayi (Gisu)
Bachemuluku	Bachemwile
Bachesoli	Bachibino
Bachoye	Baechalo
Baembo (Abanyala, Wanga, Samia, Marachi)	Baengele (Tachoni, Abanyala ba Ndombi)
Bafisi	Bafulo
Bafumbula (Gisu)	Bafumo (Gisu)
Bafuumi	Bahabiya (Tachoni)
Bahongo	Bahuma
Bakafisi	Bakamukongi (Tachoni)

---

172. One of the major linguistic differences between Babukusu and other Luyia subnations is the lack of *A* prefix so common in possessive pronouns across Buluyia. For instance while other subnations say Abaengele, the Bukusu omit the *A* and instead simply say Baengele or Babukusu instead of Ababukusu. This omission is also common among subnations in Busia region—Abakhayo, Abasamia, Abanyala, and Abamarachi.

Bakamutebi

Bakembe (Abanyala ba Ndombi)
Bakhanywinywi
Bakhekhe (Samia)
Bakhiisa
Bakhonjo

Bakhufwe
Bakhami (Wanga)
Bakibwabi
Bakimiyu (Gisu)
Bakinisu (Maasai)
Bakisebe
Bakitang'a
Bakiyabi
Bakoboolo

Bakolati
Bakoyi
Bakuta
Bakwangwa

Bakwaya (Gisu)
Balako (Banyore, Gisu)
Balende
Baliango
Balindo
Baliuli (Gisu)
Balugulu (Gisu)
Balunda (Zambia, Angola, Congo)
Balwonja
Bamaandali (Gisu)
Bamachina (Tachoni, Kabras)
Bamakambo (Gisu)

Bakangala (Samia, Bakhayo, Abanyala ba Ndombi, Kabras, Marachi, Uganda, Congo)
Bakhali
Bakhayaki
Bakhelenge
Bakhoma
Bakhoone (Abanyala, Bakhayo, Marama)
Bakhurarwa
Bakibeti
Bakikayi
Bakimweyi
Bakipemuli
Bakisiayi
Bakitwika
Bakobelo
Bakokho (Marama, Gisu, Cameroon)
Bakolongolo
Bakusi (Tachoni)
Bakuunga
Bakwangwachi (Abanyala ba Ndombi, Marachi)
Balakasi
Balanda (Abanyala ba Ndombi)
Baleyi
Baliisa
Balinduyi
Baluchwata
Balumela
Baluu
Bamaakita
Bamacharia (Bacharia)
Bamaeso (Gisu)
Bamakhanga (Tachoni)

Bamakhuli (Abanyala ba Ndombi)
Bamalicha
Bamatiri
Bameywa (Tachoni, Samia, Abanyala ba Ndombi, Uganda)
Bamoyayo (Gisu)
Bamukhongo (Abanyala ba Ndombi)
Bamukongi
Bamula
Bamulolwana

Bamulundu (Gisu)
Bamurumba (Abanyala ba Ndombi)
Bamutilu (Gisu, also called Batiilu)
Bamwalie
Banabombi
Bananjofu (Gisu)
Bang'ale (Samia, Banyore, Kabras, Butsotso, Marachi, Uganda)
Bang'oma (Abanyala)
Banywaka
Barakaru
Barefu
Basakwa
Basamo (Tachoni)
Basaniaka (Tachoni, Maragoli, Tiriki)
Baseenya (Abanyala ba Ndombi)
Basekele
Basibacho (Gisu)
Basichongoli
Basihondo

Bamalaba (Tiriki)
Bamasike (Gisu)
Bameme
Bamisoo

Bamufuni
Bamuki

Bamukoya (Gisu)
Bamulika (Gisu)
Bamululu (Abanyala ba Ndombi, Gisu)
Bamunaa
Bamusomi

Bamuyonga

Bamwayi (Samia)
Banang'anda
Banasaka (Gisu)
Bangaachi (Tachoni)

Banyangali (Gisu)
Baolo (Cameroon)
Baraki
Basakali (Isukha, Maragoli, Luo)
Basamba
Basang'alo (Tachoni)
Basaya (Abanyala ba Ndombi)

Basefu
Basekese
Basibende
Basienya
Basikula

Basiloli (Banyore, Abanyala ba Ndombi)	Basimaolia (Gisu)
Basime	Basimisi
Basiondo	Basioya (Tachoni)
Basirikwa	Basituyi
Basiukhu (Abanyala ba Ndombi)	Basoba (Maragoli, Tiriki, Suba, Gisu)
Basombi	Basonge (Abanyala ba Ndombi, Tiriki)
Batakhwe	Batanyi
Batasama	Bateecho (Abanyala ba Ndombi)
Batemulani	Batilu
Batinga	Batobo
Batura (Tiriki, Isukha, Bukusu, Wanga, Bakhayo, Marachi)	Bauma (Abanyala ba Ndombi)
Baundu	Baunga
Bausi	Bawabuya
Bawambwa (Gisu)	Bawandiambi
Bawaswa (Gisu)	Bawayila
Bawele	Bayaka
Bayaya (Abanyala, Abanyala ba Ndombi)	Bayemba (Gisu)
Bayilifuma (Abanyala ba Ndombi)	Bayima (Wanga, Abanyala ba Ndombi)
Bayitu	Bayonga (Kisa, Isukha, Maragoli)
Bayumbu (Tachoni)	Bayundo (Wanga, Abanyala ba Ndombi)

a. *Bukusu creation mythology*

Where biblical scriptures point to Adam as the first man on earth, Bukusu mythology posits that the first man, Mwambu was created from clay by *Wele Khakaba* (God the benefactor).[173] And

---

[173.] *Wele* (also spelt *Were*) is generic name for God among Babukusu. However, they distinguish between *Wele Khakaba* which literally means God the benefactor and *Wele Kumali* (refers to God of darkness and misfortune).

just like the biblical God created Eve as a companion to Adam, *Wele Khakaba* created Sela (Sarah) to be a wife to Mwambu. This creation is said to have taken place in quarries (*biumbwa*, singular: *siumba*). Because of the symbolic relationship with creation, the Bukusu regard quarries as sacred grounds to be approached only by the most pious or individuals in a state of ritual purity. It is a place where people can seek communion with *Wele* (*Were*) and their ancestors (*kimisambwa*, variation: *misambwa*). Anyone who is bloodied or has handled blood in recent times such as menstruous women, murderers, circumcised boys, widows, etc., are regarded as ritually contaminated and hence cannot have a séance in a quarry (Nangendo 1996: 71).

There are two theories about Bukusu creation beliefs. In the first instance, the Bukusu believe that *Wele Khakaba* caused heaven and earth to unite to create the first man. The second theory says that *Wele* took cosmic dust from the morning star *(ya Sulwe)* and mixed it with clay from the quarry to create the first man (Nangendo 1996: 70).

b. *Migration from Egypt and Maina's curses*

The quarry mythology notwithstanding oral stories about the origin of Babukusu, like other Luyia subnations, point to *Misiri* or *Misri*[174] (Egypt) as the land of primeval ancestry. From Egypt they moved southward and did not become a distinct grouping until, at the very earliest, the late eighteenth century. Over several generations, they journeyed through Ethiopia (Abyssinia) and

---

174. *Misri* is derived from the Hebrew word *Mizraim*. Ugaritic inscriptions refer to Egypt as *Msrm* while in the Amarna tablets it is called *Misri*. Assyrian and Babylonian records called Egypt *Musur* and *Musri* respectively. The Arabic word for Egypt is *Misr*. According to Genesis 10:6, Mizraim was a son of Ham and together with his brothers Cush, Put and Canaan constituted the Hamite branch of Noah's descendants of which the negroid race is putatively a part.

Sudan before reaching Uganda as part of a much larger group of people, many forming the eastern extension of the great Bantu migration out of west and central Africa. They settled in northern Uganda and in Kenya around Lake Turkana (formerly Lake Rudolf) under the leadership of Kitanga, according to some unreferenced sources. The Nilotic Turkana later occupied this place and called it Lok-Kitang meaning the place of Kitang (Lokitaung is a remote outpost in northern Kenya bordering Ethiopia). From here they settled at Embayi, said to be somewhere in Karamoja country before moving to Sirikwa.

Their stay at Sirikwa was disturbed by constant attacks by Kalenjin and Maasai tribes leading to another wave of emigration. This time they went to Bukaya in Uganda where they lived for a long time, but due to population pressure they migrated to the other side of Mount Elgon in present-day Kenya. Those they left behind are what we know today as Bamasaaba which is used interchangeably with Bagisu. Although Prof. Were categorized Bamasaaba, Bagisu and Babukusu as related but separate entities in his book, *A History of Abaluyia of Western Kenya*, the truth is Bamasaaba is a name derived from Mt. Masaba (Elgon) and clusters all Bantu clans living on the foothills of the mountain. Accordingly, all clans that fall under Babukusu and Bagisu (including assimilated non Bantu) are all Bamasaaba. The Bagisu even have a coat of arms with the inscription *Lweliswa ni Bulamu bwe Bagisu* (For the land and prosperity of Bagisu).

According to Prof. Gideon Were (1967), their leader at this time was Maina wa Nalukale who had eight wives and two sons, Namungumba and Wakhulunya. While here, Namungumba, the eldest son, fell in love with his youthful stepmother.[175] Although

---

[175] Dr. John Osogo gives the name of Chesekweli as the offending son (Osogo 1966: 80) whether this was another name for Namungumba is not immediately clear.

Gisu and Barwa elders thirsted for his blood, Teso (Wamia, Bamia) urged caution as a "woman is like a flowing river" while Babukusu said Maina should let his son copulate with his wife as he is old and suggested a cleansing rite known as *siluukhi* to restore purity (Makila 1978: 149). Maina imploded at this suggestion and pronounced a curse on Wamia to wonder aimlessly and suffer poverty. To Babukusu he foredoomed them to constant combat, circle Mt. Elgon three times, scatter to the four winds of the earth and never circumcise their children in one place. For suggesting that Namungumba should be killed, Maina blessed Barwa and Gisu with peace and prosperity.

After uttering his curses and blessings, Maina levitated into thin air with his barren wife, Nabusambia never to be seen again, alive or dead. Then one day, people had a strange voice which they recognized as Maina's. As the party approached the spot from where the sound came, the voice commanded them to stop, identified itself as Maina and invited them to come closer and have a look. The creature they saw was half human half snake. Terrified but transfixed to the spot, Maina directed them to brew alcohol and drink it at the spot they had encountered him. While drinking *kamalwa* (alcohol) they also placed Maina's favorite beer pot on the spot. This pot later turned into a rock while *kamalwa* turned into a pool of water forming a small lake. Both the rock and lake (*Ubukobero*) exist as shrines for *Dini ya Musambwa* adherents. Other shrines of religious significance include Mwiala wa Mango (Mango's cave), Mwibale lya Namakanda (Namakanda's rock) in Sang'alo, River Malaba (Lwakhakha) and Buyemba Hill in Bugisu, Uganda (Makila 1978: 151-152).

Maina's curse went deep into the inner sanctum of Bukusu culture. For the next several generations they suffered the effects of Maina's commination. Unable to circumcise and therefore assemble a platoon of warriors, they suffered defeats at war with the Teso who kept up cattle raids and dislodged them from their territories. The war with Iteso only ended after the two sworn enemies participated in a ritual peace pact known as *khulia imbwa* (dog eating) just before imperial conquest late nineteenth century.

There are two versions regarding the revival of circumcision among Babukusu. One presupposes that a man known as Kolongolo was reminded of the tradition while visiting his uncle in Bugisu. But the more popular version ascribes the resurrection of circumcision rituals to one, Mango, a Mukhurarwa clansman, who singlehandedly decapitated a dreaded serpent (*yabebe*) that had terrorized the land for a long time. His heroic exploits earned him the ritual honor of circumcision, until then a preserve of Nilotic Sabaot which made him a decorated warrior (Bulimo 2013: 272).

Another version of Bukusu migratory story traces their origin to one, Muntu we Entebbe who lived in Tabasya, south of *Misri*. His son Mwambu married Sera (Sela) the daughter of Wasiela the son of Samba Ambarani, believed to be the biblical Abraham. Mwambu founded the cities of Kush, Nubia, Namelu (Meroe), Rwa (Alwa), Saba, and Balana. He sired Mwaabini who in turn begat Kongolo and Saba. According to this narrative, Kongolo is the *pater familias* of all Bantu tribes west of River Nile and Saba those to the east (Kingdom of Sheba). His great-granddaughter called Nakuti of Saba (Queen of Sheba) married a prince from the house of Samba Ambarani (Ibrahim) and bore him a son whom they named Maina wa Nakuti. It is believed it is this Maina whom the Arabs call Ibn Malik and Ethiopians refer to as Menelik. Maina grew to become the ruler of Saba until hostile Arabs invaded his kingdom and drove some of his people southward. The exodus from Saba was led by Muntu Mkhulu who sired Saba II (Masaba) under whose leadership the Bukusu came to Tabasya north of Lake Turkana. Here they lived for a long time, but following repeated attacks from the Balana (Borana or Galla) and harsh weather conditions, they resolved to migrate again. Masaaba, the father of Bukusu and

Gisu, led the people to Embayi and Sirikwa. At Sirikwa, the people disobeyed *Wele Khakaba* who punished them by unleashing a giant boulder from the sky which destroyed the habitat. He then sent swarms of stinging insects to attack them followed by epidemics. These calamities caused Babukusu to scatter in different directions with the main body settling around Cherenganyi Hills and Mount Elgon, their present abode.

c. Largest Luyia subnation

Bukusu are the most populous of the Luyia subnations forming about 17-20 percent of the estimated six million Luyia with more than two hundred clans (Simiyu 1997: 1). They live mainly in Bungoma (derived from Bongamek, a Kalenjin tribe that originally roamed this territory), Trans Nzoia and Uasin Gishu (no relationship with Gisu which means striped cattle in Maasai) and Lugari Settlement scheme. Pockets of Bukusu also live across the border in Uganda's Mbale District, specifically in Yembe and Cheptui divisions. Bagisu of Uganda are cousins of Babukusu sharing many cultural traits, not least traditional circumcision rituals (*sikhebo*). Among clans straddling both sides of Mount Elgon that anchor the cousinage are Bamoyayo, Babuutu, Bakokho, Balako, Bachemayi, Bamutiilu (Batiilu or Batiiru), Bamasike, Balugulu (Balukuliu), Bamululu, Bawaswa, Bawambwa, Bamaeso, Bamulika, Bafumo, etc.

The colonial government called Babukusu *Kitosh*,[176] a derogatory term meaning "the terrible ones" first used by Nandi and Bakwavi (Uasin Gishu Maasai). Babukusu were feared by these tribes for their ruthlessness in warfare and cattle raids. Following protests, the name was eventually expunged from official literature in mid 1950s. But just who is a Mubukusu? The question of who is

---

[176.] Tachoni ethnographer, Demmahom Lihraw (2010), posits that the original *Kitosh* (*Kitoki*) people were Tachoni rather than Bukusu.

a true Mubukusu arouses patriotic emotions among various clans and is as difficult a question as asking who is a true Englishman? The people we now call Babukusu are a confederation of various clans and range from the primordial to assimilated and migratory clans. Bukusu ethnocultural heritage is a mishmash of pygmoid, Bantu, Nilotic (Kalenjin, Maasai), and Abyssinian ancestries (Namulundah 2005: 28). Because of the ability of Babukusu to assimilate all and sundry without upsetting the epicenter, they are described as solid as the "thigh of the elephant."

Nonetheless, there are six core clan clusters (*chibolo2i*) which can be described as "blue-blooded" out of whom have sprang several clans (*chikholo*) and subclans. These are Basilikwa, Bamalaba, Banabayi, Bamwalie, Baneala, and Bakikayi which all have special oath (*sisiilao*) that defines their ethno-historical origins and characteristic traits. Basilikwa and Bamwalie invoke Namurwa while Bamalaba, Baneala and Bakikayi swear to Munyole. Bakikayi have two oaths—Naluwa and Nawanga because they are divided into two clusters with Nawanga implying their mother came from Wanga (Makila 1978: 53).

Basilikwa and Bamwalie clan clusters swear to Namurwa because the mother of Mukisu and Mubukusu, the eponymous tribal founders was a Kalenjin (*omurwa*). Basilikwa were named after Mubukusu's youngest son Silikwa while Bamwalie are so called because they lived among Barwa around Mwalie hills in present-day Malakisi location. The main *chikholo* (clans) falling under Basilikwa cluster are Bakitwika, Bakimeyi, Babuulo, Bakiyabi, Basefu, Bachemayi, Bakolati, Babichachi, Babambo, Batilu, Basimisi, Baliango, and Barwa. The main *chikholo* under Bamwalie clandom include Bachambachi, Bamuhongo, Bamululu, Bameywa, Basioya, Bakafisi, Bakamutebi, Bamarakalu, Barefu, Basonge, Babangachi (clever), Bahabiya, Basang'alo, Bamakina, Bawayila, Bamakhuli, Baengele, Basaniaka, Bakusi, Basamba, Basamo, Balukulu, Bakobolo (fish lovers), Babichu, Bamalicha,

Bamacharia (Bacharia), Bakamukongi, Bayumbu, and Banyangali (Makila 1978: 55). According to Makila (1978), Bamwalie were "lost" Bukusu clans which had wandered off in a different direction from Silikwa and lived among Barwa (Kalenjin) with whom they intermarried widely adopting some of their customs such as *khulicha* (initiation and oathing rituals). They, however, reunited with the main body of Babukusu following a chance discovery by Kitimule okhwa Wetoyi who was on a reconnaissance mission up the Mwalie hills. Babukusu baptized the "lost" tribes Bayumbu, but those not reunited with Babukusu became the founders of Tachoni subnation as we know it today.

However, this account was dismissed as an emasculation of the Tachoni by Lihraw (2010) who claimed several of the clans listed as Bukusu are in fact Tachoni and have no relationship with Silikwa migration theory. The `stolen` Tachoni clans included in the Bamwalie cluster are Basioya, Bakafisi, Bakamutebi, Bamarakalu, Babichu, Bamacharia (Abacharia), Bahabiya, Bamukonga (Bamukongi), Bakobolo, Bakusi, Bamachina, Bamakhuli, Banyangali, Barefu, Basamba, Basamo, Basang`alo, Bawayila, and Bayumbu. According to Lihraw (2010), the Tachoni are not the only subnation to lose clans to Makila`s Bukusu list. He lists the following clans as Abanyala rather than Bukusu: Abaafu, Ababuya, Abaemba (Abayemba), Abahengele, Abakangala, Abakembe, Abakhalenge, Abakisembe (Abayemba), Abalanda, Abaliango, Abalindo, Abalunda, Abamisoo, Abamuki, Abamuyemba, Abameywa, Abasienya, Abaswuhu, Abatasama, Abatecho, and Abayaya (Lihraw 2010: 8).

Bamalaba, Banabayi, and Baneala clandoms take the Munyole oath whose main plank is disavowal of circumcision. Living in Bunyole country, Uganda they adopted some local customs such as *obusinde* (non circumcision) although they now participate in *sikhebo* (circumcision) rituals. Bamalaba clans are descendants of Malaba, who is part of the divine trinity, according to Bukusu creation mythology where *Wele Khakaba* (Providence) had two messengers—*Malaba* (protector) and *Mukhobe* (light). Some major clans under Bamalaba cluster includes Balwonja, Bayemba, Bayundo, Babuya, Baala, Bakuta, Basakali, Baliuli, Babasaba, Bakunga, and Bakhonjo. The clan of Bakuta is a progeny of Babasaba and the two clans do not intermarry to this day.

Besides swearing the Munyole oath like Bamalaba and Baneala, Banabayi (Babayi) clandom had a special role in Bukusu society. Members of this clanal sept were entrusted with shepherding duties (of both man and beast). Before tribesmen settled in a new area, an elder of Banabayi was summoned to offer blessings for the people and cattle in the new settlement. For this purpose, he thrust a spear into the ground and held a lump of soil upward beseeching gods to protect the homestead. After construction of *olukoba* (fort), he went round the village sprinkling a protective medicine on the huts, pastures, and water points. The main clans under Banabayi cluster include Bayaya, Basombi, Balunda, Baumba, Basime, Baleyi, Basekese, Batecho, Bakangala, Basichongoli, Balisa, Bayitu (Baitu), Bakoyi, and Bameywa (Makila 1978: 58-59). Other accounts indicate that Bayaya were originally known as Bakhabocha, part of the mystical Abakhabotsa clan of Bunyala largely associated with the Sumba legend (see p.210). The man who led Bayaya migration to Bungoma was Welemuyaya who settled at Tulumba hill in the eighteenth century. Then they called themselves Bakhabocha but later adopted the name Bayaya apparently because they did not want to stir old animosities with enemy clans like Bakhoone that had fled from Busia during *Esiatikho* wars and settled in Bungoma. Bayaya links with Abakhabotsa remained a top secret as late as 1970s as elders still feared reprisals from enemy clans in the polity (Florence 2011: 45).

Baneala cluster includes clans that settled at Neala in Bugisu country after immigrating from Silikwa. From here they settled at Mwiala near Amukura. The fact they take a Munyole oath like

Bamalaba and Banabayi indicates they too lived in Ebunyuli, Uganda, before settling at Mwiala. Among the major clans in this cluster include Bameme, Batakhwe (nomads), Bakongolo, Bakisiayi, Bamunaa, Bakhurarwa, and Bachibino.

The Bakikayi cluster first lived on the foothills of Kikayi Hills in Bugisu. The group is divided into two: each with a separate oathing according to ancestral origins. The first group takes the oath of Naluwa, the leader who led them out of Bugisu. Some of the major clans in this sub sept include Balako, Baechalo, Bamuyonga (blacksmiths), Bachemwile (captivating conversationalists), Bakokho, Basimaolia, Batemulani, Basituyi, Bamusomi, Bakhoma, and Bakisebe. The second group swears to Nawanga, a maternal ancestor from Wanga and includes clans like Bamukoya, Basibacho, and Bakhwami (Makila 1978: 60).

d.   Solemnized introduction and spread of Babukusu

Because of or, in spite of clanal pride, rivalries and suspicions, Babukusu devised a system of introduction that involved not merely stating one's name but also lineage, clan, and totems by which clansmen solemnly swear (Makila 1978: 49). By *khukhwitacha* (declaring one's name) and *khukhwilaa* (stating ancestry), a Bukusu tribesman is declaring that he is not a stranger (read enemy or spy) and also precluding endogamous liaisons. Despite Bukusu society being a patriarchy, Babukusu men are known to have a strong dose of Oedipus complex phenomenon. We find a manifestation of this affinity in the nomenclatural system. Men who are high achievers often use their mother's name as a title of honor, e.g., Masinde Muliro was known in Bukusu circles as Okhwa Makinia, i.e., son of Makinia, his mother. Another example is Wachiye wa Naumbwa, a historical figure in Bukusu renowned for performing miracles (see p.358). Although his father's name was Lwasaka, it was by his mother's moniker (Naumbwa) that he was better known. When a Bukusu man is really angry, he swears by his mother's name or clan which is a signal that he has reached the end of his wits and is ready to fight to death, if need be.

We have already seen how clans are interleaved across several subnations. In the case of Babukusu, we can single out clans like Bakhoone, Bang'ale (Bang'are), Basaniaka, and Batura. Originally Bakhoone came from Busoga in Uganda and settled in Busia among Abakhayo and Abanyala. They were feared and ruthless warriors who terrorized other clans but met their comeuppance when smaller clans outmaneuvered them by poisoning their soldiers (see p.206). Their defeat sent shockwaves across Buluyia and to escape further annihilation, they scattered in different directions taking refuge among friendly tribes. This is how some ended up among Babukusu where they are largely renowned in the art of circumcision.

Bang'ale originally came from Samia and settled in Bukusu, Butsotso, Tachoni, and Bunyore where they are associated with iron smithing trade. Basaniaka are scattered across Tachoni, Maragoli, and Tiriki. In Maragoli, they are associated with *obung'osi* (dream prophesy). Bayonga are also found in Maragoli (Avayonga), Kisa, and Isukha. Besides Bang'ale, Batura also have one of largest interspatial in Luyialand—living among the Tiriki, Wanga, Marachi, Isukha, and Bakhayo. Some scholars even classify Batura as a separate Luyia subnation, but having no significant geographical locality of their own, it is difficult to justify this taxonomy. Several Bukusu clans are of Nilotic origin. These include Balako (Bok), Bakwabi (Maasai), Bakimweyi, Bakibeyi, Bakamukongi, and Bang'oma. Similarly, the Bukusu are also closely related to Abatachoni with at least twenty common clans. One popular theory posits that Abatachoni were created through the union of Babukusu and Kalenjin tribes (see p.297).

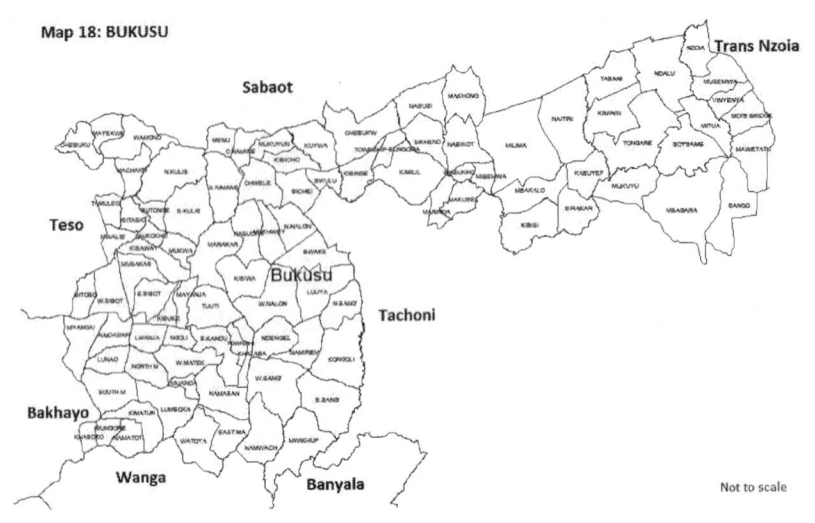

Map 18 shows the main administrative locations in
Bukusu, Bungoma County.

Although immigrant or assimilated clans retain ties with
mother clans and continue to observe taboos or prohibitions
that are clan-specific,[177] if they live among Babukusu, they call
themselves Babukusu irrespective of their place of origin. For
instance Bang'ale (Abamang'ali) in Bukusu are Babukusu; in
Samia they are Abasamia, and in Bunyore, they are Abanyole. So
Mubukusu, like an Englishman is a mix of various clans sharing
a common territorial boundary. Some clans are associated with
certain trades, traits, or peculiarities. For instance circumcisers
come from Bamasike, Babasaba, and Bakhoone clans while Bakoi
are renowned for being peacemakers; Babutu, Bakwangwa, and
Basaniaka are dream prophets (*bang'osi*), and Bakitwika (Maina's
clan) are associated with magic powers. One of the most famous
magicians since Maina is Wachiye wa Naumbwa who is said to have

---

177. Some clan specific customs condoned include burial, arts and crafts, secret
oaths and songs, nomenclature, circumcision, and cliteridectomy. This
includes the direction in which an individual faces when being circumcised
or buried.

performed not only dazzling magic but also miracles. Bakwangwa split from Bakitwika and like Babutu and Basaniaka are known to be *bang'osi* while Baliuli are magic busters. Bakwangwa and Bameywa consider reedbuck (*esunu*), a cultural totem; they don't eat meat from this antelope. Be that as it may, clans that are directly descended from Mubukusu, the tribal ancestor consider themselves more Bukusu than assimilated or immigrant clans. As a result the pedigree Bukusu clans include Bamalaba, Bamwalie, Babikayi, Basilikwa, Banabayi, and Baneala. These "mother" clans are considered the original *chibololi* (clandoms) of the people we know today as Babukusu.

Basilikwa spawned up to fifty clans while the Bamwalie begat thirty-six and Bamalaba nine. But the largest clan in terms of numbers is Bakitwika whose former subclans Bakitang'a, Banambobi, Basakha, Bakwangwa, and Baluleti have spawned several other autonomous clans. Clans with dynamic leadership qualities which have dominated Bukusu political and military life are split into two tiers. In the first tier, you find Bakitwika, Bayemba, Bakiyabi, and Bakhurarwa while the second tier includes Baliuli, Babuya, Balwonja, Balanda, Bakimweyi, Basombi, Bameme, Bamutilu, Bamuki, Bakhoone, and Babichachi. The rope (*omukoye*) is an object of totemic significance for Baliuli and Bamutilu who believe that on their migratory journeys southward, they crossed a big river (believed to be River Nile) using a bridge made of ropes. One of their favorite girl names is Nekoye in recognition of the rope that saved them from drowning (Makila 1978: 104).

Bamusomi have given rise to two clans—Bamae and Bayesele while Babuya have Baolo and Bakhufwe whose characteristic peculiarity is timidness. Babwoba have the following subclans—Banabwema, Banakhalundu, Basiabulili, Batuta, and Bananyenje while Baechalo have Baminyi, Bachebasa, Banakhungu, Batoya, Banabalayo, and Bamangoye. Balwonja subclans include Banawanga, Bakheyana, Bakutolo, and Bamusabi while Babuya have Basikulu, Baholo, Bakabo, Bakhufwe, Bahambwa, and Bamwonja. Baala subclans include Bakoyabe, Balubiri, and Babaangura while Bakiyabi have Babikeyo, Banelima, and Balokiywa. Babuulo have Banabukhisa, Babatelema, Baweswa, and Banakoyonjo while Bamusomi have Bamahe, Bayasere, Basomi, Basiuma, Batoboso, Bamasiukha, Batunguya, and Bamabechu. Balako subclans include Bababweywe, Bakhandia, Bakelo, and Basiambo (Makila 1978: 88). Baata have five subclans—Bafumbula, Bawele, Bamulekhwa, Bakhatumu, and Bachema of which the first three are fully fledged septs but otherwise exogamous, in Kenya at least. Oral sources indicate the clan founder, Moli, was an elder brother of Wanga, the eponymous founder of Wanga kingdom. He settled at Siritanyi in Bungoma and later emigrated to Bugisu settling among Babulo clansmen. It was in Bubulo that he begat five sons that constitute the Baata clandom. He returned with some of his brethren to Bungoma where he died. The Baata clans in Bugisu are fully fledged septs and do not observe rules of exogamy, but their Kenyan brethren resolved in a ritual ceremony in 1963 not to intermarry.

Baala Bakoyabe do not wear *omukasa* (copper bracelet), the ultimate symbol of leadership in Buluyia. They lost the right to high office following an incident in which a gluttonous Omukoyabe sauntered into the kitchen of his hosts at night to eat more food despite having eaten to the fill the previous night. In his haste, *omukasa* dropped in the pot, but for fear of attracting attention, he abandoned it there. When the hostess discovered it while tending to her pots, the following morning she went round asking if anyone had lost *omukasa*, but no one, including the loser, owned up. Embarrassed by the incident, Baala Bakoyabe disavowed the bracelet thereby ruling them out of leadership positions (Makila 1978: 105). Another clan that does not wear *omukasa* and therefore cannot be leaders is Balende.

Although all clans observe rules of exogamy, where subclans split from mother clans seven generations ago, these rules are cast aside, and clansmen may intermarry so long as there is no living member interlocking the two consanguineous clans. For instance although Bakitang'a, Baluleti, Basakha, Banambobi, and Bakwangwa were subclans of Bakitwika, they now consider themselves independent enough to intermarry with each other. The same case applies to Bamusomi, the mother clan of Bamae and Bayasele and so are Bayuya who gave birth to Baolo and Bakhufwe. In both cases, clansmen are no longer ritually endogamous.

The Bukusu bury their dead facing east, the direction from which their ancestors came. Clan elders and warriors are buried with their weapons. Three clans, Balunda, Bayaya, and Bafumi as well as Bakhibi, a subclan of Batura, bury their dead in a sitting position. In explanation of this custom, clansmen aver that the sitting position means the deceased continues to play a supervisory role in the welfare of the family while a lying position signifies defeat (Bulimo 2013: 519). This burial mode is now at a crossroads with the church which wants it ended or the clergy will not preside over requiem mass. In July 2012, the Catholic Church called this type of burial quaint in the twenty-first century, but clan elders fired back aiming their ammunition at Father Sebastian Mang'oli whom they accused of being disrespectful of their culture.[178] Balunda are also famed as the "owners of rain" because the first rain magician (*omukimba*) among Babukusu was Omulunda just like Nganyi commanded a similar reputation in Bunyore and neighboring territories.

[178.] Article on *Westfm* website on July 2, 2012, written by Protus Simiyu entitled *Balunda, Batura Bakhibi cultural history of burying the dead while seated at crossroads with religion.*

Table 40: Bukusu population distribution by administrative units, surface area, and density

Admin Unit	Total	Area (sq km)	Density
Bungoma South	**408,598**	**666.4**	**613**
Township	**43,516**	**13.9**	**3,133**
Township	19,017	5.1	3,739
Khalaba	24,499	8.8	2,784
Musikoma	**37,933**	**44**	**863**
Namasanda	12,682	23.6	538
South Kanduyi	25,251	20.4	1,240
Kibabii	**35,781**	**48.5**	**738**
Tuuti	16,385	22.3	736
Marakaru	19,396	26.2	740
East Bukusu	**65,411**	**125.1**	**523**
West Sang'alo	18,822	33.4	563
Namwacha	14,301	25.8	554
East Sang'alo	15,434	32.5	475
Mwikhupo	16,854	33.4	505
Bukembe	**47,060**	**87.1**	**540**
North Sang'alo	14,330	21.7	662
Ndengelwa	10,774	17.8	606
Namirembe	9,537	17.9	534
Kong'oli	12,419	29.8	417
Bumula	**178,897**	**347.8**	**514**
Bumula	**12,589**	**27.3**	**460**
Bumula	7,600	15.8	488
Lunao	4,989	11.8	424
Napara	**16,354**	**31.4**	**521**
Bitobo	5,771	10.3	560
Khasolo	10,583	21.1	502
Kimaeti	**20,185**	**35**	**576**
Siombe	12,068	21.6	560
Nakwana	8,117	13.5	602
Khasoko	**14,035**	**24.9**	**563**

Khasoko	4,024	6.1	665
Namatotoa	6,448	11.9	541
Mungore	3,563	7	511
Kabula	**20,756**	**41.7**	**497**
Kabula	10,360	18.7	555
Watoya	10,396	23.1	450
Siboti	**18,210**	**32.9**	**553**
East Siboti	8,730	15.6	558
Musakasa	9,480	17.3	549
Mukwa	**14,297**	**27.2**	**526**
Mukwa	5,623	10.7	526
Kisawayi	8,674	16.5	525
Kibuke	**5,111**	**8.6**	**594**
Mayanja	4,891	9.6	507
Lwanja	5,961	12.4	480
Ng'oli	4,039	8.3	488
South Bukusu	**23,135**	**48.3**	**479**
Muanda	8,452	18.7	452
Lumboka	11,672	24.4	479
Mateka	3,011	5.3	569
Mabusi	**19,334**	**40**	**483**
Kimatuni	9,012	17.7	510
Mabusi	10,322	22.4	462
Bungoma North	**320,300**	**559.5**	**572**
Tongaren	**187,478**	**378.4**	**496**
Tongaren	**42,674**	**77.9**	**548**
Tongaren	24,970	46.2	540
Soysambu	17,704	31.7	559
Ndalu	**24,745**	**59.6**	**415**
Ndalu	13,630	38.1	357
Mituwa	11,115	21.5	518
Kiminini	**16,455**	**48.7**	**338**
Kiminini	8,937	27.9	320
Tabani	7,518	20.8	361
Naitiri	**51,880**	**106**	**489**

Naitiri	18,528	41.4	448
Milima	33,352	64.6	516
Mbakalo	**32,229**	**50.2**	**642**
Mbakalo	14,903	23.3	639
Kibisi	17,326	26.9	654
Kabuyefwe	**19,495**	**36**	**542**
Sirakaru	10,355	18.7	553
Kabuyefwe	9,140	17.3	529
Kimilili	**132,822**	**181.2**	**733**
Kimilili	**36,267**	**42.1**	**861**
Kimilili Rural	22,338	33.1	675
Township	13,929	9	1,543
Maeni	**24,209**	**41**	**591**
Nasusi	13,525	23.3	580
Sikhendu	10,684	17.7	604
Kamukuywa	**37,888**	**46.2**	**821**
Makhonge	16,147	23.6	683
Nabikoto	21,741	22.5	966
Kibingei	**34,458**	**51.9**	**664**
Kibingei	9,385	17.1	550
Chebukwabi	25,073	34.8	720
Bungoma East	**230,253**	**404.3**	**570**
Webuye†	**152,654**	**270.4**	**565**
Webuye	**47,413**	**51.3**	**924**
Maraka	11,368	21.2	535
Township	24,106	13	1,853
Matulo	11,939	17.1	699
Sitikho	**30,055**	**80.1**	**375**
Sitikho	11,073	21.6	513
Milo	9,587	20.5	468
Khalumuli	9,395	38	247
Bokoli	**32,891**	**68.9**	**477**
Mahanga	6,806	14.9	456
Matisi	7,515	13.7	548
Miendo	10,314	24.4	422

Bokoli	8,256	15.9	521
Misikhu	**42,295**	**70.1**	**604**
Misikhu	21,862	33.2	658
Kituni	9,520	17.9	533
Malaha	10,913	19	576
Ndivisi†	**77,599**	**133.9**	**580**
Ndivisi	**15,251**	**20.5**	**745**
Sitabicha	10,744	13.7	785
Magemo	4,507	6.8	666
Namarambi	**20,722**	**34.3**	**603**
Wabukhonyi	2,807	4.6	605
Marinda	8,590	10.4	828
Misemwa	4,491	7.1	634
Makuselwa	4,834	12.2	395
Chetambe	**23,620**	**41.5**	**569**
Mihuu	15,369	27	570
Mitukuyu	8,251	14.6	566
Lugusi	**18,006**	**37.5**	**480**
Misimo	9,681	17.7	546
Lutacho	8,325	19.8	420
Bungoma West	**243,535**	**445.5**	**547**
Sirisia	**55,952**	**111.8**	**501**
Sirisia	**28,399**	**64.6**	**439**
North Kulisiru	15,876	34.4	461
South Kulisiru	12,523	30.2	414
Namwela	**27,553**	**47.2**	**584**
Central Namwela	7,602	9.7	782
South Namwela	13,931	27.8	501
Menu	6,020	9.6	627
Malakisi	**46,470**	**101.4**	**458**
Malakisi	**17,533**	**39.2**	**447**
Sitabicha	4,292	9.8	440
Tamulega	3,111	8.1	382
Bukokholo	4,252	9.1	469
Butonge	2,416	6.7	360

Mwalie	3,462	5.6	621
Namubila	**14,552**	**36.4**	**400**
Wamono	9,327	23.4	399
Machakha	5,225	13	403
Lwandanyi	**14,385**	**25.8**	**558**
Mayekwe	6,477	11	588
Chebukuyi	7,908	14.8	536
Nalondo	**84,420**	**150.4**	**561**
Kabuchai	**23,710**	**41.6**	**570**
Kabuchai	10,485	19.1	551
Kisiwa	13,225	22.5	587
North Bukusu	**15,847**	**29.1**	**545**
North Nalondo	9,182	16.3	562
Mukhweya	6,665	12.8	522
Sirare	**19,905**	**32.4**	**614**
West Nalondo	19,905	32.4	614
Luuya	**24,958**	**47.3**	**528**
Luuya	13,618	26.1	522
Bwake	11,340	21.2	535
Chwele	**56,693**	**81.9**	**692**
Chwele	**32,983**	**41.5**	**635**
Sichei	9,818	15.5	635
Chwele	18,705	17.9	1,045
Sikulu	4,460	8.2	547
Mukuyuni	**23,710**	**40.4**	**587**
Kuywa	11,094	19.1	580
Mukuyuni	6,048	9.9	612
Kibichori	6,568	11.4	577

†. Majority of people in Webuye and Ndivisi divisions are Tachoni.

Adapted from Kenya Census 2009, *Kenya National Bureau of Statistics, Nairobi, August 2010.*

e. Traditional and modern government

Unlike neighboring Wanga, the Bukusu did not have a centralized system of government although leaders came from certain designated clans foremost of which are Bakitwika. However, Bakitwika lost their pedigree status following a curse by Maina when one of his descendants passed over all royal insignia to Bakhoone. Although all these happened in the distant past, it still remains a point of rivalry between Bakitwika and Bakhoone to this day (Makila 1978: 153). Nonetheless, a village headman called Omukasa, usually elected by elders, was the highest-ranking figure of authority in Bukusu society although some healers and prophets were venerated for their deep knowledge of tribal tradition and medicines. Foremost among these adepts was Elijah Masinde, Omubichachi clansman deified as a prophet (*omung'osi*) who founded *Dini ya Musambwa*.[179] In 27 August 2011, he was formally honored as a national hero by the Kenya government along with Masinde Muliro, the quintessential Bukusu politician.

The few clans like Babichachi that produce pedigree individuals occupy an exalted position in the magico-cultural hierarchy of Babukusu. Most of the respected elders come from these clans and, among other duties, officiate at important community events like funerals. Known as *basala kimise* (singular: *oswala kumuse*), these individuals are highly venerated for their deep knowledge of Bukusu culture and traditions (Simiyu 1997: 2). During the *kumuse* funerary rituals, they wear the hut of peacemakers (*bakayi*, singular: *omukayi*). Among other things, they are chief custodians of the history, culture, and customs of Babukusu. In this leadership role, they hold

---

[179.] *Dini ya Musambwa* literally means religion of ancestors. Elijah Masinde founded the sect in protest against Christian evangelism which had taken root in Buluyia since early 1900s and regarded African customary practices such as polygamy, traditional circumcision rites, and ancestral belief systems as heathen. The sect spread among the Tiriki, Wanga, Tachoni, Kabras, Batsotso, and Pokot.

the community together at a time of great grief preaching against witchcraft, admonishing youth against miscreancy, and rallying society to uphold the highest moral standards. The most famous *omukayi* in recent times is John Ngonelo Wanyonyi Manguliechi (1930-2012), Omumeme clansman who presided over the *kumuse* of Masinde Muliro in 1992. Another notable *omukayi* from historical pages is Mukite wa Nameme (Omumutilu clansman), one of the greatest Bukusu warriors and prophets of the ninteenth century. His mother came from Bameme clan which, incidentally, is the clan of Elijah Masinde's mother. He is credited with crafting an organized Bukusu army that finally defeated arch enemies like the Teso, Maasai, Sabaot, and Wanga and returned Bukusu refugees to their homeland.

The geopolitical map of Bungoma had six constituencies— Kimilili, Kanduyi, Webuye, Bumula, Sirisia, and Mt. Elgon shared between the dominant Babukusu and minority Sabaot and Tachoni. Of the six, Mt. Elgon is predominantly Sabaot while Webuye is split almost equally between the Bukusu and Tachoni. However, following adoption by Kenyan Parliament of Ligale Report in June 2011, Bungoma gained an additional three constituencies. In addition to Tongaren and Kabuchai, Webuye constituency was abolished and in its place created Webuye East and Webuye West. After the 2013 general elections, the MPs for the new ridings are James Lusweti Mukwe (Kabuchai), Dr Eseli Simiyu (Tongaren), and Dan Wanyama (Webuye West) while Alfred Sambu migrated to Webuye East.

In the colonial days, the most famous Bukusu was Sudi Namachanja (aka Wasike Lusweti) from Bakhoone clan who had forty wives. One of his wives, Rosa Namisi, was a diviner. She gave birth to Maurice Michael Otunga who rose to become head of the Catholic Church in Kenya and one of Africa's putative modern saints.[180] On the political stage, Masinde Muliro[181] from the Bakokho clan distinguished himself as a principled man who could not be corrupted into mediocrity or sycophancy. One of his defining political moments was when in 1975 as a member of the executive, he voted against the government over a report into the murder of a popular politician, Josiah Mwangi Kariuki—the only full cabinet minister to do so.[182] His vote swung the balance and the government lost the motion. Angry President Kenyatta tossed Muliro to the deep sea to meet his fate but he survived the political sharks that wanted him completely vanquished and impoverished. He died in 1992 without amassing ill-gotten riches that too often accompany the political class in Kenya but with his dignity held intact. He is immortalized by a university in Kakamega bearing his name. Before Muliro, the first Bukusu to win elections in open contest was Pascal Nabwana (Omuyemba) although his victory

---

[180.] Cardinal Maurice Otunga will become a saint once the long process of canonisation and beatification is over. As and when it happens, he will join an elite group of African saints such as St. Josephine Bakhita, a former Sudanese slave who died in 1947 and a phalanx of nineteenth century Ugandan martyrs of which St. Charles Lwanga is best known.

[181.] Henry Pius Masinde Muliro was born at Matili, Bungoma on 30 June 1920 to Muliro Kisingilie and Makinia and died on 14 August 1992 in Nairobi. He was among the five founders of FORD, the vehicle that finally broke Daniel arap Moi's one party tyranny. Others were Jaramogi Odinga Oginga, Joseph Martin Shikuku, Kenneth Matiba, and Charles Rubia. He is hailed as one of the greatest Luyia leaders and immortalized by an institution of higher learning bearing his name—Masinde Muliro University of Science and Technology (MMUST) in Kakamega in addition to Muliro Gardens also in Kakamega where civic and political activities take place. He was the first MP for Trans Nzoia (renamed Kitale East then Cherengany in 1988) and ruled for four terms (1966-74, 1974-79, 1984-88 and 1988-90). On 27 August 2011, the government declared him a national hero.

[182.] Peter Kibisu, then MP for Vihiga was also sacked from the front bench as an assistant minister for voting with backbenchers.

was overturned by colonialists in collusion with Sudi Namachanja (Omukhoone).

Kenya's first cardinal, Maurice Otunga, a Mukhoone clansman from Bungoma may yet be declared a saint once the long process of beatification and canonization is over.

Another notable Bukusu politician was Michael Kijana Wamalwa who rose to become a vice president in 2003 but sadly died only months into his prefecture. Wamalwa's passing attracted an unwelcome controversy. A Kalenjin group, Sabaot claimed that contrary to popular belief, Wamalwa was one of their own. Sabaot elders issued a press statement[183] detailing his true parentage. Although his mother, Esther Nekesa (died 27 May 2009) was a Bukusu from the Baengele clan, his father, Senator William Chemayyek Ngeywo was a Sabaot who had changed his moniker to Wamalwa to get education. Baengele are famed for being haughty and stubborn but otherwise very eloquent, a characteristic trait Wamalwa seems to have inherited for his renditions were so eloquently seamless they unarmed opponents. Nonetheless, Sabaot elders argued that in early colonial Kenya Sabaot children were discriminated against by chiefs and the only way they could get education was by changing their names. The elders said that Sabaot and Bukusu are both patrilineal societies and descent stems from the father's and not mother's clan. Although their claim had merit, the Bukusu culture also recognizes the right to nationhood of immigrant and assimilated clans and so Wamalwa was buried with full funeral rites as a Bukusu not a Sabaot.

f. Other prominent Bukusu personalities

From historical pages, we find the following people who influenced events in Bukusu society: Walumoli Sioka (Omubuya), Bukusu leader during migratory journeys at Sengeli; Sioka (Omulako), inherited leadership from Walumoli; Makutukutu (Omukhurarwa), took over from Sioka; Sanjamolu (Omubuya), succeeded Makutukutu; Maina wa Nalukale (Omukitwika Omukitang'a), said to have disappeared mysteriously; Wakhulunya, son of Maina; Namunyulubunda, son of Wakhulunya; Kitimule okhwa Wetoyi (Omukitwika Omukitang'a), reputed for discovering 'lost' Bukusu clans at Ebuyumbu (Mwalie Hills); Kaluuka okhwa Nabwonja (Omuala Omukoyabe), the postmortem specialist;

[183.] Article in the *East African Standard* August 26, 2003. The statement was issued on behalf of Sabaot Council of Elders by their chairman, Philip Chebus, 76.

and Nasokho (Omuyemba), famed for playing host to a Maasai, Masibayi (Masiribayi) who later deposed him after rescuing Babukusu from drought (see p.212).

Others are Khakula (Omumeme), a seer whose son was killed by *yabebe* serpent (Bulimo 2013: 271); Mulya (Omulunda), whose footprints (*Sikele sya Mulya*) left a permanent imprint on a rock in Sang'alo Hills which today stands as a shrine for *Dini ya Musambwa* followers; Mukite wa Nameme (Omutilu), the military strategist credited with herding Bukusu refugees back to their homeland; Mukisu Lufwalula (Omuyemba Mukhayama), credited with introducing ruthlessness in warfare that finally defeated Iteso; Maelo okhwa Khandi, a military strategist, Mutonyi okhwa Nabukelembe aka Walubengo, a dream prophet (*omung'osi*) and Sunguru (Omumuki), a diviner (*omulakusi*).

Other great Babukusu include Wachiye wa Naumbwa (Omukitwika Omukwangwa), credited with performing miracles; Lumbasi (Omutecho), a war doctor; Sikhokhone (Omuyitu), a nobleman; Wakoli okhwa Mukisu (Omuyemba Omukhuyama), a multilingual military strategist under whose command thiryt British soldiers were massacred leading to War of Lumboka in which 420 Bukusu warriors were killed and 450 cattle seized. Situma okhwa Wachiye was son of Wachiye wa Naumbwa and is credited with war prophecy that warned Babukusu against a war with Barwa but they defied him. In the ensuing battle Babukusu suffered heavy casualties, their blood turning River Kamukuywa red. To this day, Babukusu never drink water from this river (Makila 1978: 243).

Other people became famous for their social skills or over generosity. Among them was Nambo Mukho Mwami (wife of an elder) whose hospitality to a stranger led to catastrophic consequences as the child was a Suk or Turkana (Mukamulyungu) spy; Kharuba (Omuechalo), treacherously bartered a wild animal for food and Ngutuku okhwa Watila (Omukitwika Omukitang'a);

diminutive fellow famed for vivacity and humour. From the world of modern politics, famous Bukusu leaders include:

- Musikari Nazi Kombo, former leader of a political party, Ford Kenya. He served as a minister and MP for Webuye (1997-2002 and 2002-2007). Although he lost the 2007 elections to a Tachoni, Alfred Sambu he was nominated to Tenth Parliament. He is from the Balunda clan, one of the Bukusu septs that bury the dead in a sitting position.
- Wafula Wabuge—MP Kitale West (renamed Saboti in 1988; 1969-74 and 1974-79) and ambassador to the USA.
- Elijah Wasike Mwangale—former minister for foreign affairs and MP for Bungoma East (renamed Kimilili in 1988; 1969-74, 1974-79, 1979-83, 1983-88, 1988-1992). Omusombi clansman, he died from a stroke in 2004.
- Dr. Mukhisa Kituyi (Omukitwika)—former industry and commerce minister and MP for Kimilili (1992-97, 1997-2002, 2002-07).
- Moses Masika Wetang'ula—foreign affairs minister (later trade and industry) and MP for Sirisia (2002-07, 2007-13). He is Omubutu clansman from Nalondo. Wetang'ula was elected the first Bungoma County senator after flooring his main rivals, Musikari Kombo and Dr. Mukhisa Kituyi in the 2013 general elections. His Ford Kenya party won ten seats across the country and his brother, Timothy Wanyonyi Wetang'ula won the Westlands riding in Nairobi. The 2013 elections not only established a new political dynasty in Luyialand but also installed Wetang'ula as the foremost Luyia political supremo.
- Dr. David Eseli Simiyu—MP for Kimilili (2007-13). In the 2013 general elections, he was reelected to represent the newly created Tongaren constituency. He is of Bunyala origin.

- Alfred Khangati—MP for Kanduyi (2007-13) originally from Bunyala.
- John Baraza Munyasia—MP for Sirisia (1992-97 and 1997-2002).
- Joseph Muliro (Omusomi)—MP for Sirisia (1988-92) and assistant minister for foreign affairs.
- William Wamalwa—MP for Kitale West (renamed Saboti in 1988, 1966-73). He is the father of late Michael Kijana Wamalwa who also represented the constituency and rose to become a vice president and Saboti MP, Eugene Wamalwa (2007-13).
- Eugene Ludovic Wamalwa—MP for Saboti (2007-13) who was appointed minister for justice and constitutional affairs in 2012. He won the Saboti seat formerly held by his brother, Kijana Wamalwa, to continue the Wamalwa political dynasty. He did not contest any elective post in the 2013 general elections and his Saboti seat was won by David Wafula Wekesa.
- Wafula Wamunyinyi (Omukibeyi)—MP for Kanduyi (2002-07). He recaptured the seat in the 2013 general elections.
- Maurice S. Makhanu (Omukhoone)—MP for Kanduyi (1988-92) and former PC.
- Sylvester Wakoli Bifwoli (Omuyemba)—MP for Bumula (2002-07 and 2007-13). He lost the seat to newcomer, Boniface Otsyula in the 2013 general elections.
- Lawrence Simiyu Sifuna (Omutilu)—MP Bungoma South which was later split into Kanduyi and Bumula (1979-83 and 1983-1988).
- Dr. Frederick S. Masinde (Omuliango)—MP for Bungoma South (1974-79).

- George Welime Kapten (Omutilu)—MP for Kwanza (1992-97, 1997-98). He died under mysterious circumstances just a year into his second term in 1998.
- Peter Joseph Kisuya (Omukitang'a)—MP for Bungoma Central (1979-88 and 1988-92).
- Nathan Waliaula Munoko (Omulako)—Senator for Bungoma in 1963 and MP for Bungoma Central renamed Sirisia in 1988 and cabinet minister (1963-69, 1969-74, and 1974-79).
- Mark Barasa—MP Elgon East (1963-66).
- George Henry Kerre—first MP for Elgon Central (died Dec. 7, 1965). Elgon Central later became Bungoma South and is now Kanduyi.
- Saulo Wanambisi Busolo (Omutakhwe)—MP for Webuye 1994-97 (won in a by election following a successful appeal against Musikari Kombo's election).
- Joash Wamang'oli (Omubayi)—MP for Webuye (1988-1992).
- Captain Davies Wafula Nakitare (Omulako)—MP for Saboti (2003-2007). An airline pilot by profession, he won in a by election following the death of Wamalwa Kijana.
- Joseph Wanyonyi Khaoya—MP for Elgon Central (Kanduyi) who captured the seat following the death of the incumbent GH Kerre in 1965. He recaptured the seat in the 1969 elections but was defeated in 1974 by Dr. Frederick Masinde.

Beyond politics, Bukusu also boasts of an array of individuals who have distinguished themselves in various academic, administrative, and professional fields. In education, the former Alliance Boys headmaster, Christopher Khaemba, was appointed the first principal of the prestigious African Leadership Academy in South Africa; Prof. Christopher Lukorito Wanjala (Omukwangwa), the literature academic; Prof. Simiyu Wandibba (Omuyonga), the anthropologist; Fred E. Makila, the author (Omuyemba); Prof. Bonaventure Kerre of Moi University; late Prof. Edward George Kasili (Omufumi), the cancer researcher ironically killed by cancer; Dr. Joab Bwayo, the late international HIV/Aids scientist; Francis D. P Situma, the law professor; and Dr. Eusebius Juma Mukhwana (Omusakali), the academic and philanthropist.

In other fields, we have Eliud Paul Nakitare, former director, ministry of culture; Justice Roselyn Naliaka Nambuye (Omukiyabi) married in Tiriki to Justice Daniel Aganyanya; Justice Ruth Nekoye Sitati (Omuliuli); Paul Kukubo, the IT specialist; Ken Lusaka, the permanent secretary; Nancy Makokha Baraza (Omutasama) the former deputy chief justice; Dinah Khayota, former chairperson of Maendeleo ya Wanawake; Patrick Wangamati, the civic leader and chairman, Luyia Council of Elders; Topi Charles Lyambila (Omuyaya), the journalist; Dr. George Masafu, the media mogul; Suleiman Kasuti Murunga, (Omuliuli) the Nairobi businessman who became Kimilili MP in the 2013 general elections; and late David Wanjala Welime (Omuliango), former chairman of NARC electoral board.

17. Abawanga (Wanga)

Table 41: Wanga clans (brackets indicate alternative spelling or where else clan members are found)

Ababala (Tiriki)	Ababere (Marachi, Samia, Haya, Bukhayo, Uganda)
Ababongo (Bunyala, Samia)	Ababonwe (Marachi, Samia)
Ababuka (Tiriki, Marachi)	Abachero (Kisa)
Abachirinya	Abachitechi
Abaholo (Ugenya, Congo)	Abakalibo
Abakana (Ugenya)	Abakhamari
Abakhami (Bukusu)	Abakoye

Abakulubi

Abalunda

Abamale

Abambatsa

Abamuima (Abamuhima, Abamuyima)

Abamukalala

Abamukolwe (Marachi, Marama)

Abamuniafu

Abamurono (Marachi, Kisa)

Abamushechere

Abamutiru

Abanamangwa

Abarunga (Bukhayo, Marachi)

Abashibe

Abashikaawa

Abashitsetse

Abatobe

Abawali

Abayundo (Abanyala ba Ndombi, Bukusu)

Abaleka (Samia, Bunyala, Uganda)

Abamaingo

Abamani (Marama, Kisa, Butsotso, Abanyala ba Ndombi)

Abambwoli

Abamuira

Abamukalano

Abamulembo (Bunyala, Bukusu, Samia, Marachi)

Abamunyendo

Abamurumba

Abamuswa (Ugenya)

Abamwende (Marama, Butsotso)

Abanatsiri (Tiriki)

Abasereme (Uganda Nyole)

Abashieni (Marama)

Abashireka

Abatende

Abatura (Tiriki, Isukha, Bukusu, Bukhayo, Marachi)

Abaweesia

a. Aristocratic ancestry

Abawanga are named after the tribal ancestor, Wanga, a descendant of interlacustrine dynasties of the Great Lakes region. Although Wanga country is populated by many clans, historicisation of the polity was influenced by Abashitsetse, the clan of *nabongos* (kings). Abashitsetse trace their roots to Mutesa who had three sons—Muwanga (Mwanga, Wanga), Mukoya, and Kamaanya (Kamwanyi). The eldest, Muwanga, settled in Buganda while Mukoya went to Busoga and the youngest, Kamaanya, went to Ibanda on the shores of Lake Victoria. He left Ibanda and trekked through Bunyala and Samia almost unnoticed circa

AD 1500 (Osogo 1966: 34 & 64) and settled around Lake Gangu (Anyuoka) in Alego. From here his descendants went to Tiriki and subsequently Wanga. For a complete genealogy of Abashitsetse dynasty, see chart 3 (p.388). The geophysical location of Abawanga is Ebuwanga, and they speak Oluwanga, widely considered standard Luyia. The Wanga neighbor the Bukusu, Batsotso, Marama, and Marachi. Their organized system of government historicized the Wanga much more than any other Luyia subnation. Some of the historical writs are, however, either contradictory or conflicting as we shall shortly see.

In chapter 3, we saw that Abamuhima,[184] descendants of the interlacustrine Chwezi, were the original founders of what later became Wanga Kingdom. Abamuhima kingdom collapsed or was subsumed by the arrival of Wanga from Tiriki accompanied by his Abashitsetse clansmen. Since then, Abashitsetse became the royal and dominant clan upon whom power, authority, and privilege oscillated. Clans outside the royal orbit consider Abashitsetse arrogant but nonetheless acknowledge the role played by *obunabongo* in putting the Wanga polity into the international spotlight. However, the origin of Abashitsetse while widely acknowledged to be in Uganda via Tiriki was a subject of intense intellectual debate. Early anthropologists like A. T. Matson suggested that Abashitsetse may have been of Kalenjin origin as its members claimed to have been descendants of a pastoral culture.[185]

A Luo scholar, S. Malo first advanced the theory that Abashitsetse were Luo in his 1953 book entitled *Dhoudi Mag*

[184.] Pres. Yoweri Kaguta Museveni is from Abamuhima clan of Banyankole. After collapse of the Chwezi kingdom, Abamuhima spread across into Kenya, Tanzania and Rwanda where they tried establishing their kingdoms with varying degree of success.

[185.] Bahima are from Ankole which is famous for the long-horned Ankole cattle. It is probable that Matson may have made wrong conclusions basing his reasoning on Kalenjin pastoralists with whom he was acquainted.

Central Nyanza (Clans of Central Nyanza), a theory that was robustly defended by a preeminent Luo historian, Prof. Bethuel Ogot (1967). Citing cultural traits like royal insignia (copper bracelet), leopard skin cloak, ritual killing of *nabongo*, and burial of kings in a shroud of fresh bull's hide and bushbuck (*imbongo*) totem, Prof. Ogot concluded that Abashitsetse are of Luo origin. He even mistakenly linked a Luo clan, Jouyoma to Bayuma of Wanga. Bayuma was first used by Mr. Matson and most likely, he was referring to Abamuhima (Abamuima) as there is no evidence of a clan in Wanga known by that name. These theories about the true identity of Abashitsetse were dismissed as having no basis by Prof. Gideon Were (1967).

To begin with, Abawanga travelled through Bunyoro, Buganda and Busoga before arriving in Tiriki, and if they were not aristocratic then, possibly picked up royal habits from these places. For instance, the ruling clan of Basoga also hold the bushbuck in high esteem as an item of totemic symbolism. Moreover, several clans in Bunyoro, Ankole, and Buganda hold bushbuck in reverence. Secondly, the burial in a shroud of skin was necessitated by absence of barkcloth which Baganda, Banyoro, and Basoga used to inter their kings. The bushbuck is not known to be one of Luo sacred animals or totem. Finally, no one could become king or handle royal insignia if they were not circumcised, a requirement that expressly rules out the Luo who traditionally did not observe this custom. Nor is the presence of pockets of Wanga people at a place called Sakwa in Luoland an indication of a direct royal link with Nabongo Sakwa of Wanga Mukulu (Were 1967: 109-110). The Nyapambo clan in Sakwa performs sacrifices using Luyia words, a clear indication of their ancestry (Osogo 1966: 27).

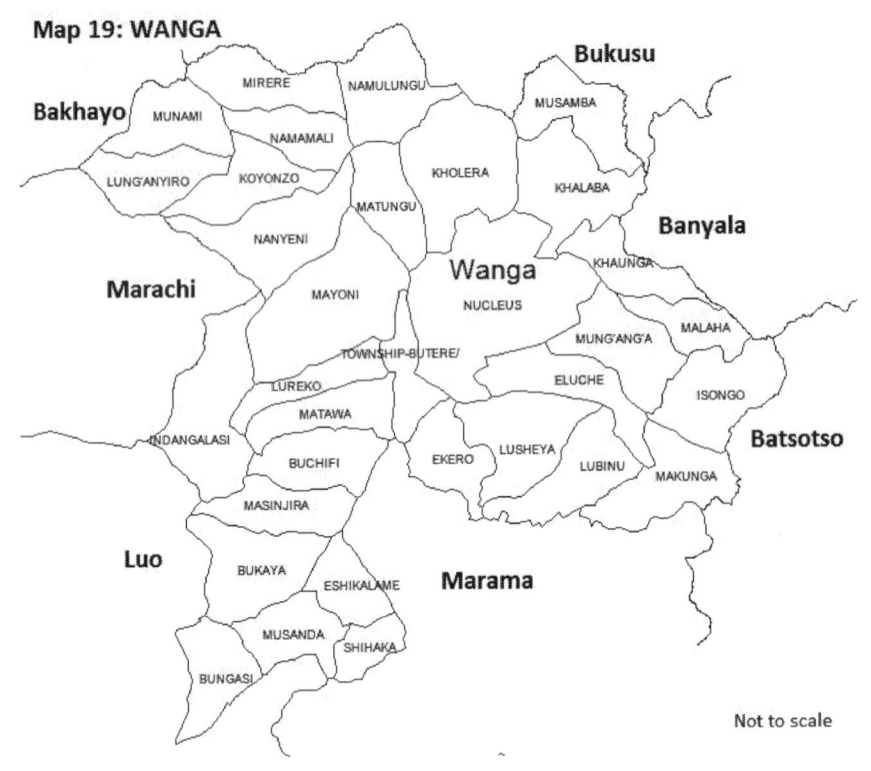

Map 19 shows the main administrative locations in
Wanga, Kakamega County.

Clan pride among Abawanga is a serious matter denoted
by how close a particular clandom is to the tribal ancestor. Only
twelve clans consider themselves direct descendants of Muwanga
with the rest being later arrivals who submitted themselves
to the political leadership of Wanga. These are Abashitsetse,
Abamurono, Abatende, Abamuniafu, Abanamangwa, Abayundo
(also found among Abanyala ba Ndombi and Bukusu), Abambatsa,
Abamushechere, Abamukalano, Abambwoli, Abasereme (also
found among Abanyole of Uganda), and Abachitechi. Abatobo are
descendant from the Nandi (Were 1967: 61). With the exception
of Abamurono and Abambatsa, the other ten clans consider
themselves too closely related to intermarry. Clans closely related

to Abashitsetse which observe rules of exogamy include Ababala, Abasereme, Abamuniafu, Abamusechere, Abamukalala, Abatende, Abanamangwa and Abambwoli.

The clan of Abakolwe deserves a special mention. Although it is generally believed the clan founder, Mukolwe, was an uncle to Wanga, other scholars say he was a Maragoli who settled among the Wanga (Osogo 1966: 72). Be that as it may, the clan is spread across Wanga, Marachi, and Marama. And even though there is no clan in Maragoli called Avamukolwe, it is instructive that the name Mukolwe is popular in Maragoli, Wanga, as well as Marama. In Wanga, Mukolwe's progeny founded the clans of Abashireka, Abachirinya, Abamale and Abakhamari. Abachirinya further spawned two autonomous clans—Abamurumba and Abamunyendo.

The autochthonous clan in Ebuwanga is Abamanga who are largely extinct followed by Abamuima (Abamuhima, Abamwima). Ebuwanga is also inhabited with large Luo populations. In 1934, Wanga mobs egged on by Walter Owen, the archdeacon of Maseno CMS, massacred Lawi Obonyo and Alfayo Odongo Mango, founders of an independent sect, JoRoho that advocated the return of land annexed by the Wanga and prophesised end of colonialism sparking a series of inter tribal warfare. The Luo, especially Kager (Abageri) clansmen lost the crusade to have their land transferred to Ugenya or Alego. Abakami (Jougem), Abamani (Jouman), Abamuswa (Joumuswa), and Abaholo clans for instance are either of Luo origin or assimilated and one finds whole sublocations inhabited by Luo in Mumias, e.g., Magoya Wang' Nyang. Abaholo also have a presence in Congo where they are known as Baholo or simply Holo.

Except for Abashitsetse, Abakalibo, and Abamurono, the nomenclatural system for Wanga clanswomen is similar to that of the Samia and Banyala. Hence a woman from Abamukolwe is known as Namukolwe; Abashikawa (Nashikawa); Abakoye

(Nekoye); Abamulembo (Namulembo); Abashiibe (Nashiibe), etc. A woman from Abashitsetse clan (*inono*) is called Bwibo; Abakalibo (Nasawa) while a Murono clanswoman is known as Oronda.

Table 42: Wanga population distribution by administrative unit, surface area, and density

Admin Unit	Total	Area (sq km)	Density
Mumias	359,381	590.2	609
Matungu	146,563	275.8	531
Matungu	79,183	150.7	526
Matungu	10,093	14.7	686
Kholera	18,895	42	450
Musamba	9,321	17	547
Mayoni	20,491	35.1	584
Khalaba	10,457	22	477
Namulungu	9,926	19.9	500
Koyonzo	67,380	125.1	538
Koyonzo	10,035	15.9	630
Nanyieni	13,791	23	599
Lunganyiro	7,924	14.3	553
Mirere	7,984	16.7	479
Indangalasia	11,986	27.9	430
Namamali	7,412	11.6	640
Munami	8,248	15.7	526
South Wanga	58,883	96	613
Etenje	35,333	60.9	580
Bukaya	10,872	21.3	511
Buchifi	9,382	15.3	615
Masinjira	7,908	14.1	563
Eshikalame	7,171	10.4	693
Musanda	23,550	35.1	672
Musanda	9,738	13.3	734

Eshihaka	6,791	7	975
Bungasi	7,021	14.8	474
Mumias	**64,211**	**82.7**	**777**
Nabongo	**64,211**	**82.7**	**777**
Ekero	11,232	13.3	843
Nucleus	15,765	35.7	441
Lureko	4,850	10.2	474
Mumias Town	22,599	9.7	2,333
Matawa	9,765	13.7	714
East Wanga	**89,724**	**135.8**	**661**
Malaha	**14,937**	**22.7**	**659**
Khaunga	7,772	12.1	645
Malaha	7,165	10.6	675
Lubinu	**26,377**	**38.5**	**686**
Lubinu	10,346	17.8	583
Lusheya	16,031	20.7	774
East Wanga	**24,571**	**35.3**	**696**
Eluche	12,380	16.5	750
Munganga	12,191	18.8	648
Isongo	**23,839**	**39.3**	**606**
Isongo	13,105	20.8	631
Makunga	10,734	18.6	578

Adapted from Kenya Census 2009, *Kenya National Bureau of Statistics, Nairobi, August 2010.*

b. *Wanga rule in Buluyia*

When colonialists arrived, they found Wanga kingdom as the only organized form of government not just in Luyialand but also the whole of Kenya. We have already discussed the role played by Nabongo Mumia in the establishment of British imperial rule in Buluyia (see p.122). The British used Wanga agents to rule over huge swathes of Luyialand and neighboring territories. In 1904, for instance, Mumia's half brother Murunga was appointed chief of Isukha and Idakho. In 1908 he was transferred to northern

Bungoma (which included Bukusu, Tachoni, Teso, and Sabaot) while southern Bungoma was ruled by Sudi Namachanja,[186] an ally of Nabongo Mumia. Mulama, another half brother of Mumia, was appointed chief of Marama (later extending his suzerainty to Kisa and Bunyore) while Kadima was sent to Samia (incorporating Bukhayo, Bunyala and Marachi). In Kabras, Shiundu Sakwa ruled over the chieftaincy and Wambani Sakwa in Butsotso while Tomia Sakwa was transplanted on Abanyala (Navakholo) although they had their own leader. Luo populated Buholo was not spared from Wanga domination either. A Wanga chief, Were, was dispatched there to look after things for Nabongo Mumia.

With his henchmen and relatives spread out across Buluyia, Mumia had extensive powers over the territory which he ruled. He was the final appeal authority on all native cases including settling boundary disputes. Wanga rule over Buluyia was, however, loathsome to most subnations and the British soon realized the system was not working. Their principal task was to collect poll tax and enforce law and order and save for Murunga and Mulama, the rest soon ran into problems due either to their inefficiency or arrogance or both. The first subnation to lead a revolt against Wanga agents was Butsotso which demanded the departure of Chief Wambani and reinstatement of their own chief. Batsotso revolt was followed by Abanyala (Navakholo) who successfully unseated Tomia and in his place, Ndombi wa Namasia was appointed by Nabongo Mumia. These developments were repeated in Kabras, Samia, Buholo, Marama, Kisa, Bunyore and Bukusu so that by 1930, all Wanga agents had been replaced. The only places Wanga agents did not penetrate are Maragoli and Tiriki; although the latter's dominant clan, Abalukhoba, is umbilical to Abashitsetse dynasty.

[186.] Sudi Namachanja was born during the slaving raids by an Arab slave trader known as Sudi wa Pangani. Under Bukusu nomenclatural system, a child is named after a season or major event that has had a major impact on people's lives.

The preeminent Wanga King, Nabongo Makokha Mumia
(1849-1949).

c. *Modern power blocs and notable clansmen*

With independence political authority shifted from *nabongo* (king) to the elected member of the Legislative Assembly. The first politician to lead the Wanga in the new political dispensation was Abraham Owori Mulama (Omushitsetse) who represented Mumias constituency from 1963-1969. He was succeeded by John O. Washika (Omushibe) in the 1969 elections who sadly died in 1972 before completing his five-year term. In the ensuing by election, Francis M. N. Obongita (Omukolwe) won and went on to recapture the seat in the 1974 elections as well. A Mombasa medical doctor, Elon Willis Wameyo (Omushitsetse), entered the race in 1979 and deposed Obongita. Dr. Wameyo (died 1998) was to rule Ebuwanga for twenty years before being dethroned by Wycliffe

Wilson Osundwa (Omushitsetse) in the 1997 elections. Osundwa managed two terms (1997-2002 and 2002-2007) until Benjamin Jomo Washiali (Omukolwe) took over in the Tenth Parliament (2007-2013). Washiali won the 2013 elections in the newly created Mumias East constituency.

In 1997, a new constituency was hived off Mumias and named Matungu. The first MP for Matungu in the 1997 elections was Dr. Joseph P. Wamukoya (Omushitsetse) who ruled for one term only. He was succeeded by David Aoko Were, *omumenya* (adopted immigrant) living among Ababere clansmen (2002-07, 2007-13). Were retained his seat in the 2013 general elections. Abawanga were allocated a third constituency in 2011 following the adoption of Ligale report. Mumias was abolished and in its place created Mumias West and Mumias East. The first MPs in the new ridings are Benjamin Washiali (Mumias East) and Niacca Johnston Manya (Mumias West).

Although traditional authority of *obunabongo* (kingship) was overtaken by modern political system of direct representation, any leader aspiring to become a law maker always seeks the blessing of Abashitsetse dynasty whose regnant *nabongo* is Peter Mumia II (Wanga Elureko). The *obunabongo* of Wanga Mukulu was revived after nearly seventy years of inactivity in 2009 with Wambani Rapando taking up the suzerainty.[187] Political leadership among the Wanga is so intense, some politicians resort to magic to bag the ultimate prize. Some witchdoctors prescribe an extreme form of secretive sacrificial offering (*omusango*) that involves the politician sleeping overnight in a bisected carcass of a cow and the meat served to potential voters the following day in one of the many feasts rendered during political campaigns. Unbeknownst to

---

[187.] Wambani Rapando was installed as *nabongo* in 2009 following exhumation of his father's bones for reburial at Eshimuli, the burial grounds of kings of Wanga Mukulu. He died January 1, 2012.

crowds, this eccentric ritual, practiced also by a Bukusu couple, caught in an endogamous marriage scandal (Bulimo 2013: 377), binds all those partaking of the sacrificial animal to a common cause.

Besides politicos, Wanga has also produced luminaries in other spheres of human endeavor. Among them are late Matayo Shiundu Mukenya, pioneer educationist (Omushitsetse) and his son Juvenal Joseph Muka Shiundu of the UN's International Maritime Organization, the first naval architect in east, central, and southern Africa; the late Prof. Festus Mutere, the academic (Omukolwe) and his son, the late Absalom "Bimbo" Mutere, a media scholar and rugby legend; Charles Bukeko (Omushitsetse), the comedian popularly known as Papa Shirandula; Dr. Daniel Don Nanjira (Omushikawa), a former UN diplomat; Edwin Osundwa (Omushitsetse), former PS; journalists Emman Omari, Edmund Ndumbi Kwena and Dorothy Kweyu, all Abakolwe clansmen; Phitallis Masakhwe, the disability rights campaigner, Dr. William Obwaka, the footballer and medical doctor; Ronald Watsiera, the footballer; and George Luchiri Wajackoyah (Omurono), a former police inspector, presidential aspirant, and key witness in Dr. Robert Ouko's murder.[188]

[188.] Dr. Robert Ouko (1931-1990) was Kenya's foreign affairs minister slain in February 1990.

Chart 3: Geneology of Wanga kings

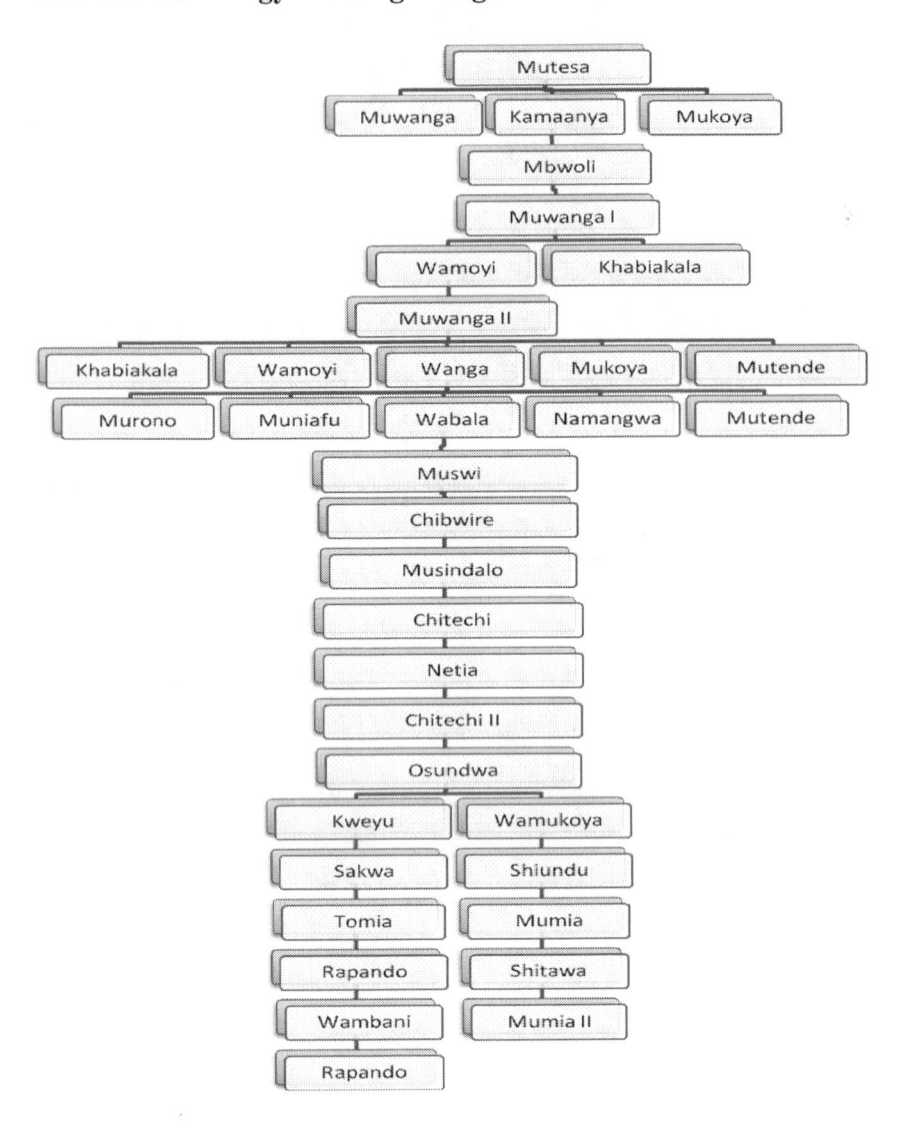

18. Abasonga (Songa)

Abasonga live in Alego-Usonga, a predominantly Luo enclave and are rather like a lost tribe of the Bantu Luyia. They neighbor Abanyala to the West and are closely related to Aberecheya of

Marama and Abagwere (Abagweru) of Uganda from whom they are descendant. Their migration into the present habitat is intertwined with that of Aberecheya which is better documented (see p.279). According to records adumbrated by Regeya Progressive Society in the 1940s and obtained by historian Prof. Gideon Were (1967), the two groups of people trace their origin to a man known as Kusesechere, a Mugweru who immigrated to Jinja where he sired a son called Musoga. Musoga moved into present-day Busia where he had two sons named Samia and Musoga, the ancestors of Abasamia and Abasonga, respectively. Musoga lived in various places including Mundika in Bukhayo, Lake Gangu (Kanyaboli) and Mbaga where his sons became ancestors of the people now called Kamenya. Although the old generation of Abasonga still speak Oluluyia, their customs are so overwhelmingly Luo that one might mistake them to be Nilotes.

According to Dr. John Osogo (1966), Abasonga are descendants of Abasonge whom we find represented in various parts of Luyialand and beyond including Bukusu, Tiriki, Kabras, Bunyala (Kakamega), Bunyoro, and Congo. They are variously referred to as Basonge, Abasonje, or Abasonge and lived at Sang'alo then Inaya in Butere before migrating to Lake Gangu in Alego (Osogo 1966: 94). They were led by a man called Songa (presumably the same as Musoga documented by Prof. Were) and over generations became assimilated by the Luo. Songa (Musoga) had three sons—Sumba, Muhango, and Siraduku—who founded the clans of Abasumba, Abamuhango, and Abasiraduku. These are the main clans in Usonga; but other Luyia clans joined them from Bunyala (Ababasi), Samia (Abaliali, Abasubo, Ababirangu), and Alego (Ababukaki). Ababirangu is a super clan that has spawned several independent clans in Samia such as Ababianga, Abadepoli, Abajapi, Abamaripo, Abayingi, Abaliro, Abadde (Abade), Abanyibomi, etc.

Despite close relationship between Abasonga and Abanyala, the two neighbors initially had an uneasy relationship with each other; often fighting over land in bruising battles. During these wars Abasonga got allies from the Luo while Abanyala received help from Abasamia (Osogo 1966: 95). The most famous son of Abasonga in recent memory is rumba maestro, Musa Juma Mumbo (1975-2011) of Orchestra Limpopo International.

APPENDIX 1

Kakamega County Administrative Units

District	Division	Location	Sublocation
Kakamega North	West Kabras	Lukume	Lukume, Lukala, Indulusia,Shikutse
		Burundu	Shimuli, Mutsuma, Kamuchisu, Sawasa
		Shirugu	Samitsi, Sheywe, Malekha, Luyeshe
		Mugai	Sundulo, Musungu, Lukala
	East Kabras	Musingu	Shitirira, Tumbeni, Masungutsa
		Chemuche	Kimangeti, Malichi, Lukhokho, Chimoroni
		Chesero	Ikoli, Kakunga, Fuvale, Luanda
	South Kabras	Mahira	Mukhonje, Mutingongo, Mwera, Shilongo
		Shianda	Lunyinya, Ifwetere, Shamoni
		Shamberere	Malimali, Sasala, Musali, Chevoso
	North Kabras	Chegulo	Namushiya, Matsakha, Chebwai, Mahusi
		Shivanga	Fubuye, Teresia, Cheptulu, Matioli
		Sirungai	Tombo, Manda, Shandiche
	Central Kabras	Matioli	Shipala, Butali, Tande, Mukavakava
		Township	Shivikhwa, Malanga, Isanjiro
Kakamega Central	Municipality	Shieywe	Sichilayi, Township
		Bukhungu	Shirere, Mahiakalo

	Lurambi	North Butsotso	Shibuli, Shiyunzu, Eshisiru
		East Butsotso	Indangalasia, Shirakalu, Murumba
		South Butsotso	Matioli, Mukaya, Shibeye
Navakholo	West Bunyala	Budonga	Bundonga, Lusumu, Sidikho, Kochwa
	East Bunyala	East Bunyala	Sivile, Namirama
	Nambacha	Nambacha	Nambacha, Buchangu
		Sirigoi	Mukhweso, Sirigoi
Kakamega South	Ikolomani North	Shesele	Mutaho, Shiseso, Shimanyiro
		Isulu	Musoli, Mukongolo, Lunerere, Shibunane
		Shirumba	Malinya, Shitoli, Shivagala
	Ikolomani South	Iguhu	Ivonda, Shiveye, Shikulu, Makhokho, Savane, Lirhembe
		Eregi	Lukose, Shisejeri, Shanjetso
		Shikumu	Madivini, Shabwali, Kaluni
Kakamega East	Ileho	Kambiri	Lubao, Bulovi, Buyangu, Ivakale
		Ivihiga	Lukusi, Ikuywa, Lunyu
	Shinyalu	Muranda	Mukulusu, Shisembe, Shiswa, Itenyi
		Khayega	Lukose, Museno, Shirulu, Shitochi, Shidodo
		Shibuye	Virhembe, Mukango, Shing'odo, Shasaba
		Ilesi	Mukhonje, Malimili, Mugomari
Mumias	Mumias	Nabongo	Nucleus, Mumias Township
		Elureko	Elureko, Matawa
		Ekero	Ekero, Kamashia
	South Wanga	Etenje	Emasinjira, Mukhuwa
		Eshikalame	Eshikalame, Eshihaka
		Bukaya	Bukaya, Buchifu

		Musanda	Musanda, Bungasi
	East Wanga	East Wanga	Eluche, Mung'ang'a
		Malaha	Malaha, Khaunga
		Isongo	Isongo, Bumini
	Shianda	Lusheya	Lusheya, Emakhwale, Lubinu
		Shianda	Eluche, Makunga
		Lubinu	Shibinga, Lubinu
Matungu	Matungu	Matungu	Namulungu, Kholera, Mayoni, Khalaba, Musamba, Matungu
		Koyonzo	Lung'anyiro, Munami, Murere, Koyonzo, Nanyeni, Namamali, Indangalasia
Butere	Butere	Butere Township	Shirotsa, Shirembe, Shinamwenyuli
		Central Marama	Ibokolo, Mutoma, Imanga
		Marenyo	Muyundi, Shikunga, Buboko
	Lunza	Marama North	Lukoye, Shiraha, Inaya, Ebishitinji
		West Marama	Shitari, Buchenya, Lunza, Bumamu
	Shiatsala	Manyala	Bushieni, Eshihenjera
		South Marama	Shibembe, Shiatsala, Masaba
Khwisero	Khwisero West	Mulwanda	Mulwanda, Khushiku, Eshirali, Mushiangubu
		Kisa Central	Wambulishe, Mundeku, Emutsesa
		Shirombe	Ebuhala, Ekomero
		Kisa West	Dudi, Muhaka, Doho
	Khwisero East	Kisa South	Emalindi, Eshibinga, Mundaha
		Kisa East	Emasatsi, Emuruba, Munjiti
		Kisa North	Mundobelwa, Mwikhalikha
Lugari	Lugari	Lumakanda	Munyuki, Mwamba
		Mautuma	Mukuyu, Mbagara
		Chekalini	Musembe, Koromaiti
		Lugari	Marakusi, Lugari

Likuyani	Likuyani	Kongoni	Kongoni, Mawe Tatu, Sango
		Likuyani	Soy, Seregeya
		Sinoko	Milimani, Namunyiri, Mwiba, Nzoia
		Nzoia	Matunda, Mois Bridge, Vinyenya, Musemwa
Matete	Matete	Luandeti	Maturu, Mahanga, Mabuye, Luandeti
		Chevaywa	Kivaywa, Kiliboti, Kulumbeni

County Summary
Districts: 12, Divisions: 27, Locations: 75, Sublocations: 233

APPENDIX 2

Vihiga County
Administrative Units

District	Division	Location	Sublocation
Vihiga	Vihiga	Central Maragoli	Chango, Ikumba, Kidundu, Emanda
		Wamuluma	Kegoye, Chambiti, Mbihi
		Lugaga	Magui, Vunandi, Muhanda
		South Maragoli	Chagenda, Lusiola, Ideleri, Masana
		Mung'oma	Madzuu, Vigulu, Mahanga, Kisienya
Sabatia	Sabatia	North Maragoli	Kivagala, Digula, Kigama, Mulundu, Mudete
		Wodanga	Gavudia, Losengeli, Vokoli, Gaigedi, Mambai
		Busali East	Itegero, Kedoli, Chavogere
		Busali West	Budaywa, Bugina, Chamakanga
	Chavakali	Izava South	Lyaduywa, Mukingi, Demesi
		Izava North	Bukulunya, Munoywa, Mbale
		West Maragoli	Kisatiru, Solongo, Kegondi, Muyundi
		Chavakali	Evojo, Walodeya, Wanondi, Viyalo, Igunga
Emuhaya	Luanda	Luanda Township	Ebusikhale, Ebusiralo, Ekamanji
		Ipali	Ebusiekwe, Embali, Itumbu Emukola, Esibakala
		Ebukanga	Mulunyenya, Emmabwi, Esikhuyu

		Ebutongoi	Emusire, Essaba, Esirulo, Essunza, Emanyinya
	Ekwanda	Ebusakami	Enyaita, Esabalu, Emutsa
		Maseno	Sunrise, Emmaloba, Kayila Mukulomoli
		Mukhalakhala	Ebwiranyi, Mwitubwi, Mwitakho
		Emasaba	Esiandumba, Ebutanyi, Ebutsimi
	Elukongo	Echichibulu	Ebunangwe, Ebusiroli, Emurembe
		Ebusamia	Ebukhunza, Emusutswi, Emuhondo, Esibuye
		Emakunda	Emmukunzi, Ebukhaya, Ebusyubi
		Ebusiratsi	Ekaita, Ebukhubi, Ematsuli Ebulonga
	Esiembero	Wekhomo	Ebuhando, Ebusundi, Emabungo
		Iboona	Ebwali, Mumbita
		Emusenjeli	Emutsalwa, Esianda, Khusikulu
		Ebubayi	Esirabe, Ematibini, Wamasiolo
Hamisi	Shamakhokho	Senende	Kaleani, Senende
		Shamakhokho	Jivovoli, Serem, Kisasi
	Shaviringa	Shaviringa	Mulundu, Jeptulu, Kaptech
		Muhudu	Muhudu, Shiru, Makuchi
	Jepkoyai	Gisambai	Gavudunyi, Gimomoi, Gamoi, Galona
		Jepkoyai	Tigoi, Kitagwa, Givole, Kapchemgung
	Tambua	Tambua	Gamalenga, Gimarakwa, Ivola, Kiptemes, Mwembe
		Banja	Kapsotik, Givogi, Gasianga, Kipchekwen

County Summary
Districts: 04, Divisions: 11, Locations: 37, Sublocations: 131

APPENDIX 3

Bungoma County Administrative Units[189]

District	Division	Location	Sublocation
Bungoma North	Central	Naitiri	Naitiri
		Milima	Milima
		Mukuyuni	Mukuyuni, Maliki
	Tongaren	Tongaren	Tongaren, Mabusi, Kakamwe
		Soysambu	Soysambu, Narati
		Kiminini	Taban, Kiminini
	Ndalu	Mitua	Muliro
		Kamakwe	Misanga, Makhanga, Nabing'eng'e
	Mbakalo	Mbakalo	Mbakalo, Karima
		Kibisi	Kibisi, Musembe
		Kabuyefwe	Kabuyefwe, Sirakaru
Kimilili	Kimilili	Kimilili	Kimilili Township, Bituyu
		Kimilili Rural	Kimilili Rural, Khamulati
		Kibingei	Kibingei, Kitai
		Chebukwabi	Chebukwabi, Kamusinga
	Kamukuywa	Maeni	Nasusi, Sikhendu
		Kamusinde	Kamasielo, Kibisi
		Kamukuywa	Kimakwa, Musembie, Nabikoto
		Makhonge	Makhonge, Mapera, Mbongi
Bungoma South	Kanduyi	Township	Township, Khalaba
		Musikoma	South Kanduyi, Namasanda
		Kibabii	Tuuti, Marakaru
		East Bukusu	Namwacha, West Sang'alo,

---

189. Excludes Mt. Elgon which is inhabited by Nilotic Sabaot (Sebei).

		Bukembe	Ndengelwa, Namirembe, North Sang'alo, Kongoli
		Mabusi	Mabusi, Kimatuni
Bumula	Bumula	Kimaeti	Syombe, Nakhwana
		Napara	Bitobo, Khasolo
		Khasoko	Khasoko, Mung'ore, Namatotoa
		Mukwa	Mukwa, Kisawayi
		West Bukusu	Kibuke, Ng'oli, Lwanja, Mayanja
		South Bukusu	Muanda, Mateka, Lumboka
		Kabula	Kabula, Watoya
		Bumula	Bumula, Lunao
Bungoma West	Malakisi	Malakisi	Butonge, Mwalie, Tamlega, Bukokholo, Sitabicha
	Lwandanyi	Lwandanyi	Mayekwe, Chepkuyi
		Namubila	Machakha, Wamono
	Sirisia	Sirisia	Kulisiru North
		Bisunu	Kulisiru South
	Namwela	Namwela	Menu
		Toloso	Namwela Central, Namwela South
Bungoma East	Webuye	Webuye	Township, Maraka, Matulo
		Misikhu	Misikhu, Malaha, Kituni
		Sitikho	Milo, Sitikho, Khalumuli
	Bokoli	Maraka	Nangeni
		Miendo	Milani
		Lutacho	Namawanga, Sirende, Manafwa, Nabuyole
	Ndivisi	Namarambi	Wabukhonyi, Makuselwa, Marinda, Misemwa
		Ndivisi	Magemo, Sitabicha
		Chetambe	Mitukuyu, Mihuu
		Lugusi	Lutacho, Misimo
Bungoma Central	Chwele	Chwele	Chwele, Sikulu, Sichei
		Mukuyuni	Kibichori, Mukuyuni, Kuywa

Nalondo	Kabuchai	Kabuchai, Kisiwa
	North Nalondo	Nalondo North, Mukweya
	Luuya	Bwake, Luuya
	Sirare	West Nalondo

County Summary
Districts: 07, Divisions: 17, Locations: 56, Sublocations: 125

APPENDIX 4

Busia County Administrative Units[190]

District	Division	Location	Sublocation
Busia	Matayos	Lwanya	Luliba, Busende, Igero
		Nangoma	Murende, Nangoma, Muyafwa
		Bukhayo West	Esikulu, Bugengi, Mundika
		Nasewa	Lunga, Buyama, Mabunge
		Busibwabo	Nakhakina, Nasira, Alungoli
	Municipality	Busia Township	Township, Mayenje
Butula	Butula	Bujumba	Bujumba, Burinda, Ikonzo, Namwitsula
		Elukhari	Kanjala, Bukati, Sikarira
		Marachi East	Tingolo, Bumala "B," Elukongo
		Marachi Central	Esikoma, Bukhalalire, Kingandole
		Bumala	Busire, Bukhakhala, Bumala "A"
		Elugulu	Bwaliro, Namusala, Bulemia, Emukhweso, Bulwani
Samia	Funyula	Nambuku	Sibinga, Ludacho, Lugala, Mango, Ganjala
		Nanguba	Bujwanga, Rumbiye, Nanderema
		Nangosia	Sirekeresi, Luchululo, Sigulu, Bukhulungu
		Agenga	Sigalame, Agenga, Bukiri, Ojibo

[190.] Excludes Teso North and Teso South districts which are populated by Nilotic Iteso.

		Odiado	Odiado, Budalanga, Wakhulungu, Kabwodo
		Namboboto	Namboboto, Buloma, Luanda, Nyakhombi, Mudoma
		Bwiri	Busembe, Hakati, Namuduru, Busijo
Bunyala	Budalang'i	Bunyala Central	Magombe West, Magombe East, Magombe Central
		Bunyala East	Budalang'i, Mudembi, Ruambwa
		Bunyala West	Bukani, Siginga, Bukoma
		Bunyala North	Sisenye, Mundere, Bulemia
		Khajula	Mabinju, Lugale, Rugunga
		Bunyala South	Obaro, Rukala, Ebulwani
Nambale	Nambale	Bukhayo East	Buyofu, Sikinga, Madibo, Mungatsi
		Bukhayo Central	Malanga, Lwanyange, Esidende
		Nambale Township	Siekunya, Kisoko, Township
		Walatsi	Musokoto, Khwirale
		Bukhayo North	Kapina, Lupida

County Summary
Districts: 05, Divisions: 06, Locations: 30, Sublocations: 99

BIBLIOGRAPHY

1. Alembi, Ezekiel. (2000). *Oral Poetry of Abanyole Children*. East African Educational Publishers, Nairobi.
2. Alembi, Ezekiel. (2002). *The Construction of the Abanyole Perceptions on Death Through Oral Funeral Poetry*. PhD Dissertation, University of Helsinki, Finland.
3. Arkell, A. J. (1974). *A History of the Sudan to AD 1821*, Athlone Press, London. First printed 1955.
4. Brunson, James. (2004). *Ethnic or Symbolic: Blackness and Human Images in Ancient Egyptian Art*. Essay published in Journal of African Civilisations Vol. 10: Egypt Revisited (Ed: Ivan Van Sertima), Transaction Publishers, New Jersey. First published 1989.
5. Bulimo, Shadrack A. (2013). *Luyia of Kenya: A Cultural Profile*, Trafford Publishing, Bloomington, Indiana.
6. Burgman, Hans. (1979). *The Early History of Mumias Mission*. National Printing Press, Kisumu.
7. Davidson, Basil. (2004). *Ancient World and Africa, Whose Roots?* Essay published in Journal of African Civilisations Vol. 10: Egypt Revisited (Ed: Ivan Van Sertima), Transaction Publishers, New Jersey. First printed 1989.
8. Diop, C. A. (2004). *Origin of Ancient Egyptians*. Essay published in Journal of African Civilisations Vol. 10: Egypt Revisited (Ed: Ivan Van Sertima), Transaction Publishers, New Jersey. First printed 1989.
9. Falola, Toyin and Aribidesi Usman. (2009). *Movements, Borders, and Identities in Africa*. University of Rochester Press, New York.
10. Florence, Namulundah. (2005). *From Our Mothers' Hearths*. Africa World Press Inc, Trenton, New Jersey.
11. Florence, Namulundah. (2011). *The Bukusu of Kenya*. Folktales, Culture and Social Identities, Carolina Academic Press, Durham.
12. Grinker, R. R., Lubkemann, S. C., and Steiner, C. B. (Eds, 2010). *Perspectives on Africa: A Reader in Culture, History, and Representation*. Blackwell Publishing Ltd, Chichester, UK.
13. Hoehler-Fatton, Cynthia. (1996). *Women of Fire and Spirit: History, Faith, and Gender in Roho Religion in Western Kenya*. Oxford University Press, New York.

14. Kabaji, Egara S. (1992). *The Maragoli Folktale: Its Meaning and Aesthetics.* MA Thesis, Kenyatta University, Nairobi.

15. Kabaji, Egara S. (2005). *The Construction of Gender Through the Narrative Process of the African Folktale: A Case Study of the Maragoli Folktales.* PhD Dissertation, University of South Africa, Pretoria.

16. Kanyoro, Rachel A. (1983). *Unity in Diversity: A Linguistic Survey of Abaluyia of Western Kenya.* Afro-Pub, Wien (Vienna).

17. Kay, Stafford. (1979). *Early Educational Development in East Africa: A Case Study.* Comparative Education Review, Vol. 23(1) pp. 66-81, published by University of Chicago Press on behalf of Comparative and International Education Society, Chicago.

18. Kenya National Bureau of Statistics. (2010). *2009 Kenya Population and Housing Census.* Republic of Kenya, Government Printer, Nairobi.

19. Lihraw, Demmahom O. (2010). *The Preindependent Kenya Tachon Peoples: History, Culture and Economy.* PERC-PACE International, Nairobi.

20. Lloyd, Albert D. (1921). *Dayspring in Uganda.* Church Missionary Society, London.

21. Makana, NE. (2010). *Peasant Response to Agricultural Innovations: Land Consolidation, Agrarian Diversification and Technical Change: The Case of Bungoma District in Western Kenya (1954-1960).* Journal of Third World Studies, Spring, New York.

22. Makila, F. E. (1978). *An Outline History of Babukusu of Western Kenya.* Kenya Literature Bureau, Nairobi.

23. Makila, F. E. (1982). *The Significance of Chetambe Fort in Bukusu History.* Unpublished Research Paper, Nairobi.

24. Matsuda, Motoji. (1984). *Urbanisation and Adaptation: A Reorganization Process of Social Relations among the Maragoli Migrants in their Urban Colony, Kangemi, Nairobi, Kenya.* MA thesis published in African Study Monographs 5: 1-48, Center for African Area Studies, University of Kyoto, Kyoto.

25. McGeoch, Lauren. (2004*). "Plant Ecology in a Human Context: Mondia Whytei in Kakamega Forest, Kenya,"* undergraduate thesis submitted in partial fulfillment of BSc Degree in Environmental Science, Brown University, Rhode Island

26. M'Imanyara, Alfred M. (1992). *Restatement of Bantu Origin and Meru History*, Longmans, Nairobi.

27. Mirimo, Abraham K. L. (1988). *Luyia Sayings: With an English Translation.* Oxford University Press, Nairobi.

28. Mumia II, Peter Nabongo. (2010). *History of Wanga Kingdom AD 1000-2010.* Unpublished manuscript, Nabongo Cultural Center, Matungu, Mumias.

29. Mwayuuli, M. S. and Nakabayashi Nobuhiro. (1989). *The History of the Isukha and Idakho Clans among the Abaluyia of Western Kenya.* Kanazawa University, Kanazawa, Japan.

30. Nandwa, Jane. (1976). *"Oral Literature among Abaluhya,"* MA Thesis, University of Nairobi, Nairobi.

31. Nangendo, Steve. (1986). *Pottery Taboos and Symbolism in Bukusu Society, Western Kenya.* African Study Monographs 17(2), 69-84, Institute of African Studies, University of Nairobi, Nairobi.

32. Ng'ang'a, Wanguhu. (2006). *Kenyan Ethnic Communities: The Foundation of a Nation.* Gatundu Publishers, Nairobi.

33. Ochieng', William R. (Ed 2002). *Historical Studies in Social Change in Western Kenya: Essays in Memory of Prof. Gideon Saulo Were.* East African Educational Publishers, Nairobi.

34. Ochieng', W. R. and Maxon, R. M. (Eds, 1992). *The Economic History of Kenya.* East African Educational Publishers, Nairobi.

35. Ochwada, Hannington. (2007). *Negotiating Difference: The Church Missionary Society, Colonial Education and Gender among Abaluyia and Joluo Communities of Kenya 1900-1960.* PhD dissertation, Department of History, Indiana University.

36. Ogot, Bethwell. A. (1967). *History of the Southern Luo.* East African Publishing House, Nairobi.

37. Ogot, Bethwell. A. (2003). *My Footprints on the Sands of Time: An Autobiography.* Trafford Publishing, Victoria, Canada.

38. Osogo, John. (1966). *History of the Baluyia.* Oxford University Press, Nairobi.

39. Otwelo, A. (1998). *A Short History of the Abanyole.* Unpublished Research Paper, Nairobi.

40. Padwick, Timothy J, Spirit. (2003). *Desire and the World: Roho Churches of Western Kenya in the Era of Globalization.* PhD Thesis, University of Birmingham, Birmingham.

41. Peek, Philip M. and Kwesi Yankah. (Eds 2004). *African Folklore: An Encyclopaedia.* Routledge, New York.

42. Purvis, John B. (1900). *Handbook to British East Africa and Uganda.* Swan Sonnenschien & Co Ltd, London.

43. Republic of Kenya. (1963-1966). *The National Assembly, House of Representatives Official Report (Hansard)*, Vol I Part II, Vol IV and Vol VII, Government Printer, Nairobi.

44. Sangale, Simani. (2005). *Tiriki Community Customs and Traditions.* Kul Graphics, Nairobi.

45. Sangree, Walter. H. (1966). *Age, Prayers and Politics in Tiriki, Kenya.* Oxford University Press, New York.

46. Schmidt H, B. Hornetz, R. Jaetzold and C. Shisanya. (2005). *Farm Management Handbook of Kenya Vol. II, Second Edition Part A, West Kenya.* Ministry of Agriculture in conjunction with Germany's GTZ, Nairobi.

47. Shilaro, Priscilla M. (2000). *A Failed Eldorado: British Trusteeship, Luyia Land Rights and the Kakamega Gold Rush*, 1930-52, PhD Dissertation, West Virginia University, Morgantown.

48. Somo, Ferg. (2010). *The Bantu in Ancient Egypt.* Retrieved from http://www.kaa-umati.co.uk on March 2, 2010

49. Wagner, Gunter. Vol 1&2 (1970). *The Bantu of Western Kenya.* International African Institute, Oxford University Press, London. First printed 1949 as *Bantu of North Kavirondo.*

50. Were, Gideon S. (1967). *A History of Abaluyia of Western Kenya 1500-1930.* East African Publishing House, Nairobi.

51. Were, Gideon S. (1967). *Western Kenya Historical Texts.* East African Publishing House, Nairobi.

52. Were, Gideon S. and DA Wilson. (1968). *East Africa through a Thousand Years—from AD 1000 to Present Day.* Evans Brothers, Nairobi.

53. Werner, Alice. (1968). *Myth and Legends of the Bantu.* Frank Cass, London.

54. Williamson, Kay. (1989). Benue-Congo Overview: In *The Niger-Congo Languages.* J. Bendor-Samuel (Ed) pp. 246-274, University Press of America, Lanham, Maryland.

55. Wolf, de J. J. (1980). *The Diffusion of Age-Group Organization in East Africa: A Reconsideration.* Journal of the International African Institute, Vol. 50(3) pp. 305-310, Edinburgh University Press, Edinburgh.

INDEX

D

E

M

O

Edwards Brothers Malloy
Oxnard, CA USA
May 29, 2013